Environmental Law Handbook

SEVENTH EDITION

The College of Law
of England and Wales

LIBRARY SERVICES

PLNG

Other titles available from Law Society Publishing:

Conveyancing Checklists (2nd edn)
Frances Silverman and Russell Hewitson

Conveyancing Handbook (17th edn)
General Editor: Frances Silverman

Freedom of Information Handbook (2nd edn)
Peter Carey and Marcus Turle

Information Sharing Handbook
Editor: Claire Bessant; Consultant Editor: Phil Tompkins

Planning and Compulsory Purchase Act 2004
Stephen Tromans, Martin Edwards, Richard Harwood and Justine Thornton

Property Development
Gavin Le Chat

Stamp Duty Land Tax (9th edn)
Reg Nock

Titles from Law Society Publishing can be ordered from all good bookshops or direct (telephone 0870 850 1422, email **lawsociety@prolog.uk.com** or visit our online shop at **www.lawsociety.org.uk/bookshop**).

ENVIRONMENTAL LAW HANDBOOK

SEVENTH EDITION

**Valerie Fogleman, Trevor Hellawell
and Andrew Wiseman**

The Law Society

© The Law Society 2011

ISBN-13: 978-1-85328-819-7

Sample environmental search report is reproduced in Appendix A3 with the permission of Landmark Information Group Limited.
Crown copyright material is reproduced in Appendix F with the permission of the Controller of Her Majesty's Stationery Office.

First edition published in 1995; second edition published in 1996; third edition published in 1998; fourth edition published in 2000; fifth edition published in 2002; sixth edition published in 2005
This seventh edition published in 2011 by the Law Society
113 Chancery Lane, London WC2A 1PL

Typeset by Columns Design XML Ltd, Reading
Printed by Hobbs the Printers Ltd, Totton, Hants

The paper used for the text pages of this book is FSC® certified. FSC (the Forest Stewardship Council®) is an international network to promote responsible management of the world's forests.

FSC
www.fsc.org
MIX
Board from
responsible sources
FSC® C020438

Contents

About the authors		xi
Preface to the seventh edition		xii
Table of cases		xiii
Table of statutes		xv
Table of statutory instruments		xvii
Table of international instruments		xix
Abbreviations		xx

1 Environmental liabilities   **1**

1.1	Introduction	1
1.2	Enforcing authorities	2
1.3	Regulatory liabilities	3
1.4	Criminal proceedings	11
1.5	Civil sanctions	17
1.6	Clean-up liabilities	21
1.7	Nature conservation and biodiversity liabilities	24
1.8	Tort liabilities	26
1.9	Protecting a client against criminal liabilities	30
1.10	Protecting a client against clean-up/biodiversity liabilities	34
1.11	Indirect costs	35

2 Contaminated land   **36**

2.1	Introduction	36
2.2	Inspection and investigation	37
2.3	Determination	39
2.4	Consider whether the works are urgent	41
2.5	Identify interested persons	42
2.6	Formulate a scheme	42
2.7	Notify and consult	42
2.8	Finalise and agree scheme	42
2.9	Exclusion and apportionment	43
2.10	Cost recovery and hardship	54
2.11	Service of remediation notice	55

2.12 Carrying out remediation works   56
2.13 Time limits and appeals   57
2.14 Prosecution for non-compliance with remediation notice   59
2.15 Local authority complete works and recover costs   59
2.16 Registers   61
2.17 Interaction of contaminated land legislation with other legal regimes   62
2.18 Dealing with contaminated land in legal transactions   66
2.19 Specific issues   69
2.20 Protecting the client   70
2.21 Conclusion   70

3 Environmental Damage Regulations   **72**

3.1 Introduction   72
3.2 Structure of regime   72
3.3 Overall summary of procedures   73
3.4 Supplementary nature   73
3.5 Who is liable?   74
3.6 Environmental damage and thresholds   75
3.7 Joint and several liability   77
3.8 Limitation periods   78
3.9 Exemptions   78
3.10 Enforcing authorities   80
3.11 Interested parties   81
3.12 Investigations   82
3.13 Information notices   83
3.14 Preventing environmental damage and further environmental damage   83
3.15 Duty to notify   83
3.16 Determination of environmental damage   84
3.17 Notification of environmental damage   84
3.18 Remedial measures   85
3.19 Appeals to notifications   87
3.20 Remediation notices   88
3.21 Appeals to remediation notices   89
3.22 Costs   89
3.23 Charges on premises   89
3.24 Duty to grant and pay compensation   90
3.25 Offences and sanctions   90

4 Climate change   **92**

4.1 Introduction   92
4.2 Zero carbon buildings   92

4.3	Energy certificates	93
4.4	The CRC Energy Efficiency Scheme	95

5 Obtaining and interpreting environmental information **108**

5.1	Introduction	108
5.2	Access to environmental information	109
5.3	Environment Agency searches	111
5.4	Local authority searches	111
5.5	Environmental data search reports	112
5.6	Environmental investigations and audits in commercial transactions	117

6 Residential property transactions **121**

6.1	Introduction	121
6.2	Potential environmental problems in residential cases	122
6.3	Law Society's Contaminated Land Warning Card	126
6.4	Practical considerations in residential freehold transactions	127
6.5	Advice to sellers	137

7 Commercial property transactions **138**

7.1	Introduction	138
7.2	Potential problems in commercial real estate	139
7.3	Law Society's Contaminated Land Warning Card	145
7.4	Commercial freehold transactions	146
7.5	Advice to sellers	157
7.6	Leasehold transactions	158

8 Corporate transactions **164**

8.1	Introduction	164
8.2	Question of liability	164
8.3	Practical steps	165
8.4	Problems identified: what approach to take?	166
8.5	Documenting the transaction	168

9 Planning and development **174**

9.1	Introduction	174
9.2	Planning implications of property transactions	174
9.3	Undertaking the works	180
9.4	Passing risk to purchaser	180
9.5	Tax considerations	182

10 Use and engagement of environmental consultants   **183**

    10.1   Environmental investigations and audit   183
    10.2   Risks of having an investigation   183
    10.3   Carrying out an investigation   186

11 Funding and borrowing transactions   **194**

    11.1   Environmental impact on funding and security   194
    11.2   Protection for the lender   195

12 Insolvency   **200**

    12.1   Introduction   200
    12.2   Disposal of land   200
    12.3   Land containing waste   200
    12.4   Prosecutions during administration   201
    12.5   Insolvency practitioners   202
    12.6   Protection for insolvency practitioners concerning
           contaminated land   207

13 Environmental insurance   **208**

    13.1   Introduction   208
    13.2   Public liability policies   208
    13.3   Professional indemnity insurance policies   211
    13.4   Property policies   212
    13.5   Homeowners policies   213
    13.6   Environmental insurance policies   213
    13.7   Finite risk programmes   222
    13.8   Self insurance   222
    13.9   Captives   223
    13.10 Major environmental insurers and brokers   223

Appendix A: Precedents   **225**

    A1   Clauses intended to pass liability for contaminated land to a
           purchaser   225
    A2   Precedent agreement on liabilities under Part IIA   227
    A3   Sample environmental search report   229
    A4   Standard questions to ask following an environmental
           search report   250
    A5   Clauses to include in client care letter regarding
           environmental risks   252
    A6   Enquiries of the seller   253
    A7   Sample lease clauses   257

A8   Illustrative environmental clauses for inclusion in a share
      purchase agreement   260
A9   Illustrative terms for inclusion in a facility agreement   266
A10   Terms and conditions of engagement   271

Appendix B: Contaminated Land Warning Card   **279**

Appendix C: CON 29R Enquiries of Local Authority (2007)   **283**

Appendix D: CON 290 Optional Enquiries of Local Authority (2007) **289**

Appendix E: CON 29DW Standard Drainage and Water Enquiries (2007) **295**

**Appendix F: Model planning conditions for development on land affected by
contamination**   **299**

Appendlx G: Contacts   **305**

Index   315

About the authors

Valerie Fogleman is a consultant at Stevens & Bolton LLP and a professor of law at Cardiff University, where she teaches environmental and climate change law and insurance law. She has practised and taught environmental law for nearly 25 years in England and the USA. Valerie is listed as a leading environmental lawyer in *Chambers UK*, *Legal 500*, *Legal Experts*, the *International Who's Who of Environment Lawyers* and the *Guide to the World's Leading Environment Lawyers*. She has written three books and co-authored others on environmental law and insurance. Valerie is an honorary member of the Royal Institution of Chartered Surveyors. Her membership of professional organisations also includes the United Kingdom Environmental Law Association and the Association of Insurance and Risk Managers. She is vice chair of the City of London Law Society Planning and Environment Committee.

Trevor Hellawell is a solicitor and legal training consultant with 20 years' experience of training and consultancy in environmental law. He works with BPP, the College of Law, lawyers and other professionals, Landmark Information Group, the Ministry of Defence and several other clients, particularly in the engineering sector. Trevor was formerly with Eversheds in the environmental law team and is a regular contributor of articles for magazines and other publications. He is a former member of the Law Society Planning and Environmental Law Committee and is the author of *Blackstone's Guide to Contaminated Land* (OUP/Blackstone, 2000) and previous editions of the *Environmental Law Handbook*.

Andrew Wiseman is head of the environmental law team at Stephenson Harwood and has 20 years' experience in advising on environmental law. He is listed in *Chambers UK* and *Legal 500* as one of the country's leading environmental lawyers. Andrew is a past chair of the UK Environmental Law Association and has been appointed by the Secretary of State to chair the Advisory Council of the Export Credits Guarantee Department. He has written for various publications and been interviewed on television and radio including BBC News 24, Watchdog, Radio 4 and Radio 5.

Preface to the seventh edition

As with most publications – and most subjects about which they are written – time moves on and things get more complex. For some years now, the fundamentals of environmental law have remained largely static, the foundations of the building having been laid down in the 1990s and subsequent years merely adding layers of bricks. This handbook has always been intended as a guide for the general practitioner needing a brief (and hopefully readable) introduction to the basics.

Much has changed in the last five years. The advent of new Environmental Permitting Regulations and Environmental Damage Regulations, the increased awareness of flooding as a real environmental hazard, the emergence of carbon emissions as a deep political issue and the introduction of the CRC Energy Efficiency Scheme as a step along the way to saving the planet have all precipitated the production of this new edition. It has become a more complicated work.

Having gargled, but rarely drunk, from the fountain of environmental knowledge over the years, the time has come for me to acknowledge that this handbook needs more erudite contribution than I alone can offer. I have thus involved the services of far greater intellects than my own to assist me in the production of this edition, over which I retain a largely editorial oversight. Andrew Wiseman and Valerie Fogleman will need little introduction to anyone familiar with the environmental area and they offered, and have agreed, to review and revise substantial areas of the existing work, as well as contributing key new sections on the vast and complex developments that have taken place since the last edition. To them both I am very grateful. This handbook is a substantially better work for their involvement.

I would like once more to take this opportunity to thank all the editorial and administrative staff at Law Society Publishing and all those professional colleagues with whom I have had many discussions over the years and who have allowed me to use their thoughts and ideas as the foundation for earlier editions.

For those who follow my private life through the prefaces to successive editions of this book, my children continue to flourish at school and, besides forging their own unique talents, demonstrate a wonder and an engagement with life that never ceases to amaze. The world without them would be like a world without birdsong or waterfalls – I hope our legacy to them is worthy of their enthusiasm and trust.

The law is stated as at 1 November 2010.

Trevor Hellawell, Crediton
November 2010

Table of cases

Bartoline Ltd v. Royal & Sun Alliance plc and Heath Lambert Ltd [2006]
EWHC 3598 (QB); [2007] 1 All ER (Comm) 1043 .... 13.2.3
Blue Circle Industries plc v. Ministry of Defence [1999] Ch 289; [1998] 3 All
ER 385, CA 1.8.4, 11.1
Bolton MBC v. Municipal Mutual Insurance Ltd [2006] EWCA Civ 50;
[2006] 1 WLR 1492, CA 13.2.1
C v. Imperial Design Ltd [2001] Env LR 593, CA.. 1.8.4
Cambridge Water Co v. Eastern Counties Leather plc [1994] 2 AC 264, HL......... 1.8.1,
1.8.3, 6.2.2, 7.2.2, 12.5.1
Celtic Extraction Ltd v. Environment Agency [2001] Ch 475, CA 12.2
Circular Facilities (London) Ltd v. Sevenoaks DC [2005] EWHC Admin 865;
[2005] All ER (D) 126 .... 2.9.2, 2.9.3, 2.17.1, 6.2.1, 9.3
City Equitable Fire Insurance Co Ltd, Re [1925] Ch 407, CA............................ 8.2
Corby Group Litigation, Re [2008] EWCA Civ 463; [2009] QB 335, CA........... 1.8.2
Corby Group Litigation v. Corby DC [2009] EWHC 1944, TCC............... 1.8.2, 1.8.5
Delaware Mansions Ltd v. Westminster City Council [2001] UKHL 55; [2002]
1 AC 321 .... 1.8.1
Dennis v. Ministry of Defence [2003] EWHC 793 (QB); [2003] Env LR 741,
QBD 1.8.7
Durham v. BAI (Runoff) Ltd [2010] EWCA Civ 1096................................. 13.2.1
Empress Car Co (Abertillery) Ltd v. National Rivers Authority [1998] 2 WLR
350, HL 1.3.1
English Partnerships v. Mott MacDonald (ENDS Report, April 1999). 7.4.7, 10.3.5, 11.1
Environment Agency v. Hillridge Ltd [2003] EWHC 3023 (Ch); [2004] Env
LR 633 .... 12.3
Getty v. Getty and Treves [1985] QB 956, QBD....................................... 10.2.2
Goldman v. Hargrave [1967] 1 AC 645, HC (Aus)....................................... 1.8.1
Holbeck Hall Hotel Ltd v. Scarborough BC [2000] QB 836, CA....................... 1.8.1
Hunter v. Canary Wharf Ltd; Hunter v. London Docklands Development Corp
[1997] AC 655, HL 1.8.1, 9.3
Jan de Nul (UK) Ltd v. NV Royale Belge [2002] EWCA Civ 209; [2002] 1
All ER (Comm) 767, CA; affirming [2000] 2 Lloyd's Rep. 700 .... 1.8.1
Khatun v. United Kingdom (1998) 26 EHRR CD212, EuCommHR.................. 1.8.7
Leakey v. National Trust [1980] QB 485, CA.. 1.8.1
McKenna v. British Aluminium Ltd [2002] Env LR 30, ChD............................ 1.8.3
Margereson v. JW Roberts Ltd; Hancock v. JW Roberts Ltd [1996] Env LR
304, CA 1.8.5
Mineral Resources Ltd, Re; Environment Agency v. Stout [1999] 1 All ER
746, ChD 12.5.3
Norman v. Theodore Goddard [1992] BCLC 1028, ChD.................................. 8.2
Post Office v. Aquarius Properties [1987] 1 All ER 1055, CA........................... 7.6.1

R v. Anglian Water Services Ltd [2003] EWCA Crim 2243............................ 1.4.4
R v. F Howe & Sons (Engineers) Ltd [1999] 2 All ER 249, CA........................ 1.4.4
R v. Milford Haven Port Authority [2000] Env LR 673, CA..................... 1.4.4, 1.9.3
R v. Thames Water Utilities Ltd [2010] EWCA Crim 202....................... 1.4.4, 1.9.3
R (on the application of OSS Group Ltd) v. Environment Agency [2007]
    EWCA Civ 611 .... 1.3.1
R (on the application of Technoprint plc, Mark Snee) v. Leeds City Council
    [2010] EWHC 581 (Admin), QBD 9.2.1
Raffineries Mediterranee (ERG) SpA v. Ministero dello Sviluppo economico
    (Joined Cases C-378–C380/08), ECJ 3.9.1, 3.9.2
Rhondda Waste Disposal Ltd (In Administration) v. Clark [2001] Ch 57, CA........ 12.4
Rylands v. Fletcher (1868) LR 3 HL 330, HL 1.8, 1.8.3
Sandridge appeal (app/cl/05/01 & 02).. 2.13.3, 2.18.1
Schulmans Incorporated Ltd v. National Rivers Authority [1993] Env LR D1........ 1.3.1
Sedleigh-Denfield v. O'Callaghan [1940] AC 880, HL........................... 1.8.1, 7.2.2
Three Rivers DC v. Bank of England [2004] UKHL 48................................ 10.2.2
Transco plc v. Stockport MBC [2004] 2 AC 1, HL.............................. 1.8.3
Van de Walle v. Texaco (Belgium) SA (Case C-1/03), ECJ.......................... 1.3.1
Wandsworth LBC v. Railtrack plc [2001] EWCA Civ 1236; [2002] QB 756,
    CA 1.8.1, 1.8.2
Wheeler v. JJ Saunders Ltd [1996] Ch 19; [1995] 3 WLR 466, CA............... 1.8.1, 9.3
William Morrison Supermarkets v. Wakefield MDC [1991] JPL 985.................... 9.2.2
Williams v. Natural Life Healthfoods Ltd [1996] 1 BCLC 288, QBD.................. 8.2
Wilmott Trading Co, Re (No.2) [2000] Env LR 54, ChD............................... 12.3

Table of statutes

Civil Liability (Contribution)
  Act 1978
    s.1(1) 3.7
Clean Neighbourhoods and
  Environment Act 2005 .... 1.6.1, 2.13.1
Climate Change Act 2008................ 4.1
Companies Act 2006.................... 4.4.4
    s.1161(1), (5) 4.4.4
Countryside and Rights of Way
  Act 2000 .... 1.7.1, 6.2.1, 7.2.1
Defective Premises Act 1972.......... 1.8.4
Environment Act 1995.................. 2.3.1
    s.108 .... 3.12
        (4)(j) 3.12
    Sched.22, para.89 .... 1.6.1
Environmental Protection Act
  1990 ...... 2.9.3, 2.11.3, 2.15.1, 2.16.2,
                  7.2.5, 9.2.4, 12.5.1
    Part I 1.4.1, 6.2.5
    s.27 .... 2.11.1
    Part II 1.3.1, 1.3.2, 1.4.1, 1.6.1,
                 6.2.5, 7.2.1, 12.5.1
    s.33 .... 1.3.2, 7.2.1, 12.5.1
        (6) 12.4
        (7) 1.3.5, 12.5.1
    s.34 .... 1.3.2, 1.8.2
    s.57 .... 2.1.1
    s.59 ..... 1.6.1, 3.4, 7.2.3, 12.5.1
    s.59ZA 1.6.1, 12.5.1
    s.73(6) 1.8.4
  Part IIA ... 1.2.1, 1.2.2, 1.4.2, 1.6.1,
      2.1.1, 2.3.3, 2.9.3, 2.17,
      2.17.1, 2.17.2, 2.17.3,
      2.17.4, 2.17.5, 2.17.6,
    2.17.7, 2.18, 2.18.1, 2.18.2,
    2.18.3, 2.19.2, 3.4, 3.6.1,
    3.8, 3.18.1, 3.23, 5.4, 5.5.2,
    6.2.1, 6.2.3, 6.4.3, 6.4.4,
    6.4.5, 6.4.8, 7.2.1, 7.2.3,
    7.4.4, 7.4.5, 7.4.6, 7.4.7,
    7.6.1, 8.4, 8.5.1, 8.5.3,

Part IIA - *continued* 9.2, 9.3,
    9.4, 10.3.2, 11.2.2, 12.1,
    12.6, 13.2.3, 13.6.4
    s.78A 2.9.1
        (2) 2.3.1
        (7) 2.11.1
        (9) 2.9.1
    s.78E 2.11.1
        (2), (3) 2.9.1
        (4)–(6) 2.11.1
    s.78F(3), (6), (7) 2.9.1
    s.78G 2.12.1
        (3) 2.12.1
    s.78H(1) 2.7.1
        (4) 2.7.1, 2.11.1
        (5) 2.8.1, 2.11.1
          (d) 2.10
          (6) 2.11.1
    s.78J 2.9.5
        (2) 2.9.5
    s.78K(1), (3), (4) 2.9.6
    s.78L 2.13.1
    s.78M 2.14.1
        (2) 1.3.5
    s.78N 1.6.1
        (3)(e) 2.10
    s.78P(1) 2.10
    s.78R 2.16.1
        (8) 2.16.1
    s.78S 2.16.1
    s.78X 2.2.1, 2.13.2, 2.19.2,
                  12.6
        (3) 2.9.1
          (a) 2.9.1
    s.78YB 2.11.1
  Part III .. 1.6.1, 2.17.6, 6.2.5, 12.5.1
    s.79 .... 1.6.1
    s.80 .... 1.6.1, 7.2.1
        (7) 1.3.5
    s.81 .... 1.6.1, 7.2.3
  Part IV 1.4.1

Environmental Protection Act
1990 – *continued*
  Part VI 1.4.1
  Part VIII
    ss.140–142 .... 1.4.1
    s.143 .... 2.16.2
  Part IX
    s.157 .... 1.4.1, 12.5.1
    s.158 .... 1.4.1, 12.5.1
Explosives Act 1875..................... 7.2.4
Finance Act 1996...................... 2.17.4
Finance Act 2001...................... 2.17.4
Freedom of Information Act
2000 .... 5.2, 5.2.1
  s.3(1)(a) 4.4.5
Health and Safety at Work etc.
Act 1974 .... 2.17.2
Human Rights Act 1998.................. 1.8
Insolvency Act 1986.......... 12.5.1, 12.5.2
  s.11 .... 12.4
  ss.29, 44 .... 12.5.1
  s.178(2) 12.2
Interpretation Act 1978.................. 3.23
Latent Damage Act 1986............... 1.8.5
Law of Property Act 1930.............. 12.5
Local Government Act 1985............. 5.2
Marine and Coastal Access Act
2009 .... 1.7.2
Merchant Shipping Act 1995
  s.181(1) 1.8.4
National Parks and Access to
the Countryside Act 1949 .... 2.3.2
Natural Environment and Rural
Communities Act 2006 .... 1.7.1
Nuclear Installations Act 1965
  s.12 .... 1.8.4
Nuclear Installations Act 1969........ 7.2.4
Occupiers' Liability Act 1957......... 1.8.4

Planning (Hazardous
Substances) Act 1990 ...... 1.3.4, 7.2.4
Police and Criminal Evidence
Act 1984 .... 3.12
Proceeds of Crime Act 2002........... 1.4.3
Radioactive Substances Act
1993 .... 1.3.4, 7.2.4
Regulatory Enforcement and
Sanctions Act 2008 .... 1.5, 1.5.1
Salmon Act 1975.......................... 1.1
Salmon and Freshwater
Fisheries Act 1975 .... 1.1
Town and Country Planning Act
1990
  s.72 .... 9.2.4
  s.102 .... 9.2.7
  s.106 .... 9.2.8
  s.187A 9.2.4
  ss.187B, 215, 219 .... 9.2.6
  Sched.5 .... 9.2.4
Unfair Contract Terms Act
1977 .... 10.3.5
Water Act 2003................. 2.3.1, 2.17.7
Water Industry Act 1991.............. 12.5.1
  s.118 .... 1.3.3, 6.2.5, 7.2.1
  s.210 .... 1.4.1, 12.5.1
Water Resources Act 1991 3.4, 3.6.2, 6.2.5
  s.85 .... 1.4.4
  ss.85–89 .... 1.3.1
  s.161 .... 2.9.5
  ss.161–161D 1.6.2, 3.4, 12.5.1
  s.161A 6.2.1, 6.2.3, 7.2.1, 7.2.3
  ss.161A–161D 2.17.7
  s.217(1), (3) 1.4.1
Wildlife and Countryside Act
1981 .... 1.7.1, 2.3.2, 3.4
  Part I 6.2.1, 7.2.1
  Part II 3.9, 6.2.1, 7.2.1
  s.31 .... 1.7.1

Table of statutory instruments

Anti-Pollution Works Regulations 1999, SI 1999/1006.................................... 1.6.2
Conservation (Natural Habitats etc.) Regulations 1994, SI 1994/2716............ 1.7.2, 3.9
   reg.10 .... 2.3.2
Conservation of Habitats and Species Regulations 2010, SI 2010/490................. 1.7.2
   reg.29 .... 1.7.2
Contaminated Land (England) Regulations 2006, SI 2006/1380........ 1.6.1, 2.1.1, 2.13.2
Control of Major Accident Hazards Regulations 1999, SI 1999/743... 1.2.4, 1.3.4, 1.4.3,
                                                  1.5, 2.17.3, 3.4, 3.5.2, 7.2.4
CRC Energy Efficiency Scheme Order 2010, SI 2010/768.............................. 4.4.1
   Part 5
      art.50 .... 4.4.3
   Part 6
      art.53 .... 4.4.3
   Part 9
      art.74(1) 4.4.7
   Part 14 .... 4.4.7
   Part 15
      art.106 .... 4.4.6
   Sched.3, para.2 .... 4.4.5
   Sched.9 .... 4.4.7
Energy Performance of Buildings (Certificates and Inspections) (England and
   Wales) Regulations 2007 .... 4.3
Environmental Civil Sanctions (England) Order 2010, SI 2010/1157
   Sched.5 .... 1.5.1
Environmental Damage (Prevention and Remediation) Regulations 2009, SI
   2009/153 ... 1.2.1, 1.2.2, 1.2.3, 1.5.1, 1.6.3, 1.7, 1.7.3, 3.2, 3.4, 3.5, 3.6, 3.7, 3.8, 3.9,
                          3.9.1, 3.10, 3.10.4, 3.11, 3.12, 3.15, 3.18.1, 3.18.2, 3.19,
                                 3.21, 3.22, 3.23, 3.25, 13.1, 13.6.4
   Sched.1 .... 3.6.3
   Sched.2 .... 3.5, 3.5.1, 3.5.2, 3.6.1, 3.6.2, 3.15
   Sched.3 .... 3.19
   Sched.4, Part 1 .... 3.18.2
Environmental Damage (Prevention and Remediation) (Wales) Regulations
   2009, SI 2009/995 .... 3.2, 3.5.1
Environmental Information Regulations 2004, SI 2004/3391.. 5.2, 5.2.1, 5.4, 6.4.4, 7.4.4
Environmental Permitting (England and Wales) Regulations 2010, SI
   2010/675 .... 1.3, 1.3.1, 1.5, 1.5.1, 1.10, 3.4, 3.10.1, 6.2.5, 7.2.1, 9.3, 12.5.1
   reg.38 .... 1.3.1, 1.3.2, 1.3.3, 1.3.4
      (1) 6.2.1, 7.2.1
   reg.40 .... 1.3.5, 12.5.1
   reg.41 .... 1.4.1, 12.5.1

Environmental Permitting (England and Wales) Regulations 2010, SI
2010/675 – *continued*
    reg.44 .... 12.5.1
Groundwater Regulations 1998, SI 1998/2746... 7.2.1
Hazardous Waste (England and Wales) Regulations 2005, SI 2005/894........ 1.3.1, 1.3.2
Magistrates' Courts (Advance Information) Rules 1985, SI 1985/601.................. 1.9.1
Pollution Prevention and Control (England and Wales) regulations 2000, SI
2000/1973 .... 1.3.1
    Part A1 .... 1.3.1
    Part A2 .... 1.3.1
    Part B 1.3.1
Producer Responsibility Obligations (Packaging Waste) Regulations 2007, SI
2007/871 .... 1.3.2, 8.4
Radioactive Contaminated Land (Modification of Enactments) (England)
Regulations 2006, SI 2006/1379 .... 1.6.1
Radioactive Contaminated Land (Enabling Powers and Modification of
Enactments) (England) (Amendment) Regulations, SI 2010/2147 .... 1.6.1
Site Waste Management Plans Regulations 2008, SI 2008/314........................... 9.3
Town and Country Planning (Environmental Impact Assessment) (England
and Wales) Regulations 1999, SI 1999/293 .... 8.5.1, 9.2.5
    regs.5, 7 .... 9.2.5
    reg.13(2) 9.2.5
    Sched.1 .... 9.2.5
    Sched.2 .... 9.2.5
    Sched.4 .... 9.2.5
Town and Country Planning (General Development Procedure) Order 1995, SI
1995/419
    art.10 .... 9.2.3

Table of international instruments

Convention on Wetlands of International Importance (Ramsar 1971) 1.7.1
Directive 92/43/EEC (Natural Habitats Directive) 1.7.1, 3.6.3
Directive 2000/60/EC (Water Framework Directive) 1.3.3, 3.6.2, 3.9
Directive 2002/91/EC (Energy Performance of Buildings Directive) 4.3
Directive 2002/92/EC (Insurance Mediation Directive) 13.6.2
Directive 2004/35/EC 3.2
Directive 2008/98/EC (Revised Waste Framework Directive) 1.3.1
Directive 2009/147/EC (Birds Directive) 1.7.1, 3.6.3
European Convention on Human Rights
    First Protocol 1.8.7
UNECE Convention on Access to Information, Public Participation in
    Decision-Making and Access to Justice in Environmental Matters (Aarhus
    Convention) 5.2

Abbreviations

ABI	Association of British Insurers
BAT	best available technique
CES	chartered environmental surveyor
CLG	Department for Communities and Local Government
CML	Council of Mortgage Lenders
COMAH Regulations	Control of Major Accident Hazards Regulations 1999, SI 1999/743
CRC Order	CRC Energy Efficiency Scheme Order 2010, SI 2010/768
CRC Scheme	CRC Energy Efficiency Scheme
DEC	Display Energy Certificate
DECC	Department of Energy and Climate Change
Defra	Department for Environment, Food and Regional Affairs
ECJ	European Court of Justice
EIA Regulations	Town and Country Planning (Environmental Impact Assessment) England and Wales Regulations 1999, SI 1999/293
ELD	Directive 2004/35/CE of the European Parliament and of the Council on environmental liability with regard to the prevention and remedying of environmental damage
EP	environmental permitting
EPA 1990	Environmental Protection Act 1990
EPC	Energy Performance Certificate
EU ETS	EU Emissions Trading System
Environmental Damage Regulations	Environmental Damage (Prevention and Remediation) Regulations 2009, SI 2009/153
Environmental Permitting Regulations	Environmental Permitting (England and Wales) Regulations 2010, SI 2010/675
FMP	fixed monetary penalty
FRI	full repairing and insuring
GMO	genetically modified organism
HHM	half hourly electricity meter
HSE	Health and Safety Executive

IA 1986	Insolvency Act 1986
IED	Industrial Emissions Directive
IEMA	Institute of Environmental Management and Assessment
IPC	integrated pollution control
JV	joint venture
LIP	licensed insolvency practitioner
LPA	local planning authority
OS	Ordnance Survey
PFI	private finance initiative
PII	professional indemnity insurance
PPC	pollution prevention and control
RICS	Royal Institution of Chartered Surveyors
SGU	significant group undertaking
SPL	significant pollutant linkage
SSSI	site of special scientific interest
TCPA 1990	Town and Country Planning Act 1990
VMP	variable monetary penalty
WAC	waste acceptance criteria
WIA 1991	Water Industry Act 1991
WCA 1981	Wildlife and Countryside Act 1981
WRA 1991	Water Resources Act 1991

CHAPTER 1

Environmental liabilities

1.1 INTRODUCTION

All environmental considerations – in whatever type of circumstance – are, ultimately, liability driven. What liabilities may an owner, a buyer of land or a company, a developer or their associated investors, officers or advisers be facing?

Much has been said and written about the extent, and potential cost, of environmental liabilities over recent years. Much of the rhetoric could be said to have caused some overreaction in the financial and business community. Although such liabilities can be expensive, and one may have to take a decision to fund improvements, close operations, back out of a deal or walk away from a purchase if the risks are too great, equally, there may be many instances where the perception of the risk is much worse than the reality.

Full information is needed – about the legal position, the practical stance taken by the regulatory bodies, and the actual state of contamination or other environmental damage. With such knowledge, one can take informed decisions about risk assessment or about proceeding with a transaction, and take all the necessary steps and precautions to secure the appropriate protection.

Conversely, a pollution incident such as a spill of heating oil or petrol from a storage tank may result in clean-up costs of many thousands of pounds, sometimes even exceeding a million pounds, if the spill occurs above a major aquifer or near a reservoir. The owner of the tank may also face a criminal prosecution for causing water pollution. Insurance that provides cover for clean-up costs and defence costs (not for a criminal fine) is available but this must be purchased separately; most public liability policies do not provide the requisite cover (see Chapter 13).

This chapter is intended to set out the basic legal position. First, it briefly describes the main governmental environmental and nature conservation bodies. It then highlights the current regulatory, clean-up, nature conservation/biodiversity, and tort liabilities and indicates the key criminal and civil liabilities which may arise. It then provides practical pointers for protecting a client against criminal and clean-up/biodiversity liabilities. The discussion deals with the vast majority of the possibilities, although other associated legislation, such as the Salmon and Freshwater Fisheries Act 1975 and the Salmon Act 1986, for example, is not discussed in detail.

1

Later chapters deal with the practical considerations involved in specific types of transaction, and discuss the steps to take to assess the actual or potential contamination or pollution issues.

1.2 ENFORCING AUTHORITIES

It is important to consider not only the legal regime itself, but also the regulatory body that enforces it. Various governmental bodies enforce environmental and nature conservation/biodiversity laws in England. The main enforcing bodies are local authorities, the Environment Agency and Natural England (and equivalent authorities in Wales, Scotland and Northern Ireland). The Health and Safety Executive (HSE) also plays a role.

1.2.1 Local authorities

Local authorities have duties and responsibilities under pollution control regimes, mainly for air pollution, statutory nuisance and noise, as well as planning duties and responsibilities. In addition, they are the primary enforcing authorities for Part IIA of the Environmental Protection Act (EPA) 1990 and have enforcement powers in respect of land damage under the Environmental Damage (Prevention and Remediation) Regulations 2009, SI 2009/153, as amended (the Environmental Damage Regulations). Some local authorities employ contaminated land officers; in others, the environmental health office has responsibilities for investigating and remediating contaminated land in addition to other responsibilities.

1.2.2 Environment Agency

The Environment Agency is a non-departmental public body of the Department for Environment, Food and Regional Affairs (Defra). The Agency's duties and responsibilities in respect of pollution control regimes include:

- environmental permitting (other than air quality but including pollution prevention and control, waste management, mining waste, surface and ground water discharges, radioactive substances and batteries);
- water resources and water quality (including recreation, fisheries and flood risk management);
- a sub-set of contaminated land known as 'special sites' under Part IIA; and
- environmental damage to water and activities permitted by the Environment Agency under the Environmental Damage Regulations.

The Agency is also the enforcing authority for the CRC Energy Efficiency scheme (see Chapter 4).

The Environment Agency has published an Enforcement and Prosecution Policy and Guidance for that policy. The policy and guidance are updated from time to time and are available on the Agency's website (**www.environment-agency.gov.uk**).

1.2.3 Natural England

Natural England is the main enforcing body in England for implementing nature conservation legislation and, as part of that implementation, prosecuting offences under it (equivalent authorities exist in Wales, Scotland and Northern Ireland). Natural England also enforces the Environmental Damage Regulations for land in sites of special scientific interest (SSSIs) and protected species and natural habitats.

Natural England has published an Enforcement Policy that sets out its approach to enforcement and prosecution. It has also published an Enforcement Strategy. Both documents are updated from time to time and are available on its website (**www.naturalengland.org.uk**).

1.2.4 Health and Safety Executive

In addition to its duties and responsibilities under health and safety legislation, the HSE is the enforcing authority, together with the Environment Agency, for the Control of Major Accident Hazards Regulations 1999, SI 1999/743, as amended (COMAH Regulations). The HSE's Enforcement Policy Statement is updated from time to time and is available on its website (**www.hse.gov.uk**).

1.3 REGULATORY LIABILITIES

The scope of environmental regulations is ever increasing. The regulations now affect not only petrochemical companies and companies that are considered to be traditional polluters; they also affect many small and medium-sized businesses and individuals.

The main regulatory regime in England and Wales is the Environmental Permitting (England and Wales) Regulations 2010, SI 2010/675 (the Environmental Permitting Regulations). Other regimes exist for waste, water and hazardous substances other than those activities that are regulated under the Regulations.

It should be noted that, increasingly, environmental legislation is in the form of regulations rather than primary legislation. The change reflects the continuing influence of the EU on UK environmental law. About 90 per cent of environmental law in the UK is derived from the EU. As such, the debates on the enactment of the legislation do not occur in Parliament. They occur mainly in the Council and the European Parliament with the input of the European Commission. Debates on the legislation do occur during the transposition of the legislation into UK law but these

3

generally take the form of comments to consultations on proposed regulations by Defra and other UK government bodies with, in some cases, workshops and public meetings.

1.3.1 Environmental Permitting Regulations

The Environmental Permitting Regulations apply to a broad range of activities including water discharges, groundwater activities, radioactive substances, waste, mining waste and 'installations' (a term that includes factories and many other industrial and commercial facilities). The first Environmental Permitting Regulations came into force in 2008 and combined controls over pollution prevention and control and waste management licensing. In 2010, the regulations were expanded to transpose or recast various pieces of EU legislation and to include activities that had formerly been controlled under many different regulatory regimes.

The Environment Agency has published guidance for the following sectors that are covered by the Environmental Permitting Regulations. The list illustrates the breadth of the permitting system beyond what may be considered to be the more polluting industries:

- intensive farming (pigs and poultry);
- mining waste;
- surface and ground water discharges;
- pollution prevention and control (PPC);
- waste treatment and storage;
- paper, pulp and cardboard manufacturing;
- chemicals;
- waste incineration;
- energy industry including oil refining;
- printing and textiles;
- metal production and processing;
- coke, iron and steel manufacturing;
- cement and lime activities;
- power stations and other large combustion plants;
- groundwater;
- landfills;
- radioactive substances; and
- clinical waste.

Pollution prevention and control

The Environmental Permitting Regulations replace, among other things, the Pollution Prevention and Control (England and Wales) Regulations 2000, SI 2000/1973, as amended. They incorporate the three-tier system from those regulations, comprising Part A1, Part A2, and Part B processes, the first regulated by the Environment Agency, the latter two by local authorities.

The conditions of an environmental permit under the subsumed pollution prevention and control regime require 'emission limit values', that is, discharges (emissions) that are authorised under a permit, to be based on 'best available techniques' (BAT). The purpose of applying BAT is the prevention or minimisation of polluting discharges. Emission limit values must also 'take account of the technical characteristics of the particular installation …, its geographical location and the local environmental conditions'. The technological benchmarks are, as with the prior regimes, set by reference to industry-wide standards agreed centrally. Other conditions include 'housekeeping' conditions regarding monitoring, record-keeping and reporting. There is also an increased emphasis on minimising the use of energy and other resources such as water.

Site reports are required at the start and end of any A1/A2 installation. The purpose of the reports is to identify any soil and groundwater contamination that is attributable to the operations carried out under the permit. When a permit for an A1/A2 installation is surrendered, the land at the installation must be returned to a 'satisfactory state'. That is, any pollution that occurred during the pendency of the permit must be remediated if it poses a risk to human health and the environment.

The subsumed pollution prevention and control regime will expand again in about 2012 when the Industrial Emissions Directive (IED) is transposed into the law of the UK (and other Member States). Among other things, the IED will require further investigations of soil and groundwater at installations controlled under it.

Waste management

The Environmental Permitting Regulations also modified Part II of EPA 1990 which governs the system for the regulation of waste. An environmental permit from the Environment Agency is required by anyone who is in the business of dealing with, treating or disposing of 'waste', as defined in the Regulations. This regime is essentially aimed at those operating landfill sites, incinerators, waste treatment and recycling facilities and waste transfer stations, though any permanent treatment of waste is caught, for example, scrapyards.

A solicitor needing to advise in respect of waste should carry out further research in this area because it is fraught with complexities and difficulties; the legislation governing waste, and cases on it, are voluminous. The complexities and difficulties include knowing when a material is 'waste' and when it ceases to be 'waste'.

Waste is anything which is, is intended to be, or is required to be, 'discarded', i.e. abandoned, dumped, disposed of or put in its final resting place, or subjected to a recovery operation without which it is useless. The definition is particularly broad and confusing. Carnwath LJ described the complexities well in *R (OSS Group Ltd) v. Environment Agency* [2007] EWCA Civ 611, as follows:

a search for logical coherence in the [European Court of Justice] case law [on waste] is probably doomed to failure. A fundamental problem is the court's professed adherence to the ... definition [of waste], even where it can be of no practical relevance. The subjective 'intention to discard' may be a useful guide to the status of the material in the hands of the original producer. However, it is hard to apply to the status of the material in the hands of someone who buys it for recycling or reprocessing; or who puts it to some other valuable use. In no ordinary sense is such a person 'discarding' or 'getting rid of' the material. His intention is precisely the opposite.

The notion of discarding was also confused, among other things, by the September 2004 case of *Van de Walle* v. *Texaco (Belgium) SA* (Case C-1/03). In that case, the European Court of Justice ruled that unexcavated soil which included spillages and leakages of waste was waste.

The Revised Waste Framework Directive (Directive 2008/98/EC on waste), which has a transposition deadline of 12 December 2010, clarifies that unexcavated soil is not waste. The Directive also includes new, in addition to existing, waste prevention and recycling measures as well as statutory targets for reducing waste (50 per cent reduction of waste from households and 70 per cent reduction of construction and demolition waste, both by 2020). Further, the Directive has implications for the statutory duty of care for waste, including requiring separate collections for waste paper, metal, plastic and glass by 2015.

Another complex area of environmental law involves prohibitions and/or restrictions on the landfilling of specified waste, such as liquid waste and tyres, and the implementation of waste acceptance criteria (WAC). WAC set out treatment measures that must be carried out before a particular type of waste may be accepted and disposed of at a landfill (if, indeed, landfilling is lawful for that waste).

It is also critical to know when waste is hazardous waste, because the handling and disposal of such waste is subject to more stringent provisions. Hazardous waste is controlled by the Hazardous Waste (England and Wales) Regulations 2005, SI 2005/894, as amended. Again, this area is fraught with complexities, including knowing when an activity is exempt from hazardous waste producer registration.

General offences

Regulation 38 sets out the offences under the Environmental Permitting Regulations. In addition to commencing proceedings in respect of the above offences, the Environment Agency or, for some environmental permits, the relevant local authority, may serve an enforcement notice or a suspension notice.

It is an offence to:

- carry out a permitted activity without a permit;
- carry out a permitted activity in breach of the conditions of a permit or otherwise than in compliance with such conditions;
- fail to comply with an enforcement notice, a prohibition notice, a suspension notice, a landfill closure notice or a mining waste facility closure notice;
- fail to comply with an information notice;

- make a false or misleading statement in respect of matters specified in the regulation;
- make a false entry in a record that must be kept according to a condition in an environmental permit;
- commit deception, forgery or the like in any application or other documentation; and
- fail to comply with specified record-keeping requirements or to fail to make an entry in specified records.

The Regulations also provide that if an offence committed by a person under the Regulations is due to the act or default of another person, the other person is also guilty of the offence regardless of whether proceedings have been brought against the first person.

Water-related offences

It is also an offence under the Environmental Permitting Regulations to commit the following water-related offence:

- to cause or knowingly permit a water discharge activity or a groundwater activity other than for an exempt facility.

Water discharge activities include the following:

- the discharge of poisonous, noxious or polluting matter or solid waste matter into surface water, coastal water and relevant territorial water;
- the discharge of trade or sewage effluent into surface water, coastal water and relevant territorial water; and
- the cutting or uprooting of substantial quantities of vegetation in surface water, without reasonable steps having been taken to remove the vegetation from the water.

Groundwater discharge activities are unlawful direct or indirect discharges into groundwater.

In addition to bringing a prosecution in respect of the above offences, the Environment Agency or, for some environmental permits, the relevant local authority, may serve an enforcement notice or a suspension notice.

Water pollution offences under the Environmental Permitting Regulations are similar to those that were previously set out in ss.85–89 of the Water Resources Act (WRA) 1991. Although the Environmental Permitting Regulations repealed the offences, the similarity – or, in some cases, the identical nature of – the new offences means that prior case law is still relevant.

The offence of 'causing' water pollution requires proof of a positive act or omission on the part of the defendant; dumping, leaking, overfilling, operating inefficiently, breaching bund walls, hosing excess chemicals down broken drains and the like. It is not necessary to prove knowledge, negligence or fault. All that is needed is a causal link between the activity and the pollution. Being part of the cause is also sufficient.

Note also *Empress Car Co. (Abertillery) Ltd* v. *National Rivers Authority* [1998] 2 WLR 350, in which the House of Lords affirmed the conviction of a site owner for a water pollution offence notwithstanding intervention by a vandal. The site owner maintained an unbunded and unsecured oil storage tank on its premises. One night, a vandal opened the tap on the tank, causing the oil to flow onto the ground and enter the nearby river. The House of Lords concluded that both the site owner and the vandal caused the pollution and that it would have needed an 'extraordinary' event such as a terrorist bomb to break the chain of causation between the site owner and the pollution. This judgment has been followed in many subsequent cases with the result that most businesses that are prosecuted by the Environment Agency for water pollution enter a guilty plea accompanied by a plea in mitigation.

'Permitting' pollution can consist of merely allowing pollution to remain, i.e. not removing it, if it was possible to do so. The offence is that of 'knowingly' permitting. What degree of knowledge is required?

There is some authority (*Schulmans Incorporated Ltd* v. *National Rivers Authority* [1993] Env LR D1) for the view that, in addition to actual knowledge of the circumstances, turning a blind eye to the obvious or deliberately refraining from enquiry for fear of the truth, may attract liability.

This ambiguity over the definition of knowingly permitting means that a purchaser or current owner may be liable for ongoing water pollution caused originally by someone else.

Clients must not imagine that deliberately contrived ignorance of the fact and extent of pollution will get them off the hook. A defence of 'I didn't want to know, so I didn't bother looking' will not work. If the client could have found out about the pollution (e.g. by a survey or investigation) and could have done something to correct it but failed to take those steps, they may be said to have 'knowingly permitted' it.

Solicitors should also note cases involving the run-off of fire-fighting water into controlled waters. The courts have decided that this is still the offence of 'causing' water pollution committed by the site owner, not the Fire Service.

1.3.2 Other waste legislation

Although the Environmental Permitting Regulations include the waste permitting regime, they are not the sole source of waste legislation. In addition, Part II of EPA 1990 sets out waste offences.

Under EPA 1990, s.33, as amended, it is an offence for a person:

- to deposit controlled waste or extractive waste, or knowingly cause or knowingly permit controlled waste or extractive waste to be deposited in or on any land without or in breach of a permit;

- to submit controlled waste, or knowingly cause or knowingly permit controlled waste to be submitted, to any listed operation in or on land, or by means of a mobile plant, without or in breach of a permit unless the waste operation is exempt; or
- to treat, keep or dispose of controlled waste or extractive waste in a manner likely to cause pollution of the environment or harm to human health.

A person convicted of an offence may also be liable for the costs of cleaning up the waste.

There is also the statutory duty of care contained in EPA 1990, s.34, in relation to persons who merely produce waste as a natural concomitant of a process or activity. Section 34 requires those generating and holding waste temporarily, pending its ultimate removal elsewhere, to:

- accurately identify the different types of waste generated and, ideally, segregate them (the key differentiation to be made being that between non-hazardous waste and 'hazardous' waste within the meaning given in the Hazardous Waste (England and Wales) Regulations 2005, SI 2005/894, as amended – which catches, among other things, oily, toxic, flammable or dangerous waste, and includes items such as TV and computer monitors and fluorescent light tubes);
- store it securely (against leakage and interference);
- label it accurately, using the appropriate paperwork;
- complete transfer notes for the waste (if non-hazardous) or consignment notes (if hazardous) for it;
- hand it over to a registered carrier for removal, with the relevant paperwork; and
- take reasonable steps to ensure that no offence is committed by anyone dealing with the waste at any time (a potentially onerous element requiring supervision of other people's actions and activities).

Yet more waste legislation has been enacted since the mid-1990s due, among other things, to obligations under EU law to minimise the creation of waste as well as to maximise its re-use and recycling. Current legislation also includes regulations concerning:

- packaging and packaging waste;
- waste electrical and electronic equipment;
- end-of-life vehicles; and
- site waste management plans (applicable to construction projects with an estimated cost greater than £300,000).

The Environment Agency may bring proceedings under the above legislation, for example, the failure of a business to register as a producer of packaging waste or otherwise to comply with the Producer Responsibility Obligations (Packaging Waste) Regulations 2007, SI 2007/871, as amended. In some cases, the business may first discover that it is in breach of the Regulations and subject to fines when it receives a request for information on its compliance with the Regulations from the Environment Agency. If the Environment Agency proceeds with a prosecution, it typically brings charges for three offences for each year during which the business has not registered. There is no real defence to such a prosecution. If a business meets the criteria for a producer of packaging waste for a given year and it has not registered, it has committed offences for each year of non-compliance.

Other waste-related legislation includes registration requirements for waste carriers and brokers, as well as obligations for the shipment of waste.

1.3.3 Other water-related legislation

In a somewhat similar manner to waste-related legislation, the Environmental Permitting Regulations are not the sole source of water-related regulatory legislation.

In addition, the Water Industry Act (WIA) 1991 sets out the powers and duties of the privatised water companies. Under s.118, it is an offence for an occupier of trade premises to discharge trade effluent into a public sewer without or in breach of the sewerage undertaker's consent as to the nature and composition and the quantity and rate of the discharge, and identification of the sewers into which the discharge can be made.

Other water-related legislation pertains specifically to agriculture such as regulations to prevent nitrate pollution and the control of pollution from silage, slurry and agricultural fuel oil. Yet other regulatory water-related legislation is more general such as requirements concerning the storage of oil. There is also legislation concerning fisheries.

There is also a vast body of legislation arising from the Water Framework Directive (Directive 2000/60/EC establishing a framework for Community action in the field of water policy) as well as legislation concerning, among other things, water quality and quantity.

1.3.4 Hazardous substances

Miscellaneous legislation covers offences relating to hazardous substances; it includes the Planning (Hazardous Substances) Act 1990 and the Radioactive Substances Act 1993.

The keeping, use, accumulation and disposal of radioactive substances in Great Britain is regulated by the Radioactive Substances Act 1993. The main purpose of this Act is to provide radiation protection to members of the public. As noted above, activities concerning radioactive substances are also regulated under the Environmental Permitting Regulations.

Storage of hazardous substances relates to the granting of consents under the Planning (Hazardous Substances) Act 1990. Hazardous substance consents are designed to ensure that hazardous substances can only be kept or used in significant quantities after the responsible authorities have had the opportunity to assess the risk to surrounding areas.

Under the COMAH Regulations, as amended, sites storing above specified amounts of hazardous substances and those carrying out particularly toxic or hazardous activities must provide information to the public on the nature of the hazard and action to be taken in the event of an accident. The Regulations mainly apply to chemical and petrochemical industries and to those that produce or use substances with flammable, toxic or explosive properties.

1.3.5 Defences

Some statutory environmental offences have defences. The defences are, however, continuing slowly to be narrowed. The following are examples to illustrate the main types of defences available for some, but not all, environmental offences.

EPA 1990, s.33(7) contains defences if the defendant can show that, in the process of depositing waste illegally:

- all reasonable precautions were taken and the defendant exercised due diligence to avoid the offence being committed; or
- the activities were undertaken in an emergency to avoid harm to human health, the defendant took all reasonably practicable steps to minimise the pollution and provided particulars of the acts to the Environment Agency as soon as reasonably practicable after they occurred.

A similar defence to that under the second bullet point above is available under reg.40 of the Environmental Permitting Regulations for, among other things, causing or knowingly permitting a water discharge activity, non-compliance with a permit condition and failure to comply with an enforcement notice, a prohibition notice, suspension notice, landfill closure notice or mining waste facility closure notice.

Under EPA 1990, s.80(7), it is a defence to a prosecution in respect of a statutory nuisance on industrial, trade or business premises to show that the best practicable means were used to counteract the effects of the nuisance.

Under EPA 1990, s.78M(2), it is a defence to a prosecution for failure to comply with a remediation notice to show that the reason it was not complied with was that a joint polluter could not or would not pay their allocated share of the cost of compliance.

1.4 CRIMINAL PROCEEDINGS

Nearly all environmental offences are criminal offences. In addition, virtually all environmental offences, with the major exception of public nuisance, are derived from legislation. Further, most environmental offences are triable either way although the vast majority of prosecutions for such offences take place in magistrates' courts.

It is worth noting that the Environment Agency and other enforcing authorities do not always bring charges for an environmental offence. Depending on the nature and severity of the offence, they may issue a warning letter or a formal caution. The Guidance for the Enforcement and Prosecution Policy, published by the Environment Agency, sets out the Agency's normal approach to specific offences.

A distinguishing feature of many environmental offences is their basis in strict liability. A business or other person may, therefore, be subject to imprisonment or an unlimited fine if they commit an offence despite a lack of knowledge, intent, recklessness or other mental element normally associated with traditional criminal offences. That said, however, there is a significant knock-on effect to strict liability offences in that, due to there being no need to prove that a defendant is culpable, judges have been reticent to sentence individuals to long – or, in most cases, any – terms of imprisonment and have also been reticent to impose substantial fines.

1.4.1 Prosecutions

The vast majority of prosecutions for environmental offences are brought by the Environment Agency. It should be remembered, however, that private prosecutions can also be brought. Private prosecutions have been brought by Fish Legal (previously the Anglers Conservation Association) and other non-governmental organisations and individuals, in particular, for water pollution offences.

Directors and officers

Slightly over 60 per cent of prosecutions each year are brought for waste offences; compared to about 26 per cent for water pollution cases. The remaining 14 per cent consist of air pollution, fishing and other environmental offences.

Between 2000 and 2007, the Environment Agency commenced proceedings for about 1,600 environmental offences each year. The number of proceedings in each year was fairly constant, with the number of prosecutions accounting for approximately half that number, with the remainder being cautions and formal warnings.

Although the vast majority of prosecutions are brought against companies, directors and others may be made directly liable for the various criminal liabilities mentioned above if they can be said to fall within the statutory wording creating the offence (e.g. by causing or knowingly permitting a water discharge activity).

Directors and other company officers may, in addition, be made indirectly liable for many of the criminal offences of their companies by virtue of provisions such as EPA 1990, s.157, which provides that:

> Where an offence under any provision of this Act committed by a body corporate is proved to have been committed with the consent or connivance of, or to have been

attributable to any neglect on the part of, any director, manager, secretary or other similar officer of the body corporate or a person who was purporting to act in any such capacity, he as well as the body corporate shall be guilty of that offence and shall be liable to be proceeded against and punished accordingly.

Similar provisions are to be found in most other environmental legislation, see, for example, WRA 1991, s.217(1), Environmental Permitting Regulations, reg.41, and WIA 1991, s.210.

It follows that whether or not the company is prosecuted for an offence, its directors can be, and they can also be imprisoned, depending on the offence. Prosecutions against directors and officers for environmental offences are, however, relatively rare and have been brought mainly for waste offences concerning small companies with few assets.

Any other person, such as employees, contractors, parent companies and lenders, may also be made liable by virtue of EPA 1990, s.158 if they are involved in the activities of the company. It provides:

Where the commission by any person of an offence under Part I, II, IV or VI or section 140, 141 or 142 above is due to the act or default of some other person, that other person may be charged with and convicted of the offence by virtue of this section whether or not proceedings for the offence are taken against the first-mentioned person.

This does not include statutory nuisances.

A similar provision is to be found in WRA 1991, s.217(3); there are no similar provisions in WIA 1991.

A director or other employee, a contractor or even a parent company, may be caught by this provision if they commit some act or default which results in an offence being committed.

Lenders, such as banks, may potentially be indirectly liable under provisions such as EPA 1990, ss.157 and 158 if they become so involved in the running of the business, for example, by issuing instructions to the management team, that they could, in effect, be said to be acting in the capacity of an officer of the company, or someone whose act or default caused the offence.

1.4.2 Penalties

Depending on the offence and the identity of the defendant, the potential maximum penalties for environmental offences are:

- six months' imprisonment, or a £50,000 fine in the magistrates' court:
- two to five years' imprisonment, or unlimited fines in the Crown Court.

Under the contaminated land provisions in Part IIA of EPA 1990, daily default fines may be imposed for non-compliance with a remediation notice.

1.4.3 Level of fines

The level of fines for environmental offences is rising, albeit slowly. This is partly due to urging by the Environment Agency and others. The fines, however, tend to be lower than those for health and safety and other more traditional offences with far fewer custodial sentences imposed. The average level of fines for environmental offences between 2000 and 2007 was about £6,700 for each water offence conviction and £3,700 for each waste offence conviction.

In 2008, the Environment Agency brought 722 prosecutions against companies and individuals, resulting in fines and costs totalling £5.3 million. The waste management industry accounted for one third of all serious pollution incidents in 2008, agriculture accounted for a quarter, and water companies accounted for one sixth of such incidents. In 2008, the average fine imposed against a company for an environmental offence was £10,080; in 2007, it was £8,229.

At the time of writing (2010), an average fine for a first offence, with good mitigation, was generally between £3,000 and £20,000 plus costs, but this very much depends on the facts, the magistrates and the number of charges which are brought.

Illustrative fines imposed by courts for environmental offences in mid-2010 are as follows:

- £19,500 with £8,447 costs imposed by Lincoln Magistrates' Court on a plastic bottle recycling company that pleaded guilty to polluting a dyke with oil;
- £4,000 with £3,210 costs imposed by Plymouth Magistrates' Court on a china clay company that pleaded guilty to polluting a brook after heavy rain caused sediments to run off an area of moorland cleared by the company;
- £3,000 with £4,833 in costs imposed by Crawley Magistrates' Court on a water company that pleaded guilty to polluting a stream with sewage from a broken pipe;
- £27,000 with £27,837 in costs imposed by the Crown Court on a water company that pleaded guilty to causing a release of sewage into a river;
- £225,000 with £3,230 in costs and £2,486 in compensation to the Environment Agency imposed on a wine merchant by Telford Magistrates' Court for breaches of the packaging regulations between 2003 and 2005;
- £32,000 with £60,000 in costs and a £15 victim surcharge imposed on the operator of a garden centre and composting site by Stafford Magistrates' Court for its treatment of composting material, breach of a waste management licence, and knowingly allowing waste to be deposited at the site while the licence was suspended; and
- £15,000 with £2,568 in costs imposed on a manufacturer and distributor of organic chemicals by Bradford Magistrates' Court for breaches of an environmental permit.

At the highest end of the scale, the fines and costs imposed by St Albans Crown Court in the joint prosecution by the Environment Agency and HSE for environmental and health and safety offences arising out of the Buncefield Oil Terminal explosion in 2005 were about £9 million. The explosion was caused after petrol that was being pumped into a storage tank overflowed and spilled over the top of the bund. The petrol exploded resulting in a vapour cloud of about 200 square metres wide by 4 metres deep. The explosion measured 2.4 on the Richter scale. The following are the fines and costs:

- £3.6 million with £2.6 million costs on the oil company Total – £3 million fine for health and safety offences; £600,000 for water pollution offences;
- £1.4 million with £1 million costs on Hertfordshire Oil Storage Limited – £1 million fine for health and safety offences; £450,000 for breaches of the COMAH Regulations;
- £300,000 fine on British Pipeline Agency Ltd with £480,000 costs for breaches of the COMAH Regulations; and
- £1,000 fine with £500 costs each on TAV Engineering Ltd and Motherwell Control Systems for health and safety offences.

The level of fines for environmental offences is likely to continue to rise because, among other things, the Environment Agency still considers that the level is too low to be a serious deterrent for some businesses.

Another type of environmental prosecution to be aware of, especially in waste cases, is the use of the Proceeds of Crime Act 2002, as amended. For example, in July 2010, Teesside Magistrates' Court ordered two directors of a skip hire company to pay £124,393 and £110,000, respectively, within 12 months or face three years' imprisonment. The directors each received a conditional discharge. The sum of £234,393 was the amount of the unlawful benefit received by the company and the two directors. The court ordered the confiscation of assets from the directors to the value of that amount. It also ordered the company to pay £3,755 in costs and compensation of £6,854 to the Environment Agency. The company had pleaded guilty to operating a site as a waste transfer station without a permit. The directors had pleaded guilty in Hartlepool Magistrates' Court in 2007 to committing the offence with their consent, connivance or negligence.

In many cases, the cost of cleaning up contamination or paying claims caused by it is a greater deterrent to a business than the amount of a fine. For example, Total faced an estimated £750 million in civil damage claims arising from the Buncefield explosion. In another case, a manufacturer of detergents in Lancashire caused substantial damage to the aquatic life of a river in 2009 when bleach escaped from its facility. The manufacturer pleaded guilty to causing the bleach to enter the river and was fined £6,600 and ordered to pay over £4,800 costs. The cost of investigating the pollution, stopping it and improving the site, however, cost nearly £70,000. As noted in the introduction to this chapter, the cost of remediating groundwater pollution may exceed £1 million. Remediation costs for groundwater pollution in the hundreds of thousands are not unusual.

1.4.4 Reduction of fines

The Court of Appeal has a tendency to reduce fines for environmental offences, finding that they are 'manifestly excessive'.

For example, in *R* v. *Milford Haven Port Authority* [2000] Env LR 673, the port authority was convicted in Cardiff Crown Court under WRA 1991, s.85 for a water pollution offence arising out of the *Sea Empress* oil spill disaster. The port authority was fined £4 million (four times the previous highest fine). It appealed against the amount of the fine and in March 2000 the Court of Appeal agreed that the original fine was 'manifestly excessive' and reduced it to £750,000.

The Court of Appeal took the opportunity to set out the factors relevant to penalty, and echoed its original advice given in *R* v. *F Howe & Sons (Engineers) Ltd* [1999] 2 All ER 249, CA (a health and safety case).

The factors, amongst others, are:

- the degree of deliberacy or intention involved;
- the presence or absence of a profit motive;
- whether harm to persons was caused and its degree;
- whether an immediate plea of guilty was entered; and
- the adequacy of relevant management systems.

The Court of Appeal considered that the *Milford Haven* reduction was justified on the grounds that, though serious, it was unintentional and no loss of human life resulted.

At around the same time, the Home Office Sentencing Advisory Panel also reported. It expressed the view that environmental penalties were inconsistent, and generally, too low. However, the Court of Appeal declined to follow its recommendations on the approach to sentencing in such cases, preferring to follow its earlier views as expressed in *Howe*.

Since that time, the Court of Appeal has continued to reduce fines for environmental offences (see, e.g. *R* v. *Anglian Water Service* [2003] EWCA Crim 2243).

A recent reduction example of a fine for an environmental offence is *R* v. *Thames Water Utilities Ltd* [2010] EWCA Crim 202, in which the Court of Appeal reduced a fine for a spill of industrial strength chlorine into the River Wandle from £125,000 to £50,000. The spill polluted nearly 5 kilometres of the river and destroyed 20 years of work in restoring the river. The water company, which had 82 convictions between 1991 and 2008 for water pollution by sewage from its premises, had paid or pledged £500,000 to restore the river and improve the local environment.

In reaching its conclusion, the Court of Appeal considered aggravating and mitigating factors (see **1.9.3**). It then set out the following approach that a court should take in calculating the fine, plus any compensation order(s), for a single offence such as the water pollution offence at issue:

- assess the seriousness of the offence by considering all relative aggravating and mitigating facts;

- identify the amount of a notional fine to combine punishment and deterrent elements;
- add to, or deduct from, the notional fine the amount of any appropriate compensation order(s) to be made (considering any offer by the offender to submit to such an order(s));
- consider the extent to which the offender has taken corrective measures, with the failure to do so generally being a significant aggravating factor, and with the carrying out of substantial voluntary corrective measures being regarded as a significant mitigating factor – with any deduction for voluntary measures not generally reducing the notional fine below the amount of its punishment element;
- consider whether there are any further mitigation features that could result in a further reduction of the notional fine; and
- deduct the appropriate percentage of discount for the guilty plea.

1.5 CIVIL SANCTIONS

In 2010, the Environment Agency and Natural England (and the Countryside Council for Wales) became the first regulators to be granted the power to impose civil, as well as criminal, sanctions for some offences. They gained these powers as a result of the Regulatory Enforcement and Sanctions Act 2008, which authorises the relevant Minister to issue an order that provides a regulatory authority with access to such sanctions following set procedures. The introduction of the Act followed detailed reports on regulatory enforcement by Sir Philip Hampton and Professor Richard Macrory.

The introduction of civil sanctions did not create any new environmental offences. Instead, it authorises the Environment Agency and Natural England to impose civil sanctions for some, but not all, existing offences instead of bringing prosecutions in relation to them.

The Environment Agency will begin using its civil sanction powers on 4 January 2011. Initially, it intends to use them mainly for hazardous waste, water resources and packaging waste offences committed in England after 6 April 2010 (after 15 July 2010 in Wales). Civil sanctions for breaches of the Environmental Permitting Regulations are anticipated to be in use by April 2011. Natural England is less advanced in introducing sanctions than the Environment Agency.

At the time of writing (2010), there are no plans to authorise civil sanctions for breaches of the COMAH Regulations and other areas in which the Environment Agency has joint enforcing powers with HSE. HSE has consistently opposed the use of civil sanctions for health and safety offences, considering that they are inappropriate for such serious offences.

1.5.1 Types of sanctions

The following civil sanctions created by the Regulatory Enforcement and Sanctions Act 2008 are to be applied by the Environment Agency and Natural England: compliance notice; restoration notice; enforcement undertaking; fixed monetary penalty (FMP); variable monetary penalty (VMP); stop notice; and enforcement undertaking.

It should be noted that not all civil sanctions apply to all environmental offences. The Environmental Civil Sanctions (England) Order, SI 2010/1157, which provides the Environment Agency and Natural England with authority to impose civil sanctions, lists the offences for which civil sanctions may be applied in Schedule 5. The Schedule also lists the civil sanctions that may be applied for each offence.

The Environment Agency may issue a VMP, a restoration notice and a compliance notice for the same offence. The Agency's website sets out details of the way in which it will use civil sanctions, together with detailed descriptions of them. See **www.environment-agency.gov.uk/business/regulation/116844.aspx**.

All civil penalties are paid into the Government's Consolidated Fund. Professor Macrory, who proposed the various categories of sanctions, considered that this would prevent regulators from taking monetary reasons into account in imposing a sanction.

The following is a description of the types of civil penalties as they will be applied by the Environment Agency.

Compliance notice

A compliance notice specifies measures that must be taken by the offender within the time specified in the notice to terminate the breach or to ensure that it does not occur again. A compliance notice is somewhat similar to an enforcement notice under the Environmental Permitting Regulations.

Restoration notice

A restoration notice specifies measures that must be taken by the offender within the time specified in the notice to restore harm caused by non-compliance with environmental legislation, generally to its state before the harm occurred. The measures need not necessarily be taken at the damaged site but may include measures to restore, say, a fish population to the state it would have been in without the damage, at another site if it is more appropriate to do so.

A restoration notice may not be issued in respect of environmental damage under the Environmental Damage Regulations (described in Chapter 3).

Fixed monetary penalty

An FMP is issued, like a fixed penalty for a road traffic offence, for minor breaches of environmental law.

The offences for which the Environment Agency may issue an FMP are those that do not involve significant environmental harm or a risk of such harm. There is a maximum limit of £100 for an FMP for an individual or sole trader and a maximum of £300 for a company. These amounts may be reduced by 50 per cent for payment within 28 days or increased by 50 per cent for payment after 56 days.

Variable monetary penalty

A VMP may be imposed for several reasons. These include:

- evidence of negligence and mismanagement on the part of an offender but for which the Agency decides that prosecution is not in the public interest;
- removal of a financial benefit such as permit fees or operating costs as a result of non-compliance with environmental legislation; and
- in addition to a restoration notice when there has been significant environmental damage.

The purpose of a VMP is to change an offender's behaviour and to act as a general deterrent.

The calculation of a VMP is a three-step process in respect of which the Environment Agency has published guidance. If the offence for which the VMP is imposed may only be heard in the magistrates' court, its cap is the maximum that may be imposed for that offence. The maximum for a VMP for all other environmental offences is £250,000.

Appeals against VMPs are likely, particularly if they result in fines that are above the average imposed by courts for environmental offences.

Stop notice

In order to serve a stop notice, the Environment Agency must reasonably believe that the activity that is being, or is likely to be, carried out involves an applicable offence or is causing, or is likely to cause, serious harm to human health or the environment. The stop notice orders the business or other person on whom it is served immediately to cease carrying out the relevant activity(ies) until the person has complied with applicable legislation or has removed the risk of serious harm by carrying out measures specified in the notice. The failure to comply with a stop notice is a criminal offence.

A stop notice may be issued in combination with any other civil penalty except an FMP. The Environment Agency may withdraw a stop notice. If it does so, or there is a successful appeal against it, the Agency is obliged to compensate the business. Due to the seriousness of stop notices, there is a fast track procedure for their appeal.

Enforcement undertaking

An enforcement undertaking is an offer by an offender to carry out measures to make amends for non-compliance with environmental legislation and its implications. An enforcement undertaking differs from the other civil sanctions in that the offender, rather than the Environment Agency, proposes its application. Also in contrast to the other civil sanctions, there is no need for the Agency to be satisfied beyond a reasonable doubt that an offence has been committed. If the Agency reasonably suspects the commission of the offence, the person may offer the undertaking to it. The Agency may then accept the offer, in which case it may not impose another civil sanction or bring a prosecution. Alternatively, the Agency may reject the offer of the undertaking and impose another civil sanction or commence a prosecution.

1.5.2   Procedure

Following the commission of a potential offence, the Environment Agency will investigate it. If the Agency considers that the offence warrants a sanction, it may select either a criminal or a civil sanction. As a general rule, it is not possible to change from the criminal sanction to the civil sanction procedure – or vice versa – after a selection has been made.

The 'beyond a reasonable doubt' standard of proof applies to compliance notices, FMPs, VMPs and restoration notices.

If the Agency decides to pursue a civil sanction, it issues a notice of intent to impose the sanction on the offender. The notice of intent must set out, among other things, the grounds for proposing the sanction and the right to make representations and objections to it within 28 days from its receipt.

The offender may make representations and objections to the proposed imposition. In the case of a compliance notice, restoration notice and/or VMP, the Agency must serve a final notice that sets out, among other things, the grounds for imposing the sanction, any early payment discounts or late payment penalties, the right to appeal the notice and the consequences for failure to comply with it.

If the Agency decides, nevertheless, to impose the sanction (whether modified or not), the offender may appeal it to the First-tier tribunal (Environment). If an issue in the appeal is the commission of the offence, the burden of proof is 'beyond a reasonable doubt'. This burden of proof, which is on the regulator and not the offender during an appeal, does not apply to stop notices.

If the offender is unsuccessful, it must pay the penalty together with the costs set out in an enforcement cost recovery notice, that is, a notice that sets out the Environment Agency's investigation, administrative costs and related costs.

If the offender does not pay a monetary penalty, it becomes a civil debt for which the Agency may bring an action to enforce payment. If the offender does not comply with a restoration notice or a stop notice, the usual procedure is prosecution.

The Agency is required to publish the results of all enforcement actions for which a civil penalty is imposed or an enforcement undertaking is accepted by it.

1.6   CLEAN-UP LIABILITIES

A novel type of liability for so-called 'clean-up costs' arises in the environmental context. The term 'clean-up costs' is not limited to the actual costs of cleaning up pollution but generally includes investigation, assessment, monitoring and other remedial action costs; in some cases, the remedial action may not involve a clean up at all but may, for example, be monitored natural attenuation.

A business may be liable for two main categories of clean-up costs: the cost of remediating current and future pollution, and the cost of remediating pollution caused by historic events. There are at least two major differences between the two categories. For example, current and future pollution must generally be cleaned up in its virtual entirety whereas pollution caused by historic events must generally be cleaned up to a 'suitability for use' standard that takes account of the current nature of the land use or the use for which planning permission has been granted, for example, residential or commercial and industrial.

Further, causing or knowingly permitting current and future pollution is generally also an offence for which the Environment Agency or other enforcing authority may bring a prosecution. In contrast, a person may be required to clean up past pollution regardless of whether the incident resulting in the pollution was lawful and the person complied with all good business practice involving the pollution at the time.

The following briefly describes the main pieces of legislation that impose a duty to clean up pollution.

1.6.1   Environmental Protection Act 1990

Part II – Waste

Under EPA 1990, s.59, if any controlled waste is deposited in or on any land so as to constitute an offence, the Environment Agency may by notice require the occupier to remove the waste, and if he does not, can do the required work and recover the cost from the occupier or, in some circumstances, from the person who deposited the waste or who knowingly caused or permitted it to be deposited. The owner of the site may be liable under s.59ZA if there is no occupier or the local authority would incur 'unreasonable expense' in locating the occupier.

Part IIA – Contaminated land

Part IIA of EPA 1990, discussed fully in Chapter 2, contains the contaminated land provisions (ss.78A–78YC). Part IIA is supplemented, not only by the statutory guidance set out in annex 3 to Defra Circular 01/2006, but also by the Contaminated Land (England) 2006 Regulations, SI 2006/1380, as amended, the Radioactive Contaminated Land (Modification of Enactments) (England) Regulations SI 2006/1379, as amended, and the Radioactive Contaminated Land (Enabling Powers and Modification of Enactments) (England) (Amendment) Regulations, SI 2010/2147.

In addition to imposing clean-up liabilities on persons who cause or knowingly permit contamination – and owners and occupiers of the sites if such persons cannot be found – Part IIA authorises a local authority, or the Environment Agency for 'special sites', to carry out such works itself. Under EPA 1990, s.78N, a local authority, having identified contaminated land in its area, may carry out such works as are appropriate by way of remediation to the relevant land in such circumstances as the section permits, mainly non-compliance with a remediation notice, or in an emergency. If works are carried out, the authority can recover reasonable costs from the appropriate person, subject to the statutory guidance and any hardship caused.

It should be remembered that although Part IIA imposes only civil liability, a responsible person may commit a criminal offence by failing to carry out measures specified in a remediation notice that is served on him. That is, it is an offence for the person served with a remediation notice by a local authority or the Environment Agency in respect of contaminated land to fail, without reasonable excuse, to comply with any of the requirements of the notice. The 'person served' is the appropriate person as defined in Part IIA and the statutory guidance, that is, the person who caused or knowingly permitted the presence of the contaminant, or the owner or occupier if the 'polluter' cannot be found, subject to complex exclusionary tests outlined in the statutory guidance.

Despite being in force since April 2000, the regime has been slow in making its effect felt. Between June 2001 (following preparation of inspection strategies by local authorities) and June 2008, only 200 determinations of contaminated land had been made affecting around 750 properties in the UK (depending on how they are counted) and some 75 remediation notices served. Many relate to special sites including former landfills, water pollution sites and sites formerly occupied by the Ministry of Defence. Several high-profile instances involving domestic properties have also emerged (Sheffield, Sevenoaks, Wigan and Hartlepool) due to the focus on such properties by local authorities as a result of their application of health criteria in determining contaminated land.

Part III – Statutory nuisances

Part III of EPA 1990 codifies the law on statutory nuisances – smoke, dust, odour – or premises or accumulations, etc. which are a health or pollution risk. The nuisances also include noise from alarms, insects and artificial light by virtue of the provisions of the Clean Neighbourhoods and Environment Act 2005.

Under ss.79 and 80 of EPA 1990, it is an offence for the person served with an abatement notice by a local authority in respect of a statutory nuisance, to fail to comply with the notice. The 'person served' is the person responsible for the nuisance or, if they cannot be found, the owner or occupier of the premises. FMPs can now be used for certain types of statutory nuisance.

Proceedings under Part III of EPA 1990 cannot be brought, other than in very limited circumstances, once an environmental permit has been issued because the environmental permitting regime is designed to control all aspects of regulated emissions, including nuisance aspects.

Under s.81, where an abatement notice has not been complied with, the local authority may abate the nuisance, and recover the cost from the person by whose act or default the nuisance was caused, or from the owner for the time being of the land.

Moreover, once land is in a 'contaminated state' within the meaning of para. 89 of Sched. 22 to the Environment Act 1995, it cannot, to that extent, also be regarded as a statutory nuisance.

The definition of 'contaminated state' catches land which, by reason of substances in, on or under it, is in such a state that there is a possibility of harm. This is not the same as 'contaminated' for the purposes of Part IIA (where the risk of harm must be 'significant') and one is therefore left in the position where polluted land where the pollution is not serious enough to be designated as contaminated, is not able to be called a statutory nuisance either. A local authority is therefore left powerless to deal with it.

Arguably, this is a defensible position given that if land is not so dangerous as to be officially 'contaminated' it is, by definition, not going to cause any significant harm and can therefore safely be ignored, but in the authors' view this is an unwelcome oversight, as there may be sites which are harmful in some sense, but not so harmful as to warrant official determination as a contaminated site. To leave an authority legally powerless to deal with such problems seems odd and undesirable.

1.6.2 Water Resources Act 1991

Sections 161–161D of WRA 1991 authorise the Environment Agency to require a person who caused or knowingly permitted 'any poisonous, noxious or polluting matter or any solid waste matter' to enter 'controlled waters' to remediate it. If the person fails or refuses to do so, the Anti-Pollution Works Regulations 1999, SI 1999/1006, authorise the Environment Agency to serve a works notice that requires the responsible person to carry out the works. The definition of 'controlled waters' is broad and includes surface, ground and coastal waters.

Also, 'so far as it is reasonably practicable to do so', the Environment Agency may require the responsible person to restore the waters 'including any flora and fauna dependent on the aquatic environment, to their state immediately before the matter became present in the waters'. Such works typically involve restocking rivers with fish such as salmon and trout.

The Environment Agency does not serve a works notice immediately; instead, it 'requests' the responsible person to clean up the pollution. Only if the person fails or refuses to comply does the Environment Agency serve a notice.

In some cases, for example, when oil is discovered in a stream, the Environment Agency may clean it up itself as an emergency measure. The Agency is authorised to do so by WRA 1991, ss.161 and 161A which provide that where it appears to the Environment Agency that any poisonous, noxious or polluting matter or any solid waste matter is likely to enter, or to be or to have been present in, any controlled waters, the Environment Agency may carry out works to prevent its entry, remove it and remedy any damage if:

- the Environment Agency considers immediate works to be necessary; or
- nobody can be found on whom the Environment Agency could serve a works notice requiring remediation of the problem; or
- a works notice is served but is not complied with.

The Environment Agency can recover any costs reasonably incurred by it from the responsible person.

1.6.3 Environmental Damage Regulations

Chapter 3 describes liability under the Environmental Damage Regulations for preventing and remediating pollution and other environmental damage to land, water, SSSIs and protected species and natural habitats.

1.7 NATURE CONSERVATION AND BIODIVERSITY LIABILITIES

Liability for restoring natural resources has existed in England for many years. More recently, it was supplemented – and massively expanded – by the Environmental Damage Regulations.

1.7.1 Wildlife and Countryside Act 1981

The key nature conservation legislation is the Wildlife and Countryside Act (WCA) 1981, as amended by the Countryside and Rights of Way Act 2000 and the Natural Environment and Rural Communities Act 2006. The Countryside and Rights of Way Act is also the vehicle for the implementation of several international and EU – as well as national – legal initiatives to protect species and ecosystems, such as wetlands and wild bird habitats.

The EU legislation is the Birds Directive (Directive 2009/147/EC on the conservation of wild birds) and the Natural Habitats Directive (Directive 92/43/EEC on the conservation of natural habitats and of wild fauna and flora). Sites protected under the Directives are known as special protection areas and special areas of conservation, respectively. They are known as European Sites and, together with such sites in other Member States, form the Natura 2000 network.

The designations used in the UK legislation include SSSIs, Areas of Outstanding Natural Beauty (AONBs), and national and local nature reserves. The designations frequently overlap, with all European Sites also being designated as SSSIs. Generally, any actions that upset or disturb the species or areas designated for protection constitute a criminal offence. It should be noted that development is severely restricted in any areas of protection.

Under WCA 1981, s.31, a person who is convicted of damaging an SSSI may be ordered to restore it to its former condition. It is a criminal offence to fail to comply with such an order.

It is also a criminal offence intentionally or recklessly to kill, injure, take, disturb, disrupt or damage the environment of specified protected species of bird, plant or animal.

Further, it is a criminal offence to carry on operations in, or intentionally or recklessly to disturb or disrupt the function of, specified areas, e.g. SSSIs or Ramsar wetland sites. A Ramsar site is a wetland that is included in the List of Wetlands of International Importance under the Convention on Wetlands of International Importance especially as Waterfowl Habitat (adopted on 2 February 1971 in Ramsar, Iran).

1.7.2 Conservation of Habitats and Species Regulations 2010

The Conservation of Habitats and Species Regulations 2010, SI 2010/490, consolidate the Conservation (Natural Habitats etc.) Regulations 1994, SI 1994/2716 and implement aspects of the Marine and Coastal Access Act 2009 for England and Wales.

Regulation 29 of the 2010 Regulations provides, among other things, that a person who commits an offence by breaching a special nature conservation order may be served with a restoration order that requires the offender to restore the site to its former condition. It is a criminal offence to fail to comply with a restoration order without a 'reasonable excuse'.

1.7.3 Environmental Damage Regulations

As noted in respect of liability to clean up pollution, Chapter 3 describes liability for preventing and remediating pollution and other environmental damage to land, water, SSSIs and protected species and natural habitats under the Environmental Damage Regulations. It should be noted that liability under the Regulations supplements other legislation imposing environmental liabilities; it does not replace it. Situations may, therefore, arise in which both the Regulations and other legislation apply to the same pollution or other environmental damage.

1.8 TORT LIABILITIES

The presence of contaminated land or polluted water may result not only in a penalty and/or a requirement to clean it up; it may also lead to claims for compensation for bodily injury and property damage. Such claims may also arise from a third party's exposure to pollutants from other sources, such as airborne pollutants.

Tort actions may be brought under:

- private nuisance;
- public nuisance;
- strict liability under the rule in *Rylands* v. *Fletcher*;
- negligence;
- statutory causes of action;
- trespass, but only to a very limited degree; and
- the Human Rights Act 1998.

1.8.1 Private nuisance

A private nuisance is an unlawful interference with a person's use and enjoyment of land or some right over or in connection with it. The tort is based on reasonableness between neighbours, that is, the use and enjoyment of a person's own land so that it does not unreasonably interfere with the neighbours' use and enjoyment of their land, and vice versa. The mere interference with a neighbour's use and enjoyment of their land is not necessarily a nuisance.

The only person who may bring an action in private nuisance is the person(s) who has the right to exclusive possession of the land (*Hunter* v. *Canary Wharf Ltd; Hunter* v. *London Docklands Development Corporation* [1997] AC 655, HL). In the case of surface water affected by a nuisance, a riparian owner may bring an action in private nuisance but not a person who only has a licence concerning the water (*Jan de Nul (UK) Ltd* v. *NV Royale Belge* [2000] 2 Lloyd's Rep 700, *aff'd* [2002] 1 All ER (Comm) 767, CA).

The landmark private nuisance case is *Cambridge Water Company* v. *Eastern Counties Leather plc* [1994] 2 AC 264, in which the House of Lords concluded that the owner and occupier of a tannery that spilled organochlorines that polluted groundwater was not liable to a water company that abstracted the groundwater because the operator could not reasonably have foreseen, when the spills occurred, that they would cause groundwater pollution. The tannery had regularly spilled the organochlorines, which it used to degrease pelts, prior to 1976. The organochlorines seeped into the underlying chalk aquifer and migrated 1.4 miles to a public water supply borehole operated by the water company. The water company subsequently discovered that water abstracted from its borehole was not 'wholesome' under revised EU law. As a result, the water company closed the borehole and constructed a new one at a cost of over £1 million. It then claimed against the tannery for damages for that amount.

Moreover, in the judgment, the House of Lords implied that whilst an owner/ occupier is not generally liable for unforeseeable historic contamination, he nonetheless could be liable for its consequences if, since the time the damage became foreseeable, it was possible to stop the nuisance, and no such steps were taken. See also *Holbeck Hall Hotel Ltd* v. *Scarborough Borough Council* [2000] QB 836, CA. It seems therefore, that even if a person is not liable for starting a nuisance, the person can be liable for not stopping it after the person became aware of it provided that it has the resources to stop it. See also *Wandsworth London Borough Council* v. *Railtrack* [2002] QB 756, CA.

To this extent, *Cambridge Water* merely equates the position of existing landowners with the position of buyers, which has been settled law for many years. Buyers of contaminated land, and those enforcing security over it, are only liable for continuing nuisances created by predecessors in title if they knew or ought to have known of the nuisance, could reasonably foresee it causing harm and could have taken reasonable steps to prevent or abate it, but failed to do so (*Sedleigh-Denfield* v. *O'Callaghan* [1940] AC 880, HL; *Goldman* v. *Hargrave* [1967] 1 AC 645, HC (Aus); *Leakey* v. *National Trust* [1980] QB 485, CA). Practitioners may also care to note *Delaware Mansions Ltd* v. *City of Westminster* [2001] UKHL 55 which emphasised that nuisance is an ongoing cause of action and successors in title have the right to sue the causer of the nuisance even if they acquired the affected property after the damage was caused. Moreover, changes in the ownership of the land causing the problem do not sever the chain of causation.

It should also be noted that compliance with an authorisation or lawful planning permission does not provide a defence against a civil action for nuisance (*Wheeler* v. *Saunders* [1995] 3 WLR 466, CA, confirmed (amongst other interesting points) by *Hunter* v. *Canary Wharf*).

Solicitors should further note the added difficulty surrounding limitation. The appropriate limitation date, which is subject to a long-stop of 15 years, may be long after the creation of the original nuisance, or the original incident. There is also the potential for pollution to be considered to be a continuing nuisance.

1.8.2 Public nuisance

A public nuisance, which is a criminal offence as well as a civil cause of action, is an unlawful act or the failure to discharge a legal duty to act when the effect of the act or omission materially affects the reasonable convenience and comfort of a class of people or their health, lives or property. See *Wandsworth London Borough Council* v. *Railtrack plc* [2002] QB 756, CA.

In *Corby Group Litigation* v. *Corby District Council* [2009] EWHC 1944, the Technology and Construction Court concluded that the local authority was liable in public nuisance for causing, allowing or permitting the dispersal of dangerous or noxious contaminants, and in breach of its statutory duty under EPA 1990, s.34. The causation issue, which was scheduled for subsequent proceedings, was not decided due to settlement of the case (see **1.8.5**).

Although damages for personal injury are not generally recoverable in private nuisance actions, they have not been ruled out of public nuisance actions (see *In re Corby Group Litigation* [2008] EWCA Civ 463, [2009] QB 335, CA).

1.8.3 Liability under the rule in *Rylands* v. *Fletcher*

Under the rule in *Rylands* v. *Fletcher*, a person who controls land is strictly liable for the natural consequences of the escape of a substance that is brought onto, or that accumulates on, the land provided that the use of the land is 'non-natural'.

The rule is a sub-set of nuisance and, thus, a claimant must have an interest in land to bring a claim under it (*McKenna* v. *British Aluminium Ltd* [2002] Env LR 30, Ch D). Reasonable foreseeability also applies, as in private nuisance (*Cambridge Water Company* v. *Eastern Counties Leather plc*).

In the early 2000s, arguments were made that the rule should be abolished. The House of Lords, however, confirmed that the rule should continue to exist. The court also confirmed that *Cambridge Water Company* was the classic type of case of non-natural use to which the rule applies (*Transco plc* v. *Stockport Metropolitan Borough Council* [2004] 2 AC 1, HL).

The position of the defendant – who could be the owner of the land, the occupier, the controller of the source of the nuisance or the creator of the nuisance itself – is made more precarious by the fact that liability under the rule is strict. It does not matter what steps were taken to prevent the harm: if an escape occurs and causes foreseeable damage, the defendant is liable for all the ensuing consequences.

The only prerequisites to liability are:

* a non-natural/non-reasonable use of the land; and
* harm of the relevant type having been reasonably foreseeable at the time of creation of the nuisance, or the collection of the harmful material.

1.8.4 Statutory torts

The two main statutory torts that apply to personal injury involving environmental damage are EPA 1990, s.73(6) and the Nuclear Installations Act 1965, s.12.

One should also note the possibility of a claim for oil pollution from a ship under the Merchant Shipping Act 1995, s.181(1), and a claim based on statutory duty, e.g. under the Occupiers' Liability Act 1957 or the Defective Premises Act 1972.

EPA 1990, s.73(6)

A person may be liable in damages if he commits a statutory tort under EPA 1990, s.73(6). This section provides that, where any damage is caused by waste deposited in or on land in such a manner as to constitute an offence, the person who deposited it, or who knowingly caused or permitted it to be deposited, is liable for the damage. See *C* v. *Imperial Design Ltd* [2001] Env LR 593, CA.

Nuclear Installations Act 1965, s.12

Section 12 of the Nuclear Installations Act 1965 authorises a claim for compensation in the case of an injury or property damage from nuclear matter at a nuclear installation. In *Blue Circle Industries plc* v. *Ministry of Defence* [1999] Ch 289, the Court of Appeal awarded over £6 million to Blue Circle for damage caused to its property by plutonium that had been washed from ponds on the adjacent Atomic Weapons Establishment during heavy rain in July 1989.

1.8.5 Negligence

To sue in negligence, the claimant must show a duty of care owed to him by the defendant and breach of that duty which resulted in foreseeable harm to the claimant or his property. This would be the main head of claim in any case involving allegations of personal injury, though public nuisance may be another avenue (see **1.8.2**).

The duty of care may be hard to establish in most situations involving pollution incidents. There is the additional problem that any latent damage caused by a negligent act is statute-barred after 15 years from the date of the original incident by the Latent Damage Act 1986.

Claimants have prevailed in negligence actions for harm caused by exposure to asbestos. See *Margereson* v. *JW Roberts Ltd* and *Hancock* v. *JW Roberts Ltd* [1996] Env LR 304, CA.

In *Corby Group Litigation* v. *Corby District Council* [2009] EWHC 1944, the Technology and Construction Court concluded that the local authority had breached its duty to take reasonable care to prevent the dispersal of contaminated mud and dust during the lengthy clean up of a former steelworks site in the 1980s and 1990s. Pregnant women had been exposed to the contaminants. The court did not determine that the local authority's actions actually caused the deformities in the later-born children. Proceedings regarding such determinations did not occur due to the settlement of the case.

1.8.6 Trespass

The claimant must show direct entry onto, and damage to, his land by the emissions of the defendant. This has usually proved difficult to show.

1.8.7 Human rights cases

A few cases based on human rights issues have been heard by the courts.

A case alleging that the London Docklands development had caused excessive levels of dust failed due to the now-defunct European Commission of Human Rights concluding that the interference by the dust was necessary to respond to a social need and was proportionate when considered with the development's economic aims (*Khatun* v. *United Kingdom* (1998) 26 EHRR CD212 (Eu Comm HR)).

In *Dennis* v. *Ministry of Defence* [2003] Env LR 741, QBD, Buckley J concluded that if the common law of nuisance had not provided a remedy for a landowner's loss of amenity and capital value of his country estate by the noise of jet fighters, he would have been entitled to damages under the first Protocol to the Human Rights Convention.

1.9 PROTECTING A CLIENT AGAINST CRIMINAL LIABILITIES

Regarding penalties for criminal liabilities, the first piece of advice must be 'forget insurance'. One cannot insure against fines for criminal offences although insurance for the cost of defending a prosecution for an environmental offence is available. If a client is prosecuted for any of the offences listed earlier in this chapter, the main 'protections' are those familiar to criminal practitioners everywhere: avoidance and mitigation.

1.9.1 Avoidance

If one accepts, as is the case in a large number of environmental offences, that the offences are offences of strict liability, is there anything that one can do to avoid prosecution and conviction? It would be wrong to assume that there is no way out of a conviction, and there follows a list of matters to consider.

Identity of the defendant

It is conceivable, especially within complex corporate groups, that the prosecutor has inaccurately identified the defendant company which actually carries on the process that has caused the discharge. Although mere typographical errors will not invalidate the proceedings, if the legal person prosecuted is wholly different from the one that ought to have been prosecuted, the proceedings will have to be withdrawn and recommenced.

Statutory defences

Some of the offences carry with them statutory defences and, of course, it is essential to check the statute to see whether the client could benefit from any of these defences, which tend to involve emergency circumstances and the defendant having taken measures to prevent the offence from occurring (see **1.3.5**).

Common law defences

There may be some common law defences. These are limited in scope, but if one can show that some natural event was the initial cause of a discharge, a defence may be made out if one can prove that the natural event was so extraordinary and exceptional as to be unforeseeable.

Duplicity of informations

The prosecutor may need to take care in the drafting of the informations to ensure that they are not duplicitous. This is particularly so when the discharge complained of has been an intermittent one. If an information charges a defendant with numerous discharges occurring between certain dates, it is at least arguable that the information contains allegations of more than one offence and is therefore invalid.

Evidential gaps

As most environmental offences are triable either way, advance information is available under the Magistrates' Courts (Advance Information) Rules 1985, SI 1985/601. All the defendant need do is request copies of the prosecution evidence in advance, and it will be provided. It is always worth checking to see whether the prosecution evidence actually sustains the allegations made in the proceedings.

There have been difficulties in proving the entry of noxious or polluting matters into 'controlled waters', as the testing of the discharge was performed at an inappropriate point (e.g. in a sewer). There have also been difficulties in proving the initial source of a particular contamination. Clearly, if the prosecution evidence is deficient, it is not entitled to a conviction.

Relationship with regulatory bodies

It may be worth negotiating with the prosecuting body on the basis that the defendant has always in the past had a constructive and responsible approach to the environment, taking advice and measures to prevent discharges of the type complained of. It may persuade the prosecuting authority not to proceed if one can point out that this good relationship is in danger of suffering, and the client's responsible attitude along with it.

The aim of discussing these possibilities is, of course, to persuade the prosecutor to withdraw the proceedings altogether, but another alternative to consider is agreeing with the prosecution to the imposition of a warning letter or a formal caution rather than going through the full litigation and conviction process. Some of the regulatory bodies have proceeded along this line in the past.

1.9.2 The hearing

If one cannot avoid a prosecution, the next question is how should the client plead at the hearing itself? The short answer is that the client should plead not guilty if there are evidential gaps or procedural problems which would deny the prosecution a conviction. There is no ethical problem in pleading not guilty, as that merely puts the onus on the prosecution to prove its case. If the prosecution is unable to discharge the burden of proof, the client is entitled to an acquittal.

If the evidence looks watertight, the standard advice is probably to plead guilty and to mitigate, putting forward the best explanation of the event that one can. As discussed above, guilty pleas with pleas of mitigation are the standard for most water pollution prosecutions.

Bear in mind also the discount to be received by a plea of guilty (standard advice in most cases), particularly early in the proceedings.

1.9.3 Mitigation

The standard approach to mitigation adopted by criminal practitioners is fairly easily adapted for use in environmental cases. Broadly, the age and history of the defendant, the circumstances surrounding the offence, the behaviour since the offence and the indirect effect of conviction or sentence are all matters on which the magistrates can be addressed. Practitioners should, of course, bear in mind the key factors set out by the Court of Appeal in cases such as *Milford Haven* and *Thames Water Utilities* and tailor their mitigation accordingly.

The Court of Appeal discussed the following factors in *Thames Water Utilities*. As aggravating the seriousness of the offence:

- the noxious, widespread or pervasive nature of the pollutant, or its ability to spread widely and have long-lasting effects;
- adverse effects on human health, animal health or flora, in particular harm to protected species and designated ecological sites;
- the need for extensive clean up, site restoration or animal rehabilitation operations; and
- the prevention or significant interference caused by the pollution to other lawful activities.

As general aggravating features:

- the degree of the offending company's culpability;
- intentional breach of a duty in order to maximise profit;
- skimping of appropriate precautions in order to make or save money, or to gain a competitive advantage;
- repetition of conduct or failure to heed advice, caution, concern or warnings from regulatory authorities, employees or others;
- a poor attitude and/or response following the incident; and
- any previous convictions.

As mitigating factors:

- a good record of compliance with the law;
- a good attitude and/or response following the incident (including prompt reporting, cooperation with enforcing authorities, taking prompt and effective measures to rectify any failures, and the payment of compensation); and
- timely admission of guilt and a guilty plea at an early opportunity.

Age and history of the defendant

The magistrates should be informed about the history of the company and its activities, how long it has occupied its site and its record in relation to previous incidents and accidents. In addition, one can concentrate on the client's commercial attitude to the environment, its past record of taking advice and preventative measures to avoid damaging discharges and its past relations with the regulatory bodies, in an attempt to persuade the court that the client is a responsible citizen, not an 'amoral calculator' who is prepared to discharge into the environment if that is the best commercial decision at the time.

Circumstances surrounding the offence

It is always worth pointing out that, since the offences require no fault on the part of the defendant, in fact there was no fault present on the part of the defendant. It is also worthwhile pointing out the facts and the effects of the incident in context. In this regard, a keen appreciation of the chemical effects of the polluting discharge is helpful. For example, how much oxygen does the chemical strip from a watercourse at a given temperature and flow rate, and how much oxygen do trout, plants, etc. need to survive? How much damage was in fact done? In appropriate cases, it is worthwhile pointing out that the company derived no financial benefit from the fact of the discharge and there was no cover-up of the incident either.

This begs a question as to whether the client should report an incident as soon as it occurs, notwithstanding the privilege against self-incrimination. The authors', perhaps rather purist, view is that if the company is a responsible environmental citizen, then it should, as a matter of policy, report incidents so that the damaging effects can be minimised as soon as possible, and then use this fact in mitigation at a later date. There is, in addition, the commercial consideration that the value of the company's land will be reduced if it is polluted and the company may find it difficult to sell the land at a later date if the pollutant has not been cleaned up to the Environment Agency's satisfaction.

Behaviour since the offence

Credit will be given for the plea of guilty (if that has indeed been the plea), and it will also be given for immediate voluntary clean up and restocking of fish and plants, etc., voluntary payment of costs and expenses, and the taking of further advice and remedial and preventative measures to ensure non-recurrence. It would also help if the company can demonstrate that it has comprehensively reviewed its internal operating procedures, made any necessary investments in new plant and machinery and even that it has supported local initiatives which may not be directly connected with this specific incident.

Indirect effect of conviction or sentence

In appropriate cases, mention the potential damage to relations with the regulatory bodies, the financial and cash-flow effects of a harsh penalty and the knock-on employment implications in the locality if a company is forced out of business as a result of harsh fines.

See also the Court of Appeal's comments in the *Milford Haven*, *Thames Water Utilities* and other cases in which the courts have considered whether a fine for an environmental offence is 'manifestly unjust'.

1.9.4 Other steps

It would be foolish for a client, or a solicitor, to underestimate the impact of a conviction on a company's reputation. It is therefore essential that the client be prepared for the barrage of questions that may follow from a conviction on a guilty plea. Depending on the seriousness of the offence, the preparation of press and other media releases should be considered and clients should be counselled in how to deal with press questions which may be put to them on the steps of the court.

Senior officials of the company should be present in court during the hearing to demonstrate to the magistrates or judge that the company is taking the offence seriously.

As a follow-up, solicitors should give any necessary advice to their clients about environmental compliance and, of course, the clients should take any remedial steps which may have been promised in the plea in mitigation in order to prevent recurrence of the incident.

1.10 PROTECTING A CLIENT AGAINST CLEAN-UP/BIODIVERSITY LIABILITIES

One possibility is insurance – this subject is discussed more fully in Chapter 13. If the client does not have an environmental insurance policy, it will most likely have a potentially large gap in its insurance cover for clean-up costs (see **13.2.3**).

If the client is responsible for the contamination or other environmental damage, the main way to reduce the costs of remediating it and reputational damage is cooperation with the Environment Agency or other enforcing authority. If, say, the client refuses to cooperate in a case involving water pollution, the Agency may serve a works notice or, in certain cases, remediate the contamination itself and seek reimbursement from the client. In addition, the Agency may bring a prosecution for water pollution under the Environmental Permitting Regulations.

If the client considers that they are not liable for the contamination, the main protection will be in the form of expert evidence. An environmental investigation should be carried out to ascertain the exact state of land or operations at a given point in time, e.g. on a purchase of land or the purchase of the shares of a company that has a lease.

The investigation will inform the client:

- of the current state of contamination; and
- whether there are any obvious problems which need attention.

The client will be liable in the future for the consequences of any contamination which he could have discovered and remediated. Although it is not possible to prove a negative, an expert's report which states that at a specific date, testing for a certain contaminant did not locate it should exonerate, or at least assist, a client in future litigation over the effects of that historic contamination.

Chapter 10 deals with the considerations to be borne in mind when engaging consultants.

1.11 INDIRECT COSTS

Environmental liabilities comprise not just the risks mentioned above, but other factors such as:

- legal costs;
- adverse press coverage, which can affect both consumers and purchasing decisions;
- reputational risks associated with the new consumer awareness of social and environmental responsibility;
- reduced profitability;
- downward pressure on a company's share price;
- effect on the company's cash flow and thus its ability to service its debt burden; and
- insolvency and potential closure.

CHAPTER 2

Contaminated land

2.1 INTRODUCTION

2.1.1 General

Section 57 of the Environment Act 1995 inserts the contaminated land regime, Part IIA (ss.78A–78YC), into EPA 1990. This requires local authorities to identify land which needs attention, and then serve notice on the person liable to clean it up, non-compliance with which would be a criminal offence.

The provisions on contaminated land are complex, and yet do not provide certainty on what precisely is contaminated land. Like so much legislation in this area, the governing legislation is little more than a set of guiding principles, the detailed operation of which is left to be specified by regulations or guidance from Defra.

The contaminated land regime came into force on 1 April 2000. The current regulations and guidance are the Contaminated Land (England) Regulations 2006, SI 2006/1380 and Defra Circular 01/2006 (see also Scottish and Welsh equivalents). In February 2010, Defra announced a review of the statutory guidance. Depending on the outcome of the review, this may result in an overhaul of the circular.

In the first 10 years of its existence, remediation notices have only been served in a few cases, most clean ups having been effected in an informal and voluntary way.

2.1.2 Overall summary of procedure

The regulatory bodies are obliged to follow the sequence of steps set out below:

1. Inspect
2. Investigate
3. Identify/determine as contaminated land or special site
4. Consider: Are works urgent?

If yes:

5A. Do works and seek to recover costs

If no:

5B. Identify interested persons
6. Formulate proposed remediation scheme
7. Notify/consult for a minimum of three months
8. Finalise/agree scheme
9. Consider exclusionary tests
10. Apportion liability
11. Consider cost recovery/hardship
12. Consider: Can/must a remediation notice be served?

If no:

12A. Do works and seek to recover costs, in so far as possible

If yes:

12B. Serve remediation notice
13. Deal with any appeal
14. Wait for the specified period
15. Prosecute for non-compliance
16. Do works and recover costs, in so far as possible

Each of these steps will be considered more fully in turn.

2.2 INSPECTION AND INVESTIGATION

2.2.1 The Act

Primary responsibility for identifying contaminated sites rests with local authorities, i.e. the district council or unitary authority. They must consult with the Environment Agency if water pollution is involved.

They are obliged to inspect land in their area from time to time for the purpose of identifying contaminated land, and any such land as is liable for designation as a 'special site'.

In the case of the latter category – sites which may be particularly hazardous – the local authority must refer the site to the Environment Agency for a decision on whether it should be determined as a 'special site'. If it is so determined, only the Environment Agency has the power to determine when and how it should be remediated, and by whom. The Agency now becomes the 'appropriate authority' for enforcement purposes.

When identifying sites, the enforcing authority is entitled to take into account the cumulative impact of two or more sites when assessing the 'significant harm' or pollution' (s.78X).

No further statutory assistance is given in defining the duty to inspect, but the application of the duty is again the subject of the Guidance.

2.2.2 The Guidance

The authority is required to have a written strategy for the inspection process ensuring a consistent, ordered approach to the task, taking into account the information already in its possession and any additional matters brought to its attention by third parties.

Specifically, the authority is required to have established the likelihood of a pollutant linkage – the presence of a target, a source and a plausible pathway – before undertaking any intrusive ground investigations. It is required to obtain 'sufficient information' to enable it to form a judgement as to the extent of contamination. The authority need not produce a complete characterisation of the nature of the contamination, but only as much as is sufficient for it to make the determination that the land in question is contaminated.

The Guidance suggests that once land has been so determined, a remediation notice can be served requiring the appropriate person to carry out further, more specific investigations to determine where to go next.

In making the determination, the authority is required to indicate the basis on which the designation is made (significant harm being caused, risk of water pollution, etc.) and to specify what pollutant linkage gives rise to the designation.

Authorities are not provided with specific numerical values of concentrations of pollutants to determine whether land is contaminated. They have to develop risk-based criteria on a site-by-site basis to enable them to justify a conclusion that significant harm is being caused in accordance with the Guidance.

Land shall not be regarded as contaminated in relation to water pollution risks if risk management arrangements are already in place to prevent such pollution.

2.2.3 Comment

Initially, the strategies had to be prepared by June 2001. Some local authorities have reviewed these. The strategies prioritised those areas which, in the authority's view, required the most urgent action. Copies of the strategies should be available from the relevant local authority and some are published on local authority websites. Practitioners should seek to obtain a copy as it may give some indication of where the key local problems lie or at least how local authorities are approaching contaminated land in their area.

The Guidance requires the local authority to be very specific in its reasons for determining land as contaminated, and this would give much scope for argument and appeal by the person served with the notice. It will also require the authority to take much scientific evidence into account in order to be sure of its ground.

2.3 DETERMINATION

2.3.1 The Act

Contaminated land is defined in s.78A(2) as being:

> land which appears to the local authority in whose area it is situated to be in such a condition, by reason of substances in, on or under land, that –
>
> (a)   significant harm is being caused or there is a significant possibility of such harm being caused; or
> (b)   [significant – *see below*] pollution of controlled waters is being, or is likely to be, caused
>
> and in determining whether any land appears to be such land, the local authority shall act … in accordance with guidance issued by the Secretary of State.

'Harm' is defined as:

> harm to the health of living organisms or other interference with the ecological systems of which they form part and, in the case of man, includes harm to his property.

There are several features to note about the new definition:

* if there is no significant harm or the significant possibility of such harm, land is not 'contaminated' within the meaning of the section, despite the presence of harmful matter;
* land is 'contaminated' only if the harm, or risk of harm, to the non-aquatic environment is significant; it is 'contaminated' if there is any risk of water pollution, however small.

The Water Act 2003 contains provisions, still not in force at the time of writing (2010), that alter the definition to provide that pollution of water must also be 'significant' to enable an authority to determine that a site is contaminated.

Each authority is under a duty to have regard to any guidance issued by Defra or the Environment Agency when assessing whether land in its area is contaminated. There is express provision within the Environment Act 1995 for such guidance to make provision for different weight to be attached to different descriptions of harm to health or property and other factors.

The definition of 'harm' and 'significant' – and therefore the practical impact of the whole provision – is the subject of the Guidance.

2.3.2 The Guidance

The Guidance indicates the approach to be adopted. The definition is to be interpreted in the following way.

'Harm' is to be regarded as significant only if it is of the following types:

- death, disease, serious injury, genetic mutation, birth defects or impairment of reproductive function in humans (a 'human health' effect): this is further defined as including an 'unhealthy' condition of the body or part of it and can include, for example, cancer, liver dysfunction or extensive skin ailments, or even mental dysfunction attributable to some pollutant's effect on the body;
- irreversible adverse change in the functioning of an ecological system (or any species of special interest sustained by such a system) in a location protected under WCA 1981, European Sites protected under reg.10 of the Conservation (Natural Habitats etc.) Regulations 1994, SI 1994/2716, sites afforded policy protection under para.13 of PPG 9 or nature reserves established under the National Parks and Access to the Countryside Act 1949 (an 'ecological system' effect);
- death, disease, other physical damage to livestock, crops, produce or domesticated or wild animals subject to hunting rights, amounting to 20 per cent or more of their value (an 'animal' or 'crop' effect);
- substantial damage to, or structural failure of buildings, or interference with rights of occupation, such that they can no longer be used for the intended purpose (a 'building' effect).

An authority must confine its identification of targets to those likely to be present due to the current use of the site only.

In assessing 'risk', local authorities are to assess the possibility of harm, and its significance by reference to:

- the effects of the contamination; and
- fundamental principles of risk assessment.

Risk assessment involves an actual determination of the extent of contamination in a piece of land, i.e. the contaminants present and their concentration, their tendency to migrate, the geo-technical ground conditions in the locality (how might they contribute to the movement of the contaminant), the likely effects of an escape or migration and, in particular, how quickly harm may be suffered after exposure to the contaminant.

The essence of the question for the authority is: how likely is it that an escape will actually occur; and what harm will follow if it does?

Substances, the routes by which they move and the entity which may be affected are described in terms of 'contaminant pathway receptor' or 'source–pathway–target', and when all three elements are present, a 'pollutant linkage' is present.

In general, the more severe the harm, the greater its degree, the shorter the timescale for it to occur or the greater the vulnerability of the target, the more significant is the risk. When a pollutant linkage gives rise to a significant risk of harm (as defined) a 'significant pollutant linkage' exists. This is what can lead to a determination that land is contaminated.

In determining the risk of water pollution, the local authority is to liaise with the Environment Agency in the determination of whether a water pollution risk is present.

In 2006, the Guidance and Regulations were amended to bring land contaminated by radioactivity into the framework.

2.3.3 Comment

The operation of the regime is profoundly curtailed by the lack of funding to local authorities and uncertainty and confusion as to how the Guidance is to be interpreted.

Only the receptors mentioned are recognised by the legislation, and all others are to be ignored by the authorities.

One notable omission from the list is land itself – premises and buildings are recognised receptors but land itself is not. Subterranean migration of a contaminant from one site to another would not, of itself, give the recipient landowner any right to complain that his site is now contaminated under this legislation (though he would have remedies in civil law). An authority would have to wait until a recognised receptor did emerge and then require the clean up of the site giving rise to the problem. If this was the 'recipient' site, it would nevertheless be the polluter of the original site that would have to foot the bill. It seems, though, that the regime is not to be used to prevent the actual migration itself.

Likewise, the recognised types of harm are very limited and this limits the use of the Part IIA powers (intentionally, no doubt) to those sites that give rise to real and imminent risks to health.

However, the definitions do pose problems of their own, for instance, with regard to human health effects, is asthma a disease in the same league as cancer or liver dysfunction? If so, land giving rise to such an impact on health is contaminated; if not, it is not. Whether land is contaminated is as much a product of medical debate as it is a product of chemistry or geology.

If an authority determines that land is contaminated, it must give notice of that fact to all interested parties. At this stage, land will be identified by searches of the local authority as being subject to determination (see form CON 29R).

2.4 CONSIDER WHETHER THE WORKS ARE URGENT

If so, the authority will have power to do the necessary works and recover the costs of so doing from the appropriate person in due course.

If not, move on to the next stage.

2.5   IDENTIFY INTERESTED PERSONS

That is, anyone who is or may be:

- an appropriate person;
- an owner of the land;
- an occupier of the land;
- anyone who may have to give permission to allow entry to carry out works; or
- anyone else affected by the remediation notice if it were to be served.

2.6   FORMULATE A SCHEME

The authority must put together a scheme using the best practicable means to cause the significant pollutant linkage to cease to exist. Consideration must be given to the costs and the benefits at this stage. The cost-benefit analysis may lead the authority to conclude that a full site remediation is necessary, but other cheaper strategies may be workable – removing the receptor or target, or severing the pathway.

2.7   NOTIFY AND CONSULT

2.7.1   The Act

The authority is under a duty to carry out a formal consultation exercise before the remediation notice is served (s.78H(1)).

This duty does not apply in cases where it appears to the authority that there is an imminent danger of serious harm or pollution of controlled waters (s.78H(4)).

A minimum of three months' notice of the intention to serve a notice must be given to:

- the appropriate person(s) on whom a notice would be served;
- the owner of the land; and
- any person who appears to be in occupation of the whole or part of the land.

2.8   FINALISE AND AGREE SCHEME

2.8.1   The Act

A remediation notice 'must not' be served where the authority is satisfied that appropriate steps are being, or will be, taken without the service of a notice (s.78H(5)).

In such circumstances, the person who would have received the notice is required to prepare, within a reasonable period, a remediation statement setting out what works will be carried out, and within what period.

2.8.2 Comment

The consultation and waiting periods incorporate lengthy delays into the system.

A cynic may suggest that appropriate persons could delay the service of a remediation notice by engaging the authority in long, technical debates over the suggested measures, offering voluntary schemes or even applying for planning permission to redevelop the site. Such permission need not be implemented for up to five years, but the fact that planning requirements may be being negotiated may be taken to satisfy the authority that works 'will be' carried out, thus preventing it from serving a notice for the length of the permission.

Pleading a plausible defence of poverty at this early stage may result in the authority being unable to serve a notice.

This period should also be used to identify other persons who should bear a share of the blame.

More realistically, it is certainly in the interests of all concerned to use the consultation period constructively and to resolve the steps to be taken and by whom, as the only alternative to an agreed strategy is the service of a notice, which is likely to result in increased costs for all parties.

2.9 EXCLUSION AND APPORTIONMENT

2.9.1 The Act

Under the legislation, the remediation notice must be served on the 'appropriate person', that is:

- the person(s) who caused or knowingly permitted the contaminating substances to be in, on or under the land in question (to be referred to as the 'original polluter'); or, if there is no such person, then
- the owner for the time being of the contaminated land; and
- the occupier for the time being of the contaminated land.

This is consistent with the 'polluter pays' principle, but has a number of defects in practice.

The original polluter

The identity of the original polluter may, of course, be complicated by a long history of contamination on the site. The difficulties of actually proving who put what chemicals into the ground, and when, will be enormous, and impossible to judge without extensive and expensive intrusive investigations beneath the surface of the land in question, with all the attendant disturbance this would cause to the current occupier.

Having found a likely polluter, the primary issue is whether he or it comes into the category of 'causing' or 'knowingly permitting' the material to be present.

By analogy with a long line of criminal authorities interpreting the same form of words (see Chapter 1 for a fuller analysis), the concept of 'causing' pollution will require proof of some form of positive act on the part of the polluter.

'Knowingly permitting' amounts to allowing a state of affairs which one could have anticipated to continue in circumstances where you could have taken steps to prevent or abate it.

Whereas 'causing' substances to be on the land obviously catches the original polluter of the land, the wider notion of 'knowingly permitting' substances to remain on-site may also catch subsequent owners, lumping them into the same category of 'original polluters' and rendering them equally liable to service of a remediation notice.

The owner

'Owner' is defined in s.78A as being the person who is or would be entitled to receive the rent for the property.

Section 78A(9) excludes from the definition of 'owner' a mortgagee not in possession.

The occupier

There is no statutory definition of 'occupier'. Presumably, it will be taken to be the literal definition of someone in physical presence on the land in question.

Who is not liable?

The Act specifically exempts certain persons from the category of potential 'appropriate persons'. They are referred to as 'persons acting in a relevant capacity' (s.78X(3)).

This includes:

- a licensed insolvency practitioner (LIP);
- the Official Receiver acting as an LIP;
- the Official Receiver acting as a receiver or manager;
- a receiver appointed by statute/court order.

In respect of clean-up costs, liability can be avoided by such persons except where the contamination is present as a result of any act done or omission made by the relevant person which it was unreasonable for a person acting in that capacity to do or make (s.78X(3)(a)).

There is no guidance on the concept of 'reasonable behaviour', but merely carrying on a business pending resale is unlikely to attach the LIP with liability.

Blatant, indeed negligent, disregard of contamination or deliberate dumping of material to make a site seem more attractive as a saleable item could still give rise to liability.

Criminal liability is not imposed unless there is a failure to comply with a requirement to do something for which the LIP is personally liable as a result of his unreasonable behaviour.

Financial institutions

The position of the banks and other lenders has still not been fully resolved although the policy statements are clear. They are not specifically excluded (compare with LIPs) but the position with regard to mortgagees in possession is clarified.

Section 78A(9) excludes from the definition of 'owner' a mortgagee not in possession. This means, however that financial institutions could still be theoretically liable in two general cases:

- as original polluter; the person responsible for 'causing or knowingly permitting' the presence of the contamination if such person is in some degree of control over the day-to-day activities of the borrower; or
- as mortgagee in possession under the 'owner' category.

Multiple appropriate persons

As logic would dictate, different and separate remediation notices can require different things to be done by way of remediation by different appropriate persons in respect of different substances on the same site, or even the same substance in discrete locations where the separate depositors of the two 'lumps' of substance can be identified (s.78E(2)).

Each appropriate person may, however, only be served with a notice in connection with any remediation which is 'to any extent referable' to substances caused or knowingly permitted by that party (s.78F(3)).

It is not clear from the Act whether the same activity can be required of two persons by two notices in respect of the same substance in separate locations, but logic would dictate that it can.

Where the same remediation activity is required from different parties (e.g. presumably because the same substance has been put in the same location by a variety of people), the authority must first allocate responsibility for remediation to those persons who are potential appropriate persons, and then apportion the relative share of the cost of remediation to be borne by each.

The questions to be determined by the authority are, respectively, who is going to share the blame, and in what proportions?

In determining both these questions, the authority must first decide whether anyone can be excluded from the 'liability group' (s.78F(6)), and then decide on the share to be borne by those who remain (s.78F(7)). The remediation notice must state the relative shares to be borne (s.78E(3)).

In this pursuit, regard must be had to the Guidance, which sets out the excludable parties, and how to apportion costs.

Although the Act is not clear on the point, it is submitted that, where it is clear that two or more appropriate persons have caused or knowingly permitted the presence of different substances in the same location, the costs should be shared between the parties in the relative proportions of the substances.

A summary of these complex points may look like this:

- *two persons, two substances, two locations*: two notices each specifying remediation activity, which may be the same for both, or different;
- *two persons, two substances, one location*: one notice specifying activity and allocating proportions of costs of compliance;
- *two persons, one substance, two locations*: one notice specifying same activity for both locations, and allocating proportions of costs of compliance, or (presumably, but this is not clear) two notices specifying different activities for each location;
- *two persons, one substance, one location*: one notice specifying activity and allocating proportions of costs of compliance.

2.9.2 The Guidance

It is in the area of exclusion and apportionment that the Guidance can be seen as most controversial and complicated.

Chapter D of the Guidance sets out a series of principles on the basis of which certain persons and categories of persons can be excluded from the definition of 'appropriate persons' (exclusions), and how costs can be shared between those who remain (apportionment).

The Guidance states that the first step is to define the 'liability group', i.e. all those who may be appropriate persons by the application of the definition in the Act. That means all those who 'caused or knowingly permitted' the contaminants to be present in the land (original polluters, or 'Class A appropriate persons') or all those who are owners and occupiers, liable as such because the original polluter cannot be found ('Class B appropriate persons').

The next step is to exclude from those groups anyone satisfying any one of a number of tests set out in the Guidance. The exclusionary tests are to be applied in the order set out in the Guidance. Only those who are not excluded are liable to receive the remediation notice. The exclusionary tests are to be stopped as soon as there is only one person left in the group.

Excluded categories

CLASS A LIABILITY GROUP (ORIGINAL POLLUTERS)

1.   Anyone who is a member of Class A solely by reason of one or more excluded

activities (among other things, lending to, insuring, licensing, consenting to the activities of, advising, carrying out work for, or leasing land to another person).

2. Any member of Class A who makes a sufficient payment to another member of Class A stipulated in the contract as being for the particular remediation of land if that remediation is not carried out properly or at all, and provided the payer retains no control over the land.

3. Anyone who has sold freehold or long leasehold (more than 21 years) land at arm's length terms, the purchaser having sufficient information for him to be aware of the pollution risk which has led to the designation. The Guidance specifically provides that:

    .... in transactions since the beginning of 1990 where the buyer is a large commercial organisation or public body, permission from the seller for the buyer to carry out his own investigations of the condition of the land should normally be taken as sufficient indication that the buyer had the information [referred to above].

4. Anyone who deposits a substance A, which is, on its own, inert and of no risk, but which when combined with substance B becomes a pollutant (in this case, the depositor of substance B becomes liable).

5. Anyone who deposits a substance which will not escape without intervention, but which later escapes due to intervention (in this case, it is the intervener who is liable).

6. Anyone who deposits a substance which is not a risk due to the lack of a pathway, but which later becomes a risk due to the subsequent introduction of a pathway (in this case, it is the introducer of the pathway who is liable). On the application of this test, see *Circular Facilities (London) Ltd* v. *Sevenoaks DC* [2005] EWHC 865 (Admin) discussed below.

CLASS B LIABILITY GROUP (OWNERS AND OCCUPIERS)

Anyone occupying under licence with no value, or paying rent for the land and having no beneficial interest in the ownership of it other than the tenancy itself.

Apportioning liability and costs

Having excluded persons from the liability group, it remains for the authority to apportion liability amongst those who remain within the group, as follows:

- *Class A persons*: according to the relative degree of responsibility for the presence of the linkage; whether they caused or permitted the presence; whether they could have prevented or removed it; or in equal shares, if all else fails.

- *Class B persons*: in the proportions in which the owners or occupiers share the capital value of the land.

The costs are to be calculated on the understanding that works should be done which will be sufficient to remedy the risk of harm, but without disturbing other contaminants or making any other problems on the site worse. The costs are to include the cost of providing compensation to occupiers for any disruption.

No member of a liability group can be called upon to pay more than his share of the total liability, and if any of the costs are irrecoverable, then the authority must bear them.

Once the authority has apportioned the shares of responsibility within each liability group, the members of that group know the shares in which they must pay the costs of remediation allocated to that group – all of them if there is only one linkage and one group of persons responsible for it.

Matters become more complicated in relation to sites where a cocktail of substances and a host of polluters have all combined to create the significant pollutant linkages on the site. This is the most likely scenario to occur in practice.

Where this is so, the authority should be considering serving one notice for the whole site (see 'Multiple appropriate persons' above), but having done so, it must:

(a) apportion costs within the liability group for each individual linkage, and then;

(b) apportion shares of the total cost for the whole site between the various liability groups.

The notice may specify two alternative remediation strategies: the 'shared common action' (which is simply a combination of all the strategies that would have been appropriate for each pollutant linkage lumped together in one notice) or the 'shared collective action' (which is the one strategy that best addresses all the linkages in one fell swoop and which is usually cheaper as a result).

For a shared common action, the Guidance says that liability for the total cost of the combined measures is to be apportioned between all the Class A liability groups equally.

For a shared collective action, the Guidance suggests that the costs should be borne by the Class A groups, but unequally, the costs being allocated in so far as possible by reference to the percentage share each polluter would bear of the aggregate total had separate strategies been specified for each linkage.

The result of both of these approaches is that wherever there is one Class A polluter for any linkage anywhere on the site, all Class B polluters are exonerated and removed from liability.

Example

A site gives rise to four significant pollutant linkages (SPLs): SPL1, SPL2, SPL3 and SPL4. The authority excludes and apportions liability within each SPL as follows:

SPL1 one Class A polluter (100)
SPL2 three Class A polluters (30:50:20)
SPL3 two Class A polluters (50:50)

SPL4 one Class B polluter (100)

The total cost of a shared *common* action (should the authority decide this is the way to go) is £250,000. This will be allocated between the three Class A groups equally (i.e. £83,333 each) and then shared within the groups:

SPL1 £83,333
SPL2 £25,000
      £41,666
      £16,666
SPL3 £41,666
      £41,666

The total cost of a shared *collective* action for the site may only be £200,000. This will be allocated between the groups responsible for SPLs 1, 2 and 3 (the Class A groups) but unequally as explained above. For example, if the sole cost of dealing with SPL1 had been £100,000, the sole cost of dealing with SPL2 had been £200,000 and the sole cost of dealing with SPL3 had been £50,000, the actual (more economical) cost of £200,000 would be shared:

SPL1 100/350, i.e. £57,143
SPL2 200/350, i.e. £114,286
SPL3 50/350, i.e. £28,571

Once allocated to the group, costs are then shared between individuals in the allocated proportions.

2.9.3 Comment

The exclusionary tests may seem fine in isolation, and the intention of removing from liability those who have no real connection with the contamination is laudable, but the practicalities of the system lead to several areas of concern.

Test 1

This excludes those who are generally thought of as peripheral to the contaminating activity advisers, lenders, landlords, surveyors and the like. Clearly, those who are offering services to a polluting business would not imagine that they could be made liable for the effects of the polluting business's activities themselves. However, the fact that the exception exists at all indicates that, in the Government's view, it is possible that such peripheral service providers could be held to have at least knowingly permitted the activities in some way.

If so, they are given an immediate exemption from liability, but the exemption can only operate at all if there are others who will be left in the Class A category after its operation. If there are no others, then the lender or the adviser can be made to pay the clean-up bill.

Test 2

This excludes those who have, in some sense, already paid for the cost of a clean-up operation on the site in relation to the pollution that is now giving rise to the problem. Having paid once, you will not be required to pay again, and this test gives the necessary exemption.

Note, though, that to benefit from the exemption, the payment must have been made expressly for the purpose of the relevant clean up, and must have been of an adequate size to pay for that clean up. Moreover, the clean up need not have been carried out properly or at all. The size and purpose of the payment must be specifically set out in the contract under the terms of which the payment has come to be made.

That said, the payment could take a number of forms, and still qualify. It could be a specific payment made voluntarily or under court order or, more likely, could take the form of a price reduction on a change of ownership of property, recorded fully and specifically in the contract.

Properly evidenced price reductions thus remove a seller from the Class A category. General price reductions, not specifically evidenced in the agreement, do not.

In addition, the payer must retain no control over the land, though this would not prevent a payer retaining some form of contractual right to supervise any remedial works, which is a common desire and inclusion in many commercial transactions.

Test 3

This excludes anyone who sells land to another member of the Class A group and who ensures that the purchaser had sufficient information about the nature and extent of the contamination to enable that party to decide whether to proceed and, if so, with what price adjustments.

This is clearly an inducement to full disclosure on the part of the seller, and enables a buyer to make an informed choice on the purchase – knowing that if they proceed, it will be at their own risk as to the cost of the clean up, as the seller will be excluded from the Class.

The difficulty with this test is in the detail. The Guidance states that the sort of transaction to which the test applies is not confined to property deals pure and simple, but can involve any network of transactions as part of which property changes hands – a company share or business acquisition involving property portfolios being the obvious other instance.

Moreover, it states that in transactions where the purchaser is a large commercial organisation (defined, presumably, in accordance with company law provisions as not being a small or medium-sized enterprise), the mere offering of facilities for inspection, survey or investigation will be sufficient to fix the purchaser with all the knowledge they could have discovered had they undertaken such an investigation, whether they did or did not do so. This counts as full disclosure by the seller.

In addition, it should be noted that this aspect of the test is made retrospective and will catch any transaction entered into since 1990. This may cause considerable upset and dislocation as such transactions may not have made sufficient provision for indemnity, and recent purchasers may have to bear the full clean-up costs alone.

Tests 4–6

These tests exclude the original polluter of the site in any circumstances where the pollutant linkage is attributable to the intervention of some other factor, without which there would have been no problem.

The Guidance seems to alter the operation of the Act on this point (see Exclusion Test 6, Circular 01/2006, Annex 3, Chapter D, Part 4, paras. D68–D72). It provides that, if the migration of the contamination would not have occurred without the act or omission of some third party, then it is the third-party intervener who is the appropriate person for service of the notice, rather than the original depositor of the substance.

The Guidance proceeds on the basis that the third-party intervener must also be in the liability group to start with, i.e. they must themselves be said to have caused or knowingly permitted the substance to be present, so as between co-polluters, it is the person who causes the migration rather than the original pollution who has to remediate.

The Act proceeds on the assumption that, once you deposit a substance, you are liable for everything and anything which subsequently happens to it. For Guidance to change the express terms of the Act is a constitutional novelty, and it remains to be seen how the courts will interpret these provisions.

CIRCULAR FACILITIES (LONDON) LTD V. SEVENOAKS DC [2005] EWHC 865 (ADMIN)

One such case is that of *Circular Facilities*. In this case, the first of its kind to be brought under Part IIA, the magistrates' court was asked to apply the exclusionary tests set out above, and in particular Test 6.

The facts of the case were as follows. An owner of a former brickworks site (X) began to infill some ponds and quarries on the site with a view to developing it. The ponds were filled with plastic sheeting and organic matter such as old tree and iris roots. The site was sold to a Mr Scott, who continued to infill the land. In 1979, Scott sold the land to Circular Facilities (CF), a development company, and applied for planning permission to build eight houses on the site. At the time of the application in 1982, a site survey was undertaken which revealed that methane gas was emanating from the infilled portions of the site. Nevertheless, eight houses were built on the site by CF. In 1999, the council investigated the site, and determined it to be contaminated land. Scott by now having died, the council served a remediation notice on CF, following the application of the exclusionary tests, omitting X from the notice.

CF appealed.

The magistrates' court applied the exclusionary tests and decided that between an original owner (X), who deposited material at a time when there was no receptor or pathway present, and a developer (CF), who introduced receptors and pathways onto a site thus creating a significant pollutant linkage – the original owner was entitled to be excluded from liability by virtue of Test 6.

The upshot of this decision was to cast a heavy burden of risk onto developers of land who, as part of their operations, create pathways (houses with service ingress points and floorboards) and then introduce receptors (the purchasers of the individual houses). The subsequent introducers are to blame for the problem, and the original polluter of the site is excluded from any further liability.

This case would seem to increase the burden on developers fully to assess and address contamination issues on a site as part of the purchase decision, and as part of the development operations (a likely requirement of the planning permission in any event).

On appeal to the High Court, the High Court decided that the magistrates' court had not given sufficient reasons for its decision, and has remitted the case back to the magistrates for a full re-hearing. It has since been settled out of court on the basis that (among other things) the authority withdraw the Remediation Notice.

One slight curiosity about *Circular Facilities* is that no evidence was produced to the court about whether the purchasers of the properties knew of the contamination at the time of purchase. If they did, then it would have been open to CF to argue that they had been removed from the liability group by virtue of Test 3 (sold with information). By the time Test 6 came to be applied, CF would already have been removed from the group, thus preventing the test from applying, and forcing Sevenoaks DC to serve the notice on X and the individual purchasers, apportioning liability between them in some way. This would have been a markedly different result and reinforces the commercial and transactional effectiveness of full disclosure on sale.

Tests A–B

These simply operate to exclude from liability those who only have a short-term interest in the land, leaving those with the long-term interest to bear the clean-up cost.

2.9.4 Agreements on liabilities

The parties may wish to agree between themselves how they wish to apportion any liability for contamination. Any such agreement will be honoured by the authority, and all its decisions regarding liability will be taken with the intention of enabling the agreement between the parties to have effect.

If the effect of the agreement would be to place an additional burden of expense on a person who would benefit from any relaxation of his responsibility to pay his full share, for example, because of the hardship it would cause him, then the authority would, in principle, have to pay that share itself, at public expense. In such circumstances, the authority can ignore the whole agreement and apply the rules in the statutory guidance instead.

Such contracts therefore need to include mechanisms to ensure that, if the authority does not honour and implement the agreement as had been intended, the parties will indemnify one another to regulate the position between themselves. It would thus be the parties who bear the risk of one of them being unable to pay their share, rather than the public purse, and this is also intended as an anti-avoidance measure.

See chapters 6 to 8 for a discussion of how to deal with contaminated land in a transactional context.

2.9.5 The position of owners and occupiers

The Act

Although primary responsibility for remediation rests with the person who caused or knowingly permitted the substance to be present in land (the 'original polluter' or 'Class A appropriate person'), who may, in certain circumstances, not even be the original polluter on the ambiguous wording of the Act, there is a residual responsibility which falls upon owners and occupiers of land.

Where, after reasonable inquiry, the original polluter cannot be 'found', the owner or the occupier for the time being becomes the appropriate person.

The Guidance

No guidance has been given in respect of the definition of 'reasonable inquiry' and it is not altogether clear what is meant by the phrase. There is also some doubt about the meaning of the word 'found'. It would seem to mean 'identified, in existence and located'. An individual must still be alive, and a corporate entity must not yet have been dissolved, though solvency is not a requirement. If it 'exists', it matters not that it has no money – in that situation, the liability cannot be passed to another person or entity and the authority will have to foot the bill.

The liability of owners and occupiers is restricted as regards remediation works in relation to the pollution of controlled waters (s.78J). Where a party finds itself responsible for remediation works solely as a result of its ownership or occupation of land (as opposed to being the original polluter), that party will not be liable for any works relating to the pollution of controlled waters (s.78J(2)). This brings the contaminated land provisions into line with WRA 1991, s.161, which allows the Environment Agency to serve works notices only on original polluters, and not on landowners purely by reason of their ownership.

2.9.6 Escapes of substances to other land

The Act

As contamination does not necessarily confine itself to boundaries of ownership or occupation, there is provision for the service of remediation notices where substances have escaped from their original resting place onto other land.

The basic principle is that the original polluter of the first site (land A) is to be treated as the original polluter of any other land (land B, C, etc.) to which the substance migrates (s.78K(1)).

Owners and occupiers of lands A, B or C are not liable to carry out remediation works in respect of contaminating substances unless the original polluter cannot be found, and, in any event, could then only be made liable to clean up land within their ownership or occupation (s78K(3), (4))

The Guidance

As noted above, the Guidance seems to alter the operation of the Act quite significantly here. It provides that if the migration would not have occurred without the act or omission of some third party, then it is the third-party intervener who is the appropriate person for service of the notice, rather than the original depositor of the substance.

The Guidance proceeds on the basis that the third-party intervener must also be in the liability group to start with, i.e. they must themselves be said to have caused or knowingly permitted the substance to be present, so as between co-polluters it is the person who causes the migration (rather than the person who caused the pollution) who has to remediate.

2.10 COST RECOVERY AND HARDSHIP

The authority must now consider what the consequences would be of serving a notice and then carrying out the works itself. Can it recover all the relative shares of the costs from all those identified as being liable to pay? If not, no remediation notice can be served on anyone.

The authority must do works and recover the full amount from those who can afford it, and as much as possible from those who cannot afford it all. See ss.78H(5)(d), 78N(3)(e), 78P(l).

One of the problems here is that there is no appeal procedure available, as no notice has been served. Judicial review would be the only action open to any of the liable parties who wanted to dispute the designation or the steps taken.

Defra encourages authorities to consult over liability issues and technical matters, to try to minimise disputes.

If there is no problem in identifying those liable and able to pay for the work, the authority can proceed to serve the notice.

2.11 SERVICE OF REMEDIATION NOTICE

2.11.1 The Act

Once a site has been identified as contaminated land (or a special site), the relevant authority is under a duty to prepare a 'remediation notice' specifying what must be done by way of remediation (s.78E).

In specifying the steps required under a remediation notice, the authority can only require reasonable steps to be taken having regard to the costs of carrying out the work and the seriousness of the harm/pollution caused (s.78E(4), (5)).

The definition of 'remediation' (s.78A(7)) includes:

- assessment of the condition of land;
- the doing of any works, carrying out of any operations or taking of any steps in relation to any land or waters for preventing, minimising, remedying or mitigating the effects of significant harm or pollution;
- the restoration of land or waters to their former state;
- inspections from 'time to time'.

It is expected that the content of remediation notices will reflect the existing content of abatement notices under the statutory nuisance system. The precise requirements with regard to content and procedure are to be dealt with by way of regulations (s.78E(6)).

In addition to any regulations made under s.78E, enforcing authorities are obliged to take into account any guidance from the Secretary of State in relation to what is to be done, the standard to which it must be carried out and the definition of 'reasonable' in the context of the cost analysis.

There are, however, a number of circumstances where the duty to serve a remediation notice does not apply.

A remediation notice 'must not' be served where:

- the enforcing authority is satisfied that a site is contaminated but no remediation works can be specified to be carried out because they would be unreasonably expensive (s.78H(5)). In such circumstances, it must publish a remediation statement setting out the grounds for taking the view that remediation works cannot be specified (s.78H(6));
- the authority is satisfied that appropriate steps are being, or will be taken without the service of a notice (s.78H(5)). In such circumstances, the person who would have received the notice is required to prepare, within a reasonable period, a remediation statement setting out what works will be carried out, and within what period;
- the authority itself would be the recipient;
- grounds already exist for the exercise by the authority of its own clean-up powers in respect of the site.

These exceptions do not apply where there is imminent danger of serious harm or serious pollution of controlled waters (s.78H(4)).

A further restriction is placed upon the authority in that it cannot issue a notice where powers are available to the Environment Agency under EPA 1990, s.27 in relation to remediation of pollution caused by prescribed processes (s.78YB).

2.11.2 The Guidance

The Guidance suggests that the main purpose of notification and consultation is to enable those affected by the notice to resolve technical and liability disputes, to refine the requirements of the notice, and to agree voluntary strategies. If such can be agreed, then no notice can be served at all, provided that the authority is satisfied that works 'will be' carried out within an agreed time frame. The time frame itself must be reasonably set so as to enable the person to afford the works.

The restriction on serving a notice must also be read in conjunction with the Guidance on cost recovery, as the powers for the authority to do works can be exercised whenever it is satisfied that, at the end of the day, it would not be seeking to recover from any appropriate person all of its share of the costs of the work. In such a situation, no notice can be served on anyone. The authority must do the work itself, if at all, and then recover as much cost as possible from those responsible.

On the question of how clean is clean, the Guidance suggests that the remediation works specified should be such as to enable the identified pollutant linkage which led to the original designation to cease to exist. This may mean simply severing the pathway (e.g. by tarmacadaming a surface) rather than cleaning the subsoil. It also means, of course, that land is never given a clean bill of health as it may be redetermined as contaminated at a later stage should a new target or pathway emerge.

2.11.3 Comment

The circumstances where the duty to serve a remediation notice does not apply represent a major weakening of the regulatory powers under the Act.

2.12 CARRYING OUT REMEDIATION WORKS

2.12.1 The Act

A remediation notice can require an appropriate person to carry out works which they are not otherwise entitled to do, because, for example, they are no longer in possession of the site and have no rights of access to it. In these circumstances, the owner or occupier of land has a statutory obligation to allow remediation works to be carried out on the land or waters that they own or occupy (s.78G).

Before the remediation notice is served, the enforcing authority has to use its reasonable endeavours to consult with all those parties who might be required to grant rights to the party carrying out the remediation works (s.78G(3)), though this requirement does not apply where there is imminent danger of serious harm, etc.

No provision is made in the Act for expediting the consent of those parties should they refuse.

In many cases, the carrying out of remediation works will create an enormous amount of disruption to an occupier of land. Thus, where rights are granted, compensation will be payable by the appropriate person. The cost of compensation could, of course, be significantly greater than that of carrying out the remediation works themselves.

2.12.2 The Guidance

The Guidance provides that the cost of compensating the occupier for rights of access is to be one of the costs to be identified by the authority in, and borne by the appropriate person receiving, the remediation notice.

2.13 TIME LIMITS AND APPEALS

2.13.1 The Act

The authority must now allow the time specified in the notice to elapse.

There is a right of appeal against a remediation notice (s.78L). Previously, if a notice was served by a local authority, an appeal was heard in the magistrates' court and the appeal was to be made by way of summary application (in a similar fashion to the statutory nuisance provision). Under the Environment and Clean Neighbourhoods Act 2005, all appeals are now heard by an Inspector appointed by the Secretary of State.

Where the Environment Agency is the appropriate authority, the appeal is also heard by the Secretary of State.

The time limit is 21 days beginning with the first day of service.

The notice can be quashed if there is a 'material defect' in the notice. The notice can also be modified or confirmed.

2.13.2 The Regulations

The Contaminated Land (England) Regulations 2006, SI 2006/1380 provide the following grounds of appeal:

- the appellant is not the appropriate person;
- someone else is the appropriate person (the appellant must specify who and where they are);

- the authority failed to exclude the appellant from the definition in accordance with Guidance;
- the authority improperly apportioned the costs of remediation;
- there is some error in or connected with the notice;
- the authority served a notice when it was statutorily prevented from doing so;
- the notice requires works to be done in respect of controlled waters by an owner or occupier liable in that capacity only;
- the notice requires works to be done in respect of migrated matter on other land;
- the notice requires works to be done in respect of matters governed by other regulatory regimes (e.g. integrated pollution control (IPC));
- the land has been improperly identified as contaminated bearing in mind the relevant Guidance;
- the authority has unreasonably refused to accept that voluntary works are being or will be carried out;
- the notice's requirements are unreasonable having regard to the costs and benefits;
- the notice is served in circumstances where the authority had power to do the works itself;
- the notice's requirements fail to take account of guidance from the Secretary of State or the Environment Agency (among other things, they are insufficiently precise, etc.);
- the period of time for compliance is insufficient;
- the notice requires an insolvency practitioner to carry out works, contrary to s.78X.

The Regulations provide that an appeal suspends the operation of a remediation notice.

2.13.3 Comment

Not even the most inventive litigator could have come up with a more comprehensive set of grounds! Having said that, there have been very few appeals, with most remediation notices complied with by those responsible.

Sandridge appeal (app/cl/05/01 & 02)

The first (and so far only) appeal to be dealt with by the Secretary of State concerned a former chemical works that was run by a company purchased by Redland Minerals. Redland then sold the site to Crest Nicholson who redeveloped the site for housing over a four-year period. The Inspector (and the court following an unsuccessful judicial review of the Inspector's decision) found that although Redland had caused the contamination, Crest had also caused it by allowing it to seep further into the underlying aquifer. In addition, the 'sold with information' test did not assist

Redland as Crest did not have all the necessary information. The Inspector apportioned liability between the two parties taking into account their respective liability for different contaminants.

2.14 PROSECUTION FOR NON-COMPLIANCE WITH REMEDIATION NOTICE

2.14.1 The Act

It is an offence to fail to comply with a remediation notice without reasonable excuse (s.78M). The offence can only be tried in the magistrates' court.

Where the contaminated land is industrial, trade or business premises the maximum penalty is a fine of £20,000 with a further daily fine of up to £2,000 for every day before the enforcing authority has carried out any remediation.

In cases of other contaminated land, the maximum fine is £5,000 with a maximum daily fine of £500 (10 per cent of Level 5).

2.15 LOCAL AUTHORITY COMPLETE WORKS AND RECOVER COSTS

2.15.1 The Act

The relevant authority has the power to carry out remediation works:

- where it is necessary to prevent imminent serious harm being caused;
- where any requirement of a remediation notice is not complied with;
- where it is agreed that the authority should carry out the works;
- where a remediation notice could not have specified works of the type required;
- where the local authority would not be seeking to recover all of its share of the costs from any of the appropriate persons:
- where there is no appropriate person on whom to serve a remediation notice.

If works are carried out, the authority can recover the reasonable costs of the work (or at least a proportion of them) from the appropriate person(s), subject to the Guidance and any hardship caused.

Costs may include interest if the appropriate person is both the original polluter and the current owner of the contaminated land.

The relevant authority also has the power to serve a charging notice on the owner which will constitute a charge on the premises which consist of or include the contaminated land in question. The costs of any charge may be paid by instalments over a maximum 30-year period.

A person served with the charging notice has a right of appeal which must be made to the county court within 21 days of the receipt of the notice.

The Government's intention behind these provisions is to avoid hardship, prevent the private sector from gaining from publicly funded improvements to land and to protect the public purse. No provision is made in the Act to deal with so-called 'orphan liabilities' (i.e. where no costs can be recovered).

2.15.2 The Guidance

First, the Guidance reminds authorities that they should not even consider serving a remediation notice if they already know that they have no likelihood of being able to recover all of their allocated share of the costs from the person served, due to the hardship caused. The only option then is for the authorities to do the works themselves, and recover as much as they can.

It suggests that hardship should be given its usual dictionary meaning of 'hardness of fate or circumstance, severe suffering or privation', and should be interpreted to include injustice, suffering and anxiety as well as financial impact. Threats to business solvency and the local impact of businesses becoming unviable are general considerations.

Authorities are allowed to develop their own policies on this point along other parameters, for example, whether the person served would be financially eligible to receive a housing renovation grant.

As far as original polluters are concerned, the Guidance suggests the following considerations as being relevant:

* whether they are businesses or private individuals;
* persons made liable in circumstances where co-parties cannot be found are to be called upon to pay only so much as they would have had to pay had the other party been found;
* whether any steps have been taken to mitigate the harm;
* the role played in, and the degree of responsibility for, the creation of the risk of harm by each person (subsequent interveners, occupiers, pathway introducers, etc.).

As far as owner/occupiers are concerned, the Guidance suggests the following considerations as being relevant:

* whether the owner/occupier knew of the contamination at purchase and whether the price was reduced accordingly;
* whether the costs are likely to exceed the value of the land, bearing in mind that windfall gains in value to the current owner at public expense should be avoided;
* where trustees may be called to pay costs, the value of any trust fund used to pay them.

None of these considerations is to override the tests for allocation and apportionment of liability set out at **2.9.2** – the tests prevail.

Having determined who should pay what, where the recovery of costs is waived, the authority must bear the unpaid costs, and not reallocate them to other parties.

2.15.3 Comment

There are difficulties over the meaning and interpretation of these clauses.

Again, the terms of a land transaction may come under scrutiny to determine the state of a buyer's knowledge, and whether there were any reductions in purchase price, to see whether any hardship would be suffered by owners in having to pay.

The fact that business solvency may be threatened would seem to enable smaller and medium-sized businesses to raise the defence of poverty, particularly in recessionary times. Even without creative accounting, many businesses are on the edge financially, and a clean-up bill may be the straw that breaks. The socio-economic costs of clean up ('force me to pay and I'll lay off the staff') are vital political considerations for a local authority.

There is also the perception that, where a local authority undertakes a clean-up operation, the 'reasonable' costs always seem to be very high.

2.16 REGISTERS

2.16.1 The Act

Every enforcing authority must keep a register whenever it decides to determine land as contaminated (s.78R). The register will contain the following details:

- remediation notices;
- charging notices;
- appeals against remediation and charging notices:
- remediation statements and declarations;
- designations of special sites:
- notices terminating the designation of special sites;
- notifications by owners/occupiers/appropriate persons of any voluntary works which they claim have been carried out on the site;
- convictions for relevant offences.

The fact that information is contained on the register which specifies what voluntary works have allegedly been carried out, is not to be taken as a representation by the authority that the works have in fact been carried out, or how successfully.

Access can be had to these registers by members of the public, free of charge, and copies provided on the payment of reasonable charges (s.78R(8)).

There are certain exclusions from the register (s.78S) for:

- information affecting national security; and
- commercially confidential information.

There is an appeals system which mirrors the existing confidentiality appeal system.

2.16.2 Comment

If it had been thought that contaminated land registers had been abandoned, here they resurrect themselves in different form. The registers must be the first port of call in any conveyancing transaction from now on and, indeed, form CON 29R now includes a standard question (3.12) asking the local authority to indicate whether the target property is on the contaminated land registers or has been notified as having been determined as contaminated land.

However, an authority may have decided that a site is not so polluted as to meet the definitional criteria for designation as contaminated land within the meaning of the amended EPA 1990, and accordingly the property would not be entered onto the registers, nor would it have been notified. The response to CON 29R would therefore be in the negative, suggesting to the inexperienced that there is 'no problem'. In fact, there may be pollutants on the site which may be of concern to a purchaser and further enquiries may be needed to protect the purchaser's interests. See Chapter 7 for fuller discussion.

It would also seem that once a site is entered onto the registers, it will not be removed from them, despite a clean up having been effected. Details of the clean up can be noted on the register, but the history will remain. It was this feature of the old regime as contained in EPA 1990, s.143 that led to its abandonment amid fears of blight. Surely those fears are likely to be realised under this scheme and sellers may thus need to compile a file of evidence to reassure purchasers that works have been carried out to address the risks found on site. Local authorities will not give comfort or reassurance that those works have in fact been effective.

2.17 INTERACTION OF CONTAMINATED LAND LEGISLATION WITH OTHER LEGAL REGIMES

There are several other regimes which are intended to deal with many aspects of pollution and contaminated land, and which often overlap with the operation of EPA 1990, Part IIA. They include:

- planning law;
- health and safety;
- major accident hazards;
- landfill tax;
- environmental permitting;
- statutory nuisances;
- water pollution.

What overlaps are there, and how are they resolved?

2.17.1 Planning law

Planning law is essentially focused on future land use, and all decisions regarding planning consent and conditions are taken with that future use in mind.

Contamination in the ground on any site coming up for redevelopment is a material consideration for the purposes of the planning legislation and conditions will therefore be set by the planning authorities which take the implications of that contamination into account and which require its remediation as part of the development work. It will thus be the developer who has the task of remediating the contamination as part of the development and who must therefore take such costs into account in any purchasing decision.

Any such remediation will be policed via the planning system and not Part IIA.

Remediation under Part IIA is intended to deal with current land use only. In Planning Policy Statement 23 (PPS 23) requirements were included regarding the approach to be taken in any development of land potentially affected by contamination. The key elements of this statement are that:

- all applications for development should be accompanied by a desk survey seeking to identify potential contamination problems;
- informal discussions should then be carried out between the local planning authority (LPA) and the applicant to determine the extent of any contamination and the proposals for dealing with it;
- conditions should be set to ensure that the development achieves certain specified aims, including:

  - the avoidance of any risk to health during the development;
  - the removal of unacceptable levels of contamination;
  - the suitability of the site for any plausible future use;
  - the removal of risks to health or financial risks which may affect the future use of the land.

Model planning conditions have been issued to LPAs to be used where land may be affected by contamination.

Circular Facilities v. *Sevenoaks DC* [2005] EWHC 865 (Admin) (see **2.9.3**) emphasises the importance to developers of assessing the contamination on the site at acquisition and taking the appropriate steps to remediate any identified issues. Failure to do so will result in the developer being the person most likely to receive the remediation notice if one is served under Part IIA.

Ascertaining and verifying whether a developer has adequately complied with any planning requirements regarding contamination remains a vexed issue. Sellers attempting to reassure future purchasers that the land is safe will require assistance from developers in the provision of information regarding the works undertaken, and such information may be a sensible inclusion in any information provided by the seller.

2.17.2 Health and safety

Health and safety issues under the Health and Safety at Work Act 1974 may arise on any site where workers may be at risk of exposure to contaminants. In any such case, under Part IIA, authorities are to liaise with the HSE to ensure that no duplication of control takes place and that the most appropriate system of control is used to deal with the problem.

2.17.3 Major accident hazards

The COMAH Regulations require action plans in relation to dangerous substances stored on sites, providing for the steps to be taken in the event of an escape. Again, under Part IIA, authorities should liaise with the HSE which oversees COMAH.

2.17.4 Landfill tax

Landfill tax under the Finance Act 1996 will be payable on any wastes going to landfill. However, exemption is available for wastes from contaminated sites or those remediated as part of certain developments. This exemption will, however, *not* be available to anyone cleaning up a site as part of enforcement action under Part IIA, though it will still be available to those cleaning up a Part IIA site voluntarily. This is intended to be a fiscal incentive to voluntary clean up, although it is being phased out from April 2012. Such incentives are also supplemented by provisions in the Finance Act 2001 permitting 'super-recovery' of the costs of remediation against corporation tax in certain circumstances.

2.17.5 Environmental permitting

Integrated pollution control, pollution prevention and control, and waste management licensing have been replaced by a wider environmental permitting (EP) regime. There is a power of clean up, exercisable by the permitting authority in the event of any breach of a licence condition. To the extent that any contaminant is already subject to control under EP, EPA 1990 specifically provides that it cannot also constitute contaminated land under Part IIA.

EP clean-up powers can be used to clean land up to any extent, and they are not subject to the restrictive operative provisions of Part IIA.

Clean-up operations ordered under Part IIA may constitute regulated processes under EP.

2.17.6 Statutory nuisances

Statutory nuisances under EPA 1990, Part III are defined to include 'premises or accumulations' which could be a pollution or health risk, as well as the more routine examples such as smoke and noise.

However, this would have meant that Part III could have been used to require the abatement of any pollution risk arising on premises, which is exactly what the regime in Part IIA is supposed to be for. Moreover, the provisions of Part III have been in force in one form or another for centuries and are familiar, quick and cheap. To deal with this, the legislation has been amended to provide that land in a 'contaminated state' cannot now be a statutory nuisance.

The definition of 'land in a contaminated state' includes any land on which contaminants are present and which may cause harm, and this is *not* the same as it being contaminated within the meaning of Part IIA, which requires additional criteria to be met.

Thus, one faces the situation where land may be in a contaminated state by virtue of the presence of chemicals or pollutants on it, but is not yet so dangerous as to pose a real risk of significant harm to any recognised receptor. Such a site cannot be 'contaminated land', but neither can it now be a statutory nuisance. It seems that this lacuna in the drafting of the legislation is intentional – it is Government policy, and now the law, that unless a site is highly contaminated, it should be left alone. Land is either 'contaminated' within the meaning of Part IIA, or no form of regulatory action can be taken.

2.17.7 Water pollution

Wherever and whenever water pollution occurs, however insignificant or harmless it may have been, the clean-up powers contained in WRA 1991, ss.161A–161D come into play. These enable the Environment Agency as water regulator to serve a works notice on those responsible for the water pollution requiring them to clean it, and all its consequences, up. Moreover, the notice can be used to prevent anticipated water pollution before it occurs.

There is a clear and undesirable overlap between these powers and those under Part IIA, which can also be used whenever water pollution occurs.

In any incident of water pollution, which set of powers should be used and by whom?

Logic would suggest that it should be the WRA 1991 powers that should be exercisable by the Environment Agency – it is, after all, the water specialist. Part IIA would thus be left to deal with land-based contamination only.

Sadly, logic has not guided Government thinking on this matter and the Guidance suggests that it should be the Part IIA powers that should be used, the authorities liaising with the Environment Agency over the terms and conditions to be imposed in dealing with any water pollution.

It remains to be seen what point there is in having the works notice powers in WRA 1991, and the Government has amended the primary legislation to clarify this overlap, with provisions in the Water Act 2003. These provide that Part IIA applies only if water pollution is significant, though this provision is still not in force.

It seems that the WRA 1991 powers are of use only if and when Part IIA does not apply, i.e. when water pollution does not emanate from land or where the pollution is not significant.

2.18 DEALING WITH CONTAMINATED LAND IN LEGAL TRANSACTIONS

As illustrated, the risk of having to remediate a piece of contaminated land tends to run with the land.

This is because the definition of the 'original polluter', the person primarily liable to pay these costs, can be said to include anyone who purchases the land in circumstances where they thereafter 'knowingly permit' contaminants to remain on the land, in circumstances where they could reasonably have removed them.

Moreover, if no original polluter of the site can be found, then the owner or occupier for the time being will have to bear the clean-up cost.

It is vital, therefore, to undertake all appropriate investigations before the transaction and if contamination or other environmental factors are perceived to be a risk, to make the necessary contractual provision to deal with the allocation of that risk.

Ideally, a seller would wish to pass to a buyer all potential liabilities attaching to the land, and the exclusionary tests available in conjunction with Part IIA provide a number of ways in which this can be achieved. Conversely, a buyer will want liability to remain with the seller, or at least to provide for an assessment of the risk and an appropriate adjustment of price or other protection to take place.

These adjustments are standard procedure in commercial corporate or property transactions, but would be rare in a routine domestic conveyancing matter, for example.

Other chapters will discuss the particular application of general environmental concepts in particular transactional settings, but this section focuses on the provisions of Part IIA in particular.

2.18.1 Exclusionary tests

General

The main thrust of Part IIA from a transactional point of view is the exclusionary tests contained in Defra Circular 01/2006 on Contaminated Land.

The Guidance states that the first step is to define the 'liability group', i.e. all those who may be appropriate persons by the application of the definition in EPA 1990. That means all those who 'caused or knowingly permitted' the contaminants to be present in, on or under the land (original polluters, or Class A appropriate persons) or all those who are owners and occupiers, liable as such because the original polluter cannot be found (Class B appropriate persons).

The next step is to exclude from those groups anyone satisfying any one of a number of exclusionary tests set out in the Guidance. The exclusionary tests are to be applied in the order set out in the Guidance. Only those who are not excluded are liable to receive the remediation notice.

It is important to note that application of the exclusionary tests is to be stopped as soon as there is only one person left in the group.

The excluded categories are as set out below.

CLASS A LIABILITY GROUP (ORIGINAL POLLUTERS)

1.   Anyone who is a member of Class A solely by reason of one or more excluded activities (among other things, lending to, insuring, licensing, consenting to the activities of, advising, carrying out work for, or leasing land to another person).
2.   Any member of Class A who makes a sufficient payment to another member of Class A stipulated in the contract as being for the particular remediation of land if that remediation is not carried out properly or at all, and provided the payer retains no control over the condition of the land.
3.   Anyone who has sold freehold or long leasehold (more than 21 years) land at arm's length terms, the purchaser having sufficient information for him to be aware of the pollution risk which has led to the designation. The Guidance specifically provides:

    … in transactions since the beginning of 1990 where the buyer is a large commercial organisation or public body, permission from the seller for the buyer to carry out his own investigations of the condition of the land should normally be taken as sufficient indication that the buyer had the information [referred to above].

4.   Anyone who deposits a substance A, which is, on its own, inert and of no risk, but which, when combined with substance B, becomes a pollutant (in this case, the depositor of substance B becomes liable).
5.   Anyone who deposits a substance which will not escape without intervention, but which later escapes due to intervention (in this case, it is the intervener who is liable).
6.   Anyone who deposits a substance which is not a risk due to the lack of a pathway, but which later becomes a risk due to the subsequent introduction of a pathway (in this case, it is the introducer of the pathway who is liable).

CLASS B LIABILITY GROUP (OWNERS AND OCCUPIERS)

Anyone occupying under licence with no value, or paying rent for the land and having no beneficial interest in the ownership of it other than the tenancy itself.

Passing liability

Exclusionary tests 2 and 3 operate to pass from the person who makes a payment or provides information (a seller of land, usually) that party's share of any remediation cost. Such transfer can, to an extent, be assured by means of contractual drafting, and the precedent clauses set out at Appendix A1 suggest some clauses that might work in this fashion. As the *Sandridge* appeal (see **2.13.3**) showed, the regulator will look carefully as to what information was actually provided and what knowledge can be obtained from that information. The clauses also contain indemnities intended to achieve the same effect between the parties if the authorities fail to exclude and reapportion the costs in the way envisaged by the clauses.

2.18.2 Agreements on liabilities

General

The parties to a transaction may decide to agree between themselves how they wish to apportion any liability for contamination rather than leaving the risk to fall where it may, depending on the operation of the complex exclusionary tests. Any such specific agreement is likely to be honoured by the appropriate authority, and all its decisions regarding liability will be taken with the intention of enabling the agreement between the parties to have effect.

The language of the Guidance talks in terms of the authorities giving effect to whatever agreements the parties may have come to as to the proportions in which they intend to share any clean-up cost. Such agreements may therefore need to specify in percentage terms what proportion of any remediation work required or agreed is to be borne by the respective parties in order to conform to the language of the relevant Guidance, and a typical indemnity clause found in many forms of commercial agreement (i.e. 'I'll reimburse you your share') may not work to reallocate the liability for the shares in the way the Guidance (or the parties) may have envisaged.

Where possible, the provisions regarding contaminated land which are intended to amount to an 'agreement on liabilities' for the purposes of Part IIA of EPA 1990 should be kept separate in the documentation from other environmental provisions, since this particular piece of legislation works to such unique and complex rules which differ entirely from other regimes. Practitioners may feel that this is an unnecessarily pedantic view, and regard a specific and detailed mention of the Part IIA provisions in the general indemnity clause as being sufficient.

If the effect of the agreement would be to place an additional burden of expense on a person who would benefit from any relaxation of his responsibility to pay his full share, for example, because of the hardship it would cause him, then the authority would, in principle, have to pay that share itself, at public expense. In such circumstances, the authority can ignore the whole agreement and apply the rules in the statutory guidance instead.

Such contracts therefore need to include mechanisms to ensure that, if the authority does not honour and implement the agreement as had been intended, the parties will indemnify one another to regulate the position between themselves. It would thus be the parties who bear the risk of one of them being unable to pay their share, rather than the public purse, and this is also intended as an anti-avoidance measure.

2.18.3 Conclusion

Part IIA liability can be allocated and dealt with in transactional documentation. The main issue surrounds quantifying the cost of adequate remediation so that the relevant price adjustments can be made, and this will, for the most part, require the engagement of consultants who are skilled, able and insured enough to express a view.

The view expressed here is that Part IIA clauses should be kept separate in the documentation from other environmental provisions covering other risks, which can be dealt with by means of more traditional warranties and indemnities. Such other risks should not be overlooked, however, as it is more likely that a purchaser of a going industrial concern, a polluting property or a company would face water pollution prosecutions, waste-related enforcement action or complaints based on nuisance rather than the service of a remediation notice under Part IIA.

2.19 SPECIFIC ISSUES

2.19.1 Lenders

The financial sector's primary concern has always been that there should not be a 'deep pocket' regime in which lenders could be pursued, regardless of their responsibility for any contamination, if no directly liable party could be found. Such cases are unlikely, but it is still possible that a mortgagee in possession of a site may be looked upon as the person who 'caused or knowingly permitted' contamination to be present (the 'Class A' person), and certainly an owner or occupier of the land, thus making them an appropriate person on whom to serve a remediation notice.

The term 'owner' is defined as 'a person (other than a mortgagee not in possession) who . . . is entitled to receive the rack rent' (i.e. the yearly amount of rent that a tenant could reasonably expect to pay on the open market). A mortgagee in possession who is entitled to receive the rack rent will therefore be treated as the owner and, accordingly, as liable to be served with a remediation notice if an original polluter cannot be found.

Accordingly, lenders and their advisers need to be vigilant to potential risks in their initial lending decisions, and although (especially in the residential sector) this may not affect their decision to lend, it will enable them to take a view on the risks posed and decide how best to deal with them in the event of default.

2.19.2 Insolvency practitioners for contaminated land

Part IIA of EPA 1990 (s.78X) provides that a person acting as an insolvency practitioner will be personally liable under Part IIA (i.e. for contaminated land) only to the extent that:

(a) harm;
(b) pollution of controlled waters; or
(c) the condition of any land by reason of substances in, on or under the land,

is attributable to his negligence.

It follows that an insolvency practitioner will be in danger of liability for land contamination under Part IIA only if it is caused by some negligent act or omission on his part. Provided the practitioner acts with reasonable care while in office, he should be safe.

Even where there is a negligent act or omission, the practitioner will only be liable to the extent that the contamination is caused by that act or omission.

The main difficulty will be that of determining causation, exactly which contaminant was contributed by the practitioner and when, and which was contributed by the borrowing company. This difficulty is likely to render actions against the practitioner extremely unlikely.

However, these provisions only apply to the contaminated land provisions contained in Part IIA which will be policed by the local authority, and not to other types of liability such as water pollution policed by the Environment Agency. Nor would the defence be available to any action at common law.

2.20 PROTECTING THE CLIENT

The key to active environmental risk management, and all the advantages that flow from it, is knowledge.

The company, its individual participants and, come to that, a purchaser, lender or receiver, should be undertaking some form of environmental investigation or audit in order to assess the exact nature and extent of any polluting activities or contamination on its land, and the risks posed by its assets and operations. From these investigations, decisions can be made about the degree of risk involved and the commercial and transactional approach to the management, apportionment or insurance of such risks.

For a further discussion of environmental investigations, see Chapter 10.

2.21 CONCLUSION

Experience has shown that the regime has been used sparingly, although it would be unwise to underestimate the impact of the regime in terms of profile raising, achieving remediation through the planning process and on individual sites around the country. Residential properties in Huntingdonshire, Wigan, Sheffield, Hartle-pool and Manchester have all been remediated at a cost of ten of thousands of pounds per property.

The general perception is that the vast majority of areas of concern are being dealt with on an informal basis, especially as there are several fiscal incentives – exemption from landfill tax and 150 per cent corporation tax offsets which may be available for informal clean ups, but not for those implemented by service of a notice. Whereas this is desirable from a cost point of view, it does mean that such areas of land will not appear on the official registers and alternative steps to ascertain the problems, and the appropriate solutions, will be needed.

CHAPTER 3

Environmental Damage Regulations

3.1 INTRODUCTION

The introduction of the EU regime to prevent and remedy environmental damage has substantially expanded the scope of liability for preventing and remediating pollution and other types of environmental damage in England and Wales, respectively. Persons who cause damage to protected species and natural habitats may now be required to restore them as well as remedying damage to land and water. The regime supplements other environmental liability regimes. Its enforcement includes minor incidents involving harm to human health from petrol and other chemical vapours as well as more serious incidents.

3.2 STRUCTURE OF REGIME

The regime is set out in the Environmental Damage (Prevention and Remediation) Regulations 2009, SI 2009/153, as amended (the Environmental Damage Regulations), which transposed Directive 2004/35/CE of the European Parliament and of the Council on environmental liability with regard to the prevention and remedying of environmental damage, as amended (ELD). Separate regulations have been enacted for Wales, Scotland and Northern Ireland. This chapter will describe the Environmental Damage Regulations, noting key differences in the equivalent regulations.

The Department for Environment, Food and Rural Affairs (Defra) and the Welsh Assembly Government have published the following documents to accompany the Environmental Damage Regulations and the Welsh Environmental Damage Regulations (Environmental Damage (Prevention and Remediation) (Wales) Regulations 2009, SI 2009/995):

- Quick Guide to the Regulations;
- In Depth Guidance to the Regulations (Guidance);
- Regulatory Impact Assessment;
- Note on Transposition; and
- Frequently Asked Questions.

The above documentation, which is updated from time to time, is available on Defra's website (**www.defra.gov.uk**).

3.3 OVERALL SUMMARY OF PROCEDURES

In a nutshell, the procedure for an operator who causes an imminent threat of environmental damage, or damage that there are reasonable grounds to believe will become environmental damage, is:

- to carry out emergency actions to prevent the imminent threat of environmental damage from materialising; and
- immediately to notify the competent authority if the actions fail to prevent environmental damage.

The failure by a responsible operator to carry out preventive measures and to notify the enforcing authority, if appropriate, is a criminal offence. There is no defence to the duty to carry out actions to prevent environmental damage.

The procedure in a case in which an operator causes environmental damage, or damage that there are reasonable grounds to believe is environmental damage, is as follows:

- the operator should carry out emergency actions to prevent any further environmental damage and immediately notify the enforcing authority of the damage;
- the enforcing authority should determine whether environmental damage has been caused and, if so, notify the operator and invite the operator to submit proposals to remediate the damage by a specified deadline;
- the operator should submit proposals;
- the authority should consider the proposals and issue a remediation notice, having invited interested parties to submit observations on it; and
- the operator should carry out the measures in the remediation notice by the specified deadline, together with complementary remediation measures, if necessary, and compensatory remediation measures (as described below).

As with actions to prevent environmental damage, it is a criminal offence for an operator to fail to carry out actions to prevent further environmental damage and remedial measures. There are defences to a notification of liability to carry out remedial measures but no defence to the duty to carry out emergency actions to prevent further damage.

3.4 SUPPLEMENTARY NATURE

The Regulations supplement existing environmental legislation; they do not replace it. The main legislation supplemented by them is:

- EPA 1990, Part IIA (contaminated land);

- WRA 1991, ss.161–161D (water pollution);
- WRA 1991 (abstraction and impoundment of water);
- EPA 1990, s.59, as amended (waste dumping);
- Environmental Permitting Regulations 2010 (permits for wide range of activities including industrial emissions and waste);
- COMAH Regulations (storage of dangerous substances and preparations exceeding specified quantities); and
- WCA 1981 (damage to, and destruction of, sites of special scientific interest (SSSIs)).

This means that even if the Environmental Damage Regulations do not apply to pollution or other environmental damage due, for example, to the threshold for such damage not having been met, other legislation may still impose liability to remediate the pollution or other damage on the person who is responsible for it. In some cases such as groundwater pollution, some of which is subject to the Environmental Damage Regulations, both the Regulations and other legislation will apply.

3.5   WHO IS LIABLE?

The 'operator' of an 'activity' who causes an imminent threat of, or actual, 'environmental damage' to a 'natural resource' is liable under the Environmental Damage Regulations.

The term 'operator' means a natural or legal person, including a governmental as well as a private organisation, who actually carries out an activity or who holds a permit or authorisation for it. An 'activity' is defined broadly to include any type of profit-making or non-profit-making activity or private or public sector activity. In essence, the only activities that are not covered by the Environmental Damage Regulations are purely recreational and domestic activities.

There are four categories of 'natural resources': land, water, SSSIs and protected species and natural habitats as described below (see **3.6**). The term 'environmental damage' means damage to a natural resource that exceeds a specified threshold (see **3.6**).

There are two categories of operators: Schedule 2 operators and non-Schedule 2 operators.

3.5.1   Schedule 2 operators

A Schedule 2 operator is a person who is carrying out an activity listed in Schedule 2 of the Environmental Damage Regulations. Schedule 2 activities include operating an installation with a permit under the Environmental Damage Regulations including industrial and waste management operations, the management of mining waste, specified activities concerning dangerous substances, authorised discharges into surface and ground water, water abstraction and impoundment, the transport of dangerous goods, and activities concerning genetically modified organisms

(GMOs). The Welsh Environmental Damage Regulations specifically provide that the holder of a consent deliberately to release GMOs is an operator, as is the holder of an authorisation in respect of genetically modified food or feed.

A Schedule 2 operator is strictly liable for an imminent threat of, and actual, environmental damage to all four categories of natural resources, that is, land, water, SSSIs and protected species and natural habitats.

3.5.2 Non-Schedule 2 operators

A non-Schedule 2 operator is an operator who is carrying out any activity other than a Schedule 2 activity. Such activities include the application of pesticides, filling a heating oil tank, storing chemicals which are not controlled by the COMAH Regulations and agricultural activities such as storing slurry and burning crop rubble.

A non-Schedule 2 operator is liable only for causing an imminent threat of, or actual, environmental damage to SSSIs and protected species and natural habitats, and only if the operator is negligent or otherwise at fault.

3.6 ENVIRONMENTAL DAMAGE AND THRESHOLDS

Environmental damage includes pollution of water and contamination of land. It is not, however, limited to them in that it includes other types of damage. Examples include damage to an SSSI due to a fire started by a farmer to destroy crop rubble which burns out of control, or a fire started by a small business to burn waste materials which burns out of control, and damage to an SSSI by groundwater having been diverted from it due to the installation of wells to abstract water for nearby water-intensive agriculture.

Environmental damage by air pollution is not covered by the Environmental Damage Regulations. Such damage is covered, however, if an airborne pollutant damages water, land, an SSSI, or a protected species or natural habitat. Thus, harm to human health from, say, particulates emitted by cars or trucks is not covered. Harm to human health from exposure to vapours from petrol or heating oil in the ground is covered because the damage results from a substance in the ground rather than an airborne substance.

There are different thresholds for environmental damage to land, water, SSSIs and protected species and natural habitats.

3.6.1 Land

A Schedule 2 operator is liable for an imminent threat of, or actual, environmental damage to land if the operator contaminates the land and the contamination 'results in a significant risk of adverse effects on human health'. The contamination of the land may be by 'substances', 'preparations', or 'organisms or micro-organisms'.

The Guidance describes a 'substance' as a natural or man-made chemical element and its compounds. A 'preparation' is a mixture or solution that consists of two or more substances. An 'organism' or 'micro-organism' includes GMOs.

The term 'significant risk' is not defined. There must, however, be a significant pollutant linkage (as under Part IIA; see **2.3.1**), that is, a source, pathway and receptor. An example is petrol or an industrial chemical in the soil, the vapours from which harm an individual.

The threshold for a significant risk of an adverse effect on human health is low. In addition to death and disease, such damage includes nausea, vomiting, diarrhoea, irritation of the nose or throat, a cough, a sore throat, a headache, lethargy or drowsiness. This threshold is lower than a 'significant possibility of significant harm' to human health under Part IIA (see **2.3.1**). There is no need for a substantial number of individuals to be harmed; it is sufficient that a single vulnerable individual, for example, a child or an elderly person, is affected by the contaminant.

Examples of land damage cases that have occurred under the Environmental Damage Regulations include its enforcement by the Mid Devon District Council in 2009 against a company that had delivered kerosene heating oil to a residence. The delivery company had placed the oil into a redundant tank rather than a new replacement tank, resulting in a spill from a disused fuel pipe leading from the redundant tank. Vapours from the oil entered the residence, causing the residents to suffer nausea, headaches and sore throats. The local authority required the delivery company to pay the cost of remedial measures as well as the cost of the authority's time and its expenses.

Other land damage cases in 2009 were a leak of industrial cleaner into a residential garden and a spill of oil onto a grass verge when a road tanker overturned.

3.6.2 Water

Under the Environmental Damage Regulations, a Schedule 2 operator is liable for preventing or remediating environmental damage to surface, transitional, coastal and ground water, that is, water that is subject to the Water Framework Directive (Directive 2000/60/EC of the European Parliament and of the Council establishing a framework for Community action in the field of water policy). Most inland and coastal water is, thus, covered by the Environmental Damage Regulations except for swimming pools and ornamental water features.

The threshold for environmental damage to water under the Environmental Damage Regulations is a change that is sufficient to lower the status of a surface or groundwater body under the Water Framework Directive, whether or not the status is actually lowered. This threshold is higher than the threshold for remediating water pollution under WRA 1991.

There has been one case of environmental damage to water under the Environmental Damage Regulations at the time of writing (2010). The case involved a spill of sewage by a water company that occurred near Southport in July 2009 and resulted in the loss of a substantial number of fish. The Environment Agency also successfully prosecuted the company under WRA 1991 for polluting the river.

3.6.3 Protected species and natural habitats

An operator is liable for preventing or remediating environmental damage to species and natural habitats that are protected by Council Directive 2009/147/EC on the conservation of wild birds (Birds Directive) or Council Directive 92/43/EEC on the conservation of natural habitats and of wild fauna and flora (Natural Habitats Directive). Protected areas are known as European Sites and form the Natura 2000 network across the EU. European Sites are also protected under national legislation as SSSIs and, in some cases, are also designated as nature reserves or other protected areas.

Species that are protected are not only those with natural habitats in the land area of the UK but include species and natural habitats within the renewable energy zone, that is, within marine waters from the UK coast out to approximately 200 miles seaward. Protected species also include migratory water fowl.

The threshold for environmental damage to a protected species or natural habitat is a significant adverse effect on reaching or maintaining its favourable conservation status. Schedule 1 to the Environmental Damage Regulations sets out criteria for making this determination which, in many cases, takes considerable expert study and time to determine.

3.6.4 SSSIs

The UK Government extended the ELD to all SSSIs in England under an optional provision in the ELD. Wales and Northern Ireland have also extended the ELD to SSSIs and areas of special scientific interest, respectively; Scotland has not extended it.

There are over 4,000 SSSIs in England, covering approximately 7 per cent of the land area. By area, 75 per cent of these SSSIs are also European Sites.

The threshold for environmental damage to an SSSI is an adverse effect on the integrity of the site. This threshold differs from that for protected species and natural habitats that are outside the SSSI. Annex I of the Guidance sets out criteria to determine both thresholds.

3.7 JOINT AND SEVERAL LIABILITY

The Environmental Damage Regulations impose joint and several liability on operators who cause the same environmental damage. If, therefore, more than one operator is responsible for the damage, or for individual emissions or events that result in such damage, each operator is liable for preventing or remediating the entire damage. This means that if more than one operator causes, say, environmental damage to groundwater, and one of those operators becomes insolvent or is unable to pay for remedial measures, the remaining operators must pay 100 per cent of the cost of the measures.

The Guidance states that an enforcing authority is not required to apportion liability between responsible operators but may require any of them to remediate it. Alternatively, the authority may carry out the measures itself and seek reimbursement from any of the responsible operators.

The Guidance further states that an operator who has remediated environmental damage may seek contribution from other responsible operators. Neither the Environmental Damage Regulations nor the Guidance specify the means by which an operator may seek contribution, however. This could lead to a problem because the Civil Liability (Contribution) Act 1978, s.1(1) states that the Act applies only to 'any person liable in respect of any damage suffered by another person'.

The Scottish regulations provide various mechanisms for apportioning liability, with joint and several liability as a backstop.

3.8 LIMITATION PERIODS

The limitation period for bringing proceedings under the Environmental Damage Regulations is 30 years from the emission, event or incident that caused the environmental damage at issue. In Scotland, the limitation period for environmental damage from a release of GMOs is 75 years. The Environmental Damage Regulations thus differ from Part IIA, which has no limitation period for an incident that has caused land to be contaminated such that it must be remediated.

The limitation period for an enforcing authority to recover costs spent on carrying out preventive and remedial measures is five years after their completion or the authority's identification of the responsible operator, whichever occurs later.

3.9 EXEMPTIONS

The Environmental Damage Regulations include exemptions to liability for remediating environmental damage. The exemptions are:

- terrorism;
- an exceptional natural phenomenon, provided that the relevant operator took all reasonable precautions to protect against damage being caused by the event;
- an activity, the sole purpose of which is to protect from natural disasters;
- the application of specified oil pollution and nuclear conventions;
- an activity, the main purpose of which is to serve national defence or international security;
- commercial sea fishing provided that the operator has complied with all legislation relating to the fishing (not an exemption in Scotland);

- specified actions under the Water Framework Directive;
- acts that are specifically authorised by Natural England (or an equivalent body) under the Conservation (Natural Habitats, etc.) Regulations 1994, SI 1994/ 2716, as amended, or Part II of WCA 1981;
- diffuse pollution if it is not possible to establish a causal link between the damage and one or more activities by individual operators; and
- an incident, event or emission that occurred before 1 March 2009 (the date when the Environmental Damage Regulations came into force) unless the activity continued after that date, and environmental damage that occurred after that date.

A European Court of Justice (ECJ) case that concerns environmental damage from a large petrochemical area in Sicily has clarified the scope of the last two exemptions as described below.

3.9.1 Environmental damage after 1 March 2009

The exemption in the Environmental Damage Regulations for environmental damage that occurs after 1 March 2009 does not comply with the ELD. In two judgments handed down by the ECJ in *Raffinerie Mediterranee (ERG) SpA* v. *Ministero dello Sviluppo economico* (Case No. C-378/08), (Cases Nos. C-379/08 and C-380/08) on 9 March 2010, the ECJ concluded that the ELD:

> applies to damage caused by an emission, event or incident which took place after 30 April 2007 where such damage derives either from activities carried out after that date or activities which were carried out but had not finished before that date.

As noted above, the Environmental Damage Regulations apply only after 1 March 2009 (later for the equivalent regulations for Wales, Scotland and Northern Ireland). As also noted, the Environmental Damage Regulations may not be less stringent than the ELD. The applicable date for liability for environmental damage is, therefore, 30 April 2007 and not 1 March 2009.

If, therefore, an operator has caused environmental damage after 30 April 2007 and before 1 March 2009, the operator is liable under the ELD even though the operator cannot, of course, immediately carry out actions to prevent environmental damage or further environmental damage. In many cases, the operator may have remediated the damage under other legislation. If, however, the operator has caused environmental damage and has not remediated it (due to there being no requirement to do so under the Environmental Damage Regulations), the potential exists for liability for interim costs (as described in **3.18.2**) to be incurred from the time of the damage.

3.9.2 Diffuse pollution

The ECJ also ruled on the meaning of the diffuse pollution exclusion in *Raffinerie Mediterranee* (see **3.9.1**). The ECJ concluded that a Member State may establish a causal link between an operator's activities and diffuse pollution as follows. The authority may establish a presumption that there is a causal link between diffuse pollution and the activities of one or more operators. The presumption must be justified by plausible evidence, which may include the location of an operator's installation close to the diffuse pollution and the same substance that has been used by the operator in its activities being found at the polluted site. In order to avoid liability, an operator must rebut the presumption by proving that it did not cause the pollution.

The ruling means that there is a relatively weak causal link between diffuse pollution and an operator who may have caused it. The ECJ did not state that the enforcing authority must 'fingerprint' a substance, that is, prove that the identical substance that was used by an operator is present at the polluted site. Instead, it only stated that the authority must show that the same type of substance is present at both locations.

The ECJ has not required Member States to establish a rebuttable presumption but, due to the legislation transposing the ELD having to be at least as stringent as the ELD, a Member State may not impose a stronger causal link. Due to the imposition of joint and several liability, therefore, an operator may have difficulty in showing that he is not liable for remediating such pollution.

3.10 ENFORCING AUTHORITIES

The enforcing authority for the implementation of the Environmental Damage Regulations in England, Wales and Scotland depends on the type of environmental damage and the natural resource that is involved. In Northern Ireland, the enforcing authority is the Northern Ireland Environment Agency.

The large number of enforcing authorities makes the division of responsibilities between them complicated. In situations in which more than one authority is involved, however, one authority may transfer its enforcement responsibility including appointing another authority to act on its behalf.

3.10.1 Local authorities

The relevant local authority is the enforcing authority for land damage. It is also the authority for a site at which damage has been caused by a person who has a permit granted by the local authority under the Environmental Permitting Regulations or other legislation but only in respect of actions to prevent environmental damage or further environmental damage concerning water, SSSIs or protected species and natural habitats. The Environment Agency or Natural England (or the equivalent entities in Wales and Scotland) are the relevant authorities for remedial measures, other than for land damage, in respect of such sites, as described below.

3.10.2 Environment Agency

The Environment Agency (or the Scottish Environment Protection Agency) is the enforcing authority for environmental damage at sites regulated by it. It is also the authority for environmental damage to inland waters including water in an SSSI. The Agency is also the enforcing authority for marine waters but only if it regulates the activity that caused the damage.

3.10.3 Natural England

Natural England (or the equivalent nature conservation authority in Wales) is the enforcing authority for land in SSSIs. Natural England (or the equivalent nature conservation authority in Wales and Scotland) is the enforcing authority for protected species and natural habitats on land outside SSSIs.

3.10.4 Marine Management Organisation

The Marine Management Organisation (or Welsh Ministers) is the enforcing authority for the Environmental Damage Regulations for protected species and natural habitats in marine waters except for activities regulated by the Environment Agency.

3.11 INTERESTED PARTIES

The Environmental Damage Regulations specifically provide for the involvement of non-governmental organisations (NGOs) and other persons. They authorise a person 'who is affected or likely to be affected by environmental damage' or 'who otherwise has a sufficient interest' to send comments to the relevant enforcing authority regarding an operator who, in their opinion, has caused, or is causing, environmental damage.

The Guidance sets out examples of persons who could be affected by environmental damage as:

- bird watchers;
- ramblers;
- recreational fishermen;
- residents;
- persons whose health may be at risk from contaminants; and
- persons who are responsible for children or elderly persons whose health may be at risk.

Persons who have a sufficient interest in environmental damage include registered charities whose objectives include environmental conservation.

The Guidance sets out a minimum list of information to be provided by the person submitting the comments to show that there is a plausible case that environmental damage is being caused.

The enforcing authority must consider the comments and, if practicable, inform the implicated operator.

If the person who submitted the comments does not agree with the authority's decisions or subsequent actions, it may judicially review them. The ELD provides that the person submitting the comments may request a court or other public body to review the procedural and substantive legality of the authority's decisions, acts or failure to act.

3.12 INVESTIGATIONS

Enforcing authorities have broad powers to investigate incidents that may be covered by the Environmental Damage Regulations and to carry out inspections regarding them. These powers, which are set out in the Environment Act 1995, s.108, are the same as those available to local authorities and the Environment Agency for 'pollution control functions' in other environmental legislation.

The powers authorise an enforcing authority:

- to enter premises;
- to require all or part of the premises to be left undisturbed;
- to take photographs, recordings, soil or groundwater samples, etc.;
- to take possession of any article or substance that appears likely to have caused environmental damage;
- to inspect records and to take copies of them; and
- to question any person who, in the authority's opinion, has information that is relevant and necessary to the investigation and to require that person to sign a declaration warranting the truth of his responses to the questions (known as a s.108(4)(j) interview).

The last item is not the same as a Police and Criminal Evidence Act 1984 interview, which the authority may also require, in that a crime must be suspected in order to conduct a PACE interview. An authority may require a person to attend a s.108(4)(j) interview regardless of whether a crime is suspected. The person who is questioned is typically an employee with direct knowledge of the circumstances related to the environmental damage. That person has the right to be accompanied by another person, who is typically the solicitor for the company under investigation. The answers given by the person who is questioned may not be used against him but may be used against the company.

3.13 INFORMATION NOTICES

An enforcing authority may serve a notice on an operator to require him to provide information on whether there is an imminent threat of, or actual, environmental damage. The information notice may also concern environmental damage that has occurred or is suspected of having occurred.

3.14 PREVENTING ENVIRONMENTAL DAMAGE AND FURTHER ENVIRONMENTAL DAMAGE

If an operator's activity has caused an imminent threat of environmental damage or an imminent threat of damage that there are reasonable grounds to believe will become environmental damage, the operator has a duty 'immediately' to prevent the damage and/or to prevent further damage. This duty is self-executing. That is, the operator must carry out the necessary actions regardless of whether an enforcing authority requires it to do so.

The above duty is new in English law. Indeed, it is rare in the law of any country. If an operator does not carry out the above actions, the enforcing authority may serve a prevention notice requiring it to carry out such actions by a deadline specified in the notice. In addition, the failure to carry out the actions is a criminal offence as is the failure to comply with the prevention notice.

There is no defence to, or right of appeal against, a prevention notice.

The Guidance provides the following two examples of an imminent threat of environmental damage. First, a tank that is in poor condition is located near an aquifer. Unless the tank is made more secure, the substance contained in it will leak. Second, the substance contained in the tank has already leaked and has entered the soil; unless action is taken to contain it, it will enter the aquifer.

The Guidance further provides the example of the leaked substance having begun to enter the aquifer. Unless actions are taken to contain it, the substance will continue to migrate and cause environmental damage to the aquifer.

If an enforcing authority cannot identify the operator who has caused an imminent threat of environmental damage or the operator has failed to comply with a prevention notice, the authority may carry out the necessary measures. The authority may then seek to recover its costs (see **3.22**).

3.15 DUTY TO NOTIFY

If an operator's activities have caused an imminent threat of environmental damage, or an imminent threat that there are reasonable grounds to suspect will become environmental damage, and measures taken by the operator do not eliminate the threat, the operator must 'immediately' notify the enforcing authority that appears to it to be the appropriate authority.

If an operator's activities have caused environmental damage, or damage that there are reasonable grounds to believe is or will become environmental damage, the operator must 'immediately' notify the enforcing authority that appears to it to be the appropriate authority.

The duty to notify pollution incidents was already included in environmental permits before the Environmental Damage Regulations came into force. Thus, Schedule 2 operators may already have been required to notify the relevant authority of such incidents. The additional duty in the Environmental Damage Regulations extends the duty to activities that are not carried out under a permit and also to incidents involving environmental damage that is not pollution-related.

The failure immediately to notify the enforcing authority of an imminent threat of, or actual, environmental damage is a criminal offence. There is no defence to it.

3.16   DETERMINATION OF ENVIRONMENTAL DAMAGE

When reasonable grounds exist to believe that environmental damage has occurred, the relevant enforcing authority must assess the damage and determine whether such damage has, in fact, occurred. The determination obviously involves consideration of the thresholds for environmental damage to land, water, SSSIs, and protected species and natural habitats, described above. Annex 1 of the Guidance sets out criteria to assess and determine whether environmental damage to each natural resource has occurred. The assessment may be relatively quick in instances of land damage, or lengthy in cases of damage to water, SSSIs and protected species and natural habitats.

The relevant enforcing authority has sole responsibility for determining whether environmental damage exists. In order to assist the enforcing authority in its determination, responsible operator(s) are entitled to participate in the process. If the enforcing authority requests them to provide information or carry out assessments, they have a duty to do so.

It is obviously to the advantage of a responsible operator to have input into the enforcing authority's determination of environmental damage, especially because measures to remediate it – if the authority makes a determination that there is environmental damage to water, SSSIs and protected species and natural resources – are likely to be costly.

3.17   NOTIFICATION OF ENVIRONMENTAL DAMAGE

If an enforcing authority determines that there is environmental damage, it must serve a notification of liability for remediating the damage on the responsible operator(s). The notification should require the operators to submit proposals for remedial measures, that is, works to remediate the environmental damage, within the deadlines specified in the notification.

If a responsible operator fails to submit the proposals by the deadline for them, the authority will specify the remedial measures that must be carried out. Obviously, it is in the interests of a responsible operator to have input into the specifications of the measures it will be required to carry out.

3.18   REMEDIAL MEASURES

Remedial measures are long-term, as opposed to emergency, measures to remediate environmental damage and to compensate for the loss of the natural resource during the time that it was damaged until it is fully restored.

There is one type of remedial measure for land and three types for water, SSSIs, and protected species and natural habitats.

3.18.1   Land

The remedial measures specified by the Environmental Damage Regulations for land are the removal, control, containment or diminution of contaminants so that the land no longer poses a significant risk of an adverse effect on human health. These measures, which include natural recovery, are much the same as those specified by EPA 1990, Part IIA except that the threshold for environmental damage under the Environmental Damage Regulations is lower than that under Part IIA (see **2.3.1**).

A risk assessment must be carried out to determine the following:

- characteristics and function of the affected soil;
- type and concentration of harmful substances, preparations, organisms and micro-organisms;
- risks posed by them; and
- possibility of their dispersion.

The standard for remediating land is the lawful current use of the land when the environmental damage occurred or any planning permission that exists at that time. The Guidance states that the lawful current use is the same as that under Part IIA, that is, any current or likely use of the land that is consistent with existing planning permission or that is otherwise lawful under planning legislation.

3.18.2   Water, protected species and natural habitats and sites of special scientific interest

Whereas the remedial measures for land are much the same as those that already existed under English law, the remedial measures for water, SSSIs, and protected species and natural habitats are a substantial expansion of environmental liabilities under English law. Although they existed to a limited extent prior to the Environmental Damage Regulations, the former requirements pale into insignificance compared to the new liabilities.

The remedial measures for water, SSSIs, and protected species and natural habitats are:

- primary remediation;
- complementary remediation; and
- compensatory remediation.

Part 1 of Schedule 4 to the Environmental Damage Regulations provides details of the various types of remedial measures.

Primary remediation

The Environmental Damage Regulations describe a 'primary remedial measure' as one that 'returns the damaged natural resources or impaired services to, or towards, the state that would have existed if the damage had not occurred'. The ELD uses the term 'baseline condition' for the condition to which damaged natural resources or services provided by it to the public and other natural resources must be returned.

Primary remedial measures for pollution include clean-up measures as well as measures to restore a natural resource; two very different types of measures. Neither the Environmental Damage Regulations nor the ELD differentiate between these two types of remedial measures.

The Guidance provides examples of primary remedial measures. These include:

- removing or treating contaminants;
- restocking fish;
- seeding, planting or re-planting vegetation;
- carrying out engineering works to provide habitats such as eddies in rivers;
- removing bottlenecks in rivers such as impassable weirs and culverts;
- providing fish passes;
- providing conservation staff to manage and maintain sites;
- implementing restrictions to access or, conversely, improvements to access; and
- monitoring.

Complementary remediation

The Environmental Damage Regulations describe a 'complementary remedial measure' as a remedial measure 'to compensate for the fact that primary remediation does not result in fully restoring the damaged natural resources or impaired services to the state that would have existed if the damage had not occurred'. Complementary measures may be carried out at the damaged site or another site adjacent, or in close proximity, to the damaged site.

In some cases, it is not possible to restore a natural resource or services provided by it to its condition before the damage or to do so within a reasonable period of time. The Guidance gives as an extreme example damage to an ancient woodland. In such a case, the Guidance states that it may be preferable to improve another part of the woodland or another woodland rather than planting and managing a new woodland over a sufficient timescale.

In many cases, the responsible operator will not own the alternative site on which complementary remedial measures must be carried out. Complementary remedial measures may thus be costly, not only because they are complex and lengthy but also due to the cost of acquiring an alternative site.

Compensatory remediation

The Environmental Damage Regulations describe 'compensatory remediation' as compensation for 'interim losses of natural resources or services that occur from the date of damage until remediation has achieved its objective'. They further state that the term ' "interim losses" means losses which result from the fact that the damaged natural resources or services are not able to perform their ecological functions or provide services to other natural resources or to the public until the primary or complementary remediation has been carried out'. The Guidance provides an example of the loss of a natural resource or services rendered by it as the removal of a bird population from an area that is regularly visited by bird watchers, or the removal of a breeding ground for fish.

Compensatory measures may be carried out at either the damaged site or another site. Although the purpose of compensatory remediation differs from that of complementary remediation, the measures carried out for both may be similar. Natural recovery is generally not considered to be complementary or compensatory remediation unless it is a result of specific complementary or compensatory measures.

Compensatory remediation does not include financial compensation. That is, a responsible operator is required to spend money to provide, enhance or improve resources and services at the damaged site or an alternative site but is not required to pay a monetary sum as compensation for having caused the damage.

3.19 APPEALS TO NOTIFICATIONS

A person who receives a notification of liability for environmental damage may appeal the notification within 28 days of the date of its service. The grounds of appeal are as follows:

- the operator's activity was not a cause of the environmental damage;
- the enforcing authority acted unreasonably in making a determination that the damage was environmental damage;
- the environmental damage was a result of the operator's compliance with an instruction from a public authority and the instruction was not related to an emission or incident caused by the operator's activities;

- the operator was not at fault or negligent when its activities caused the environmental damage and the emission or event that caused them was expressly authorised by, and fully in accordance with, the conditions of a permit listed in Schedule 3 to the Environmental Damage Regulations;
- the operator was not at fault or negligent when its activities caused the environmental damage and the emission or event that caused them, or the manner of using a product in the course of an activity, was not considered likely to cause environmental damage according to the state of scientific and technical knowledge at the time that the release of the emission or the occurrence of the activity happened; and
- the environmental damage was the result of the act of a third party and occurred despite all appropriate safety measures having been taken by the operator.

The fourth and fifth grounds of appeal are known as the permit defence and the state-of-the-art defence, respectively. Neither defence applies to the deliberate release of GMOs in Wales or Scotland.

The person who hears an appeal to a notification may confirm or quash it. The various procedures are set out in the Environmental Damage Regulations and the Guidance.

The appeal procedures differ in Scotland.

3.20 REMEDIATION NOTICES

The relevant enforcing authority should consider the proposed remedial measures submitted by the responsible operator (if they have been submitted) together with any comments submitted by interested parties or the owner of the land on which remedial measures will be carried out. The authority then selects the remedial measures and serves a notice on the operator.

The remediation notice contains, among other things:

- details of the remedial measures to be carried out together with reasons for carrying them out;
- the deadline for carrying out the measures; and
- any additional monitoring or investigation to be carried out by the operator.

The authority may serve more than one remediation notice for environmental damage on an operator. Indeed, in a complex remedial scheme, it is likely that more than one notice will be served.

Further, the authority may subsequently decide that the selected remedial measures will not achieve their purpose. In such a case, the authority may select new remedial measures but must provide the operator with an opportunity to participate in the process.

As with notifications of liability, the appeal procedures for a remediation notice differ in Scotland.

3.21 APPEALS TO REMEDIATION NOTICES

An operator may appeal a remediation notice within 28 days of the date of its service. The only ground on which an appeal may be made is that its contents are unreasonable. The procedures for the appeal are set out in the Environmental Damage Regulations and the Guidance.

The Planning Inspector who hears the appeal may confirm, vary or quash the remediation notice. In doing so, the inspector must provide written notification of his final decision, reasons for the decision and, if time has elapsed since the remediation notice was served, any further compensatory remedial measures that must be carried out by the responsible operator.

Unless the Planning Inspector decides otherwise, the remediation notice is suspended during an appeal. The responsible operator must, however, immediately carry out any actions necessary to prevent further environmental damage if there are reasonable grounds to believe that this may occur.

3.22 COSTS

An enforcing authority can recover the costs of enforcing the Environmental Damage Regulations from a responsible operator. Such costs include the costs of:

- carrying out investigations;
- collecting data;
- establishing the identity of responsible operators;
- reasonable costs of carrying out preventive and/or remedial measures;
- preparing notifications of liability;
- preparing remediation notices;
- assessing environmental damage;
- carrying out a consultation for remedial measures;
- establishing appropriate remedial measures; and
- monitoring remedial measures during the time in which, and after, they are carried out.

The above costs are more extensive than those that may be claimed by an enforcing authority under other environmental legislation. As noted above, an enforcing authority has five years in which to seek reimbursement of its costs following the date on which the environmental damage occurred or identification of the responsible operator, whichever is later.

3.23 CHARGES ON PREMISES

An enforcing authority may serve a charging notice on an operator in respect of 'premises' owned by him in order to recover costs incurred by the authority. The authority must also serve a copy of the notice of every person who, to the authority's knowledge, has an interest in the premises that could be affected by the charge. Information to be included in the notice is specified in the Environmental Damage Regulations.

An operator may appeal the notice within 21 days from the date on which it was served on him.

The Environmental Damage Regulations define the word 'owner' as:

> a person (other than a mortgagee not in possession) who, whether in that person's own right or as trustee for any other person, is entitled to receive the rack rent of the premises or, where the premises are not let at a rack rent, would be so entitled if they were so let.

The above definition is materially the same as the definition of an 'owner' under Part IIA of EPA 1990 except for the word 'premises' instead of 'land'. It is likely, however, that the definition of 'premises' includes buildings as well as the land itself, as does the word 'land' under the Interpretation Act 1978.

There is nothing in the Environmental Damage Regulations or the Guidance that requires the premises in respect of which the charging notice is served to be the same premises on which preventive or remedial measures were carried out.

The Scottish Regulations do not provide for charging notices.

3.24 DUTY TO GRANT AND PAY COMPENSATION

If works to prevent environmental damage or further environmental damage, or to remediate environmental damage, are carried out on land that is not owned or occupied by the operator who is responsible for carrying them out, the person on whose land they are carried out is required to allow the works to be carried out. In such a case, the responsible operator must compensate the person who granted the right to carry out the works.

3.25 OFFENCES AND SANCTIONS

It is a criminal offence to fail to comply with the following duties in the Environmental Damage Regulations:

- immediately to carry out actions to prevent an imminent threat of environmental damage or an imminent threat of damage for which reasonable grounds exist to believe that it will become environmental damage;
- immediately to notify the enforcing authority if actions taken by the operator do not eliminate the above threat;
- immediately to carry out actions to prevent further environmental damage or damage for which reasonable grounds exist to believe that it is, or will become, environmental damage;
- immediately to notify the enforcing authority of such environmental damage;

- to comply with a prevention notice, whether to prevent environmental damage or further environmental damage;
- to comply with a remediation notice;
- to provide information demanded by the enforcing authority;
- to comply with instructions by the enforcing authority in investigating an Environmental Damage Regulations incident or to carry out inspections regarding them; and
- to provide false or misleading information to an authorised officer.

As with most other environmental offences, an enforcing authority may prosecute an Environmental Damage Regulations offence in the magistrates' court or the Crown Court. The maximum penalty in the magistrates' court is a £5,000 fine, three months' imprisonment, or both. The maximum penalty in the Crown Court is an unlimited fine, imprisonment of two years, or both.

Also, as with other environmental legislation, the Environmental Damage Regulations provide that a director, manager, secretary or other similar person of a company may be liable if the company has been convicted of the offence and if the offence was committed with that person's consent or connivance, or was attributable to any neglect on his part.

CHAPTER 4

Climate change

4.1 INTRODUCTION

Whether you believe in the science behind climate change or whether you are a sceptic, what is clear is, from a lawyer's point of view, there is an increasing body of regulation dealing with climate change matters. Much originates from Europe although some is very UK specific.

There are a number of international, European and national targets for reducing greenhouse gases. In 2008, the Government created a new department, the Department of Energy and Climate Change (DECC) which brought together the relevant sections of the Department for Business, Innovation and Skills (BIS) and Defra.

In November 2008, the Climate Change Act 2008 received Royal Assent and it came into force partly towards the end of 2008 and partly in 2009. The Act aims to set a regulatory framework for the UK's climate change policies including setting legally binding targets for emission reduction.

From a practising lawyer's perspective, there are various aspects of numerous measures aimed at reducing climate change which could impact on their work. These range from company reporting to emissions trading schemes. Whilst many of these are outside the scope of this book, there are three areas which are more likely to have an impact on the day-to-day working of most solicitors as against specialist environmental lawyers. These are: the Carbon Reduction Commitment Energy Efficiency Scheme (CRC Scheme); the aim of achieving zero carbon buildings; and the different forms of certificates dealing with energy performance and efficiency of buildings.

4.2 ZERO CARBON BUILDINGS

As part of the move to reduce carbon emissions, the Government wants all new homes and new school buildings in England to be zero carbon by 2016. It also wants all new non-domestic buildings to be zero carbon by 2019.

Currently, there is no agreed definition of what is a 'zero carbon building' but it is basically a building where its net emissions of carbon dioxide from all energy use, i.e. energy used to provide electricity and cool and heat the building, are nil.

In relation to new homes, many of the changes needed will be introduced through revisions to the Building Regulations. Reductions have been set by reference to the Building Regulation standards of 2006. A phased approach has been introduced so that, currently, new homes must emit 25 per cent less carbon dioxide, from 2013, 44 per cent less, and then zero carbon dioxide from 2016.

The Government has also introduced a new code for sustainable homes which goes further than just zero carbon, but also looks at design issues including water efficiency, waste and ecology. Although not mandatory, some local planning authorities may require housing to achieve all or some of these standards.

Relief from SDLT (stamp duty land tax) has been granted on all new zero carbon homes that cost up to £500,000. If a home costs over that amount, then the liability for SDLT is reduced by £15,000.

4.3 ENERGY CERTIFICATES

The Energy Performance of Buildings (Certificates and Inspections) (England and Wales) Regulations 2007 introduced a scheme of compulsory air conditioning inspections, Display Energy Certificates (DECs) and Energy Performance Certificates (EPCs). These Regulations aim to implement the Energy Performance of Buildings Directive 2002 (2002/91/EC).

4.3.1 Energy Performance Certificates

An EPC contains energy efficiency information about a building. This includes the rating of the building on a scale from A to G (very similar to the rating system on domestic appliances). The certificate will also include a reference value which is the benchmark against which the building can be judged against. The average dwelling in England and Wales is E and the average of commercial buildings is C.

Each EPC has to be accompanied by a report containing recommendations for the improvement of the energy efficiency of the building. These recommendations do not have to be implemented and are for information purposes only. They are divided into two categories: those viewed to be 'cost effective', and then those items which are more expensive, e.g. installing renewable energy.

Whenever a building is let or sold, the prospective tenant or buyer must be provided with a valid EPC and the recommendation report. These cannot be charged for.

The requirement to provide the EPC happens when either the landlord/seller enters into a contract, when the prospective tenant/purchaser views the building or when written information is provided to the person requesting the information (whichever of these happens first).

There are certain circumstances where a landlord or seller does not have to provide an EPC, e.g. if they have reasonable grounds to believe the prospective tenant or buyer is not genuinely interested in the property.

It should be noted that lease renewals, lease surrenders, the sale of shares in a company and the property remains in that company's ownership and compulsory purchase orders are not considered to trigger the requirement for an EPC.

Although an EPC was originally intended to be provided as part of a Home Information Pack (HIP) and the requirement to provide HIPs has been suspended, there is still a requirement to provide an EPC.

Certain buildings do not require an EPC and these include:

- temporary buildings due to last less than two years;
- agricultural non-residential buildings with low energy demand;
- those buildings with a floor area of less than 50 square metres that are non-residential;
- places of worship, workshops or industrial sites with low energy demand.

Multi-let buildings and flats have special rules in relation to EPCs.

Each individual flat that is a separate dwelling should have its own EPC. Where there are a number of separate commercial units in a building which has one heating system, either an EPC can be prepared for the whole building which is used when the part of it is sold or let or, alternatively, one can be prepared for the specific part of the building that is being rented or sold.

If a building is part of a larger building that shares a common heating system, then each part of the building that is being rented or sold is required to have an EPC.

4.3.2 Display Energy Certificates

Buildings with a total floor area of over 1,000 square metres that are occupied by institutions providing public services to a large number of persons and frequently visited by those persons are required to display a DEC. The intention is that a member of the public visiting those buildings will be aware of the energy performance of that particular building. Whether it will stop them visiting the building or change their attitude to the institution in question is highly debatable!

These buildings are either occupied by public authorities, e.g. central and local government, the executive agencies, statutory regulatory bodies, NHS Trusts, the police and school premises, or are occupied by organisations which carry out services which have traditionally been provided by the Government in the past and where the Government has a duty to provide the service.

Those buildings which are not visited frequently by members of the public do not require a DEC.

4.3.3 Inspection of air conditioning systems

Anyone who has control of an air conditioning system (with output of more than 12kw) has to ensure that the system is inspected at least every five years and that a written report of the inspection is obtained.

If the air conditioning system was put into place since 2008, the first inspection has to take place within five years of the system being put into service. If it was in service prior to 2008, then it has to be inspected prior to 4 January 2011 unless it has an output of more than 250kw, in which case it should have been inspected by 4 January 2009.

4.4 THE CRC ENERGY EFFICIENCY SCHEME

4.4.1 Introduction

The CRC Scheme came into effect on 1 April 2010. Its detail is set out in the CRC Energy Efficiency Scheme Order 2010, SI 2010/768 (CRC Order).

4.4.2 Qualification

There are two levels of involvement by public and private sector organisations in the CRC Scheme: full participation and making an information disclosure. Information disclosures are discussed at **4.4.6**.

Full participation will occur when the following 'qualification criteria' are met:

(a)   at any point during the 'qualification year' for a particular 'phase' (these terms are described at **4.4.3**), an organisation has at least one half hourly electricity meter (HHM) settled on the half hourly market; and

(b)   an organisation's total electricity supply during the qualification year through all its HHMs is at least 6000 MWh.

Participation is based on electricity *supply* received. An organisation receives a supply of electricity for CRC purposes when it has an agreement with a supplier for the supply of energy and the organisation pays for that supply of energy. The supply of electricity needs to be measured by a metering device that measures electricity supply half hourly for charging purposes.

If an organisation purchases electricity through a third party agent who procures the energy services on the organisation's behalf and pays the bills, the organisation who contracted the agent will be responsible for those supplies, not the agent.

Some types of electricity supplies are excluded from the calculation of total qualifying half hourly electricity supply. These are:

- Supply for the purposes of domestic accommodation, unless it is provided in connection with certain activities, such as education (e.g. university halls of residence), employment (e.g. nurses' accommodation), recreation (e.g. hotels) and care services (e.g. hospitals).
- Supply for the purposes of transport, subject to a few exceptions including vehicles operating without a licence (e.g. on-site vehicles).

- Energy an organisation does not consume at all for its own use. The exception to this is where a landlord is supplied with energy but that energy is partly or entirely consumed by its tenants. In this case, the landlord is still responsible for the supply.
- Electricity used for the purposes of distribution, transmission or generation by an organisation that has a licence to do so or is exempt from the requirement to hold such a licence.

If, as a result of deducting the relevant electricity supplies, an organisation's qualifying supply is below the 6000MWh threshold, the organisation does not need to fully participate in the CRC Scheme. It will instead have to make an information disclosure.

4.4.3 How CRC works

Timelines

The CRC Scheme is divided into a series of 'phases' for administrative purposes. Each phase lasts for seven years, except for the first phase (referred to as the 'introductory phase'), which lasts for three years. The introductory phase runs from 1 April 2010 to 31 March 2013. Phase two runs from 1 April 2011 to March 2018 and phase three runs from 1 April 2016 to 31 March 2023, and so on.

Phase	Commencement date	End date
Phase one	1 April 2010	31 March 2013
Phase two	1 April 2011	31 March 2018
Phase three	1 April 2016	31 March 2023
Phase four	1 April 2021	31 March 2028
Phase five	1 April 2026	31 March 2033
Phase six	1 April 2031	31 March 2038
Phase seven	1 April 2036	31 March 2043

What happens in each phase?

Apart from the introductory phase, each phase is divided into the following years:

- A *'qualification year'*: This is the year before the start of a particular phase, during which an organisation will have to assess whether it qualifies for full participation in the forthcoming phase based on how much electricity supplies it was responsible for during that qualification year.
- The *'first compliance year'* or *'footprint year'*: This is the first year of a phase during which, if an organisation has met the qualification criteria, it has to register as a CRC Scheme participant. Registration can only take place between April and September of the first compliance year. Organisations which need to

register but fail to do so or register late can face civil penalties. Participants must also monitor their total emissions from energy supplies (i.e. their 'footprint') and determine which supplies and emissions should be included in the CRC Scheme. (The emissions that must be accounted for are defined in art.50 of the CRC Order.)

- *The 'second compliance year'*: This is the second year of each phase. On the last working day of July of this year, participants have to submit their footprint reports. A footprint report will record an organisation's total emissions from energy supplies, CRC emissions, details of any exemptions and any major changes in its organisational structure. The report is submitted via the online CRC Registry. A participant who fails to submit a footprint report will face a fixed penalty of £5000 and a penalty of £500 per subsequent working day the report is not submitted, up to a maximum of 40 working days.

- *'Compliance years' or 'annual reporting years'*: The third to seventh years of each phase are known as compliance years or annual reporting years. These run from April to March. In April of each of these years, participants will have to purchase sufficient allowances to cover the amount of CRC emissions they expect to emit during that particular compliance year. Participants' allowances will be held in 'compliance accounts' in the Registry, which will be run by the Administrator of the CRC Scheme (the Environment Agency will be the Administrator of the CRC Scheme for England and Wales). Organisations must submit annual reports of their actual emissions by the end of July after each compliance year. Both footprint and annual reports will report on energy supply from electricity, gas, coal and any other fuel types (such as oil and diesel), but excluding energy from transport, domestic accommodation and unconsumed fuel supplies. Emissions that are already covered by a Climate Change Agreement or the EU Emissions Trading System (EU ETS) will be excluded. Emissions from consumption outside the UK will also be excluded. Participants will also have to surrender enough allowances to the Administrator by the end of July after each compliance year to cover their reported CRC emissions.

For the introductory phase:

- the qualification year is 2008;
- the registration period is April to September 2010;
- the footprint year and first annual reporting year is April 2010 to March 2011 (during which there will be no sale or surrender of allowances);
- the first sale of allowances takes place between April 2012 and March 2013.

The Chancellor of the Exchequer announced the postponement of the first sale of allowances from April 2011 to April 2012 in the Comprehensive Spending Review on 20 October 2010. Full details were not available when this book went to print.

Buying and surrendering allowances

The CRC Scheme is a 'cap and trade' scheme. Participants will be required to buy and surrender allowances in each compliance year of a phase to cover their CRC emissions (CRC Order, art.53). One allowance will be equal to one tonne of carbon dioxide.

An allowance is valid for the year in respect of which it was issued, although an allowance issued in the introductory phase will not be valid in respect of CRC emissions in a subsequent phase. Other than this, unused allowances from the previous compliance year may be used to cover CRC emissions in future compliance years, although there are exceptions to this rule. Allowances cannot be bought to cover emissions in a year that has already ended; they can only apply to future estimated emissions.

The rules on buying and selling allowances in the introductory phase are different from those relating to the other phases. During the introductory phase, an unlimited number of allowances will be sold by the Government at a fixed price of £12 per tonne of carbon dioxide emitted.

Sales in the introductory phase were originally scheduled to take place in April 2011 and April 2012, with the allowances covering a participant's estimated CRC emissions for the second compliance year (April 2011 to March 2012). This has obviously changed since the postponement of the first sales until April 2012. The effect of the postponement on other phases was not known when this book went to print.

From phase two onwards, the number of allowances available for sale will be capped by the Government and sold at auctions held at the start of each compliance year for the relevant phase. The first auction will be in April 2013 (during phase two). The price of each allowance will be determined by demand and only participants and their agents will be able to purchase allowances.

In addition to allowances being sold by the Government, extra allowances will be available on the secondary market from other participants or account holders (these are the persons in whose name the account is held at the Registry). Additional allowances will also be sold by the Environment Agency through a 'safety valve' if they are so requested by participants. It is called a safety valve because if a participant requests additional allowances from the Environment Agency, the Agency will obtain these allowances through the EU ETS. Allowances will only be available via the safety valve during a specific two-week period each year. The price of safety valve allowances will relate to the price of allowances in the EU ETS, but this price will always be higher than allowances bought from the Government.

League tables

At the end of each annual reporting year, the Administrator of the CRC Scheme will gather information from the reports of all the participants and use this information to compare their performance in terms of how well they have reduced their emissions. Participants' comparative performances will then be published in a league table.

The league table will be publicly available and will contain certain information from the reports submitted by participants.

Recycling payments

The CRC Scheme was originally intended to be 'revenue neutral', in that the income received by the Government by the annual sale or auction of allowances would be repaid (or 'recycled' back) to participants.

The amount of money participants would have earned back would have depended on their position in the league table. Their position in the league table, in turn, would have depended on their emissions reductions.

The Chancellor of the Exchequer announced in the Comprehensive Spending Review on 20 October 2010 that revenues from the annual carbon allowance sales would go to the Treasury and would not be repaid to participants, thus effectively changing the scheme into a carbon tax.

Evidence packs

A participant has to keep records of the information on which its reports are based (an 'evidence pack'). The evidence pack will need to be audited and certified by a person exercising management control of the participant. If it is selected for an audit, a participant will need to send its evidence pack to the Environment Agency.

4.4.4 Who the Scheme applies to

Undertakings

The CRC Scheme applies to 'undertakings' and groups of undertakings rather than individual sites.

What an undertaking or a group of undertakings is depends on its organisational structure at the end of the relevant qualification year (this day is known as the 'qualification day').

An undertaking is defined as having the meaning given in the Companies Act 2006, s.1161(1), but this definition is expanded to include unincorporated associations that carry on a charitable activity. Undertakings include companies, partnerships (including limited partnerships and limited liability partnerships) and unincorporated associations. An undertaking does not include a public body (although public bodies, per se, can be caught by the CRC Scheme).

Groups of undertakings

In order to decide whether a group exists for CRC purposes, the parent and subsidiary undertakings must be identified. The CRC Scheme draws on definitions in the Companies Act 2006 of parent and subsidiary undertakings to define the relationships within the group, specifically using the definition of 'group undertaking' as set out in the Companies Act 2006, s.1161(5).

Once identified, parents and subsidiaries will be grouped together for CRC purposes. If the group meets the qualification criteria, it will be required to register and participate in the CRC Scheme as a single participant under the 'highest parent undertaking' in the group. The 'highest parent undertaking' is the undertaking in the group that is not a subsidiary of any other undertaking in the group and will be the 'primary member' for the group unless another member of the group is nominated. The primary member will liaise with the Administrator and is the entity in the group in whose name the compliance account at the Registry is held. The primary member will also report the emissions for the group and buy, sell and surrender allowances on the group's behalf.

Each undertaking within a group is jointly and severally liable to comply with the requirements placed on the group as a whole by the CRC Scheme.

Overseas undertakings

The CRC Scheme only covers energy supplies consumed in the UK. The primary member of a group must be a UK-based organisation. If the highest parent undertaking is based outside the UK, all of the UK subsidiaries will be grouped together as a single participant and the overseas parent undertaking must nominate one of its UK group members (or a third-party agent based in the UK) to act as the primary member.

Undertakings incorporated outside the UK can still be caught by the CRC Scheme if:

(i)   they have a subsidiary undertaking in the UK that meets the qualification criteria; or

(ii) they have some other type of 'presence' in the UK that meets the qualification criteria (e.g. an office or a franchise in the UK for which it is responsible for the energy supplies to those offices for CRC purposes).

Significant group undertakings

Where there are subsidiaries within a group that would be eligible to participate in the CRC Scheme in their own right, such subsidiaries are known as 'significant group undertakings' (SGUs).

An SGU can be identified at any level of a group and can be any individual member or grouping of members of a group or a subsidiary of a member. It is not possible to group sister subsidiaries which together meet the qualification criteria unless their common parent undertaking also forms part of that SGU.

Groups with members defined as SGUs have additional administrative requirements.

In certain circumstances, it may be possible to limit the extent to which group members are jointly and severally liable for each other, by disaggregating a group's SGUs. Disaggregation can occur provided that:

(i)   doing so does not cause the parent undertaking and the remainder of the group to fall below the 6000MWh qualification threshold; and

(ii)   the SGU consents to the disaggregation and registers as a participant in the CRC.

Where an SGU has been disaggregated, it will be treated as a separate participant from the group and will be required to comply with the same obligations as any other participant in the CRC Scheme.

In deciding whether to disaggregate an SGU, one of the issues to consider is whether it would be administratively convenient to do so, as this will double the number of audits that the group will have to perform. Another issue is whether the SGU and the group are likely to perform well or badly in the CRC Scheme and what impact this may have on their brands.

In the event of a merger, acquisition or disposal involving an SGU after the qualification day, additional rules will apply (according to whether the change occurs before, or after, registration for a phase). The Administrator must be notified of a change during a phase within three months of the change (potentially sooner, if the change occurs before registration).

Landlords and tenants

If the landlord pays the energy bills, it will be responsible for the electricity use and emissions that are associated with that supply under the CRC Scheme, even if a tenant is in occupation and is billed separately by the landlord for energy. Tenants will be obliged to cooperate with their landlords for the purpose of complying with the CRC.

If the tenant is billed for the electricity supply by the electricity supplier, then the tenant will be responsible for those supplies under the CRC Scheme.

Whilst landlords and tenants are free to enter into whatever commercial arrangements they think appropriate in relation to the CRC Scheme, landlords have no automatic right to pass on the costs of compliance to tenants. They will have to absorb the costs or ensure that leases enable them to recover the costs from tenants.

If a landlord is responsible for energy supplies, it may focus on how CRC Scheme costs, penalties and financial bonuses are dealt with. Landlords may wish to review lease provisions to have more control over the tenant's use of the property so as to prevent them from increasing their energy use and emissions. To the extent that any reduced energy consumption is due to the tenant's actions, tenants may wish to address the issue of receiving a benefit from their landlords.

When new leases are being drawn up, landlords and tenants will need to clarify at the outset the costs they expect to recover from the tenant and the basis of such recovery, especially where multi-tenanted properties are concerned.

In the case of multi-let buildings, landlords will generally be responsible for the energy supply for common parts and, where tenants do not have a direct energy supply contract with the energy provider, the areas occupied by tenants, too. In this case, the landlord will be responsible under the CRC Scheme. Where the landlord is responsible for the energy supply for common parts but its tenants pay for their own energy supplies for the demised areas, the landlord is responsible for the energy used in the common parts and the tenants will be responsible for the energy used in their premises. If the landlord provides all the energy for common parts and the tenants' premises but also has sub-meters for the tenants' premises, here, too, the landlord will be responsible even though sub-metering enables the landlord to bill tenants for their actual energy use.

Franchises

Where there is a franchise for CRC purposes, franchisors are generally responsible for the energy supply of all their franchisees, even if the franchisee is legally owned by another undertaking or falls within another group of undertakings. Therefore, an undertaking which owns a franchisee must not report that franchisee's emissions as part of its own emissions.

Where there is a franchise for CRC purposes, the franchisor must consider the electricity supplies for all its franchisees to determine whether it meets the qualification criteria. If the criteria are met, the franchisor will be responsible for the franchisee's participation in the CRC Scheme.

A franchisee owes a duty of reasonable assistance to the franchisor within a reasonable time in order to participate in the CRC Scheme.

If the franchisee is a tenant and its landlord pays the energy bills, the landlord is responsible for the franchisee's CRC emissions, not the franchisor (*The CRC Energy Efficiency Scheme User Guide* (DECC, April 2010, p.16)). However, if the franchisee as tenant receives a separate and independent electricity supply that it pays for, the franchise rule applies and the franchisor will be responsible for that supply.

Joint ventures and private finance initiatives

Joint ventures (JVs) and private finance initiatives (PFIs) are treated in the same way for the purposes of the CRC Scheme.

As with any other type of undertaking, the issue of whether a JV or a PFI has to participate in the CRC Scheme as a stand-alone entity or as part of a group will be determined by reference to definitions in the Companies Act 2006 of 'parent undertaking' and 'subsidiary undertaking'.

Where a JV or PFI is not part of a group according to Companies Act tests, it will be treated in one of two ways. Either:

(i)   where the JV or the PFI has a majority owner (i.e. this owner has more than a 50 per cent stake), then all of that JV's or PFI's electricity supplies are aggregated with that of the majority owner; or

(ii)   where there is no single owner of the JV or PFI with more than a 50 per cent stake, the JV or PFI is counted as a separate undertaking that must assess if it meets the qualification criteria in its own right.

4.4.5   Public sector

In general, public sector organisations will be required to participate in the CRC Scheme if:

(i)   they are a 'public body' for CRC purposes; and

(ii)   they meet the qualification criteria during the qualification year for a particular phase.

A public sector organisation will be a 'public body' for CRC purposes if it is designated as a 'public authority' under the Freedom of Information Act 2000, s.3(1)(a) (CRC Order, Sched.3, para.2).

Mandated participants

Some Government bodies will have to participate in the CRC Scheme irrespective of their meters and electricity supply if they have been designated as 'mandated participants'.

Grouping of public bodies

Certain types of public bodies will be grouped and participate together in the CRC Scheme. For example, state funded schools in England and Wales will be grouped with their local authority for CRC purposes.

Bodies corporate as public bodies

A company, in some cases, will be deemed to be a public body for CRC purposes where another public body (such as a local authority or a government department) is a majority member of that company.

If a government department has majority control in a company, that company must participate in the CRC Scheme as a group with the government department unless there is a Government 'decision' that the company is not part of the group.

If any other class of public body is a majority member of a company, that company will be a public body for CRC purposes, but it will not participate as part of a group with the majority-holding public body. The company in this case will have to assess whether, as a public body, it has to be a full participant in the CRC Scheme or make an information disclosure.

Local authorities

Local authorities will qualify to participate in the CRC Scheme where they meet the qualification criteria. They will have to determine the extent of their 'organisation', taking into account mandatory groupings (such as with schools), companies in which they have a majority control and relevant decisions applying to local authorities.

Schools

All state funded schools in England and Wales will be grouped with the local authority that maintains them.

Academies, city technology colleges and city colleges in England will be grouped with the local authority that exercises educational functions for the area in which they are geographically located.

The local authority must consider the electricity supplies of these schools when determining whether it meets the qualification criteria and, if it does, it must then decide whether it has to fully participate in the CRC Scheme or make an information disclosure.

The Crown

The Crown will participate in the CRC Scheme but is not liable for any offence. Persons in the service of the Crown, however, are still liable for offences under the CRC Scheme.

4.4.6 Information disclosures

If an organisation has at least one HHM settled on the half hourly market in the qualification year of a particular phase, but its total qualifying electricity supplies is less than 6,000MWh, it must make an information disclosure.

When making an information disclosure, an organisation must provide the Administrator with a list of all of its HHMs settled on the half hourly market and also calculate how much electricity it was supplied through all HHMs.

Information disclosures must be made during the registration period of a particular phase (this is between April and September of the first compliance year).

Failure to make an information disclosure when required to do so within the registration period will lead to a one-off penalty of £500 per settled HHM for which that organisation is responsible.

Obligations if between 3,000MWh and 6,000MWh

If an organisation receives more than 3,000MWh of electricity in the qualification year of a particular phase, that organisation must disclose its total annual supply of half hourly electricity during that qualification year, in addition to the information described above when making an information disclosure.

Obligations if less than 3,000MWh

If an organisation receives less than 3,000MWh in the qualification year of a particular phase, it will need to provide contact details on the Environment Agency's online form.

4.4.7 Enforcement

The Administrator of the CRC Scheme may exercise its enforcement powers where it reasonably believes that there has been a failure to comply with the CRC Scheme.

The Administrator's enforcement powers are set out in Schedule 9 to the CRC Order and include powers of entry and inspection, requests for information, and the power to issue an enforcement notice on a participant who fails to comply with any provision of the CRC Order.

Both civil and criminal penalties are available for non-compliance, falsification and obstruction.

Criminal offences

Criminal offences under the CRC Scheme are set out in art. 106 of the CRC Order.

It is a criminal offence to knowingly or recklessly make false and misleading statements on material matters (for which there is no defence available) or fail to comply with an enforcement notice. The penalty for doing so is up to three months' imprisonment and/or a fine not exceeding £50,000 on summary conviction. On indictment, it is up to two years' imprisonment and/or an unlimited fine.

It is also a criminal offence to fail to provide facilities or assistance during any inspection or refusing to provide access during an inspection.

Where a criminal offence has been committed with the consent or connivance of a company officer or due to that officer's neglect, both the officer and the body corporate will be guilty of a criminal offence and both can be prosecuted. An officer includes a director, manager, secretary or other similar officer. Where a body corporate is managed by its members (e.g. a limited liability partnership) a member may be liable for a criminal offence in the same way as it were an officer of a body corporate.

Civil penalties

There are 10 civil offences set out in Part 14 of the CRC Order. These offences include a failure to register for the CRC Scheme, a failure to make an information disclosure, failure to provide a footprint report, a failure to provide an annual report, a failure to surrender allowances and a failure to maintain records.

The civil penalties for these failures involve a combination of fines, publicity of the relevant failure, a lower position in the league table and blocking a participant from certain uses of its account in the Registry.

The Administrator has to give written notice to the person affected where it has decided to impose a civil penalty and any fines imposed must be paid within 60 days of the notice being given.

Appeals

The body who hears the appeal will depend on the subject of the determination, notice or penalty and their location. The Secretary of State will hear appeals against determinations, notices and penalties relating to England given by the Environment Agency.

The appeal must be received by the appeal body by no later than 40 working days after the date of the determination, the service of the enforcement notice or imposition of the civil penalty.

The effect of bringing an appeal suspends an enforcement notice, financial penalty or publication from taking effect. The exception to this is where the appeal body has given the appellant notice that the appeal is frivolous or vexatious or otherwise has no reasonable prospect of success or that the appeal is conducted in an unreasonable or vexatious manner. The effect of bringing an appeal does not suspend an art. 74(1) determination or any other civil penalty taking effect.

Audits

The Administrator will audit approximately 20 per cent of participants every year. Audits will usually involve a review of the participant's evidence pack, although some site visits may also be carried out.

In addition, participants are also required to keep their records for at least seven years after the phase to which the records relate. Records relating to the first year a participant participates in the CRC Scheme must be kept for the whole of the time that the participant is in the Scheme.

4.4.8 Caveat

On 20 October 2010, the Chancellor of the Exchequer announced major changes to the CRC Scheme as part of the Comprehensive Spending Review. The changes are:

- postponement of the first sale of allowances from April 2011 to April 2012;
- the Treasury to retain revenue from the annual carbon allowance sales rather than repaying the revenue to participants in the scheme; and
- a potential simplification of the scheme following a consultation by DECC.

The items in the first two bullet points are noted at **4.4.3**. DECC's website will provide details of the third item in due course; see **www.decc.gov.uk/en/content/cms/what_we_do/lc_uk/crc/**.

CHAPTER 5

Obtaining and interpreting environmental information

5.1 INTRODUCTION

Information is power, and in any transaction involving property or other assets which may bring with them an environmental implication, knowing what the risks are is the first stage in the process of quantifying them and dealing with them in the documentation.

There are many sources from which environmental information can be obtained:

- the regulators (all of whom make their information on regulated activities and processes, as well as information regarding all of their statutory duties, public);
- public bodies and organisations performing public services (obliged by freedom of information legislation to make their information public);
- mapping organisations (whose information may reveal past contaminative uses as well as topographical data which may assist in assessing other risks (such as flooding));
- environmental data search companies (who sell a range of products outlining a wide variety of geospatial data intelligence – environmental, flooding, planning and stability in particular);
- local knowledge and records; or
- environmental consultants and other specialist professional advisers.

Generally, clients want information to be as comprehensive, as quick and as cheap as it is possible to make it and in the modern age much information can be obtained quickly and electronically from organisations who have already researched the public data banks for all and any relevant information, and there is usually little need to repeat their efforts and undertake comprehensive searches on an individual case-by-case basis.

Over the years, it has become increasingly commonplace to undertake environmental searches (in the form of 'desk-top studies') in almost every case. Lenders, if no others, would regard the failure to do so as potentially negligent.

This chapter outlines some considerations regarding the extraction of information from three key areas: the Environment Agency, local authorities and environmental data search companies.

5.2 ACCESS TO ENVIRONMENTAL INFORMATION

Numerous statutory provisions and treaty obligations allow access to environmental information – the Freedom of Information Act 2000, the Aarhus Convention (more directed at access to environmental justice in court and tribunal procedures) and the Local Government Act 1985, which permits access to local authority records of any meeting to which the public had access.

The most potent instrument in the arsenal of anyone seeking information about the environment, though, would be the recently amended Environmental Information Regulations 2004, SI 2004/3391.

5.2.1 Environmental Information Regulations 2004

Under these Regulations, it is possible to ask local authorities, the Environment Agency and other public bodies whether they hold any information relating to the environment, and this would include information about possible contamination of sites.

The Regulations came into force on 1 January 2005 and override any other, more restrictive, rights of access, such as the general rights contained in the Freedom of Information Act 2000.

They require that relevant persons holding past or present information relating to the environment make that information available to anyone who requests it, within a basic period of 20 days at a charge of no more than is reasonably attributable to the supply of the information. Public inspection of the information is free, the provision of copies can be charged for. The information should be provided by easily accessible electronic means if possible.

Any grounds for a refusal to give the information must be given.

'Relevant persons' are:

- public authorities;
- bodies with public responsibilities for the environment and under the control of public authorities (this may include privatised utility companies).

'Information' means records, registers, reports, etc. available in an accessible form (i.e. written, visual, oral or database).

'Relating to the environment' means relating to the state of any water/air, any flora/fauna, any soil, any natural site or other land or to any 'measures or activities' which may harm, or which may be intended to protect, anything so mentioned. It would also include measures, policies, legislation and guidance intended to affect the environment and also pertains to the protection of human health and buildings as well as the natural world.

The Regulations need not allow access to information which may affect national security, pertain to legal or similar proceedings, internal communications of an organisation, in the course of completion or relate to matters of intellectual property or commercial confidentiality. These categories give many instances where information can legitimately be refused.

Information must be withheld if disclosure would entail breach of contract/law, it is personal information and the person concerned does not consent, information is given to the relevant person voluntarily and the donor does not consent or its disclosure may harm the environment.

Information need not be given if the request is too general or vague, or manifestly unreasonable.

Thus, the Regulations may allow access to information held by relevant persons regarding:

- physical/biological state of any environmental media at any time;
- conditions in and around man-made structures;
- living and dead organisms;
- UK, EU or worldwide matters;
- human health issues;
- activities having a potentially damaging impact;
- steps/activities taken with the aim of improving the environment.

Primarily, this information will be in the form of:

- IPC, PPC or Local Authority Air Pollution Control (LAAPC) registers of applications, authorisations, permits, conditions, requests, variations and certain monitoring data;
- details of emissions, incidents, etc. required to be furnished to the Environment Agency/local authority;
- information compiled by the Environment Agency/local authority inspectors;
- Environment Agency registers of applications, licences, authorisations, permits, consents, conditions, variations and monitoring and sampling data;
- sewerage undertakers' registers of discharge consents;
- HSE reports, investigations, etc.;
- Environmental Impact Assessment statements by planning authority;
- waste regulators' records relating to waste management licences and waste carriers;
- local authority information and registers relating to statutory nuisance, especially noise, litter, sewer and drainage maps, etc.

In practice, it can be difficult to enforce the Regulations. The exemptions are wide and easily arguable; information is occasionally presented in a form which is meaningless to the lay person or even lawyers and the cost may be prohibitive. Access to the information may be free, but the cost of copies may be high bearing in mind that bodies can charge the reasonable cost of 'supplying' the information – and there are differing interpretations of the meaning of that phrase.

There is, however, an increasing realisation among local authorities and other regulators that openness has a virtue and many such bodies encourage the open access of information in order to speed up transactions and to avoid having to research the same information repeatedly in respect of a particularly troublesome location for applicant after applicant. The attitude of such bodies varies across the country and some applicants may still meet resistance.

5.3 ENVIRONMENT AGENCY SEARCHES

The Environment Agency, via its website, provides all data in relation to its statutory functions – water resource management, flooding and IPC, PPC and waste management regulation being the main ones.

Those seeking to acquire environmental information may not appreciate what to look for, however. Furthermore, Agency data does not generally include historic site information, nor any information about past or current activity which may be potentially polluting if it is outside the legally-regulated industry sectors.

Agency flood data, though much improved over the years, fails to ask the key question (often at the top of a buyer's mind) 'has this property ever been flooded?' – preferring to concentrate on bare data based on proximity to water-courses and flood-basins and the presence or absence of flood defences.

5.4 LOCAL AUTHORITY SEARCHES

Over the years, enquiries have been added to what is now called form CON 29R as a result of consultations between the Law Society and local authorities which seek to identify all the information which a local authority is required to compile for the purposes of carrying out its duties under Part IIA and compiling the official registers which they have to maintain under that legislation. It asks whether:

- the authority has notified anyone of its determination that land is contaminated;
- the property is on the registers held under Part IIA;
- a decision has been made to make an entry on the registers (even though it may not have appeared yet);
- whether any consultations have been carried out with regard to the status of the land.

These questions are more searching than previous versions, and may flush out more issues than previously, but there is still the reservation that information would only be revealed in answer to CON 29R enquiries if notifications are made that the authority deems the land to be contaminated or if formal action is taken in respect of land actually suspected of being 'contaminated'. If land is not deemed to be 'contaminated' within the strict meaning of Part IIA, no information need be revealed in answer to the new enquiries and a negative answer would be given to the enquiries.

This negative response may imply that there is no problem with the land, but this may not, in fact, be the case. There may be pollutants on the site which may give rise to troublesome issues – though not being so serious as to merit a formal determination under Part IIA.

Further, information regarding the actual state of the land (albeit not yet 'contaminated') may be in the possession of the authority and may be of interest to a purchaser. In such cases, consideration should be given to widening the scope of the enquiry and the wording of the new questions.

Information, in the widest sense, is to be made publicly available under the terms of the Environmental Information Regulations 2004 (and any later re-enactments thereof). The time limit for response is reduced from two months under the old predecessor regulations to 20 days as mentioned in **5.2.1**.

Practitioners could try questions modelled on the precedents set out in Appendix A4.

5.5   ENVIRONMENTAL DATA SEARCH REPORTS

5.5.1   Environmental data providers

The environmental search report market has developed over the last 20 years. The search providers offer a range of products for the residential property market, the commercial market and other products for use in risk assessment, mapping and due diligence work.

An environmental search report generally covers past and current environmental permits, past industrial use, past contaminative use, in-filled ground, flooding, natural stability hazards, radon sensitivity and other matters, depending on provider.

5.5.2   Reading environmental data search reports

These comments are made in reference to the sample report reproduced in Appendix A3. Obviously, practitioners must remain aware that although the same information is, broadly, provided in all varieties of report, there will be differences of presentation, order and style.

Cover sheet – risk certificate and terms of issue

Most reports offer a 'certificate' of various kinds which (depending on the product) purport to give some clearance or comfort to users that the land will not be determined as contaminated land within the meaning of Part IIA of the EPA.

However, these certificates are often based on computer-modelled or statistical risk assessments, not on any actual site inspection, do not factor in all the information contained in the search reports and are limited to opining on what are quite unlikely eventualities.

The fact that a 'certificate' has been issued, or the word 'PASSED' appears does not mean that there are no environmental problems associated with the site. Equally, a 'FAILED' report does not mean that a site is fatally contaminated. A site which does not initially get a full certificate requires further investigation and such enquiries may result in the land being given a cleaner bill of health at a later stage.

So, undue reliance should not be placed on such certificates; clients should be advised to make their own judgments based on such additional research as they or their advisers deem appropriate.

Report cover sheet

Check that the description of the property which is the subject of the search is accurate.

The first nine pages of the Report in this sample are a 'report summary'.

Page 1 – Introduction

An introductory explanation of the matters researched by the report. The matters should be compared between products so practitioners can decide which they prefer, given the balance between cost and comprehensiveness.

Page 2 – Aerial photograph

Enables the reader to assess the locality of the target property and see features not visible from the ground or any on-foot site inspection. In this sample, note the flat green area to the west of the property, the strip of land between the three cottages and the roadway to the north.

Page 3 – Schematic plan

Shows the locality in digital map format.

Pages 4/5 – Section A – Enquiries of statutory registers

This page details any entries in a 250 metre radius of the property in any of the statutory registers of potentially polluting industries and activities – IPC, PPC, Local Authority Pollution Prevention and Control, waste facilities, radioactive, hazardous, dangerous substances, COMAH sites, abstraction and discharge consents and contaminated land.

A string of 'No' answers indicates no such entries and is the ideal result.

113

Any 'Yes' entries may require further investigation as there may be amenity, noise, odour, leakage, escape or hazard risks, and associated value concerns, especially if the licensed activity is especially proximate.

See Appendix A4 for possible enquiries which could be made of the relevant register-holder or regulator (whose contact details would be provided in the report) if the client chose to pursue this matter of concern.

Page 7 – Section B – Enquiries concerning site history

This page centres on researches about past and current contaminative uses as shown by historic map data and current industry listings for those processes not caught by Section A enquiries.

A string of 'No' answers indicates no such entries and is the ideal result.

Any 'Yes' entries may require further investigation as there may be amenity, noise, odour, leakage, escape or hazard risks, and associated value concerns, especially if the licensed activity is especially proximate. The main concern would be that the purchaser or owner would suffer all or part of a clean-up bill under Part IIA.

See Appendix A4 for possible enquiries which could be made of the relevant party or regulator (whose contact details may be provided in the report) if the client chose to pursue this matter of concern.

If an entry here caused grave concern, a Part IIA certificate may not have been granted, but the matter referred for expert re-evaluation, and specific pointers given for further action, whom to approach and what to ask.

In this sample, an area of concern has been identified and later pages of the report pick this up and explain the nature of the feature.

Page 8 – Section C – Enquiries concerning mining and radon

This section contains information regarding mining, any positive answers to which should indicate a necessity to carry out mining reports. Bear in mind that other extractive industries can cause similar issues to coal mining, and further searches revealing this extra dimension are available.

It also contains information regarding the naturally occurring carcinogen – radon. Undetectable except with specialist equipment, radon occurs naturally in some areas but not others. This data indicates the percentage of houses likely to be affected in the area of the search. If less than 1 per cent, there is no cause for concern. If 1 per cent or more are affected, then the area is 'radon-affected' and tests are recommended. If 3 per cent or more are affected, venting and abatement measures have been compulsory for new build houses, and extensions, since 1999. Similar measures – simple in essence, but costly to install in older properties – might be recommended for existing dwellings.

Page 9 – Section D – Enquiries concerning natural perils

This section contains recently enhanced and improved flooding data, which includes flood defence measures, indications as to the possibility of pluvial and tidal flood and encompasses not only Environment Agency data, but also data from RMS and Aviva which incorporates insurance industry risk-based data.

The next section of the Report (pages 10–11 inclusive in the sample), provides additional information relating to any 'Yes' answers given in pages 1–9.

Page 10 – Site plan with polygon features indicated

This plan shows the exact location of any positive entries revealed in pages 1–9, together with a key outlining what the feature in fact is.

In the sample, note especially, the sub-station to the east, the potentially-infilled land to the west, and the military land to the south. In particular, the area of potentially-infilled land to the west corresponds to the strip of land identified above on the aerial photograph as now being the flat green strip of land providing access to the three cottages.

At some point in history, this search shows, that area was once a hole, which now no longer exists. However, the question remains as to what it might have been filled with – that would be the concern.

Having identified such a feature, further enquiries could be pursued to ascertain whether, in fact, there is any need for concern over that particular feature – see Appendix A4.

Page 11

This page confirms the nature of the mapping information on the strength of which the feature has been identified. It confirms, in so far as historic map information can, what the nature of the activity might have been.

Pages 12/13

These pages provide the contact details of the main agencies of whom further enquiries can be made in relation to any features identified as a risk in the main body of the report.

5.5.3 Interpreting environmental search reports

Having received a search report, clients are likely to want their advisers to interpret it in some way and explain the significance of any entries revealed. Clearly, lawyers are not environmental experts and not even the Law Society's Warning Card on Contaminated Land requires or expects them to be so.

However, whilst lawyers cannot give any definitive view on what issues are actually present, they can (and should) explain the implications of the possible presence of likely issues, and direct the client to other specialist advisers as need be.

Clear search or no perceived problem

In many cases, the search will reveal no entries of any concern whatsoever, and the practitioner may advise the client that it should be safe to proceed with any purchase transaction, say, safe in the knowledge that the information is as accurate and reliable as modern mapping and information-gathering techniques can make it.

No search service is perfect, however, and matters may still crop up which the search service could not have been expected to spot – spillages and leakages on the site, non-compliance with planning conditions, activity that came and went in between editions of the OS maps on which historic data is based and ancient historic activity pre-dating the oldest maps. These caveats should perhaps be mentioned.

Searches revealing entries

In most cases, it is likely that the search will reveal entries that may be of some concern to a client. The practitioner should discuss these issues with the client to decide how to proceed to ascertain the degree of risk posed by a revealed entry.

Certain entries always carry an inherent degree of risk with them, and certain types of land-use have particular contaminating characteristics. For example, infilled land may be structurally unstable, landfill sites may give rise to methane gas generation, old gasworks may have contaminated the land with tars and other chemicals and petrol stations may have leaking underground storage tanks. The nearer to the site the identified entry, the greater the risk that some problem may occur on the site in question.

The mere fact that information reveals an entry, or a potentially contaminative historical use, does not necessarily mean that there is a problem with the land, merely that there may be, and this possibility may require further investigation.

It cannot be over-emphasised that until the actual extent of a potential problem is investigated and revealed by an intrusive ground investigation (see **5.6**), no practitioner can fully advise on its implications, and reports are only designed to provide the information to enable practitioners to identify the next questions.

The lawyer is in no position to do anything beyond accumulating the information, explaining its potential significance and leaving the client to make a suitably advised decision.

The decision whether to proceed, undertake further investigations or withdraw from a transaction must be the client's, and it will frequently depend on factors unrelated to the environmental information revealed by the search. Factors such as the cost of the further investigations, the difficulty and delay involved in undertaking them, the accuracy and helpfulness of the further information revealed, the general timescale of the transaction and the client's attitude to risk will all influence the decision.

Often, the next step after obtaining a report is simply to acquire further information (especially as it may be easily obtainable from an obvious source), rather than to consider an actual site inspection at significant additional cost.

Obvious next steps could be to contact the relevant agency or local authority using any useful contacts section of the search report. The local authority will have assessed its area for the purposes of Part IIA and may have records of the steps taken by a developer to make the land safe, which would avoid, in most cases, the need for a site investigation. Enquiries could be directed towards the developer, too.

Practitioners should develop a range of questions which can be directed to the relevant bodies to elicit any further information that may be relevant should the client wish to proceed with further investigations. Not knowing where to turn for additional help, or not knowing the questions to ask, would cause delay. See the precedents in Appendix A4.

One feature common to all the products is that they do not involve any actual assessment of the land which is the subject of the report. They provide information from public databanks only, and no interpretation or judgment is (or could be) offered by the report providers.

5.6 ENVIRONMENTAL INVESTIGATIONS AND AUDITS IN COMMERCIAL TRANSACTIONS

The necessity for carrying out environmental investigations and audits is largely now a given in most commercial transactions, and in many private ones, too. Lenders, insurers, purchasers and enlightened managers all perceive the need for knowledge relating to a particular site or company's environmental situation, and the potential risk of incidents, accidents and claims.

Broadly, an environmental investigation or audit involves a full assessment of a site, or a company's sites, operations and installations with the intention of evaluating the potential environmental risks posed by those locations and installations, and to monitor corporate environmental performance (especially in the light of enhanced reporting obligations and duties in recent companies legislation).

An 'investigation' is an investigation for the purposes of general information gathering – maybe as a preliminary to a purchase – and will normally consist of a paper, or desk study, possibly followed by site visits, of a more or less detailed type.

An 'audit', on the other hand, involves a thorough site investigation, together with detailed monitoring operations, so that a company's performance can be measured against clearly defined criteria, which have already been determined and set by the company. It is a quantitative exercise, intended to gauge in precise terms how a company measures up to its own standards and, if not, by how far it is falling short.

This concept of 'measurability' is what distinguishes an audit from an investigation.

5.6.1 Types of investigation

There is no standard form of investigation. They are almost infinitely variable according to the circumstances and the purposes which they are required to serve.

The most common manifestations of investigations are usually said to include:

- investigations of the whole of a company's activities or operations;
- investigations of specific activities or operations;
- investigations of specific assets (e.g. prior to purchase, sale or development);
- analysis of specific environmental risks to ensure compliance with the regulatory framework;
- investigations of waste facilities;
- risk assessment investigations;
- waste minimisation strategies;
- environmental impact assessment in connection with planning consents;
- investigations as a preliminary to environmental impairment liability insurance; or
- investigations designed to assist in the production of a corporate environmental policy statement (CEPS), and management system, as part of the company's 'green' image.

It is vital to the success of the investigation to have identified its objectives, and what it is intended to achieve. Setting objectives can seem like a waste of time and effort, but a lot of money can be wasted getting a report which analyses the wrong aspects of a company's operations, or which tackles the job from a wrong perspective.

The management team, with the help of appropriate professional advice, must decide on the objectives, and inform the professional investigation team what it is they are expected to produce, how and when. Time spent setting out the terms will be time saved having to seek clarification and further information later.

The general objectives of an investigation, however, are also variable according to the company's circumstances and requirements, but will often include a combination (or even all) of the following considerations:

- introducing a proactive approach to the management of environmental aspects of the business;
- the avoidance of criminal and civil liabilities and clean-up costs;
- reporting to shareholders, bankers/lenders, insurers, employees and regulatory bodies;
- the enhancement of the company's public image;

- to safeguard authorisations, permits, licences and insurance policies;
- to avoid disruption to production or trading arising out of environmental hazards and the extraordinary costs associated with it;
- the avoidance of the devaluation of assets due to contamination; and
- to establish and maintain good relations with the local community and neighbouring residents.

There are two basic types of environmental investigation:

- the 'compliance' investigation, to look at the whole business, and its operations and processes; and
- the 'transactional' investigation, undertaken in connection with specific transactions, such as purchase or disposal of assets, or funding arrangements.

Underlying this diversity, there is a fairly common procedural approach which can be applied and adapted to meet the differing needs of the investigation and the circumstances in which it is carried out. It consists, broadly, of a three-part process.

Phase I – Desk study and historical review

A Phase I study involves a paper exercise to discover the past land-use of the site, in order to determine whether there is the potential for contamination. Study of old Ordnance Survey (OS) maps, interviewing local residents, aerial photographs and visits to the site to pick up visual clues are all sensible steps to take. Much of this effort can be saved by acquiring an environmental data search report from a commercial provider (see **5.5**).

Phase II – Site inspections/walk through the production process

Having identified the potential for contamination and other environmental problems, the process would then encompass a full site visit. This visit will usually involve the drilling of boreholes and trial pits and trenches to find out what is actually beneath the ground. It may involve geological analysis, groundwater modelling, and chemical testing of contaminants to give a final indication of the level of contamination, and degree of risk, involved.

Terms relating to site access, the precise extent of the investigations, after-care provisions and provisions relating to confidentiality and the provision of report copies should be agreed between the parties.

Phase III – Implementation of recommendations and remediation programme; further sampling if necessary, monitoring and follow-up

The final, Phase III investigation is the basis of the environmental 'auditing' process – the undertaking of the groundworks or other remediation and engineering solutions necessary to deal with the issues, the continuing investigation and measuring of a company's performance, and the comparison of the actual with the intended performance as set out in the company's environmental policy, which itself is derived from the results of the earlier investigation phase.

CHAPTER 6

Residential property transactions

6.1 INTRODUCTION

Property practitioners must, as a consequence of the publication of the Law Society's Warning Card on Contaminated Land (see **6.3**), take the whole range of environmental matters on board, and take steps to assist clients to understand and deal with relevant environmental issues in *any* land transaction. Whether the client perceives the need for such steps or not, it is now, and for some time has been, a requirement that such matters are addressed, with the attendant implications for the overall cost of the transaction and its timescale.

Of particular concern to solicitor and client alike are the potential environmental risks that:

- a costly legal liability may be inherited by a purchaser of a site;
- the value of a property or site may be adversely affected, even to the point of it being unsaleable, as a consequence of some actual or perceived environmental problem with the site or neighbouring property; or
- some non-legal effects may be felt, such as effects on the health of occupants, structural problems, flooding or subsidence.

The network of environmental liabilities is complex, and the price that buyers will pay for sites which they know or believe to be polluted is very volatile. Purchasers with experience of foreign jurisdictions may be particularly sensitised to the issue. These risks should not therefore be ignored. The legislation applies with equal rigour to both commercial and domestic transactions, so all practitioners must take care.

It is essential, however, to keep matters in perspective and it would be easy to panic and scaremonger about the extent of the risks involved. Whilst it is true that environmental liabilities can be costly when they do arise, they will not do so in the majority of cases. Recent research estimates suggest that something in the order of only 2 to 5 per cent of the domestic property stock in the UK is likely to be affected by some serious environmental problem. This equates to one transaction in 50 – however, the problem is spotting that one, as environmental problems are not geographically discrete (in the way mining activity or radon gas are), it can take a long time for creeping pollution problems to emerge, and often they are not visible. The fact that a site is green, and a field, does not make it a greenfield site.

Whilst not strictly part of a lawyer's remit, the non-legal factors mentioned (particularly flooding) are also matters which a client may expect an adviser to deal with. Whilst it is not suggested that a failure to do so would be professionally negligent, a client may nevertheless feel let down if such matters are not pointed out at some stage, and many clients perceive the solicitor as being the adviser most likely to have their interests at heart.

Solicitors and their clients should, however, take comfort from the fact that, with some relatively cheap and easy steps, an adequate (if not a perfect) view can be taken of the risks involved in any transaction, which can then be used to inform the decision whether to proceed at all and, if so, with what additional protections.

6.2 POTENTIAL ENVIRONMENTAL PROBLEMS IN RESIDENTIAL CASES

6.2.1 Criminal liabilities

Nature conservation regime

Offences under the nature conservation regime involve adversely affecting protected species or their habitats, or designated eco-systems (WCA 1981, Parts I and II, as amended by the Countryside and Rights of Way Act 2000).

The offences involve damage – deliberately or recklessly caused – to protected species and eco-systems. Any activity, or construction or development work, may have to be undertaken with special care to avoid such harms being caused.

It is useful to discover from the nature conservation bodies whether such designations have been made in the area of the target property. Such information may be included in an environmental search report.

The website **www.magic.gov.uk** also enables practitioners to search addresses, locations and properties for information relating to a vast range of conservation issues.

Contaminated land

It is an offence to fail to remediate contaminated land when instructed to do so (EPA 1990, Part IIA).

This may come about as a result of substances already in the land at completion, which are giving rise to a risk of significant harm to persons or things nearby. This may catch such commonplace matters as leakages of oil from storage tanks for domestic heating systems, or waste oils from car engines, or other polluting matter disposed of on the land from DIY activities. More likely, it will involve historic land-use issues, long since forgotten about but which emerge over time, as in Totley in Sheffield (old rolling mills), 'Chemical Fields' in Hartlepool (chemical manufacture) or in Sevenoaks (old brickworks and infilled quarry pits).

If the original polluter of the land cannot be found, the current owner or occupier may be served with a remediation notice requiring the land to be cleaned up. An offence is committed if he fails to comply, and the authorities can do the necessary works themselves and recover the costs from the person served with the notice.

As previously discussed, the problem is that a purchaser can himself qualify as the 'original polluter'. If a buyer knew, or ought to have known or realised, or could have found out, that there was contamination on the site, he may be caught, as the definition of 'original polluter' includes anyone who knowingly permits contamination to remain.

There may also be leakages of substances onto the ground after completion in respect of which the purchaser client will likely be the 'original polluter' of the land.

Residential purchasers should, however, take comfort from the fact that:

- only the most seriously polluted sites are likely to be designated as contaminated;
- most remediation would have been addressed when the site was last developed (if this has occurred in the last three to five years), though this should not be taken for granted;
- remediation strategies must be cost-effective;
- liability is likely to be shared with others;
- regulators are more likely to want to target the developers of a site than the current owners (see *Circular Facilities* v. *Sevenoaks DC* [2005] EWHC 865);
- in considering the recovery of costs, the authorities must take potential hardship to the owner into account.

On the other hand, a series of exclusionary tests to be applied by the authorities may result in the seller of property no longer being required to share the cost of remediation if the purchaser knew about the contamination of the site at completion. This provision may be interpreted as meaning that a purchaser is better off buying in ignorance of the state of the site, but this cannot be good practice.

Details of what sites are designated as contaminated would be available from the local authority (or Environment Agency, if a special site) and would be included in an environmental search report.

Details of which sites may have a history of potentially contaminative land use (and which *may*, as a consequence, be determined as contaminated under Part IIA) would also be included in an environmental search report from a private provider (though *not*, as matters currently stand, from local authorities or the Environment Agency).

Pollution of controlled waters

Offences relating to the pollution of controlled waters involve polluting water without or in breach of a licence and failing to clean up water when instructed to do so (Environmental Permitting Regulations, reg.38(1); WRA 1991, s.161A).

Any discharges to controlled waters will constitute a criminal offence unless they are consented for, and such consents should be obtained in respect of emissions from septic tanks and other non-mains waste outfalls.

Any leakages of oil from storage tanks, any washings or other deposits from garages, etc. or even fertilisers from the garden shed which get into watercourses, either directly or via the drainage system, may give rise to a liability.

The same problems afflict buyers with regard to water pollution offences occurring before completion but persisting afterwards, as it may be said that the buyer has knowingly permitted the offence to continue.

So, if a buyer ought to have known or realised, or could have found out, that there was a possibility of water pollution occurring from the site, they may be caught.

Information regarding discharge consents and past pollution incidents is available from the licencing body – the Environment Agency – and will be included in an environmental search report.

6.2.2 Civil liabilities

Nuisance (Cambridge Water v. Eastern Counties Leather [1994] 2 AC 264)

Purchasers of land giving rise to a nuisance will be liable for continuing nuisances created by predecessors in title if they knew or ought to have known of the nuisance, could reasonably have foreseen it causing harm, and could have taken reasonable steps to prevent or abate it, but failed to do so.

Purchasers must therefore take any such reasonable steps to stop ongoing pollution if they are to avoid such liability at some point in the future.

6.2.3 Clean-up liabilities

Clean-up liabilities arise under the following regimes:

- contaminated land (EPA 1990, Part IIA);
- water pollution (WRA 1991, s.161A).

These powers apply in circumstances where an offence has been committed, a notice has been served on the owner of the land, and he has failed to comply with it.

The authorities may enter onto the site and undertake any necessary works, and recover the cost from the person served with the notice.

6.2.4 Other miscellaneous provisions

The keeping, use, accumulation and disposal of radioactive substances in Great Britain is regulated.

The storage of hazardous substances is regulated by legislation designed to ensure that hazardous substances can be kept or used in significant quantities only after the responsible authorities have had the opportunity to assess the risk to surrounding areas.

Sites storing above-specified amounts of hazardous substances and those carrying out particularly toxic or hazardous activities must provide information to the public on the nature of the hazard and action to be taken in the event of an accident. The regulations mainly apply to chemical and petrochemical industries and to those that produce or use substances with flammable, toxic or explosive properties.

Explosives legislation controls the registration, storage and supply of various categories of explosive substances to ensure public safety and security. All premises where explosives are stored must be registered.

The implications for those living and operating on, or contemplating purchasing, property near such hazardous and dangerous substances may be:

- health effects and concerns;
- risk of explosion, fire or escape;
- civil liability to adjacent landowners; and
- diminution in property values as a result of blight.

Public records are available from the local authority and HSE and will often be included in an environmental search report (depending on product and provider).

6.2.5 Related legal issues

Whilst liability under other regulatory regimes will not be directly relevant to a domestic purchaser (they are not going to be purchasing an operating chemical manufacturing plant), the residential client may nevertheless want to know whether there are any potentially polluting processes in the area surrounding the target property, in case there is a history of pollution, odour, noise or other inconvenience that would detract from the enjoyment of the property, or pollute it by virtue of pollution migrating from the site of origin.

Enquiries could therefore be made of the regulatory bodies regarding:

- regulated processes under EPA 1990, Part I (IPC) or PPC (now subsumed into the Environmental Permitting Regulations);
- regulated waste operations under EPA 1990, Part II (now subsumed into the Environmental Permitting Regulations);
- statutory nuisances under EPA 1990, Part III;
- water discharge consents under WRA 1991 (now subsumed into the Environmental Permitting Regulations);
- trade effluent consents under WIA 1991, s.118.

Purchasers and their advisers should be aware that the regulatory and licensing bodies only keep and retain information regarding the legal regimes which they police. Most of these only came into being with the advent of the EPA 1990, and thus only date back to the last decade of the twentieth century. Moreover, they only apply to those activities designated for regulation under the legislation.

If a residential purchaser wanted fully to assess the potential for contamination in the target site, enquiries would need to be made about those potentially contaminative uses of the site that either pre-date, or are not included in, the legal regimes mentioned above.

Such enquiries would need to centre on trade journals, or a study of old OS maps which may reveal past uses. This information may be readily available from a commercial data provider.

6.2.6 Non-legal issues

In addition to the legal liabilities outlined above, residential buyers should also be made aware of the following, non-legal implications, which may have a bearing on the use, enjoyment and value of the site:

- health effects from the presence of pollutants, or possibly naturally-occurring substances such as radon gas;
- health and other impairments from nearby polluting activities;
- stability issues relating to past-infilled land;
- adjacence to floodplains;
- proximity of active waste facilities such as landfill sites – potentially damaging to wealth as well as health;
- proximity of overhead power lines or mobile phone masts;
- proximity of wind-farms or other noise and nuisance sources;
- client concerns regarding any substances left on-site as part of the development (however well contained);
- delay, inconvenience and wasted costs involved in dealing with problems.

6.3 LAW SOCIETY'S CONTAMINATED LAND WARNING CARD

The Warning Card was issued by the Law Society in June 2001, with copies being distributed to the profession and the full text, reproduced in Appendix B, was published in the *Gazette* in July 2001.

The feeling within the Society was that there was a potential negligence liability for solicitors who failed to address relevant issues, and that guidance was therefore required.

The issue seems to be that the legal profession is the only one with professional indemnity insurance (PII) cover for environmental matters, and solicitors are thus a prime target for complaint from those adversely affected by an incomplete assessment of the risks – clients and lenders.

The Warning Card requires practitioners to 'consider whether contamination is an issue' in every transaction.

This guidance is not intended to be a professional requirement, but can be taken into account in assessing negligence on the part of a practitioner in any given case.

It suggests, broadly, six steps to follow in every case:

STEP 1   Advise the client of the potential for problems.
STEP 2   Make full enquiries of the seller.
STEP 3   Make enquiries of the statutory and regulatory bodies.
STEP 4   Undertake independent site history investigations.
STEP 5   Consider a full site investigation by environmental consultants.
STEP 6   Consider contractual or other protections.

6.4   PRACTICAL CONSIDERATIONS IN RESIDENTIAL FREEHOLD TRANSACTIONS

6.4.1   Generally

Inheriting a costly environmental legal liability is unlikely in most typical residential conveyancing cases but 2 to 5 per cent of properties (on average) may be expected to have some sort of potentially problematic historic land-use issue associated with them. Even leaks of domestic heating oil can be costly to remediate – in the few examples to date, average 'repair bills' have been around £20,000 to £30,000 per house.

Of equal, if not more, importance to the buyer of residential property is the risk that, at some point in the future, the property may be rendered unsaleable, or its valuation significantly reduced, if it becomes known that a pollution problem exists, or has existed, on the site.

Other issues of concern to a purchaser may include:

- flooding risk;
- health risks (from radon gas, power lines or mobile phone transmitters);
- structural integrity (property on infilled ground, subsidence);
- inconvenience;
- delay;
- wasted expense.

Interpreting how future events may affect the valuation may then have to be a matter of inspired guesswork, but anticipating the problem as best one can now must be better than buying at full value now and then realising a loss later.

Close liaison with the valuation profession is required. The Royal Institution of Chartered Surveyors (RICS) only requires its members to take into account the fact or potential for pollution in conducting inspections or determining valuations if such problems are known or obvious. The surveyor will not be covered under his professional indemnity policy for such matters, and will not therefore give any advice on pollution issues. Specialist surveyors who are qualified to express opinions, backed by PII, are available.

Others may try to pass the burden of advising on such matters on to the solicitor, often by oblique means. Solicitors need to check what assumptions they are being asked to make in reports on title, for example, and qualify them accordingly (though the standard Certificate used in the Solicitors' Code of Conduct 2007, Rule 3, makes it clear that it does not include certificates regarding the environment). If advice is required, specific instructions would need to be given to the valuer in the terms of engagement, and specific top-up insurance cover purchased.

In the absence of meaningful assistance from valuers, a cost-effective investigation of historical problems and of what, if anything, has been done to alleviate those problems, should put the current client's mind at rest, and provide some evidence to give to future purchasers by way of comfort, possibly as part of an information pack for purchasers.

6.4.2   Step 1: Advise the client of the potential for problems

It is essential not to overstate the risk that a purchaser client may have to bear the cost of a clean up of contaminated land, as there is a very long road to travel before that conclusion is reached. However, to ignore this completely is potentially negligent. The possible follow-up steps which could be taken to investigate any likely risk further – and possible cost implications – should be discussed with the client at the initial stage.

Often, the problem is not that clients are resistant to paying an extra fee, though that is often the stated objection, it is rather they do not fully comprehend the enormity of the risks they may be facing unless this is sensibly explained to them. Moreover, there is so much information readily and cheaply available, that most clients, when asked the question 'do you want to know, or don't you?', would answer in the affirmative.

If such information could be obtained quickly and cheaply – which it can – would a typical client want to know about:

(a)   the proximity of, and risk associated with:

- SSSIs;
- polluting industrial processes (current or past, regulated or unregulated);
- landfill sites and waste operations (current or past);
- contaminated land (current or past);
- statutory nuisances;
- water pollution and discharges;
- hazardous, dangerous or radioactive substances;
- floodplains;
- radon gas;

- subsidence;
- overhead power lines;

(b) and possibly also information on:

- crime statistics;
- house price indices;
- OFSTED school reports;
- insurance bandings;
- council tax bandings;
- credit reference ratings;
- local council performance indicators;
- nearest amenities and services.

The information in (b) is obtainable from **www.upmystreet.com** and is comprised in some search reports.

The location and signal strength of mobile phone transmitters can be found from **www.sitefinder.ofcom.org.uk** and may also be included in search reports (depending on product and provider).

In order to get the point across to a client who is resistant to the need for such enquiries, practitioners should consider:

- a standard paragraph in a client care letter;
- a leaflet/handout which can be sent at the start of the matter;
- a face-to-face meeting to discuss the issues.

Firms seem broadly to have adopted a policy of undertaking environmental search enquiries as a matter of course, and this practice is to be commended.

Some firms have expressed the view that they have a policy of merely mentioning the issue to clients, but not undertaking any enquiries unless specifically instructed to do so, although, in the author's view, this is not complying with the wording or the spirit of the Law Society's Warning Card.

A policy of not undertaking searches as a matter of routine may also put a practitioner in breach of obligations to any lender, given the current injunction in the Council of Mortgage Lenders (CML) Handbook (paras. 5.2.1–5.2.4) to ensure that 'all usual and necessary' searches are undertaken, together with any other searches which may be appropriate given the property's location and other features'.

See Appendix A5 for clauses to include in a client care letter to explain environmental risks.

6.4.3 Step 2: Make specific enquiries of the seller

Solicitors should consider raising specific environmental enquiries of the seller, though it is recognised that this rather cuts across refinements aimed at speeding up the conveyancing process. Some suggested forms of enquiry are included in Appendix A6.

The extent of the enquiries will depend on the client's budget and attitude. From the practitioner's point of view, it is essential that the client be told how much pollution investigation (if any) is covered by his budget at the outset.

As a counsel of perfection, enquiries could deal with:

- whether the seller is aware of any potentially contaminative current or previous use of the site or neighbouring sites;
- whether the site or any adjoining sites have been used for landfill or waste disposal;
- details of previous owners or occupiers and activities carried on by them;
- whether there have been any disputes, or circumstances which may give rise to any disputes, with neighbours or regulatory bodies regarding the state of the land;
- what (if any) planning consents have been issued in respect of the site, what conditions they contained regarding contamination and its remediation, and details of any works carried out in compliance with it. It will be essential to check any such information whenever acting for a purchaser of new property from a developer. They will offer facilities for inspection of the documentation. Take the chance to read it and, if necessary, request clarification of any technical details. There is an incentive in Part IIA of the EPA for the developer to give full *and clear* information to a buyer to enable them *reasonably* to assess the risk of contamination on the site at purchase.

There are two main responses to these enquiries:

(a)   *Replies are forthcoming*: The replies may need specialist interpretation by surveyors or environmental consultants. Further, more detailed investigation may be needed of specific areas of concern.

(b)   *The seller stonewalls*: If the seller issues the blanket response 'not so far as the seller is aware, please rely on own investigations and surveys', the client must consider whether to undertake alternative investigations of his own. The seller may be making an implied warranty that he has checked before asserting his ignorance of such matters. If he has not, some contractual redress may be possible.

See Appendix A6 for further enquiries of the seller.

6.4.4   Step 3: Make enquiries of the statutory and regulatory bodies

General

The main bodies to contact are:

- Natural England (and their Northern Irish, Scottish and Welsh equivalents) (nature conservation designations);

- Environment Agency (licences, authorisations, permits, registers and prosecutions);
- the local authority (registers and information on contaminated land and any relevant planning consents, hazardous substance information);
- the HSE (incidents and accidents);
- sewerage undertakers (consents and registers);
- British Coal (mining activities and abandoned mine leakage issues);

making full searches of any public registers regarding the site and adjacent land.
One should make enquiries of these bodies regarding any:

- information held by them about the site, any investigations or inspections made of it or adjacent land, details of any accidents, incidents or complaints and an indication of whether there is any intention to serve any notices in respect of the land;
- accidents, incidents and complaints by regulators or others relating to adjacent land.

Searches from commercial search companies (see Chapter 5) will usually include details obtainable from the public registers.

Environment Agency searches

The Environment Agency, via its website (**www.environment-agency.gov.uk**), provides all data in relation to its statutory functions – water resource management, flooding and IPC, PPC and waste management regulation being the main ones.

However, Agency data does not include historic site information, nor any information about past or current activity which may be potentially polluting if it is outside the legally-regulated industry sectors, so the Agency data is not as all-encompassing as one might like and may not be as good as that available from other providers.

Local authority searches

The enquiries added to form CON 29R as a result of consultations between the Law Society and local authorities now seek to identify all the information which a local authority is required to compile for the purposes of the official registers which they have to maintain under EPA 1990, Part IIA. It also asks whether the authority has notified, or has decided to notify, anyone of its determination that land is contaminated or whether the property is, or is to be put, on the registers held under Part IIA.

However, information need only be revealed in answer to CON 29R if notifications are made that the authority deems the land to be contaminated or if formal action is taken in respect of land actually designated as contaminated. If land is not deemed to be contaminated within the strict meaning of Part IIA, no information need be revealed in answer to the new enquiries.

However, information regarding the actual state of the land (albeit not yet 'contaminated') may be in the possession of the authority and may be of interest to a purchaser. In such cases, consideration should be given to widening the scope of the enquiry and the wording of the new questions.

Information, in the widest sense, is to be made publicly available under the terms of the Environmental Information Regulations 2004 (and any later re-enactments thereof). The time limit for response is reduced from two months under the old predecessor regulations to 20 days as mentioned in **5.2.1**.

Practitioners could try questions modelled on the precedents set out in Appendix A4.

Note that the desirability of undertaking searches in relation to planning uses and applications in the neighbourhood is enhanced with the availability of search reports which provide this information.

6.4.5   Step 4: Undertake independent site history investigations

If little or no meaningful response is forthcoming from the enquiries and searches, then one must take a view on whether to take any further investigatory steps.

These may include:

- desktop studies of the site involving consideration of old maps, plans, photographs and local physical and anecdotal evidence, to evaluate potential risks;
- consideration of contaminated land profiles (obtainable from a number of sources) which outline the usual types of contamination associated with certain types of land use (e.g. landfill, railway yards, gasworks, munitions factories, etc.);
- obtaining a site investigation report from a commercial search company.

The commercial environmental data search companies have, over recent years, developed a range of information-based searches which condense in an easily-readable and accessible format all the information currently available from statutory and regulatory bodies, as well as information regarding past land-use and potential contamination risks from industrial and commercial usage. They also include information on flooding, radon, subsidence and past-infilled ground. Such searches are available quite cheaply and can be obtained very quickly indeed, offering little or no delay to the conveyancing process. Nowhere else can so much information be obtained so readily and cost-effectively, enabling a practitioner to give at least an initial view to a client on the risks posed by their new purchase.

Reports also provide an initial risk assessment of the information data. Different providers offer different forms of risk assessment on whether the issues revealed in the search are likely to result in the property being classified as contaminated land within the meaning of EPA 1990, Part IIA and, often, whether there is likely to be any effect on the value of the property – a matter of prime concern to the client and lender alike.

These professional opinions give a degree of comfort to those buying such reports, removing, in most cases, any concerns regarding blight and relieving the conveyancer from expressing a specialist view he may feel ill-at-ease about.

However, practitioners should note that any such assessment can be and is based purely on the publicly available information, as no actual site assessment is undertaken, and there are matters contained in the report which may affect a client's decision which are not taken into account in the risk assessment at all. Moreover, no mapping or information service would be able to tell whether there had been a spillage of domestic heating oil in the back garden – enquiries of the seller or the local authority may be necessary here.

Practitioners should satisfy themselves that their chosen provider and product is as comprehensive, up-to-date and as detailed as possible, as well as understanding the types of information presented and the manner of presentation, in order to increase familiarity with the product and to facilitate the explanation of the information to a client.

The lender's position

As already noted, there was some confusion as to the lender's position with regard to the need to refer commercial environmental reports to the lender (see the Law Society's *Gazette*, 31 August 2001).

On the one hand, lenders do not wish to be inundated with environmental information but, on the other hand, they demand that practitioners undertake all 'necessary and appropriate searches' and would wish the conveyancer to make them aware if there is a potential risk to the loan. Current indications are that lenders only wish to be informed of problems if there is 'independent evidence of a significant environmental risk'.

The CML Handbook has been updated frequently since and states in para. 5.2.4 that, unless practitioners are specifically instructed, in Part 2 of the standard instructions, to undertake an environmental search, there is no need to undertake one on behalf of the lender. However, the general view is that if any matters emerge which could have been identified by such a report, a practitioner may have some explaining to do. One could look to the CML's formerly stated stance on mining searches for a better guide to best practice for environmental searches. This, before its removal, effectively said, 'do a search if you think it appropriate, inform us if you find anything, but don't tell us if the search is clear'.

Moreover, it is still best practice to consider undertaking one on behalf of the borrower client, and if any entries are revealed that would be of concern to a lender, the practitioner would still be under a duty to report that feature.

6.4.6 I've received my report – what next?

For a comprehensive discussion of the interpretation of search reports, see Chapter 5.

Clear search or no perceived problem

In many cases, the search will reveal no entries of any concern whatsoever, and the practitioner can advise the client to proceed, safe in the knowledge that the information is as accurate and reliable as modern mapping and information-gathering techniques can make it. Keeping the search with the file or deeds will assist if future reference needs to be made in relation to the information disclosed. There would be no need to contact the lender over such matters.

Beware of over-reliance on the wording of the Risk Assessment Certificate.

Searches revealing entries

In some cases, the search will reveal entries that may be of some concern to a purchaser client. The practitioner should discuss these issues with the client to decide how to proceed, if necessary following consideration of any risk assessment, to ascertain the degree of risk posed by a revealed entry.

The outline steps, discussed more fully in **5.5.4**, are:

1 Check the entries, noting any positive ones.
2 Check the 'additional information' in the report to discover the nature of the identified risks.
3 Check the identity of the authority or agency that provided the data relating to the entry in the 'useful contacts' section of the report.
4 Contact the local authority for any further information it may have regarding the entry, as the authority will have assessed its area for the purposes of Part IIA and may have records of steps taken by a developer to make the land safe which would avoid, in most cases, the need for a site investigation. Enquiries could also be directed towards the developer.
5 Contact other specialist advisers if risks still remain.
6 Consider any 'further action' points in search report (if provided).

There are several important points to remember.

- Certain entries always carry an inherent degree of risk with them, and certain types of land-use have particular contaminating characteristics. For example, infilled land may be structurally unstable, landfill sites may give rise to methane gas generation, old gasworks may have contaminated the land with tars and other chemicals and petrol stations may have leaking underground storage tanks. The nearer to the site the identified entry, the greater the risk that some problem may occur on the site in question.
- The mere fact that information reveals an entry, or a potentially contaminative historical use, does not *necessarily* mean that there is a problem with the land, merely that there *may* be, and this possibility may require further investigation.
- The decision whether to proceed, undertake further investigations or withdraw must be the client's, and it will frequently depend on factors unrelated to the environmental information revealed by the search. Factors such as the cost of

the further investigations, the difficulty and delay involved in undertaking them, the accuracy and helpfulness of the further information revealed, the general timescale of the transaction and the client's attitude to risk will all influence the decision.

- It cannot be over-emphasised that until the *actual* extent of a potential problem is investigated and revealed by an intrusive ground investigation, no practitioner can fully advise on its implications, and reports are only designed to provide the information to enable practitioners to identify the next questions. This is highly unlikely ever to be undertaken in a routine domestic transaction, and thus the client will ultimately be required to take a view on the basis of information alone. The lawyer is in no position to do anything beyond accumulating the information, explaining its potential significance and leaving the client to make a suitably advised decision.

Practitioners should develop a range of questions which can be directed to the relevant bodies to elicit any further information that may be relevant should the client wish to proceed with further investigations. Not knowing where to turn for additional help, or not knowing the questions to ask, will cause delay. See Appendix A6 for some precedents.

It may be sensible to undertake the environmental search before the local authority search, so that any additional, specific queries can be added to the local authority search form prior to its submission at the start of the transaction.

If the property which is the subject of the report is to be charged as security for a loan, the practitioner should contact the lender to report the findings and indicate (if it be the case) that further investigations are ongoing. Practitioners should ask the lender whether it requires any further steps to be taken. The report should only be sent to the lender with a recommendation that it is referred to the lender's valuer for consideration in extreme cases. The report should be kept with the title deeds, along with other important searches.

6.4.7 Step 5: Initiate a full site investigation by environmental consultants

This would be rare in most routine residential cases, as the nature or value of the transaction would not usually justify the cost involved. It may, however, be relevant on larger sites. Additionally, the client may prefer to take the risk and proceed regardless.

Where there is a substantial risk of contamination, or a high-net-worth client is considering a substantial purchase, the investigation costs may well be acceptable. For sites with a lower degree of *prima facie* risk, the client may prefer to limit the investigation to obtaining an initial screening report. If the report reveals problems that need further investigation, then a thorough site survey involving test boreholes and sampling may be advisable (particularly on 'hot spots').

In that event, the solicitor should be consulted regarding the terms of engagement of the environmental consultant to ensure that the client gets a report which is useful and reliable as a basis for risk assessment.

In the majority of cases, if the risk is so great as to justify expense of this type, the client would be better advised to withdraw.

6.4.8 Step 6: Consider contractual protections against seller

These may include:

- amending conditions in Standard Conditions of Sale, especially condition 3 (regarding compliance by the buyer with public requirements, with indemnity to seller);
- reducing the price to take account of the potential liability;
- requiring remediation by the seller before completion;
- obtaining insurance cover.

Clearly, this is a matter for the relative bargaining power of the parties, but it would be rare indeed for any of the more sophisticated commercial drafting devices – warranties, indemnities, capped and phased indemnities – to find their way into domestic conveyancing documentation.

Amendment of Standard Conditions of Sale

Condition 3 requires that the buyer bear the cost of complying with any outstanding public requirement, defined, among other things, as a notice served by a body of competent authority, with an indemnity to the seller for such costs. This condition should either be deleted, or it should be made clear that this provision is not to be taken as an 'agreement on liabilities' for the purposes of EPA 1990, Part IIA.

New insurance

Several players in the insurance market now offer insurance products designed to cover the risk that land may be determined to be contaminated within the meaning of Part IIA. As to the availability and features of domestic contaminated land insurance, see Chapter 13 for a fuller discussion.

6.4.9 Withdrawal from the purchase

At any stage in the above process, a buyer must be prepared to walk away from the deal if:

- the risks are too great;
- the information is too hard to find; or
- the seller is too resistant to negotiation.

This may well occur earlier in the process than in the commercial world.

6.5 ADVICE TO SELLERS

This chapter has so far concentrated on the position of a purchaser and his solicitor. From the seller's point of view, achieving a clean break from the liabilities attaching to a site may not always be possible.

In particular, liability may continue for:

- breaches of the consents committed while the seller was the site owner and operator (commercial sites only);
- breaches of waste legislation while in possession (commercial sites only);
- contaminated land (on the person who originally caused or knowingly permitted substances to be on the site pre-sale) (commercial and residential sites);
- statutory nuisances caused or continued (commercial and residential sites);
- water pollution offences caused or knowingly permitted (commercial and residential sites);
- sewerage discharge offences (commercial sites only);
- civil liability (as co-defendant for damage caused or continued during the period of ownership) (commercial and residential sites).

In respect of most of these liabilities (all save for contaminated land), there is no easy way to shift liability onto a purchaser other than by getting the purchaser to give indemnities, which is unlikely.

A more important strategy is to ensure (perhaps by incoming and outgoing audits) what the state of play is when the site is sold on, so as to be able to successfully determine who did in fact cause a pollution incident, should there ever be a dispute.

As far as contaminated land is concerned, sellers should take close note of those clauses in the Guidance Notes that would exclude a seller from liability if:

- contract documents specifically reject the payment (often in the form of a price reduction) of a specific sum for remediation;
- the land is sold in circumstances where full information is provided to the buyer about the contamination on the site;
- the seller and buyer agree on a contractual formula for dealing with any liabilities which emerge;

and ensure that the paperwork is drafted in such a way as to maximise the chance of exclusion.

CHAPTER 7

Commercial property transactions

7.1 INTRODUCTION

This chapter, of necessity, repeats much of what has already been covered in Chapter 6, but focuses attention on those (often wider) issues of relevance in commercial property matters. Commercial property practitioners have also always had a difficult line to tread providing a cost-effective service to the client, which deals with all the likely issues of concern without costing the client an unnecessary fortune or leaving the solicitor guilty of negligence.

That position was not improved by the publication in June 2001 of the Law Society's Contaminated Land Warning Card which requires practitioners to consider 'in every transaction . . . whether contamination is an issue' and sets out some steps to deal with the salient issues which should be considered in all cases.

Practitioners must take these matters on board, and take steps to assist clients to understand and deal with relevant environmental issues in any land transaction. Whether the client perceives the need for such steps or not, it is now a requirement that such matters are addressed, with the attendant implications for the overall cost of the transaction and its timescale.

Of particular concern to solicitor and client alike are the potential environmental risks that:

- a costly legal liability may be inherited by a purchaser of a site;
- the value of a property or site may be adversely affected, even to the point of it being unsaleable, as a consequence of some actual or perceived environmental problem with the site or neighbouring property; or
- some non-legal effects may be felt, such as health effects, structural problems, flooding or subsidence.

As the previous chapters have explained, the network of environmental liabilities is complex, and the price that buyers will pay for sites which they know or believe to be polluted is very volatile. Purchasers with experience of certain foreign jurisdictions may be particularly sensitised to the issue. These risks should not therefore be ignored. The legislation applies with equal rigour to both commercial and domestic transactions so all practitioners must take care.

It is essential, however, to keep matters in perspective. Having said that, a reasonable starting point in commercial cases will be to assume that pretty much all commercial property could have some sort of contaminated history, and that to assume the site is polluted until proven otherwise is a good position to adopt.

Admittedly, it is hard to see how a leased, second-floor, city centre office suite may be affected but even there, amenity issues from adjacent sites and clean-up cost clawback via the service charge may be live issues.

The key problem is in spotting the main risks and issues, as environmental problems are not geographically discrete (in the way mining activity or radon gas are), it can take a long time for creeping pollution problems to emerge and often they are not visible. The fact that a site is green, and a field, does not make it a greenfield site.

Whilst not strictly part of a lawyer's remit, such non-legal factors (flooding, invasive weeds, public health issues, etc.) are also matters which a client may expect an adviser to deal with, and whilst it is not suggested that a failure to do so would be professionally negligent, a client may nevertheless feel let down if such matters are not pointed out at some stage, and many clients perceive the solicitor as being the adviser most likely to have their interests at heart.

Solicitors and their clients should, however, take comfort from the fact that, with some relatively cheap and easy steps, an adequate (if not a perfect) view can be taken of the risks involved in any transaction, which can then be used to inform the decision whether to proceed at all and, if so, with what additional protections. Inevitably, though, it is likely that a full-blown environmental investigation of the site will be required in all but the most benign of cases.

7.2 POTENTIAL PROBLEMS IN COMMERCIAL REAL ESTATE

7.2.1 Criminal liabilities

A purchaser can find themselves with criminal liability should there be significant problems at a site. Further discussion of these liabilities can be found in Chapter 1 but the following deal with the main areas of concern.

Nature conservation regime

Offences arise under the nature conservation regime in relation to actions that adversely affect protected species or their habitats, or designated eco-systems (WCA 1981, Parts I and II, as amended by the Countryside and Rights of Way Act 2000).

The offences involve damage – deliberately or recklessly caused – to protected species and eco-systems. Any industrial activity, or the development of an old industrial site, may have to be undertaken with special care to avoid such harm being caused.

It would be useful to know from the nature conservation bodies whether such designations have been made in the area of the target property. This information would be included in most, if not all, environmental data searches.

Environmental permitting

Offences and liabilities exist under the Environmental Permitting Regulations. The offences under the EP regime are related to carrying on prescribed processes or activities, such as chemical and metal manufacture. It is an offence to operate such a process without, or in breach of, a permit to do so. The conditions of the permit carry many house-keeping requirements regarding the operation of the plant.

For commercial buyers, it is essential to make an inspection of the public registers if the buyer is taking over the site as a going concern and intending to carry on the process, in order to ensure the transfer of the permit and the purchaser's ability to meet all its conditions. Warranties and indemnities regarding past operations would be commonplace.

If merely acquiring the site after operations have ceased, a run-down of the past track record of the site will assist in assessing the risk posed by the site, especially if any accidents or incidents are recorded.

This information is available from the permitting body – the Environment Agency or local authority. This information would be included in most if not all environmental data searches.

Controlled waste

The waste offences largely involve the disposal of waste on a site without, or in breach of, a licence (EPA 1990, s.33). This mainly, though not exclusively, relates to operative landfill sites, incinerators and treatment plants.

For commercial buyers, it is essential to make an inspection of the public registers if one is taking over the site as a going concern and intending to carry on the process, in order to ensure the transfer of the permit and the purchaser's ability to meet all its conditions. Warranties and indemnities regarding past operations would be commonplace.

If merely acquiring the site, after operations have ceased, a run-down of the past track record of the site will assist in assessing the risk posed by the site, especially if any accidents or incidents are recorded.

This information is available from the permitting body – the Environment Agency. This information would be included in most, if not all, environmental data searches.

For buyers of a closed landfill site, it is unlikely that any action would be taken against them in respect of historic events on the site, as there are defences in EPA 1990, Part II to such prosecutions available for innocent occupiers (but see Part IIA of that Act).

Contaminated land

Offences arise following failure to remediate contaminated land when instructed to do so (EPA 1990, Part IIA). The contamination may come about as a result of substances already in the land at completion, which are giving rise to a risk of significant harm to persons or things nearby. For purchasers, it is important to recognise that liability for clean up can arise from historic contamination which occurred long before they purchased the site.

This may catch such commonplace matters as historic leakages of liquids from storage tanks, washings from site plant and equipment, spillages from delivery wagons, or wastes and liquids being deposited (deliberately or inadvertently) on site from a potentially contaminative industrial process or other historic land use.

If the original polluter of the land cannot be found, the current owner or occupier may be served with a remediation notice requiring the land to be cleaned up. An offence is committed if he fails to comply, and the authorities can do the necessary works themselves and recover the costs from the person served with the notice.

A further problem is that a purchaser can himself qualify as the 'original polluter'. This is because the original polluter is defined as 'any of the persons who [caused or] knowingly permitted the [contaminating substances] to be in, on or under the land'. Allowing something to remain on land if you could remove it can amount to permitting it to be on the land.

Actual knowledge of the contamination, turning a blind eye to an obvious risk of contamination or failing to make enquiries for fear of discovering the truth would all amount to having the required knowledge. Accordingly, if buyers knew, or ought to have known or realised, or could have found out, that there was contamination on the site, they may be caught. This must be true in respect of most, if not all, commercial sites.

There may also be leakages of substances onto the ground after completion in respect of which the purchaser client may be deemed to be the 'original polluter' of the land.

The provisions relating to contaminated land are complex but, in essence, commercial purchasers should take comfort from the fact that:

- only the most seriously polluted sites are likely to be designated as contaminated;
- most remediation will have been addressed when the site was last developed (if this has occurred in the last three to five years), though this should not be taken for granted;
- remediation strategies must be cost-effective;
- liability is likely to be shared with others (e.g. predecessors in title).

On the other hand, a series of exclusionary tests to be applied by the authorities may result in the seller of property no longer being required to share the cost of remediation if the purchaser knew about the contamination of the site at completion. This provision may be interpreted as meaning that a purchaser is better off buying in ignorance of the state of the site, but this cannot be good practice.

Further exclusions take a seller out of the line of fire if a reduction in the purchase price was negotiated to take account of particular contamination and remediation.

These exclusions are likely to be relevant in most commercial transactions, the effect being that liability for contamination tends to run with the land. Buyers should beware.

Details of which sites are designated as contaminated would be available from the local authority (or Environment Agency, if a special site). This information would be included in all environmental data searches.

Statutory nuisances

Statutory nuisances are noises, smells, dust, odour, effluvia or other emissions which may be a pollution or health risk. These provisions have been interpreted in several recent cases as being limited to localised irritants, i.e. things which annoy the neighbours.

Buyers of land can be served with abatement notices in respect of any nuisances continuing after the date of purchase as it could be said that they are the person responsible for the continuing nuisance.

Otherwise, they may be liable as owner or occupier if the person responsible cannot be found.

An offence is committed if they fail to comply with any abatement notice (EPA 1990, s.80), and clean-up works can be undertaken and the costs recovered.

This information is available from the regulatory body – the local authority. This information would be included in most, if not all, environmental data searches.

Pollution of controlled waters

There are two main water pollution offences:

- to cause or knowingly permit a water discharge activity or a groundwater activity other than for an exempt facility (Environmental Permitting Regulations, reg.38(1)); and
- to fail to clean up water pollution when instructed to do so (WRA, s.161A).

If any polluting matter gets into 'controlled waters' (virtually any watercourse other than a sewer), an offence is committed, unless a discharge consent has been obtained for it. Such consents are necessary for point discharges and for diffuse discharges caused by spreading activities by virtue of the Groundwater Regulations 1998, SI 1998/2746.

Any deliberate or inadvertent leakages of substances from a site which get into watercourses, either directly or via the drainage system, may give rise to a liability. No intention to commit the offence need be shown, only a causal chain of events from the activities of the owner on-site leading to the emission into the waters.

The same problems afflict buyers with regard to water pollution offences occurring before completion but persisting afterwards, as it may be said that the buyer has knowingly permitted the offence to continue.

So, if buyers ought to have known or realised, or could have found out, that there was a possibility of water pollution occurring from the site, they may be caught.

Information regarding discharge consents and past pollution incidents is available from the licensing body – the Environment Agency. This information would be included in most, if not all, environmental data searches.

Sewers

An offence relating to sewers is committed by discharging trade effluent to a sewer without, or in breach of, a licence (WIA 1991, s.118). This offence relates to ongoing discharges of trade effluent to a sewer for an operative site and would only really be relevant when buying a business as a going concern, though it is conceivable that if substances are getting into the sewerage system by migration or leakage, an offence could be committed.

Almost exclusively relevant to the purchase of a going concern, information regarding discharge consents is available from the licensing body for the sewerage undertaker. This information would be included in most, if not all, environmental data searches.

7.2.2 Civil liabilities

A purchaser of land can find themselves liable to third parties under civil law. Such liability can arise in a number of ways, not least for the ongoing migration of contamination from the property onto a neighbouring site. A more detailed discussion on the potential liabilities can be found in Chapter 1.

The most likely liability arises from the tort of nuisance. See *Cambridge Water* v. *Eastern Counties Leather* [1994] 2 AC 264.

Purchasers of land giving rise to a nuisance will be liable for continuing nuisances created by predecessors in title if they knew, or ought to have known, of the nuisance, could reasonably have foreseen it causing harm, and could have taken reasonable steps to prevent or abate it, but failed to do so (*Sedleigh-Denfield* v. *O'Callaghan* [1940] AC 880).

Purchasers must therefore take any such reasonable steps to stop ongoing pollution if they are to avoid such liability at some point in the future. This may be a particular risk in development projects, where remediation of adverse ground conditions is likely to be a condition of planning consent, and thus, a perfectly reasonable set of steps to take. If not taken adequately or properly, and pollution ensues, an action may lie in civil law.

7.2.3 Clean-up liabilities

A liability for clean up can arise through:

- environmental permitting;
- controlled waste (EPA 1990, s.59);
- contaminated land (EPA 1990, Part IIA);
- statutory nuisances (EPA 1990, s.81);
- water pollution (WRA 1991, s.161A).

All these powers apply in circumstances where an offence has been committed, a notice has been served on the owner of the land, and he has failed to comply with it.

The authorities may enter onto the site and undertake any necessary works, and recover the cost from the person served with the notice.

7.2.4 Miscellaneous provisions

Miscellaneous provisions that may be relevant include:

- the Explosives Act 1875;
- the Nuclear Installations Act 1969;
- the Planning (Hazardous Substances) Act 1990; and
- the Radioactive Substances Act 1993.

The keeping, use, accumulation and disposal of radioactive substances in Great Britain is regulated by the Radioactive Substances Act 1993. The main purpose of this Act is to provide radiation protection to members of the public.

Storage of hazardous substances relates to the granting of consents under the Planning (Hazardous Substances) Act 1990. Hazardous substance consents are designed to ensure that hazardous substances can be kept or used in significant quantities, only after the responsible authorities have had the opportunity to assess the risk to surrounding areas.

Under the COMAH Regulations, sites storing above specified amounts of hazardous substances and those carrying out particularly toxic or hazardous activities must provide information to the public on the nature of the hazard and action to be taken in the event of an accident. The Regulations mainly apply to chemical and petrochemical industries and to those that produce or use substances with flammable, toxic or explosive properties.

The Explosives Act 1875 controls the registration, storage and supply of various categories of explosive substances to ensure public safety and security. All premises where explosives are stored must be registered.

Public records are available from the local authority and HSE. This information would be included in most, if not all, environmental data searches.

7.2.5 Related legal issues

Purchasers and their advisers should be aware that the regulatory and licensing bodies only keep and retain information regarding the legal regimes which they police. Most of these only came into being with the advent of EPA 1990, and thus only date back some 20 years. Moreover, they only apply to those activities designated for regulation under the legislation.

If a commercial purchaser wanted to fully assess the potential for contamination in the target site, enquiries would need to be made about those potentially contaminative uses of the site that either pre-date, or are not included in, the legal regimes mentioned above.

Such enquiries would need to centre on trade journals, or a study of old OS maps which may reveal past uses. Such information may be readily available from a commercial data provider.

Any development of the site will need to address issues of contamination as part of the planning requirements, and clean-up and development operations may themselves constitute a regulated activity requiring licensing or authorisation, or may create statutory nuisances or a nuisance actionable in civil law (see Chapter 8).

7.2.6 Non-legal issues

In addition to the legal liabilities outlined, commercial buyers should also be made aware of the following, non-legal implications, which may have a bearing on the long-term viability and value of the site:

- health effects from the presence of pollutants, or possibly naturally-occurring substances such as radon gas or Japanese knotweed;
- stability issues relating to past-infilled land;
- adjacent to floodplains and other potential flooding sources;
- proximity of overhead power lines or mobile phone masts;
- market perceptions regarding any substances left on-site as part of the development (however well-contained);
- delay, inconvenience and wasted costs involved in dealing with problems to the satisfaction of the planning authority and eventual purchasers.

7.3 LAW SOCIETY'S CONTAMINATED LAND WARNING CARD

The Warning Card was issued by the Law Society in June 2001, with copies being distributed to the profession and the full text, reproduced in Appendix B, was published in the *Gazette* in July 2001.

The feeling within the Society was that there was a potential negligence liability for solicitors who failed to address relevant issues, and that guidance was therefore required.

The issue seems to be that the legal profession is the only one with PII cover for environmental matters, and thus a prime target for litigation.

The Warning Card requires practitioners to 'consider whether contamination is an issue' in every transaction.

This guidance is not intended to be a professional requirement, but can be taken into account in assessing negligence on the part of a practitioner in any given case.

It suggests, broadly, six steps to follow in every case:

STEP 1   Advise the client of the potential for problems.

STEP 2   Make full enquiries of the seller.

STEP 3   Make enquiries of the statutory and regulatory bodies.

STEP 4   Undertake independent site history investigations.

STEP 5   Consider a full site investigation by environmental consultants.

STEP 6   Consider contractual or other protections.

7.4   COMMERCIAL FREEHOLD TRANSACTIONS

7.4.1   The steps to take

All land is second hand, so when buying property, it is essential to bear in mind – and provide for – the possibility that the buyer will inherit some or all of the liabilities attaching to the site, or suffer a diminution in value in the future. It is not always the polluter who pays, but occasionally the current owner, so purchasers have to be vigilant; *caveat emptor* is still very much appropriate.

The worst thing a buyer – or his legal adviser – can do, is ignore the environmental issue. Ignorance of the law has never been a defence; ignorance of the fact of pollution, or the consequences of it, may not be a defence either.

Many professional advisers called in to advise on environmental aspects of a transaction may not be covered for such advice under their professional indemnity policies. This is especially true of the surveying profession, who will need specific instruction (and top-up PII cover) before they are able to assist in advising on environmental matters.

To avoid allegations of negligence, therefore, one should:

- alert the client to the fact that there may be problems associated with a site (whether in the form of liabilities or decreased valuation);
- discuss with the client the steps which can then be taken to further assess the scale of the problem, and to solve it in the most cost-effective way.

Often, the perception of the environmental risks on a site is worse than the reality, and steps to alleviate or remove the problem may actually be less costly than imagined, and thus a less significant matter.

A choice will need to be made by the client as to how much to spend on the investigations, though commercial search organisations will now provide informative studies quite cheaply, and these should perhaps now be routinely suggested to a purchaser.

Such searches will comprise a desktop study of past land use in the area, a search of public records and a *prima facie* indication of levels of potential risk associated with the site. This information is collated from old OS information and other database sources. Average cost is in the order of £150–£250 but may be cheaper.

Information revealed by these steps will give a much clearer idea of the potential risk, which can then be pursued in a much more targeted way with the seller. The buyer can then decide whether the transaction will proceed and, if so, with what terms, assurances, price adjustments or pre-completion remediation works.

Information of this sort is now a requirement of any application for planning consent (see Chapter 9).

7.4.2 Step 1: Advise the client of the potential for problems

It is essential not to overstate the environmental risks, but to ignore them completely is potentially negligent. Having said that, most commercial clients will already be alive to the main concerns, and may already have commissioned an environmental investigation of some kind even before instructing solicitors. If this has not already occurred, the possible follow-up steps that could be taken to investigate further any likely risks and possible cost implications should be discussed with the client at the initial stage.

The client may not wish to pursue the point at all, in which case, solicitors should confirm the initial advice (and the fact that no investigations have been requested or made) to the client and any lender.

Compliance with the Warning Card should be achieved as long as the solicitor can be content that the client understands the full nature of the risks he is running before deciding not to pursue the point.

7.4.3 Step 2: Make full enquiries of the seller

Solicitors should consider including specific environmental enquiries in their standard pre-contract enquiries. Too many clearly irrelevant enquiries will often merely induce the seller to issue a blanket response indicating that the purchaser should 'rely on his own enquiries'. Specifically targeted enquiries generally get a better response.

The extent of the enquiries may well depend on the relative bargaining strengths of the parties, indications from pre-contract site surveys, and last (but not least) the client's budget. From the practitioner's point of view, it is essential that the client be told how much pollution investigation (if any) is covered by his budget at the outset.

As a reasonable minimum, enquiries should deal with:

- the need for, and compliance with, all consents, licences, authorisations and permits in relation to any activities or processes conducted on the site, etc.;
- any contact or disputes with the regulatory bodies;
- details of any pollution incidents or accidents affecting the site and copies of any reports. correspondence, court orders, notices (including, in particular, remediation, charging or works notices) or recommendations relating to such accidents or incidents and details of any remedial work carried out including certificates of satisfactory completion;
- details of any environmental impairment liability insurance or any application thereof (whether or not the proposal was accepted by the insurers);
- disclosure of any consultants' or other report on the environmental risk assessment of the property or the vendor's business;
- whether the seller is aware of any potentially contaminative current or previous use of the site or neighbouring sites. (The list of potentially contaminative uses set out in the first Department of the Environment Consultation Paper (3 May 1991) also provides an excellent checklist for the solicitor when perusing the title to a property.);
- whether the site or any adjoining sites have been used for landfill or waste disposal;
- details of previous owners or occupiers and activities carried on by them;
- what (if any) planning consents have been issued in respect of the site, what conditions they contained regarding contamination and its remediation, and details of any works carried out in compliance with it.

The Commercial Property Standard Enquiries (CPSE) are perfectly adequate for this purpose and their use is to be commended (see **http://property.practicallaw. com/6-502-2923**).

There are a number of possible responses to these enquiries:

(a) *Replies are forthcoming*: The replies may need specialist interpretation by surveyors or environmental consultants. Further, more detailed investigation may be needed of specific areas of concern.

(b) *The seller stonewalls*: If the seller issues the blanket 'not so far as the seller is aware, please rely on own investigations and surveys', the client must consider whether to undertake alternative investigations of his own.

7.4.4   Step 3: Make enquiries of the statutory and regulatory bodies

General

The main bodies to contact are:

- Natural England (and their Northern Irish, Scottish and Welsh equivalents) (nature conservation designations);
- the Environment Agency (licences, registers and prosecutions);

- the local authority (registers and information on contaminated land and any relevant planning consents, hazardous substance information);
- the HSE (incidents and accidents);
- sewerage undertakers (consents and registers);
- British Coal (mining activities and abandoned mine leakage issues);

making full searches of any public registers regarding the site and adjacent land.

One should also make enquiries of these bodies regarding any:

- information held by them about the site, any investigations or inspections made of it or adjacent land, details of any accidents, incidents or complaints and an indication of whether there is any intention to serve any notices in respect of the land; and
- accidents, incidents and complaints by regulators or others relating to adjacent land.

Searches from commercial search companies (see Chapter 5) will usually include details obtainable from the public registers.

Local authority searches

The enquiries added to form CON 29R in 2007 as a result of consultations between the Law Society and local authorities now seek to identify all the information that a local authority is required to compile for the purposes of the official registers which they have to maintain under EPA 1990, Part IIA. It also asks whether the authority has notified anyone of its determination that land is contaminated or whether the property is on the registers held under Part IIA.

However, information need only be revealed in answer to CON 29R if notifications are made that the authority deems the land to be contaminated or if formal action is taken in respect of land actually designated as contaminated. If land is not deemed to be contaminated within the strict meaning of Part IIA, no information need be revealed in answer to the new enquiries.

However, information regarding the actual state of the land (albeit not yet 'contaminated') may be in the possession of the authority and may be of interest to a purchaser. In such cases, consideration should be given to widening the scope of the enquiry and the wording of the new questions.

Information, in the widest sense, is to be made publicly available under the terms of the Environmental Information Regulations 2004 (and any later re-enactments thereof). The time limit for response is reduced from two months under the old predecessor regulations to 20 days as mentioned in **5.2.1**.

Practitioners could try questions modelled on those set out in Appendix A4.

Note that the desirability of undertaking searches in relation to planning policies, emerging local plans, uses and applications in the neighbourhood is enhanced with the availability of search reports which provide this information.

7.4.5   Step 4: Undertake independent site history investigations

If little or no meaningful response is forthcoming from the enquiries and searches, then one must take a view on whether to take any further investigatory steps.

These may include:

- desktop studies of the site involving consideration of old maps, plans, photographs and local physical and anecdotal evidence, to evaluate potential risks;
- consideration of contaminated land profiles (obtainable from a number of sources) which outline the usual types of contamination associated with certain types of land use (e.g. landfill, railway yards, gasworks, munitions factories, etc.);
- obtaining an environmental screening report from a commercial search company.

The commercial environmental data search companies have, over recent years, developed a range of information-based searches which condense in an easily-readable and accessible format all the information currently available from statutory and regulatory bodies, as well as information regarding past land-use and potential contamination risks from industrial and commercial usage. They also include information on flooding, radon, subsidence, past infilled ground, overhead power-lines and the location of radioactive and explosive substances. They can be supplemented by additional, more detailed reports relating to:

- flooding;
- planning; and
- land stability,

though some of these enhanced products may not be available on commercial property, or sites above a certain dimensional area.

Such searches are available for around £150–£300 and can be obtained very quickly indeed, offering little or no delay to the conveyancing process.

In addition, different providers offer different forms of risk assessment on whether the issues revealed in the search are likely to result in the property being classified as contaminated land within the meaning of EPA 1990 Part IIA and, often, whether there is likely to be any effect on the value of the property, a matter of prime concern to the client and lender alike.

These professional opinions give a degree of comfort to those buying such reports, removing, in most cases, any concerns regarding blight and relieving the conveyancer from expressing a specialist view he may feel ill-at-ease about.

However, practitioners should note that any such assessment can be, and is, based purely on the publicly available information, as no actual site assessment is undertaken, and there are matters contained in the report which may affect a client's decision which are not taken into account in the risk assessment at all. Moreover, no mapping or information service would be able to tell whether there had been any spillage, incidents or accidents on-site or nearby, for example, and enquiries of the seller or the local authority may be necessary here.

Some report providers also offer a one-stop service, encompassing information, a professional assessment and further consultancy relating to site-specific solutions at an enhanced price and these comprehensive providers may be more attractive to the practitioner.

The lender's position

As noted in Chapter 13, the stance of the commercial lender is usually to require an exhaustive site inspection, rather than to be content with a basic screening report only. A screening report may nonetheless pinpoint areas of particular concern and should be regarded as a pre-requisite of any search or investigation on the site itself.

7.4.6 I've received my report – what next?

Clear search or no perceived problem

In some, rare cases, the search will reveal no entries of any concern whatsoever, and the practitioner can advise the client to proceed, safe in the knowledge that the information is as accurate and reliable as modern mapping and information-gathering techniques can make it. There would be no need to contact the lender over such matters.

Beware of over-reliance on the wording of the Risk Assessment Certificate.

Searches revealing entries

In most cases, the search will reveal entries that may be of some concern to a purchaser client. The practitioner should discuss these issues with the client to decide how to proceed, if necessary following consideration of any risk assessment, to ascertain the degree of risk posed by a revealed entry.

The outline steps are:

1. Check the entries, noting any positive ones.
2. Check the 'additional information' in the report to discover the nature of the identified risks.
3. Check the identity of the authority or Agency that provided the data relating to the entry in the 'useful contacts' section of the report.
4. Contact the local authority for any further information it may have regarding the entry, as the authority will have assessed its area for the purposes of Part IIA and may have records of the steps taken by any earlier developer to make the land safe which would avoid, in most cases, the need for a site investigation. Enquiries could be directed towards any earlier developer, too.

5.   Contact other specialist advisers if risks still remain – to instruct an environmental consultant or engineer would be most likely.

6.   Consider any 'further action' points in the search report (if provided).

There are several important points to remember.

- Certain entries always carry an inherent degree of risk with them, and certain types of land-use have particular contaminating characteristics.

- For example, infilled land may be structurally unstable, landfill sites may give rise to methane gas generation, old gasworks may have contaminated the land with tars and other chemicals and petrol stations may have leaking underground storage tanks. The nearer to the site the identified entry, the greater the risk that some problem may occur on the site in question.

- The mere fact that information reveals an entry, or a potentially contaminative historical use, does not *necessarily* mean that there is a problem with the land, merely that there *may* be, and this possibility may require further investigation.

- The decision whether to proceed, undertake further investigations or withdraw must be the client's, and it will frequently depend on factors unrelated to the environmental information revealed by the search. Factors such as the cost of the further investigations, the difficulty and delay involved in undertaking them, the accuracy and helpfulness of the further information revealed, the general timescale of the transaction and the client's attitude to risk will all influence the decision.

- It cannot be over-emphasised that until the *actual* extent of a potential problem is investigated and revealed by an intrusive ground investigation, no practitioner can fully advise on its implications, and reports are only designed to provide the information to enable practitioners to identify the next questions. The lawyer is in no position to do anything beyond accumulating the information, explaining its potential significance and leaving the client to make a suitably advised decision.

Practitioners should develop a range of questions which can be directed to the relevant bodies to elicit any further information that may be relevant should the client wish to proceed with further investigations. Not knowing where to turn for additional help, or not knowing the questions to ask, would cause delay. See Appendix A6 for some suggested questions.

It may be sensible to undertake the environmental search before the local authority search, so that any additional, specific queries can be added to the local authority search form prior to its submission at the start of the transaction.

If the property which is the subject of the report is to be charged as security for a loan, the practitioner should contact the lender to report the findings and indicate (if it be the case) that further investigations are ongoing. Practitioners should ask the lender whether they require any further steps to be taken.

7.4.7 Step 5: Initiate a full site investigation by environmental consultants

This should be commonplace in most commercial cases, as the nature or value of the transaction, and the size of the potential liabilities, would usually justify the cost involved.

Clearly, the scope for detailed surveys of potentially contaminated sites is enormous. Clients will naturally wish to avoid unnecessary additional costs in relation to their acquisition. Nevertheless, the risks can be great and the costs of the detailed site investigation may well be justified in certain circumstances. It is estimated that full site investigation costs around £15,000 per hectare, but this is a very rough guess and the cost will depend on the precise problems.

As it may be in the seller's interests that the purchaser knows the state of the site at completion, an investigation at joint expense may be negotiable.

Where there is a substantial risk of contamination, the investigation costs may well be acceptable to an intending purchaser or lessee. For sites with a lower degree of *prima facie* risk, the client may prefer to limit the investigation to a 'desk survey'. If the desk survey reveals problems that need further investigation, then a thorough site survey involving test boreholes and sampling may be advisable (particularly on 'hot spots'). These might be identified by a commercial screening report from a commercial search company. For previous landfill sites, methane monitoring over a reasonable period of time may be required to ascertain whether the site or watercourses flowing from or under the site are carrying methane.

In these events, the solicitor should be consulted regarding the terms of engagement of the environmental consultant to ensure that the client gets a report which is useful and reliable as a basis for risk assessment. This is covered further in Chapter 10. To realise the potential cost of errors in the engagement process one need look no further than the £18.5m judgment in *English Partnership* v. *Mott MacDonald* (ENDS Report, April 1999), a dispute arising out of unclear terms of engagement. An 'outcomes' approach would be best – explaining clearly what the client expects from the consultant by way of deliverables should alleviate these problems.

It is important that the client is made aware of the risks of having no survey, or a survey that does not cover contamination issues.

Cost may not be the only factor limiting the extent of surveys and investigations on-site which may be possible; if the site is in current use and occupation and is covered by buildings, there may be difficulties in obtaining complete access for the purpose of carrying out the necessary physical examinations.

From the seller's perspective, requests for investigations of this nature are hard to resist and, from the point of view of Part IIA's exclusionary tests, much to be commended. Allowing access for investigations will attach the large commercial buyer of property with all the knowledge of on-site contamination which an investigation would reveal – even if none is actually conducted. Access agreements would be commonplace, however, and the basic terms on which investigations should be permitted should include requirements to make good any works or damage undertaken on the site (trial pits, boreholes, etc.), providing copies of any reports to the seller, limited circulation of the reports within the buyer's organisation, use of the report for a limited range of purposes and provision for destruction of the report and all copies in the event of the transaction not going ahead. It is now increasingly common for indemnities to be sought by a seller – and therefore also by the buyer client – against any liabilities triggered by the investigation itself.

7.4.8 Step 6: Consider contractual protections against seller

These may include:

* requiring the seller to make a specifically quantified and earmarked payment or price reduction, to take account of the potential liability;
* requiring the seller to provide full information about the contamination to the buyer in the contract;
* agreeing a formula whereby remediation costs are shared between potential polluters;
* seeking appropriate warranties as to the state of the site at completion;
* seeking an indemnity against future liabilities or reductions in value due to the state of the land at completion;
* requiring remediation by the seller before completion;
* obtaining assignment of any environmental insurance policies which may cover the site (or obtaining fresh cover).

This is a matter for the relative bargaining power of the parties. It is increasingly common for buyers or lessees to insist upon warranties and indemnities in respect of contamination issues. The liabilities that can arise on pollution incidents can be heavy and therefore the value of such contractual terms may be limited by the financial means of the seller or any guarantor.

Specific payments or price reductions

The buyer may seek a reduction in the price (as opposed to a retention) to cover the cost of remediation or clean up, or any perceived blighting effect on value. Alternatively, the buyer may want the seller to make a payment towards the cost of remediation.

The buyer should be aware that if such payments are made, this may have the effect of removing the seller from the category of persons eligible to receive a remediation notice in respect of contaminated land. If this occurs, the buyer would have to foot the seller's share of any clean-up costs, in addition to any liability of its own.

Buyers may not wish this to occur (though a seller will) and should therefore note the following.

For a price reduction to be sufficient to count as a 'relevant payment' for remediation so as to exclude the seller from the category of appropriate persons for receipt of a remediation notice, it must be explicitly stated in the contract that the reduction is for the purpose of particular remediation in respect of specific contamination. Indeed, it must relate to the specific 'significant pollutant linkage' identified by the regulator, and not some other problem or issue.

Further conditions which must be met for this exclusion to apply are that:

- the payment would have been sufficient to pay for the remediation in question at the date it was made;
- the remediation specified would have been effective to cause the land to cease to be contaminated by the specific significant pollutant linkage in question;
- the remediation has not been carried out effectively or at all;
- the payer retained no control over the condition of the land (though this does not prevent contractual clauses enabling a payer to supervise works).

If, for lack of compliance with these specific requirements, a payment does not have the effect of removing the seller from the relevant category, any payment made would be likely to be taken into account in any decision on the apportionment of the costs of any clean-up works.

See Chapter 2 for further discussion.

Requiring the provision of full information

This may seem to add little to the information-gathering process already undertaken. However, it is a way in which a seller can establish precisely that full information has been given to a buyer in relation to the presence of contaminants on the site, their nature and concentration. What amount of information, and the form in which it is offered, may be a source of dispute between the parties, as the purchaser must be put in a position reasonably to be able to ascertain the existence of the relevant contaminants and the broad measure of their presence.

The provision of this information would have the effect of removing the seller from the category of persons eligible to receive a remediation notice in respect of contaminated land, thus leaving the buyer to foot the seller's share of the cost in addition to any the buyer would already have to bear. There is thus a clear incentive for a seller to give the information and a corresponding incentive for the buyer to know exactly the state of the site and take decisions about whether to proceed and, if so, at what price.

The Guidance, however, provides that the mere offer of inspection facilities may be sufficient to fix the buyer, where they are a 'large commercial organisation', with all the relevant knowledge necessary to exempt the seller, so the seller may take the view that there is no need to go into print on the point in the contract, other than the evidential reason mentioned above.

It should be noted that this exclusion only allows a seller the exemption if:

- the sale was at arm's length terms;
- no material misrepresentation was made;
- the seller retained no interest in the land after completion.

See Chapter 2 for further discussion.

Agreements on liabilities

The parties may wish to agree between themselves how they wish to apportion any liability for contamination. Any such agreement will normally be honoured by the authority (subject to certain anti-avoidance provisions), and all its decisions regarding liability will be taken with the intention of effecting the agreement.

See Chapter 2 for further discussion.

Insurance

Insurance is available to the buyer and the seller against the risks of liability resulting from contamination or pollution of a site from past pollution events. The market for such environmental insurance policies, called property transfer policies, began developing in the 1990s. It is now an integral part of many commercial transactions, particularly those in which the buyer and the seller cannot agree to the allocation of liabilities arising from known or unknown past pollution events. Circumstances that have changed from the 1990s include substantially lower premiums due to the entry of new insurers into the market, flexible policies, a wider range of policies and the willingness of insurers to underwrite risks arising out of contamination or pollution that is known to the insured.

A property transfer policy provides cover for liabilities arising out of: (a) pollution or contamination which has not been caused by the insured and which is unknown to the insured; and (b) pollution or contamination which is disclosed to underwriters, provided that they agree to cover it. The liabilities include clean-up costs and claims for bodily injury or property damage, together with related legal expenses.

Unless a buyer or seller purchases, or both purchase, a property transfer policy, they are not protected by insurance against clean-up liabilities and claims for injury and damage from contamination or pollution that is subsequently discovered – or known contamination or pollution that subsequently results in liabilities – at their site or which has migrated from their site. This is because most public liability policies do not provide cover for clean-up costs and, since 1990, do not provide cover for harm from gradual pollution.

Further, property policies do not provide cover for cleaning up contamination or pollution of the insured's site. For a fuller discussion of environmental insurance policies and the gaps in public liability and property policies for pollution and contamination, see Chapter 13.

Retention by buyer

Alternatively, the buyer may prefer to complete on the basis of a retention from the price sufficient to cover any likely costs of remediation or clean up. This will enable the buyer to carry out the remediation works rather than rely upon the seller and this has advantages in terms of quality control and project management.

Indemnities

The seller might be required to indemnify the buyer against the costs of remediation or clean up or against any damages, loss or injury resulting from any past contamination or pollution of the soil or any watercourses or aquifers.

Caps on the level of indemnity are common, and the indemnities are only as good as the credit of the person giving them.

Phased indemnities are becoming more common – an arrangement whereby the seller remains liable for the first year, but the buyer gradually assumes part of the risk as the years go by until after, say, 10 years, the buyer is wholly liable.

Of general note is the fact that an indemnity carries with it no obligation on the part of the recipient to mitigate any losses suffered, so if one is desired, it should be built in to the wording of the indemnity itself, along with a restriction on reporting matters to the authorities in the latter years (sometimes done to trigger a clean up at the expense of the indemnity's giver). Indemnities from parent companies in a corporate group may be desirable, but rarely obtainable.

7.4.9 Withdrawal from the purchase

At any stage in the above process, a buyer must be prepared to walk away from the deal if:

- the risks are too great;
- the information is too hard to find; or
- the seller is too resistant to negotiation.

American and continental purchasers, in particular, are often not prepared to accept the environmental risk associated with the contamination of sites. This will become a more common occurrence as public awareness of the issues grows and the courts and public authorities impose more and more liability on property owners and occupiers.

Where there is a portfolio of properties comprised in the assets of a company, it may be necessary to hive off the clean ones for disposal purposes.

7.5 ADVICE TO SELLERS

This chapter has so far concentrated on the position of a purchaser and his solicitor. From the seller's point of view, achieving a clean break from the liabilities attaching to a site may not always be possible.

In particular, liability may continue for:

- breaches of the consents committed while the seller was the site-owner and operator (commercial sites only);
- breaches of waste legislation while in possession (commercial sites only);
- contaminated land (on the person who originally caused or knowingly permitted substances to be on the site pre-sale) (commercial and residential sites);
- statutory nuisances caused or continued (commercial and residential sites);
- water pollution offences caused or knowingly permitted (commercial and residential sites);
- sewerage discharge offences (commercial sites only);
- civil liability (as co-defendant for damage caused or continued during the period of ownership (commercial and residential sites)).

In respect of most of these liabilities (all save for contaminated land) there is no easy way to shift liability on to a purchaser other than by getting the purchaser to give comprehensive indemnities, which is a matter for the bargaining power of the parties and general market conditions and may be unlikely.

A more important strategy is to ensure (perhaps by incoming and outgoing audits) what the state of play is when the site is sold on, so as to be able successfully to determine who did in fact cause a pollution incident, should there ever be a dispute.

As far as contaminated land is concerned, sellers should take close note of those clauses in the Guidance Notes that would exempt a seller from liability if:

- contract documents specifically reject the payment (often in the form of a price reduction) of a specific sum for remediation;
- the land is sold in circumstances where full information is provided to the buyer about the contamination on the site;
- the seller and buyer agree on a contractual formula for dealing with any liabilities which emerge;

and ensure that the paperwork is drafted in such a way as to maximise the chance of exemption.

7.6   LEASEHOLD TRANSACTIONS

See Appendix A7 for sample lease clauses.

7.6.1   Standard lease

Existing leases

As currently drafted, most full repairing and insuring (FRI) leases will not contain provisions specifically requiring the tenant to clean up or remove any contamination which may from time to time exist on the site. For many sites, it may well be inappropriate to suggest that the tenant should be responsible for handing back to the landlord demised premises which have been cleaned up to a polished earth standard as this would render the lease extremely onerous. Onerous leases have knock-on effects in terms of assignability and rental growth.

The case law currently relating to repairing covenants in leases is confusing enough as it stands, particularly in the area of inherent defects. The added dimension of contaminated land will certainly not help to clarify issues.

Repairing covenants

The relative lack of sophistication of older FRI leases is likely to mean that the question of liability for clean up is between landlord and tenant and will have to be debated within the context of the repairing covenant. The temptation for the judiciary to produce a just result in individual cases is likely to produce a body of law which is inconsistent and difficult for practitioners to apply with any certainty.

Cases like *Post Office* v. *Aquarius Properties* [1987] 1 All ER 1055, CA would suggest that landlords are going to have great difficulty in imposing obligations upon tenants to make good any ground contamination existing prior to the start of the lease, not least because most leases envisage the repairing covenant to apply to buildings rather than the land itself.

There must, therefore, be doubt as to whether the repairing covenant would cover contamination of the site during the term, where the premises remain fit for occupation and use for the permitted user. This position may differ if the contamination affects the actual structures on the land in some physical sense.

It has been suggested that a covenant to keep the demised premises 'in good condition' may add weight to the landlord's contention that contamination of the premises is the responsibility of the tenant. It is unlikely that such a covenant would be interpreted as being intended to refer to, e.g. the sub-soil of the property, and therefore it would probably not add weight to the landlords argument except in so far as it is necessary to keep the premises in the condition contemplated at the start of the lease as being necessary for the fulfilment of the lease. Covenants to keep the property 'clean' are unlikely to assist, as they almost exclusively relate to appearance only.

Covenants to comply with statutory obligations

It is not uncommon for leases to require the tenant to comply with statutory and other regulations relating to the premises and to comply with notices served by the appropriate authorities. Such clauses would indicate that the tenant and its successors in title would be responsible for any contamination that had arisen during the term as a result of any such breach. It would also indicate as between landlord and tenant that the tenant will be responsible for pollution or clean-up notices received from public bodies (although this would not fetter the ability of the authorities to serve such notices on the landlord also).

Covenants not to commit waste

Some leases will contain a tenant's covenant not to commit waste. In the absence of an express covenant, the ancient law of waste creates obligations in tort rather than contract and will exist alongside the tenant's obligations in the lease. This would mean that only the tenant committing the waste will be liable in respect thereof. The right to sue for damages in respect of the tort of waste may not be assignable, on the grounds of public policy, and so the successor in title to the reversion may be unable to recover damages from the tenant in respect of earlier torts.

In many leases, covenants not to commit waste have been superseded by covenants not to carry out alterations or additions. In view of the derivation of such clauses, they may be sufficient to enable the landlord to recover damages from the tenant in respect of contamination arising during the term. Widely drafted alterations (and waste) clauses may also impose responsibility on the tenant in respect of contamination caused by third parties or migrating from adjoining property.

Clauses restricting user

Clauses dealing with the permitted user of the property will usually be expressed in general terms (often by reference to the relevant use class) and are likely to add little. Specific, restrictive user clauses will restrict the rental stream and possible resale.

Covenants not to create nuisance, etc.

Provisions relating to nuisance and, more especially, annoyance are more likely to give the landlord an effective lever where there is a risk of migration of contamination from the site, whether this is from contaminants placed there before or after the grant of the lease.

Prohibition on assignment, etc.

If premises are being demised for a use where there is a substantial risk of contamination, then the standard alienation clause is unlikely to provide adequate comfort to the landlord. Provisions can be inserted dealing with the experience and competence of assignees. To put the matter beyond doubt, however, 'offer back' clauses may be appropriate. Again, in situations of high risk, it is appropriate for the alienation provisions to be invoked where there is a change in the control of the tenant company

Indemnities

Perhaps the most significant clause in most modern leases will be the indemnity clause, which is often drafted very widely indeed and will frequently require the tenant to indemnify the landlord in respect of all losses as may arise directly or indirectly out of the state and condition of the property. Whilst this may not necessarily require the tenant to be responsible for a full clean up, it is quite possible that it could face a claim for loss of profits if, at the end of the term, the landlord would otherwise be able to sell the property for, e.g. residential redevelopment. Indemnities in respect of contaminated land liability under EPA 1990, Part IIA will need careful consideration and drafting (see Chapter 2).

It is apparent that the modern FRI lease does not deal with the issue of contamination in a satisfactory way. The extent to which additional clauses are required will depend primarily upon the condition of the property at the commencement of the term, the intended use of the property and the likelihood of contamination arising.

Whilst some provisions may sit relatively easily alongside existing lease clauses, e.g. aftercare conditions contained in any consents obtained by the tenant, it is generally most appropriate to consider pollution control and environmental protection as a separate and self-contained issue within the lease. For some suggested clauses, see Appendix A7.

This separate section of the lease will need to deal with:

- compliance by the tenant with pollution control legislation and all the terms of any consents, licences, guidance, industry best practice, etc.;
- prior to implementation, obtaining consultant's report (approved by landlord) and fully complying with all recommendations;
- provision of a bond (if applicable) to cover aftercare/proper performance;
- procuring surrender of licences before the end of the term, alternatively transferring to, or at the direction of, the landlord (if required);
- notification of all contaminating events at the site and the carrying out of a remediation programme as recommended by the landlord's consultant;
- notification of any proceedings in relation to pollution control legislation brought against the tenant/employees;
- obligations to maintain environmental impairment liability insurance;
- indemnity for state and condition/operations/contaminating events plus cost of remedial action/preventative measures to protect the demised premises/ neighbouring property;
- rights for the landlord to enter and carry out works (and recover cost);
- continuation of liability of the tenant under this clause beyond the expiry of the term.

The landlord retains an interest in the property so it inevitably risks liability in respect of the actions of its tenant. Because of the 'deep pocket' syndrome, the landlord needs to be fully satisfied as to the quality of the tenant's covenant and the degree of control that it can exercise over the way in which processes are carried out on the property if there is any material risk of contamination.

Landlords may be excluded from the categories of appropriate person for receipt of remediation notices in respect of contaminated land if they are not in 'effective control' of the activities of the tenant. Guidance Notes currently provide that one is not in effective control merely by leasing land to someone else.

Equally, tenants are not to be treated as appropriate persons in their capacity as 'occupiers' if they pay rent, but have no beneficial interest in the property.

New leases

Having considered the effects of more familiar terms, it is appropriate to look at negotiating a new lease for the acquisition of land which may be contaminated. The lease is a useful mechanism for allocating the risks associated with past or present contamination between vendor and purchaser; operating company and holding company; lender and borrower. It may therefore be appropriate to adopt a leasehold structure where a freehold sale cannot proceed because contamination is discovered as part of pre-contract investigations.

The lease may allow the existing owner of a contaminated site to get an income from it even if it is not disposable on a freehold basis, and if there is an existing liability for clean up and total clean up is not practicable (so that there will be a residual legal liability after the remediation has been carried out), the rent-stream may be able to fund or support the cost of remediation.

In the traditional lease arrangement, the tenant takes a lease of the whole site with no special arrangements to exclude the contaminated sub-soil. The tenant is therefore potentially an 'owner' of the contaminated land and, as such, may be liable for clean up and other liabilities arising out of the contamination. Before setting up such an arrangement, careful pre-lease investigations are vital.

Moreover, the lease should contain:

- covenants by the landlord (or the tenant) which identify specifically the responsibility for carrying out any remediation works, the standards to be applied, the notification, inspection and reporting procedures as between the landlord and the tenant and the obligations in respect of compliance with all relevant legislation;
- provisions dealing with containment, interception, dissipation and monitoring of the contamination, depending on the appropriate engineering solutions;
- rent suspension if contamination prevents the tenant from using and enjoying the site;
- break clauses;
- guarantees and sureties;
- covenants to maintain environmental impairment liability and other insurances.

7.6.2 'Pie-crust' leases

The purpose of the 'pie-crust' lease is to leave the contaminated soil out of the demised premises so that the tenant does not become the owner of the contamination and therefore has no liability to third parties for its escape. The demised premises will consist of everything (buildings and airspace) above the surface of the ground, plus the layer or layers of clean soil, hard core and surfacing material above the impermeable capping layer.

As noted above, tenants are not to be treated as appropriate persons in their capacity as 'occupiers' if they pay rent, but have no beneficial interest in the property. As regards the contaminated sub-soil, they have no beneficial interest in it and pay no rent either, so it is doubly difficult to see how they could be classed as its 'occupier' under the terms of the Guidance. Common sense may, however, suggest a different view.

Whilst this is not a complete panacea as the landlord retains control over the sub-soil and the tenant loses a degree of flexibility for future use and development, it has provided considerable comfort to banks taking security. This is particularly so where continuity of occupation is essential to the value of the business.

Where the landlord is the original polluter, it may be advisable to retain control and ownership of its pollution for two reasons:

(a)   it may yet be primarily liable for that pollution and thus benefit from greater control over the clean-up costs; and

(b)   as polluter, the likelihood is that it will be more familiar with the contaminants thereby being better able to quantify the risk. The cost to the landlord of assuming that risk should be significantly lower than the premium required by any purchaser, tenant or insurer.

There is still a need for the covenants in the lease to be carefully drawn to reflect the contamination of the sub-soil (e.g. landlord to comply with all requisite standards: indemnify tenant against the claims and liabilities arising; suspension of rent if the tenant's use and occupation is interrupted; right for the landlord to enter and remain to carry out the remediation works; possibly a break clause; guarantees and sureties; restrictions upon alterations by tenant or anything that may affect the pollution control measures taken by the landlord).

In addition, the easements and rights reserved and granted need to be very carefully drawn to ensure that both the landlord and the tenant are able to use and enjoy or control the respective parts of the land held by them.

While the concept of a pie-crust lease often sounds attractive, and has been well rehearsed in many articles and publications, in practice they are rarely used, being viewed to be an extremely complicated mechanism to deal with such issues.

CHAPTER 8

Corporate transactions

8.1 INTRODUCTION

Corporate clients of all sorts and sizes are now wise to the fact that there is a need to consider environmental issues arising in relation to specific transactions which involve the acquisition of an interest in an existing business. They may have implications for the future operation of the business, and a share purchaser's bankers will no doubt wish to make further enquiries before they will be prepared to fund any acquisition.

The risks and liabilities must first be fully assessed. This may involve the commissioning of an environmental audit or investigation by either party to the transaction or both of them, ideally at an early stage of the transaction, and the disclosure of potential liabilities by the vendor.

The risks will then be allocated between the purchaser and the vendor (or transferred by insurance) and the result will be dependent on who has the commercial upper hand. This will involve the negotiation of warranties and indemnities, a consideration of whether insurance can be obtained to cover the relevant risks or possibly the performance of remedial work by the proposed vendor before or after completion of the transaction, price retentions or reductions or a restructuring.

This chapter focuses mainly on the considerations which may be especially relevant on a share purchase, as the acquisition of a business or a group of assets can be structured to carve out any unnecessarily risky assets. On a share purchase, however, the concern is to anticipate and deal with risks which may affect the value of the company (a contribution to clean-up costs of a current or past site being the most acute) and thus, the value of the shares.

8.2 QUESTION OF LIABILITY

As discussed in Chapter 1, breach of environmental statutes carries criminal sanction. Commonly, few defences are available for offences under such legislation so even companies which regard themselves as blameless can still find themselves penalised. In addition, there may be responsibility for clean-up costs, which may be significant, and civil liability may be owed to other third parties.

The legislation also allows for officers of a convicted company to be held personally liable where the offence is proved to have been committed with the consent or connivance of, or is attributable to, any neglect on the part of any director, manager, secretary or other similar officer of that company. It is not yet clear whether the standard of care usually required by a director in relation to his civil liability (i.e. that set out in *Re City Equitable Fire Insurance Co. Ltd* [1925] Ch 407, CA), which is that he must exhibit such skill as can reasonably be expected from the person with that director's knowledge and experience, will be applied in this situation, though indications in cases such as *Norman* v. *Theodore Goddard* [1992] BCLC 1028 would suggest that those with particular expertise in environmental matters should show higher standards.

Solicitors should note *Williams* v. *Natural Life Healthfoods Ltd* [1996] 1 BCLC 288 which indicates that directors can be liable for the torts of their companies (including pollution nuisance) if they 'direct or procure' the commission of the tort by the company.

In most instances, it is the person who causes or knowingly permits pollution to occur who is potentially liable. However, owners/occupiers of land may be liable under certain provisions and principles. Therefore, it is not simply a question of the polluter paying.

The key point for a purchaser is to appreciate the costly and complex liabilities flowing from operating a process, or even merely from owning or occupying land, and which he may be buying in a corporate acquisition.

8.3 PRACTICAL STEPS

When advising a purchaser or vendor, the solicitor must ensure that he understands the nature of the business and the processes that are being, and have been, carried on at its sites and, accordingly, that he has the appropriate questions in mind in order to identify problems at the outset.

He should also have the necessary contacts on call in the event that the questions of insurance (see Chapter 13) or the appointment of environmental consultants (see Chapter 10) are raised.

The following issues should be considered:

1. *The product* – the product itself may have dangerous, hazardous or polluting properties and may need careful management after manufacture, but even if it does not appear to be polluting, this must not be the end of the enquiry.
2. *Raw materials* – it is necessary to consider the components used in the production process since in any of these there may lurk the potential for an environmental breach. If toxic materials are used in the manufacturing process, how are they being dealt with? A prospective purchaser should seek details of the current environmental policy operated by the company together with details of its implementation and how compliance is monitored. Under the environmental permitting (EP) regime, operators may be required to

monitor raw material and other input usage (such as electricity and water). It may be the case, over time, that certain conditions are attached to the use of such materials which may affect the operation of the process in the future.

3.   *The process* – the onus is on the purchaser as part of its due diligence exercise to find out whether the process will result in emissions to environmental media and, if so, what steps are being taken to minimise their effects. At the end of an EP process, the operator will have to remove any contamination not discovered in the land assessment done at the start of the process, so a copy of that assessment should be made available and suitable indemnities obtained.

4   *Disposal of waste* – the waste management responsibilities (especially the duty of care) dealing with its storage, transportation and disposal must be complied with.

5.   *Historical use of the site* – old processes may give rise to current liabilities and a clear understanding of historical use may give warnings as to whether or not the land is currently contaminated.

6.   *Licences* – it is important to check that all appropriate environmental permits, consents and licences have been obtained, to note the conditions attaching to them and to determine whether these conditions are being complied with. Certain licences are subject to review by the relevant regulatory authority and it is important to identify whether this is pending. It is also helpful to see copies of correspondence with the regulators and others to assess the local climate of opinion regarding the industry in question. Consideration needs to be given as to whether there are any restrictions in the licence conditions should there be a change in control of the company.

7.   *Site and local inspection* – a significant concern is the risk of discharge or loss of fluids to groundwater via, for example, cracked concrete or soakaways. The position of the drains and the route of rainwater run-off will also need to be considered. The local sub-surface hydrogeology and uses of groundwater are also of significance. Site inspections should be carried out by reputable specialists. A desk survey or report similar to those commissioned in property transactions will inform the investigation process and assist in identifying particular risks for further investigation.

8.   *Occupation of former sites* – if the operator has conducted his polluting operation on other premises in the past, there may be a contingent liability and risk that it may be called upon to contribute to the cost of remediating those other sites as the 'original polluter'.

8.4   PROBLEMS IDENTIFIED: WHAT APPROACH TO TAKE?

The first issue is whether a purchaser should acquire the assets or some or all of the issued share capital of a company. A purchaser may choose to take certain of the assets off-site and limit the liabilities it assumes by not acquiring a contaminated property.

A process that is licensed or authorised by the appropriate regulators is permitted (subject to conditions) to operate in that location and no other. To relocate such a process is to risk difficulties with fresh licence applications. In practice, therefore, this may not be a real option to achieve the desired objective of being able to continue the business but leave behind environmental contamination. This will be especially difficult in relation to EP processes, where land assessments will have to be carried out on any relocation. For this reason, in essence, most of the issues relevant to a share purchase apply equally to an assets transaction where the purchaser intends to carry on the existing business. In the latter case, however, concerns about a company's liability in relation to previous environmental offences, and the occupation of previous sites, can be set aside.

If the purchaser wishes to acquire the company, perhaps for tax reasons, the company is acquired with all of its liabilities (subject to any reorganisation which the vendor can be persuaded to undertake prior to completion of the transaction).

The main practical solution for a purchaser faced with a large environmental liability which has been properly identified, whether on an assets transaction or share purchase, is to negotiate suitable warranties, to seek an appropriate indemnity and to feel that the price paid reflects the acceptance of potential liabilities.

In practice, warranties may be of little contractual benefit (due to various limitations and disclosures). It is always preferable to undertake as full an environmental due diligence exercise as possible and to use environmental warranties as a means of sparking disclosure and filling the gaps.

To the extent that matters are highlighted before signing the contracts, they may be omitted from the warranties, and, in such cases, the due diligence process becomes paramount in order to elicit as much information as possible, rather than trying to sue for the lack of it.

There may be difficulties in limiting the acquisition to an 'assets' purchase, as it may be the site that is licensed, and the land may therefore have to be acquired in any event. If this is so, then some sophisticated conveyancing solution may be needed (a 'pie-crust' lease, for example – see **7.6.2**) to leave contaminated ground out of the transaction.

It is worth noting that the exclusionary tests relating to contaminated land exempt from liability anyone making a 'sufficient payment' for remediation in the contractual documentation transferring assets (but not shares in the company owning the property).

The exemption relating to 'sales with information' relates to any deals as part of which land portfolios may change hands, and would, therefore, apply to a business or assets acquisition which includes such properties. Full contractual apportionment and indemnity is, however, still the best way to proceed to eradicate any ambiguity, and to ensure that the liabilities fall where the parties expect and provide.

Any agreement which apportions responsibility for the cost of contaminated land within the meaning of EPA 1990, Part IIA should generally be honoured by the regulatory authority.

If acting for the vendor, you will obviously try to avoid giving an indemnity to the purchaser. This may not be possible if a specific problem has been identified and in these circumstances you should seek to put a ceiling on the vendor's liability under the environmental warranties and/or indemnities, as well as excluding liability for post-completion matters. The vendor will also want a time limit on his potential exposure and the ability to control the conduct of any claims.

In certain circumstances, an indemnity may not be appropriate or at least still not provide a full solution. Certain breaches, e.g. failure to register under the Producer Responsibility Obligations (Packaging Waste) Regulations 2007, SI 2007/871, may be a criminal offence which the purchaser will require to be remedied.

Insurance is an alternative, either for the purchaser in respect of future claims, or for the vendor in respect of liability under warranties and indemnities. The availability of environmental insurance is discussed further in Chapter 13.

Finally, it may be possible for either the purchaser or the vendor to carry out remedial work to resolve or reduce the problem. This will, however, depend on the nature of the contamination, the intended use of the land, the cost of the work required and the negotiating strengths of the parties.

8.5   DOCUMENTING THE TRANSACTION

Illustrative environmental clauses for inclusion in a share purchase agreement are set out in Appendix A8. They are provided for illustrative purposes only and are not intended to be used as precedents.

The definitions in the sample warranties and indemnities have been extremely widely cast. That of 'environmental contamination' is aimed at catching all types of contamination whether accidental or gradual, toxic or merely excessive in quantity.

The definition of 'waste' also repays careful attention. Waste can give rise to a liability without being toxic or dangerous. Removing substances will generate a disposal cost, which, if excessive or above the norm, should be shifted to the other side.

8.5.1   Environmental warranties

Sample warranties are given in Schedule I in Appendix A8. The purpose of the warranties is to elicit as much information about the operations of the business as possible. They may often be supplemented by the right of recourse against a vendor under the environmental indemnity, but in themselves provide a network of contractual promises which can be sued upon if they turn out to be false.

Where there is to be a sale of shares of a company, the purchaser cannot avoid taking the company subject to all existing liabilities and continuing commitments. This is to be contrasted with the purchase of a business where liabilities do not pass unless specifically taken over.

It has therefore always been the custom for the purchaser to receive some form of assurance from the vendors as to the liabilities attaching to the target company or assets in a business sale. The process of checking the warranties will bring out potential problems and provide information on the business to be purchased and the parties will be able to negotiate as to what impact these should have on the transaction.

However, another purpose of the warranties is to allocate risk as between the vendors, the parties giving the warranties, and the purchaser, in relation to the possibility of the target company or assets being subject to undisclosed liabilities or obligations. To the extent that warranties are given, the warrantors accept the liability; in so far as the warranties are not given or are restricted in their scope by limitations or disclosures in the disclosure letter, the purchaser takes the risk.

The remedy normally sought by a purchaser where there is a breach of a warranty is compensation by way of payment of damages which may be difficult to quantify. The basic rule is that the purchaser should be compensated for its loss of bargain: however, it will be under an implied duty to mitigate any loss suffered and he will not be able to recover for any losses which are too remote. In contract, under the indemnity, the purchaser can claim for a specified sum, in certain circumstances, on a pound-for-pound basis, subject to any cap or limitations placed upon this and is not subject to any duty to mitigate his or its losses.

Warranty 1.1 seeks to obtain details of all permits, licences, authorisations, consents or other approvals required under the relevant environmental legislation in order to carry on the business of the company or to use the property where it is located and to gain an indication of the costs of such compliance. This is also dealt with in Warranty 1.11.

The definition of 'environmental law' is deliberately made very broad, and is intended to catch laws not yet in force but which may have retroactive effect, as was the case with the contaminated land provisions in EPA 1990, Part IIA. It is intended to cover both statutory and common law liabilities of all types and to catch health and safety laws.

Warranty 1.2 has the aim of eliciting details of any breach of environmental law or environmental licences or the conditions attaching thereto. This is expanded in Warranties 1.5–1.9. The key concern of the purchaser here is to ensure that the company or business is capable of carrying on its processes or manufacturing its products in compliance with its licences and consents and without annoyance to its neighbours. The important areas to be borne in mind here are discharges to air, water and sewer, storage and disposal of waste (whether by third parties or otherwise), noise and odours. These are all the subject of 'environmental law'.

Warranty 1.3 is included to glean information as to the state of knowledge of the vendor in respect of recently granted consents and licences and in respect of periodic rights of review by the relevant regulatory authority. It also requires the vendor to confirm, in effect, that the licences and consents relating to the business or the company are held on acceptable terms.

Warranty 1.4 deals with environmental assessments and investigations. Currently, a statutory 'assessment', pursuant to the Town and Country Planning (Environmental Impact Assessment) (England and Wales) Regulations 1999, SI 1999/293, is only required for the purposes of certain particularly significant planning applications, but this warranty also aims to discover whether a private voluntary investigation, or remedial work, has been undertaken by the vendor. Any such assessment or investigation report will assist a purchaser's understanding of the site.

When acting for the purchaser, there are a number of consulting organisations which can give competent technical advice in relation to environmental problems and can undertake an environmental investigation. It may be preferable for lawyers to instruct one of these consultants personally so that their report is privileged. If the client company deals directly with them, they may run up against disclosure problems, for example, to inspectors appointed by the regulators.

All environmental reports must be private to the purchaser and a common argument put forward by the purchaser is that the report should not be disclosed to the vendor. The vendor, if it obtained a copy, would usually attempt to disclose any such report back to the purchaser by way of the formal disclosure letter to limit its liability under any warranty or indemnity. The contents of the disclosure letter serve to amend or contradict the warranties and, possibly, the indemnity and therefore if an environmental report is annexed to it, the purchaser will take the risk of liabilities revealed therein and will not be able to claim for such losses under the warranties or the indemnity if it is so limited. Clearly, disclosure of the report is a matter for commercial negotiation between the parties.

Warranty 1.5 is designed as a catch-all warranty to enable the purchaser to discover facts relating to latent environmental problems within the knowledge of the vendor but not yet the subject of actual or threatened proceedings.

Warranty 1.6 is self-explanatory and could be one to give away in the course of negotiations.

Warranties 1.7–1.9 all relate to waste management. Warranty 1.8 is onerous and consequently would usually be qualified by the vendor's awareness.

Warranty 1.10 seeks to repeat certain of the warranties in respect of persons occupying adjoining land. A vendor will obviously seek to exclude this warranty and buyers would be very lucky to win this. Chapters 1 and 2 deal with the potential liabilities arising from migration in some detail, against which the operation of these warranties becomes clear.

8.5.2 Environmental indemnity

It is not uncommon for a purchaser to seek an indemnity from a vendor in connection with environmental liabilities. The purchaser will be concerned that it is buying a contingent liability that results from the fault of the vendor or its predecessors in title. As a first step, it is necessary to identify what liabilities this will cover. For example, if the vendor is to pay only the 'costs of clean up', what does this actually mean? Should this involve merely removing the affected material to landfill elsewhere, or does it also include making good the land, i.e. remediation? The vendor will be concerned that such an indemnity might be a blank cheque and that it will suffer if environmental legislation grows more strict, and will thus wish the indemnity to be limited to covering laws in force at the time or imminent.

It is sometimes argued that the purchaser should only be indemnified against costs and damages that it is actually ordered to pay and that the vendor should have conduct of any such claims. This may affect the purchaser's ongoing relationships with the environmental regulators and its neighbours. Possible compromises include the appointment of an independent environmental consultant whose opinion binds both parties and stipulations that the purchaser must take all reasonable steps to mitigate the liability (though care needs to be taken here that such a form of words is not taken to imply that the purchaser must undertake preventative or precautionary remediation works).

If an indemnity against clean-up costs is given, the vendor will want to ensure that this provision is not used by the purchaser to effectively demand payment for works that were unnecessary or excessive in relation to complying with the strict legal requirements.

In the sample agreement, there is a suggestion for a 75 per cent/25 per cent split of liability between vendor and purchaser. This is a suggested compromise which attempts to deal with a vendor's concern over the betterment argument. Whether an apportionment is included is a matter of negotiation. The limitations in the indemnity are for illustration only.

The provision for a 75 per cent cap on the vendor's liability also aims to prevent the purchaser from using the indemnity as an excuse to upgrade the site at the vendor's expense. Such costs as are recoverable from the vendor ought to represent the bare minimum necessary in order to bring the property into a state of compliance with environmental law. Again, an independent environmental consultant may be useful in order to give effect to provisions of this sort.

Environmental indemnities commonly give protection for longer than would be normal for other kinds of indemnity: five years is by no means unusual. This, of course, results from the long lead-time between environmental incidents and their effects.

Environmental law is likely to change during the lifetime of a reasonable environmental indemnity. The question of whether the vendor should be liable under an indemnity in respect of liabilities payable pursuant to laws not in existence at completion is frequently the subject of debate and is rarely won by the purchaser's adviser.

Possible sources of compromise in other areas include the cap on liability, a requirement for the purchaser to bear a certain percentage of costs (thus meaning the purchaser will bear some of the pain in an attempt to discourage it from making frivolous claims), provisions apportioning liability in respect of certain kinds of problem, phased indemnities which provide for the progressive take-over of responsibility by the purchaser (say, at the rate of 10 per cent per annum for 10 years), duration of the indemnity, *de minimis* provisions and requirements to notify the vendor in certain ways.

The indemnity in Appendix A8 also seeks to indemnify the purchaser in respect of civil and criminal actions brought against the purchaser on the basis of facts associated with acts/omissions of the vendor. It is important to include legal costs in such clauses. It should be borne in mind that an indemnity in respect of criminal sanctions is not enforceable.

8.5.3   Effect of contaminated land provisions in EPA 1990, Part IIA

The principles applicable in a corporate transaction appear to be largely unaffected by the Part IIA provisions in that, on an assets transaction, contaminated land would often be left out of the acquisition anyway. However, although on a share acquisition there is no land acquisition as such, the buyer steps into the shoes of the seller and inherits all the seller's potential liabilities, and this may include liability in respect of formerly-occupied sites. For this reason, it is suggested that there does need to be some due diligence relating to sites previously owned or occupied by the target, particularly when the target currently or previously carried out activities which have the potential to cause contamination.

It is provided that the exemption from liability for those making full disclosure of any contamination (or offering the facility for inspection) does apply to any series of transactions as a result of which property portfolios change hands. If land is included in an assets or business acquisition, all the considerations enumerated in Chapter 7 in relation to commercial property transactions should be borne in mind in relation to full investigations (possibly at joint cost), specific payments (in the form of price reduction) and sales with information, these latter devices working to pass to the purchaser any Part IIA liability which would have fallen on the seller. This result is not necessarily what the purchaser would want and indemnities and agreements may alter the position.

Moreover, as has already been pointed out in earlier chapters, the regime does provide that any agreements on liabilities be honoured by the regulators. The language of the Guidance talks in terms of the authorities giving effect to whatever agreements the parties may have come to as to the 'proportions in which they intend to share' any clean-up cost. Such agreements may therefore need to specify in percentage terms what proportion of any remediation work required or agreed is to be borne by the respective parties in order to conform to the language of the relevant Guidance, and a typical indemnity clause ('I'll reimburse your share') may not work to reallocate the shares in the way the Guidance (or the parties) may have envisaged.

One is tempted to suggest that any indemnities regarding contaminated land which are intended to amount to an 'agreement on liabilities' for the purposes of Part IIA be kept separate in the documentation from other environmental provisions, since this particular piece of legislation works to such unique and complex rules which are different entirely from other regimes. They also apply solely to Part IIA liabilities, and other more general provisions will be guarding against other risks, too. See Chapter 2 for a fuller discussion.

CHAPTER 9

Planning and development

9.1 INTRODUCTION

The development of previously developed land (brownfield sites) is at the heart of government regeneration and development policy.

It is not the purpose or function of this book to look in detail at the planning system, or the full implications of urban regeneration, but this chapter mentions the key issues to be borne in mind by developers in particular, when contemplating building on land that is suspected of being, or that actually is, contaminated.

Other chapters discuss each of these matters in more detail.

In outline, though, any development of the site will need to address issues of contamination as part of the planning requirements. In addition, clean up and development operations may themselves constitute an 'industrial' activity requiring permitting or authorisation, create a statutory nuisance or a nuisance actionable at common law, and may require the production of evidence of compliance with such conditions to purchasers and tenants of the completed project.

9.2 PLANNING IMPLICATIONS OF PROPERTY TRANSACTIONS

In the various policy documents issued in conjunction with the introduction of the regime to remediate contaminated land set out in Part IIA of the Environmental Protection Act 1990 (EPA 1990), it became clear that the Government still saw planning control of development as one of the major ways of dealing with contaminated land. Following the slow implementation of Part IIA, it is clear that the Government has increasingly regarded planning control as the major way to deal with contaminated land. Planning controls are familiar, they deal with less dangerous sites at a time when works would be carried out anyway and, arguably, work in a more just fashion than the contaminated land regime (that is, the person who gets the profit from the site has to spend money remediating it).

Indications over the past 10 years or so are that the planning system will play an ever larger role in the future, especially in the development of new homes. Much of this development (60 per cent) will have to take place on brownfield sites, raising the spectre of how to deal with contamination as part of the redevelopment.

The section of the Planning Policy Statement 23 (PPS 23) on development of land potentially affected by contamination has been in force since 2004 (see **9.2.9**). Corresponding advice for Wales is contained in the third edition of *Planning Policy Wales* (July 2010).

Other Planning Policy Statements that are relevant to environmental matters include PPS 9 on Biodiversity and Geological Conservation and PPS 25 on Development and Flood Risk.

9.2.1 Contamination: a 'material consideration'

The presence of contamination on land is a 'material consideration' for planning purposes and, in serious cases, may restrict or prevent the development of the land; for instance, if the development cannot be carried out without tangible and serious harm to the environment.

In less serious cases, the local planning authority (LPA) may impose stringent conditions to protect the environment (including current and proposed occupiers of the land in question) or neighbouring residences.

Many authorities have for some time included in consents a condition that prohibits development until a scheme for investigating potential contamination and, if contamination exists, requiring its remediation as approved by the LPA before the development may proceed. Such a condition is a condition precedent; a development completed without adherence to this process is unlawful, unauthorised and liable to enforcement action.

To address the inconsistency in approach between LPAs on this matter, the Department for Communities and Local Government (CLG) issued guidance in May 2008 on the form of model planning conditions for development on land affected by contamination (see Appendix F; available at **www.communities.gov. uk**). The purpose of the conditions, which should be adapted to individual situations, is to support effective implementation of the policy set out in PPS 23. The conditions replace those contained in Annex 2 of PPS 23 as well as those in paras. 56–59 of Appendix A of Circular 11/95, entitled 'Use of conditions in planning permission'.

In some cases, an LPA should obtain information on contamination before granting consent subject to conditions. In *R (on the application of) Technoprint plc, Mark Snee* v. *Leeds City Council* [2010] EWHC 581 (Admin), QBD the judge quashed planning permission for the demolition of a building and its replacement with flats on several bases. In respect of contaminated land, a technical officer had recommended obtaining information on contamination before planning permission was granted. When all the requested information was not submitted, the planning officer imposed six detailed conditions. The judge considered that a reasonable LPA would have demanded more information before deciding to grant permission instead of granting permission subject to conditions when the extent of any potential land contamination problem was unknown.

9.2.2 Opportunity as well as a threat

There may be circumstances when a distinction is drawn between different categories of occupier and the perceived level of sophistication.

For example, supermarkets may be regarded as sufficiently sophisticated to warrant giving planning permission for a supermarket development on a former landfill site with methane migration problems with which the proposed building will cope by technologically advanced monitoring and ventilation controls (see the appeal decision of the Secretary of State in *Wm. Morrison Supermarkets* v. *Wakefield MDC* [1991] JPL 985).

On the other hand, development of a similar site for residential purposes might be considered inappropriate because the residential occupier is less likely to ensure that the buildings and outbuildings are adequately maintained and operated to avoid the risk of methane accumulation.

The existence of contamination problems on a site may in fact militate in favour of development which would otherwise be unacceptable. For an example, one need only look at the Secretary of State's decision on a called-in application by British Airways for planning permission for a corporate headquarters and business centre on 5.1 hectares in the metropolitan greenbelt at Prospect Park near Harmondsworth. In this case, planning permission was granted mainly because the development would lead to remediation of methane problems which were affecting a nearby residential estate ([1993] JPL 268).

9.2.3 Requirement for notification

Article 10 of the Town and Country Planning (General Development Procedure) Order 1995, SI 1995/419, requires the LPA to consult with other statutory bodies in specified circumstances. For example, the LPA must consult with the relevant waste regulation authority in respect of any application for planning permission within 250 metres of existing or past waste disposal sites. The LPA must also consult with the Environment Agency for development involving the carrying out of works in the bed, or on the banks, of a river or stream.

9.2.4 Planning obligations, aftercare and restoration conditions

Even before the EPA 1990, it was not uncommon for LPAs to impose 'aftercare conditions' to ensure the safe clean up and landscaping of a site used for environmentally harmful uses.

In particular, land at mining and landfill sites must frequently be graded and landscaped at the end of the works, but may (especially in relation to landfill sites) include remediation works, e.g. methane venting or capping and grading.

Anyone who buys a site which is subject to these conditions may unexpectedly find themselves saddled with expensive obligations. It is therefore essential to check all planning consents carefully to ensure that any aftercare conditions in existing consents have been complied with fully.

Under s.72 of, and Schedule 5 to, the amended Town and Country Planning Act (TCPA) 1990, the powers to impose aftercare and restoration conditions were increased in the case of mineral and waste-tipping operations.

Practitioners should be aware of the power to serve breach of condition notices contained in s.187A of the amended TCPA 1990. Such notices are enforceable by planning authorities through magistrates' courts; there is no right of appeal.

9.2.5   Environmental impact assessment

Environmental assessment is largely governed by the Town and Country Planning (Environmental Impact Assessment) (England and Wales) Regulations 1999, SI 1999/293, as amended (the EIA Regulations) and is explained in DETR Circular 02/99 and Welsh Assembly Government Circular CL-02-02.

An environmental assessment is required by the EIA Regulations in all cases of development proposals falling within Schedule 1 to those Regulations and also in cases of development proposals falling within Schedule 2 if that development would be likely to have significant effects on the environment due to factors such as its nature, size or location.

Schedule 1 development covers major industrial developments such as crude oil refineries, thermal or nuclear power stations, certain iron, steel, asbestos, chemical and waste disposal installations and certain roads, railways, aerodromes and ports.

Schedule 2 lists 13 categories of development, most of which list at least six types of development within that category. The categories cover agriculture, the extractive industry, the energy industry, metals processing, glass-making, the food industry, textile, leather, wood and paper industries, the rubber industry, certain infrastructure projects such as industrial or urban estates or tramways, and certain other projects such as holiday villages and hotel complexes.

To guide developers and LPAs as to when Schedule 2 development proposals might require an environmental assessment, Circular 02/99 sets out both general tests and also specific indicative criteria and thresholds for each of the categories of development in Schedule 2. The three main categories of Schedule 2 projects which require an environmental assessment are:

- major projects which are of more than local importance;
- smaller-scale projects in a particularly sensitive or vulnerable location;
- in a small number of cases, where the project has unusually complex and potentially adverse environmental effects and where detailed analysis of those effects would be desirable.

Development which would otherwise be permitted development (e.g. under a GPDO (General Permitted Development Order) or the SPZ (special planning zone) scheme) will not be so permitted if it constitutes Schedule 1 or Schedule 2 development. Developers can apply to the LPA for an opinion on whether a proposed development which would have constituted permitted development requires an environmental assessment (see the EIA Regulations).

Because of the uncertainty as to whether Schedule 2 development requires an environmental assessment and because the preparation of an environmental statement involves a lot of time and expense, there is provision in the Regulations for a developer to ask the LPA whether, in its opinion, an environmental assessment is required. If the LPA states that one is required and the developer is not happy with this, the developer can apply to the Secretary of State (or, to the Welsh Assembly Government in Wales) for a direction on the matter. The procedure for requesting an opinion is set out in reg.5 of the EIA Regulations.

There is no prescribed form, as such, for an environmental statement. However, Schedule 4 to the EIA Regulations specifies what it must contain. The contents are too long to list here but it should be noted that the information required is very detailed and will require much time and expense to prepare.

When an environmental statement is submitted with a planning application, the applicant must observe special rules regarding additional documentation and publicity for the application. In addition, the LPA is under a duty to send the application and environmental statement with accompanying documents to the Secretary of State or Welsh Assembly Government and must consult with various bodies specified in reg.13(2) of the EIA Regulations.

Where an environmental statement is not submitted with the planning application but the LPA considers that one is necessary, it must notify the applicant within three weeks. If the applicant disagrees, he can, within three weeks of the notification, apply to the Secretary of State or Welsh Assembly Government for a direction on the matter.

Where an environmental statement is required, the LPA, or the Secretary of State or Welsh Assembly Government, cannot grant planning permission until it has been supplied and an environmental assessment has been carried out (reg.7).

In reaching a decision on the planning application, the LPA has 16 weeks (instead of the usual eight) in which to notify the applicant of its decision.

9.2.6 Enforcement powers

Under TCPA 1990, s.215, the LPA has power to serve notice on the owner and occupier of land if it appears to the LPA that the amenity of a part of its area (or of an adjoining area) is adversely affected by the condition of land in its area.

The notice will require such steps for remedying the condition of the land as may be specified in the notice to be taken within such period as may be specified (which may not be less than 28 days from service). There is a right of appeal against the notice to the magistrates' court and there are criminal penalties for failing to comply with the notice. Under TCPA 1990, s.219, the LPA may enter on to the land and take the necessary steps to comply with the notice and recover from the person who is then the owner of the land any expenses reasonably incurred in doing so. In the past, this power was rarely used but amendments have made it easier to use and LPAs may be prepared to use these powers in the future for the improvement of the environment.

Practitioners should also note the power, under TCPA 1990, s.187B, for an LPA to obtain an injunction if it considers such action to be necessary or expedient to prevent any actual or apprehended breach of planning control. Unlike under previous legislation, an authority need not show that it has exhausted all other possibilities before following this line.

9.2.7 Powers of revocation and modification

Under TCPA 1990, s.102, LPAs have power to require the discontinuance of the use of land or the removal of buildings or works. These powers are very rarely used because they involve rights of compensation, but it is possible that pollution problems arising from contamination may give rise to the exercise of these powers.

9.2.8 Planning obligations

Under TCPA 1990, s.106, the LPA can enter into contractual arrangements with the developer, which will bind the land and all subsequent owners.

This is a useful delivery mechanism to ensure that a remediation package for a contaminated site, say, is appropriately designed and implemented and that there are adequate arrangements for monitoring and testing, maintenance, insurance (in so far as it is available), repairs and renewals. Advice and guidance on the use of s.106 in England is contained in ODPM (now CLG) Circular 05/2005.

9.2.9 Planning Policy Statement 23

Annexe 2 to PPS 23 sets out requirements regarding the approach to be taken in any development of land potentially affected by contamination. The key elements of this statement are:

- all applications for development should be accompanied by a desk survey seeking to identify potential contamination problems;
- informal discussions should then be carried out between the LPA and the applicant to determine the extent of any contamination and the proposals for dealing with it;
- conditions should be set to ensure that the development achieves certain specified aims, including:
  - the aversion of any risk to health during the development;
  - the removal of unacceptable levels of contamination;
  - the suitability of the site for any plausible future use; and
  - the removal of risks to health or financial risks which may affect the future use of the land.

9.3 UNDERTAKING THE WORKS

Development works themselves may constitute:

- a pollution prevention and control (PPC) permitted activity (that is, an activity under the PPC regime that was subsumed into the Environmental Permitting Regulations) such as crushing or grinding;
- a regulated waste management process (removing or treating contaminated soil or relocation of rubble as hardcore); the Site Waste Management Plans Regulations 2008, SI 2008/314 require construction projects of over £300,000 to have site waste management plans in place;
- a contaminated land issue – the works may trigger a problem by introducing a pathway that was not formerly present, thus creating a significant pollutant linkage. The statutory guidance to Part IIA of the EPA 1990 provides that the introducer of the pathway is liable and that the original polluter is exonerated from further liability (see Exclusion Test 6 and *Circular Facilities (London) Ltd* v. *Sevenoaks District Council* [2005] EWHC 865 (Admin), [2005] All ER (D) 126, QBD (Admin)):
- a statutory nuisance – see *Wheeler* v. *JJ Saunders Ltd* [1996] Ch 19, CA and *Hunter* v. *Canary Wharf Ltd* [1997] AC 655, HL;
- a water pollution problem, by releasing polluting substances (dust, silt, etc.) to controlled waters;
- a common law nuisance, if damage is foreseeable.

9.4 PASSING RISK TO PURCHASER

From the seller's point of view, achieving a clean break from the liabilities attaching to a site may not always be possible.

In particular, liability may continue for:

- breaches of any permits or consents committed while the seller was the site-owner and operator;
- breaches of any legislation while in possession;
- contaminated land (on the persons who originally caused or knowingly permitted substances to be on the site pre-sale);
- statutory nuisances caused or continued;
- water pollution offences caused or knowingly permitted;
- sewerage discharge offences; and
- common law liability (as co-defendant for damage caused or continued during the period of ownership).

In respect of most of these liabilities (all save for contaminated land), there is no easy way to shift liability onto a purchaser other than by getting it to give indemnities to the seller against all liabilities attributable to environmental risks no matter when the events giving rise to the risk took place (i.e. an indemnity given on completion against any risks arising post-completion due to environmental incidents or accidents occurring pre- or post-completion).

This has been insisted upon by some sellers, but it is unlikely that most sophisticated buyers would tolerate the burden depending, of course, on their negotiating position. More limited indemnities (to the seller for liabilities due to post-completion incidents only) or phased, sliding or capped indemnities are more common and acceptable.

A more important strategy is to ensure (perhaps by incoming and outgoing audits) what the state of play is when the site is sold on, so as to be able successfully to determine who did in fact cause a pollution incident, should there ever be a dispute.

As far as contaminated land is concerned, sellers should take close note of those clauses in the statutory guidance that exempt a seller from liability if:

- contract documents specifically reflect the payment (often in the form of a price reduction) of a specific sum for remediation;
- the land is sold in circumstances where full information is provided to the buyer about the contamination on the site; or
- the seller and buyer agree on a contractual formula for dealing with any liabilities which emerge;

and ensure that the paperwork is drafted in such a way as to maximise the chance of exemption.

Note that in sales to 'large commercial organisations', permission to inspect is normally sufficient to pass information for the purposes of Exclusion Test 3 of the statutory guidance to EPA 1990, Part IIA. This should be evidenced in writing and should be an express and explicit permission to enter the property and undertake all and any investigations (including intrusive investigations) as the purchaser and seller shall agree. An assertion that the purchaser must rely on his own inspections would not, of itself, amount to permission to enter and inspect.

Moreover, Exclusion Test 3 requires that the information be sufficient to enable the purchaser to reasonably be aware of the nature and broad measure of the contaminants on the site, so providing information only upon request and in a form not readily comprehensible to a lay recipient is unlikely to be adequate.

As buyers have continued to become more aware and sophisticated, it has become much more common for them to demand some sort of credible proof of compliance with planning conditions, and that previously identified risks have been dealt with adequately. Without such proof or verification, sites have become more difficult to sell, though LPAs are unlikely to offer any definitive confirmation of this kind, and developers who use special purpose vehicles (SPVs, i.e. a company that is established specifically for one site, financial transaction or series of related transactions), in particular, may no longer be around to give their view on what was carried out on site. To the extent that such information can be obtained, it could be provided to buyers.

9.5 TAX CONSIDERATIONS

Practitioners should be aware of the tax implications of remediating contaminated land. There are two main areas of tax: land remediation tax relief and landfill tax.

9.5.1 Land remediation tax relief

Tax relief for remediating contaminated land was introduced in 2001. In the late 2000s, the relief was being extended to include long-term derelict land and land containing arsenic, arsenical compounds, radon and Japanese knotweed.

The scheme works by providing relief from corporation tax so as to provide a 100 per cent deduction plus an additional 50 per cent reduction to qualifying expenditure incurred by a company in remediating land that has been acquired from a third party in a contaminated state.

The definitions of various terms are critical in order not only to determine whether the tax relief applies, but also the works to which it applies. Such works extend beyond those typically considered to be remedial measures for contaminated land. Further research is thus necessary to determine whether the tax relief applies to a client. The website for HM Revenue & Customs should thus be consulted (see **www.hmrc.gov.uk/manuals/cirdmanual/cird60015.htm**).

9.5.2 Landfill tax

Landfill tax is a tax on waste that is disposed in landfills. It was introduced in 1996 with the purpose of minimising waste and encouraging its re-use, recovery and recycling as an alternative to landfill. Whereas the persons who need to register are landfill operators, the tax is obviously passed on to persons who send waste to landfill not only individually but also through waste collections by local authorities. In particular, the tax can have a significant impact on the cost of development and re-development projects.

There are two tax rates: one for inactive or inert waste such as rocks and soil, and a standard rate for any other waste. The rate for inactive or inert waste was initially £2 per tonne. It was increased to £2.50 per tonne for 2010–2011.

The standard rate was originally £7 per tonne with an annual increase of £1 per tonne per year. The rate has risen substantially. The rate for 2010–2011 is £48 per tonne; the annual increase is £8 per tonne per year until at least 2014–2015. This means that by 2014–2015, the standard rate will be £80 per tonne. VAT applies to the entire charge for landfilling waste including the landfill tax itself.

An exemption from the tax for waste from the remediation of contaminated land is being phased out. The final date for the disposal of waste that qualifies for the exemption is 31 March 2012. Critically, HM Revenue & Customs will not accept applications for exemption certificates for such waste after 30 November 2008. Exemptions for dredging and mining waste still apply.

CHAPTER 10

Use and engagement of environmental consultants

10.1 ENVIRONMENTAL INVESTIGATIONS AND AUDIT

The necessity and desirability of carrying out environmental investigations and audits has grown rapidly in recent years. Lenders, insurers, purchasers and enlightened managers all perceive the need for knowledge relating to a particular company's environmental situation, and its potential exposure to liability for historic contamination, incidents, accidents and claims.

An environmental investigation or audit can take a number of forms. They can involve a full assessment of a company's sites, operations and installations with the intention of evaluating the potential environmental risks posed by those installations, and to monitor corporate environmental performance. Such an audit is often used when purchasing an existing business. When looking at potential liability from historic activities, a Phase 1 or 2 environmental survey may be commissioned. A Phase 1 survey will include looking at the historic and current use of the site and the surrounding area, enquiries of relevant regulators and statutory bodies and a basic site walk over. A Phase 2 site investigation will include intrusive investigations which involves physically taking soil samples and carrying out an analysis of those samples to ascertain if they contain high levels of contaminants.

10.2 RISKS OF HAVING AN INVESTIGATION

10.2.1 General

One of the main risks of an environmental investigation is that it may provide damaging information which could be the basis for civil or criminal liability, or write-downs on the values of assets.

Such results may have a damaging impact on public perception and confidence, which may in turn affect the company's share price. It may also affect a company's position with its bankers, in that loan facilities may be withdrawn or renegotiated.

The problem is that investigation reports commissioned by a company from, say, an environmental consultant, and submitted by the consultant to the company, would not be secret, confidential or in any way protected from having to be shown to inspectors and officers of the regulatory agencies.

Nor would it be possible to avoid having to show these documents to an opponent in any civil court proceedings which may be brought. It would be highly embarrassing to have to reveal the contents of a damaging investigation report in court.

Many clients do not appreciate that the concept of 'confidentiality' is not protected by English law. Merely calling a document 'confidential' does not make it secret in the way that the company might want.

A typical investigation report is almost inevitably going to contain potentially damaging information about the company's site operations and installations, and may even point out specifically the potential danger for a pollution offence or explosion.

Most formal environmental management systems, like ISO 14001, will require not only the documentation and recording of the corporate environmental policy, but also the monitoring of records and results of later audits, which will spell out the ways in which company performance is inadequate, and in breach of stated policy.

Clearly, the company may wish to keep this information confidential, particularly from public-interest groups, regulatory authorities or opponents in a civil action.

10.2.2 Can consultants' reports be privileged?

There are ways in which protection for this documentation can be maximised, though never fully guaranteed, by the use of legal professional privilege.

The only documents protected from disclosure to any of these parties or bodies is documentation which is protected by legal professional privilege. Only if a document attracts legal professional privilege can it truly be called confidential or secret, because it is only such documents which are protected from disclosure.

The main category of privilege is solicitor–client communications, which breaks down into two sub-categories:

- communications passing between a solicitor and his client; and
- communications between third parties and a solicitor which are privileged only if they are made in anticipation of contemplated or pending litigation and the dominant purpose of the communication was to prepare for the proceedings.

Communications between a lawyer and his client will be privileged provided they are confidential, made between a lawyer in his professional capacity and his client, and made for the purpose of either seeking or giving legal advice (see the affirmatory comments of the House of Lords in *Three Rivers District Council* v. *Bank of England* [2004] UKHL 48). No opponent or inspector can have access to them or use them in subsequent proceedings. Clearly, this is a very valuable protection for a client, but it is available only if the client instructs the solicitor to give 'legal advice'.

In the context of an environmental investigation, therefore, the ideal situation would be for the client to contact the solicitor and instruct the solicitor to advise the client on compliance with legal environmental duties and responsibilities.

Particular problems arise in dealings with third parties, such as environmental consultants, in that an investigation report commissioned by a company without involving its lawyers would not be privileged, as it would not be 'legal advice', nor would it be prepared 'for the dominant purpose of anticipated or pending litigation', unless, of course, criminal or civil proceedings had already been started against the company by the time the report was commissioned.

However, there is some authority (see *Getty* v. *Getty and Treves* [1985] QB 956) for the proposition that privilege extends to information which a solicitor receives in his professional capacity from a third party, for onward transmission to the client as part of the legal advice which the client has sought.

This suggests that there is some mileage in arguing that if a solicitor is engaged by a company to give legal advice, and that solicitor feels it necessary to take further advice from other consultants and specialists in order to advise the client of the full and true legal position, then the advice by the third-party consultants to the solicitor should be privileged, just as much as the solicitor's own advice to the client would be.

In the context of an environmental investigation, one would seek to argue that the technical consultants and, maybe, the management consultants or accountants, were merely undertaking investigations and expressing opinions in order that the solicitor could fully and accurately assess the legal position, in particular, the requirements for the company's compliance with its legal obligations.

To be able to argue this point successfully, it would be necessary for the solicitor to engage the third-party consultants, whether they be technical engineering consultants or accountants and management consultants, as it would be, in effect, the solicitor who required their services.

Such reports would therefore be commissioned by the solicitor, and be addressed to the solicitor to ensure consistency with this approach. The solicitor would then collate all the information, and provide the necessary advice to the client company.

By this means, the consultants' reports to the solicitor, and the ultimate advice to the client from the solicitor, may attract legal professional privilege and thus be safe from disclosure.

However, this approach has not been tested in court, and cannot be guaranteed to be successful. Moreover, there are severe dangers for any solicitor who is in the 'hub of the wheel' in this way. In particular:

- solicitors may be liable in negligence for the quality of the advice they are passing on, and if the consultant gets it wrong, it may be the solicitor who is sued by the client;
- there may be insurance difficulties in passing on information in this way;

- the client and any future purchaser/funder may wish to rely on the contents of the report so provision needs to be made for a collateral warranty/duty of care letter.

It may be thought best, therefore, for the solicitor to engineer the appointment of the consultant directly by the client, subject to suitable advice on the terms and conditions of that appointment. A draft set of terms and conditions is set out in Appendix A10.

In addition, precautions should be taken as to the storage of any such report, so that it is not inadvertently handed over to an inspector by a member of staff, as part of an official investigation.

10.3 CARRYING OUT AN INVESTIGATION

10.3.1 Internal matters

It is assumed, for the following discussion, that a company undertaking a compliance investigation genuinely wishes to take proactive steps to manage its risks, and is therefore committed to implementing the suggestions made in the final report.

A company without such a commitment is wasting its money undertaking the investigation in the first place.

For compliance investigations, conducted with a view to introducing (or improving) the management of businesses in respect of environmental issues, ISO 14001 sets out the practices to adopt.

Whilst not all compliance investigations are commissioned with a view to ISO accreditation, it nonetheless provides a helpful guide to the sort of issues that should be addressed in a compliance investigation.

The essential elements of an investigation are numerous and involve, as a fundamental condition, full management commitment to the process and the implementation of the findings and recommendations.

Accordingly, the company should appoint a main board director with specific responsibility and accountability for environmental issues, and the implementation of the environmental policy. This individual will be charged with the responsibility for commissioning the investigation, and implementing its recommendations in due course. The same individual will also be responsible for the follow-up audits in due course.

There must be a dedicated team (accountable to the responsible director and the board) to formulate and implement the company's environmental policy, comprising any relevant internal or external technical and scientific experts, line managers and legal advisers, whether internal or external.

The investigation itself should produce a written document setting out the findings of the investigation and any recommendations.

The investigation should include a careful environmental impact study of each area of production activity in the business and should set out specific, measurable objectives and targets, and a timetable for achieving them.

Facilities for monitoring and investigation should be programmed in as part of the policy, as should systematic records of performance, so that achievement can be monitored and investigated effectively.

The investigation itself, and perhaps the follow-up audits, will very often be undertaken by an external, independent environmental consultant.

10.3.2 Using environmental consultants

Environmental investigations have for some time been a growth area and the number of consultancies has mushroomed. There are now several hundred different consultancies in the UK, and choosing one should not be difficult. However, picking one at random is unlikely to be the best solution, and close thought must be given to the selection process.

Shop around – not all consultancies do the same things, charge the same fees, or are of a comparable standard. Look at what experience they have of similar projects, the degree to which they understand the nature of the business in question and who is actually going to carry out the work.

The term 'environmental consultant' covers a vast range of technical and scientific disciplines, e.g. geology, hydrogeology, acoustics, chemistry, biochemistry, ecology, etc.

There are a wide variety of consultancies available, ranging from the very common, small domestic consultancy (turnover £100,000 or less) at one end of the market, to UK divisions of large foreign engineering and environmental consultancies at the other. In addition, many of the UK engineering companies have set up dedicated divisions within their overall operating structure to provide these services.

It is important to recognise that they are the experts and you are relying on their expertise. In view of this, consideration should be given to what you are asking them to do. Rather than providing a detailed specification to the consultants for the work they are to carry out, it may be better to provide them with the required outputs, e.g. a report detailing the risk of the property being identified as a Part IIA site and allow the consultants to decide what work is appropriate to achieve the desired output.

10.3.3 Do I need to appoint a consultant at all?

There is no need to appoint a consultant to achieve the purposes of an investigation. Companies may well be able to solve their environmental problems and achieve their aims by developing their own in-house expertise.

However, appointing a specialist consultant is certainly the easiest and commonest way of addressing the issues, and almost the only option in a purchase transaction.

10.3.4   Selecting and appointing consultants

Prior to appointing a consultant to carry out an investigation, the business should have a clear idea of the objectives which it wishes to achieve in the investigation. Some of the possibilities are mentioned above.

It should then select and appoint the investigation team which will best provide the service required by the company. This may sound obvious, but only when the company has addressed this question will it be able to choose the right consultancy for the job. Without such analysis, the company stands a much smaller chance of getting the right product. Using consultants is too expensive to take that sort of risk.

Solicitors can often provide useful advice at this stage in helping to specify the investigation service required and the quality standards that will need to be achieved.

Choosing a consultancy can be done by the tried and trusted method of word-of-mouth recommendation, though this is not always a fail-safe and speedy method. Many consultancies also offer new or potential clients the opportunity to speak to former or existing clients, to ascertain how certain projects were carried out. Some clients request client references as part of the tender process. This kind of third-party testimonial is an invaluable method of endorsement to the consultancy and of reference to the client.

Various directories are now available which list the consultancies, and specify their level of expertise and technical coverage. The *ENDS Directory of Environmental Consultants* (published by Environmental Data Systems Ltd (ENDS), see Appendix G for address) is the obvious publication to consult, though the Institute of Environmental Management and Assessment (IEMA) would be another useful contact or, when looking at potential issues around historic contamination, whether the person carrying out the work is a Specialist in Land Condition (SiLC) (see **www.silc.org.uk**).

Inviting a selection of consultants to attend a 'beauty parade', and to tender for work is another method favoured by many. Contacts through parent companies, trade associations, seminars and professional advisers are all useful sources of information and contacts.

Some banks and other lending institutions tend to have their own panel of approved consultants, and will insist on the report being compiled by one of them. A client may not therefore have a totally free choice.

There are several systems of formal accreditation or registration for organisations, individuals, or both, which give an independent technical certification to those involved in environmental consultancy work. There are also accrediting organisations within the environmental consultancy industry which accredit the professional standard of consultancy work, including IEMA and the United Kingdom Accreditation Service (UKAS).

Increasingly, professional institutions such as the RICS, the Institution of Civil Engineers (ICE), the Royal Society of Chemistry (RSC) and the Institution of

Chemical Engineers (IChemE) maintain registers of professional consultancies and individuals who are competent in environmental and other disciplines.

The Environmental Consultants Group (ECG) of the Environment Industries Commission (EIC) has been established to give information on the expertise of its members. It assesses their competence in a range of technical areas rather than simply publishing self-certified information on the expertise of consultancy companies.

There is a further class of surveyor known as the chartered environmental surveyor (CES). Part of the appointment brief for a CES is to provide an overview reflecting the outputs of the project team in a market context, for example, to be able to produce a Land Quality Statement which is designed to create the bridge between technical issues relevant to brownfield sites and the marketplace.

10.3.5   Considerations on appointment

There are a number of considerations which need to borne in mind in the appointment of the consultants. A non-exhaustive list of the more important ones follows.

Type of consultancy

An early decision needs to be taken as to what type of consultancy is required. Does the company need engineering or analytical advice, or does it need management consultancy? Consultants from both ends of the spectrum are available, and the answer to this question will limit the options.

The history and background of the consultancy, and the core business of its parent company will also affect the angle taken by the consultant on the project, and again will limit the options.

One large consultant, or many small ones?

In the vast majority of cases, the company will want the whole investigation process and the whole project to be handled by one consultant.

With this in mind, employing a multi-disciplinary practice may be preferable to employing a series of specialists, particularly when one bears in mind the logistical difficulties in getting all the reports in the right form, at the right time, at the right price and on the right terms from a variety of different suppliers.

On the other hand, it would be foolish to employ a consultancy on the grounds of convenience if it does not have the specific expertise required and, in any event, the larger consultancies tend to be more expensive.

Previous experience and details of relevant projects

The ability of the consultancy to do the job is what counts. There are few better indicators of this than experience. Even where a consultancy says it has the relevant experience, it is worth checking that the key personnel who may have significant experience and reputation are working on your job.

Moreover, in professional and business life, there are those for whom practice does not make perfect, and who may still perform badly despite plenty of opportunity to improve.

One should consider taking references from previous clients.

Membership of professional bodies

One should ideally choose a consultant that has some independent accreditation of quality. The Institute of Environmental Assessment launched a quality standard in 1991. This has now been superseded by the IEMA version. Registration with IEMA should carry a degree of confidence in the quality of the consultancy.

It is worthwhile checking if the individual is a member of a relevant professional body and is 'chartered'.

There is, of course, the possibility of accreditation to ISO 9000 or equivalent standards, though this is not necessarily an indication of the quality of the investigating, merely of the management of the business. It is possible to perform a bad investigation very effectively.

Professional indemnity insurance – are there any restrictions on cover?

Adequate insurance coverage should be insisted upon. Bad advice from a consultant may expose a company to huge potential liabilities, and recourse may be had against the adviser. It would be unfortunate if there were no fund with which to pay the bill.

Most professional indemnity and public liability insurers include pollution exclusion clauses in all their policies, and the surveying profession has had its PII cover removed for such risks.

It should be routine to check the cover available to the consultant. Even if the consultant is insured, there may be limits on the level of cover offered which may be too low for the comfort of the employer company. In addition, exclusions in the policy may result in the specific project not being covered, the specific contaminant not being covered, or an excess being required.

If a claim has already been made against the consultant by another client, it may have exhausted the aggregate limit of funds available under the policy leaving no funds for the next claimant. Also, has the renewal date passed?

These points need to be checked directly with the insurer, if possible.

Many large consultancies carry perfectly adequate cover because of their size and reputation in other fields, and many take a responsible view of their obligations although some have a more cavalier attitude.

In any event, cover can usually be purchased on a project-specific basis.

Beware of 'standard contracts', as some do not give adequate protection to the client company

Many consultancies work on standard terms of engagement, and those terms are frequently biased in favour of the consultant. Often, they are based on foreign versions, often American, and are vaguely worded to the point of being meaningless and unenforceable.

Particular restrictions to be wary of are:

- clauses which restrict the amount that can be claimed to a set sum (often £50,000) or to a sum equivalent to the contract price. These limitations are inadequate, as the value of the decisions taken on the strength of the advice is significantly greater than the price paid for the initial investigation report itself;
- clauses which limit the limitation period within which claims can be brought. The normal period of six years can be reduced by agreement between parties of equal standing to a contract. Many standard contracts reduce the period to three years, two years or even one year; and
- clauses which require the client to indemnify the consultant against all liability whatsoever for all matters arising in connection with the investigation.

Such terms are not affected by the Unfair Contract Terms Act 1977, which in many contexts has the effect of rendering void any terms which purport to restrict remedies in contract (limitation clauses), or at least subjects them to a reasonableness test before they can be relied upon. These legal restrictions on limitation clauses only apply to clauses purporting to limit liability for personal injury and death due to negligence, consumer contracts or contracts entered into on standard terms and conditions. Freely negotiated contracts between commercial organisations of equivalent bargaining strength would not normally be affected by such legal restrictions and a consultant could therefore include limitations on liability and expect to be able to rely on them.

Giving a precise specification of works required

Having decided what is required by the investigation, the company and its advisers must ensure that the message is adequately and clearly communicated to the consultant.

English Partnerships v. *Mott MacDonald* illustrates the huge expense which misunderstandings at this stage can create (ENDS Report, April 1999).

In particular, depending on the purpose behind the investigation, the methodology adopted by the consultant may be required to correlate with that required to be adopted by local authorities in the identification of contaminated land.

Requiring detailed information on costs

It is essential to ensure complete understanding of the basis on which the fees are to be assessed and paid. This would include finalising details of any fixed-cost preliminary investigations, the provision of regular progress reports with costs limits, or the delivery of interim invoices linked to specific tasks, and time sheets and a final account with a full statement of work done.

Assignability of rights

If the client has engaged the consultant directly, it is essential to insist, if possible, that the right to use, and sue upon, the report is transferable to anyone else involved in, or affected by the project.

Normally, only the company which engaged the consultant would be allowed to sue, as it is only the company which has a contract with the consultant. There may be times, however, when others (e.g. purchasers of a reclaimed site, tenants, funders, or potential shareholders) are affected by the inadequacy of the service offered by the consultant, and want to sue. They would need to have the right to sue assigned to them specifically.

The right of the employing company to assign this right should be retained in the contract with the consultant.

This is frequently resisted, and the matter dealt with on an ad hoc basis by means of collateral warranties or a duty of care letter between the consultant and the person purportedly relying on the report.

Readable reports produced in a form accessible to the company

One problem often encountered with investigation reports is that they are produced in a technical way, using graphs, read-outs and technical language which is incomprehensible to a company manager.

The consultant should be aware of the need for clear, simple language, and clarity of expression. Nevertheless, the company should make clear its requirement for clear and readable presentation, perhaps confining technical documentation to an appendix.

Copyright and other intellectual property rights associated with the investigation to be owned by the company

The terms of engagement should provide that any technical information disclosed to the consultant remains the property of the company, and also that any novel or inventive discoveries made by the consultant in the process of the investigation also belong to the company.

Likewise, there should be company access to all source material and data generated by the consultant. This is to ensure that any inventions, trade marks, designs, patents and other confidential information are not misused.

Confidentiality

All matters relating to the investigation must be treated with the strictest confidentiality by the consultant, and not revealed to anyone without the express authority of the company.

Discipline of this nature is essential to ensure that there is no undue reliance on the contents of the report by anyone to whom it is not directed, and also to ensure that copies of the report do not fall into the wrong hands, thus waiving any privilege which may otherwise have attached to it.

Privilege

All correspondence, draft documents and other papers including the final report, all technical or other confidential information learned by the consultant in the course of the investigation about the company's business, and all correspondence between solicitors and the consultant and other documents should be retained by the appointing solicitor in order to maximise the protection afforded by the solicitor–client privilege.

CHAPTER 11

Funding and borrowing transactions

11.1 ENVIRONMENTAL IMPACT ON FUNDING AND SECURITY

The ever increasing burden of environmental regulation has affected lenders as well as polluters. In particular, lenders are concerned about environmental risk for the following reasons:

- it can reduce the creditworthiness of the borrower by imposing additional costs on its business, for example, liability for clean-up costs, or the tightening of environmental systems by the introduction of new technology;
- it can reduce the value of the security held by the lender;
- there can be a reputational risk in lending to a business that is perceived to be 'dirty';
- it can, in certain circumstances, create direct liability on the lender.

In the first two examples, the impact of the environmental regime may serve to put the borrower in breach of its bank agreements (perhaps non-compliance with financial covenants) which will put lenders on notice of problems with the borrower's financial stability.

Lenders will have at the forefront of their minds the possibility that their security may be jeopardised, not only by direct pollution, but by indirect contamination; for example, where an adjacent site is contaminated or the property is in an area of high pollution where the mere possibility of creeping pollution is usually sufficient to depress the market value of a property. Disposal of a site (even though it is 'clean') in these circumstances may be extremely difficult (see *Blue Circle Industries plc* v. *Ministry of Defence* [1998] 3 All ER 385 (a judgment in excess of £6 million attributable to lost property value), and *English Partnerships* v. *Mott MacDonald*, reported in ENDS Report, April 1999 (a judgment in excess of £18 million, turning on the interpretation of the term 'clean')).

The subject of direct liability faced by lenders in respect of contamination has already been discussed in Chapter 1.

11.2 PROTECTION FOR THE LENDER

What steps can lenders take to restrict the impact of the environmental regime and the other liabilities discussed earlier?

11.2.1 Risk evaluation

The view taken by the Council of Mortgage Lenders (CML) in relation to the domestic property market seems to be largely to ignore the risk of contamination in lending decisions, in order to avoid the problem and issue of blight. However, those representing the lender's interests are obliged to take all reasonable steps to ascertain the extent to which there may be a risk to the security and advise accordingly in appropriate cases.

Most commercial lenders will have addressed the issue of environmental risk in their lending criteria and sanction authority.

Lenders will consider issues such as:

- the environmental record and standing of the borrower:
- environmental auditing and control systems;
- environmental planning and continuing measures;
- the extent to which pollution (particularly known risks) would impact on the value of the security;
- assessment of the risk of pollution or contamination in the light of the nature of the business and the locality in which it operates.

Lenders will generally factor into the lending decision the environmental risk and the terms of the loan will reflect it, perhaps by taking increased security, a higher interest rate margin or tighter covenants and monitoring.

Environmental investigations or audits

Risk evaluation cannot take place without information. Historically, only if a proposal involved a contaminative industry, would lenders require an environmental investigation. This is now common practice in almost any case involving land which may have a history of contaminative use, regardless of the current or future user. The lender's satisfaction with the investigation report should be a condition precedent to the drawdown of the facility. The choice of environmental consultant is discussed in Chapter 10.

Certificate of title

Provisions may be included in a certificate of title produced by the borrower's solicitors dealing with the environmental condition of the land. However, the solicitors acting for the business may be reluctant to include it in the certificate. Nevertheless, if instructions require it, it must be provided.

In these circumstances, the lender may require the management of the business to confirm that the business is not subject to environmental problems or enforcement actions. This type of confirmation will usually be qualified to the best of the management's knowledge.

The standard certificate issued by the City of London Law Society which is used in the majority of transactions contains representations regarding environmental permits. It does not deal with environmental reports although the notes do flag this up as an issue that the lender may wish to consider.

Consents and licences

The lender should investigate, particularly in relation to facilities granted to contaminative industries, whether all consents and licences have been obtained, whether they are all in full force and effect and are being complied with, and whether any notices (prohibition, enforcement, remediation, abatement, works, etc.) have been served.

Environmental management systems

The lender should ensure that adequate management systems are in place to cope with pollution or contamination problems and, more importantly, to try and prevent environmental problems arising. Increasingly, this means an externally verified and accredited system such as ISO 14001 or EC Eco-Management and Audit Scheme (EMAS).

Representations and warranties

The inclusion of appropriate representations or warranties in the facility letter should ensure that further information is disclosed to the lender against those warranties. This is a very useful source of information and is discussed in further detail below.

11.2.2 New proposals and ongoing protection

New proposals create an opportunity for lenders to face environmental issues head on and deal with them in any manner which gives them some protection and comfort for the duration of the facility. The facility agreement and security documents should make provision for the lender's protection. The following are some rudimentary steps which can be taken to safeguard the interests of the lender.

Conditions precedent

Prior to any funds being drawn down, the lender should have sight of, and be happy with, all environmental reports, consents and licences. The lender is likely to require a collateral warranty so that it can rely on the contents of the environmental report. Appendix A9 sets out the issues which should be on a lender's list of conditions precedent from an environmental point of view.

Representations and warranties

The representations and warranties, if drafted thoroughly, should provide a lender with information about environmental risks at an early stage.

The representations and warranties are first given by the borrower immediately before drawdown. Certain representations and warranties (relevant to environmental problems) are set out in the examples at Appendix A9. Briefly, these warranties are that:

- the environmental report (if one has been produced) is true and the borrower is not aware of anything material omitted from the report or anything else which would be likely to give rise to any material liability on the part of the borrower under any environmental legislation;
- the borrower complies with all environmental laws;
- the borrower has all the necessary consents and licences to operate the process, that no notice has been served on the operator relating to any breach of licence or consent condition and that such consents can be transferred;
- the borrower has maintained all necessary assets;
- the borrower is not subject to any compliance or enforcement orders;
- the borrower is not subject to any claim, demand or notice alleging responsibility for any clean-up or other costs or property or personal damage or fines or penalties arising out of the presence of any hazardous or polluting matter or violation of any environmental law.

As mentioned, the representations and warranties should be certified by the borrower to be true immediately before drawdown of the facility. They should also be repeated at regular intervals to ensure continued compliance and so that the lender obtains swift warning of any problems. If acting for the borrower, annual repetition is satisfactory; more frequent repetition is preferable when acting for a lender if there are believed to be environmental issues.

The impact of the representations is diluted if they are not monitored and policed properly. Lenders must ensure that the information is provided punctually.

Covenants and undertakings

Representations and warranties provide a snapshot of the borrower at any particular moment. Covenants are ongoing obligations of the borrower which usually persist for the entire period of the facility.

There is a degree of overlap between the representations and warranties and the covenants, particularly if the representations and warranties are repeated on a regular basis. Appendix A9 sets out some illustrative covenants that the lender might ask for.

There is a provision for the production of a certificate, within 60 days of the financial year end, from an officer of the company confirming that there have been no changes to any of the matters set out in the environmental report and if that certificate is not given, the lender has the right to undertake a further environmental investigation.

Where the lender receives notice of a claim under any environmental law, there is a covenant requiring a more comprehensive delivery of information. This should ensure that the lender is kept fully aware of the potential problem enabling it to assess its position fully.

The insurance covenant in the facility letter could be expanded to ensure that it covers environmental risks to the extent that such cover is available in the marketplace. Environmental insurance can be a difficult issue and is discussed in Chapter 13.

It may be prudent to restrict the borrower from acquiring assets or commencing a new business which may be an environmental risk. The difficulty here is that the lender does not wish to get involved in relatively minor asset acquisitions, but the lender needs to recognise that the potential liability for the company could be large, even though the consideration for the asset is insignificant.

Events of default

A specific event of default may not be necessary as a breach of a representation, warranty or covenant will usually be a default anyway. But a specific environmental default may be required due to the fact that the full impact may be difficult to assess and the liability to the borrower may not be calculable for some considerable time. This may give rise to arguments about whether a general event of default clause is applicable. In these circumstances, a specific default clause would be preferable.

The occurrence of an event of default under a facility agreement will generally give rise to the right to demand repayment of the facility and enforce security. Lenders must be wary about enforcing security unless they are fully aware of the environmental problems with land over which they have security. As discussed in Chapter 1, the lender risks direct liability in respect of contaminated land in certain restricted circumstances. If a site over which the lender has security is particularly contaminated, the lender may be forced to release the tainted security.

Uniquely, in respect of contaminated land under EPA 1990, Part IIA, an insolvency practitioner is released from potential liability save in respect of his own negligent acts. Appointing a receiver over a tainted security would seem to be preferable to entering into possession, but the receiver may still be liable for other matters and may not therefore be willing to take the risk of appointment.

Recovery of clean-up costs

The greatest concern for lenders is the direct liability for clean up in respect of contaminated sites over which they held security. Chapter 1 discusses the circumstances where this may arise. Even if the lender is not automatically responsible for clean up, a sale of a contaminated site will be unlikely unless clean up occurs. The lender may have to bear this cost. Therefore, it is essential that the lender's facility or security documents incorporate an appropriate clause to enable it to recover such costs. An illustration is set out in Appendix A9.

11.2.3 Existing facilities

Lenders may be restricted in the options available by the terms of existing facility letters, most of which will not address the issues of environmental default.

Facilities which are uncommitted may be withdrawn and demand made for outstanding liabilities. Practically, the lender will not be able to take this course without jeopardising the customer relationship. Term facilities which are not in default are even more of a problem.

Once again, it is important for the lender to acquire information. The existing information covenant contained in the facility letter should be carefully examined to see whether it can be used to demand the relevant information. If not, it will often be possible to agree with a borrower to expand certain terms of the facility agreement to incorporate more extensive information covenants. This can be formalised very readily by the signature by the lender and borrower of an amending agreement.

The flow of information is crucial. If, for example, the borrower is operating in a highly contaminative sector, the lender may decide that despite a desire to enforce its security, it will not do so because, on the basis of its intelligence, there is a significant potential direct liability for clean up and other issues.

Armed with the relevant information at an early stage, lenders have sufficient weapons in their armoury to protect themselves. It is the unexpected major problem which sends lenders scurrying for their security documents.

CHAPTER 12

Insolvency

12.1 INTRODUCTION

The interaction between environmental law and insolvency law is an uneasy fit that may lead to difficult situations. These include a client who encounters financial difficulties itself or who has leased land to a company that becomes insolvent after having stored or disposed of waste on the leased site. In addition, solicitors may serve as insolvency practitioners and thus face potential liability depending on the environmental responsibilities and liabilities of the insolvent company.

This chapter describes cases that involve the interaction of environmental law and insolvency law. It then describes the potential environmental liabilities of insolvency practitioners. Finally, it discusses the statutory protection for an insolvency practitioner for remediating contaminated land under EPA 1990, Part IIA.

12.2 DISPOSAL OF LAND

Solicitors should ensure that their clients do not dispose of land without also transferring or surrendering any environmental permit for that land. A classic case is the sale of a former landfill without transferring or surrendering the environmental permit for the landfill. In such a case, the company remains liable for complying with the terms and conditions of the permit even though it neither owns the site nor has access to it.

In a case in which a company holding a waste management licence (now an environmental permit) became insolvent, the Court of Appeal held, in *Re Celtic Extraction Ltd* v. *Environment Agency* [2001] Ch 475, that the liquidator may disclaim the licence as onerous property under the Insolvency Act (IA) 1986, s.178(2).

12.3 LAND CONTAINING WASTE

Another classic example of the interaction between environmental law and insolvency law involves a company that encounters financial problems and does not have sufficient funding to remove waste from its site or to clean up contamination at it.

In *Re Wilmott Trading Company (No 2)* [2000] Env LR 54, a company that operated a scrap metal recycling facility under a waste management licence occupied a site that contained 1,600 tons of waste. After the company ceased trading, insufficient funds remained to comply with the terms and conditions of the licence. Neuberger J concluded that the licence ceased to exist when the company was dissolved.

Legislation has been enacted to avoid the situation in which the operator of a landfill has insufficient funding to comply with the terms and conditions of the landfill permit. The Environmental Permitting Regulations require an operator to provide evidence of adequate financial provision for the costs of complying with the permit including post-closure care to ensure that waste at the landfill does not pose a risk of harm to human health and the environment after the operational phase has ended and the landfill has been closed.

The Environment Agency has ensured that its requirements for the establishment of a financial provision do not result in a situation in which the Agency cannot access the funds if the landfill operator becomes insolvent. This situation arose in *Environment Agency* v. *Hillridge Ltd* [2004] Env LR 633, in which Blackburne J concluded that the liquidator had disclaimed the insolvent company's interest in the trust fund that had been established to satisfy the financial provision requirements when the liquidator disclaimed the waste management licence. As a result, the Agency was not entitled to the money in the trust account because the Agency ceased to have powers under the licence when the liquidator of the company that operated the landfill disclaimed it.

Clean-up costs enjoy no preference in an insolvency proceeding.

12.4 PROSECUTIONS DURING ADMINISTRATION

Section 11 of IA 1986 provides that 'no other proceedings and no execution or other legal process may be commenced or continued' against a company in respect of which an administration order is in force except with leave of court or the administrator's consent. In *Re Rhondda Waste Disposal Ltd (In Administration)* v. *Clark* [2001] Ch 57, the Court of Appeal concluded that criminal proceedings are included in the term 'other proceedings' in s.11.

The Environment Agency had alleged that a waste disposal company had failed to comply with a condition of its licence that required it to cap waste at a landfill in breach of EPA 1990, s.33(6). Two days before the Agency laid the information against the company, the High Court made an administration order over it.

The Court of Appeal concluded that the High Court, which had refused leave to the Agency to bring a prosecution against the company, had failed properly to exercise its discretion. Scott Baker J commented that leave of court is necessary due to the Environment Agency not having details of the financial information regarding the company that is available to the administrator and the court. The Court of Appeal further concluded that the High Court had failed adequately to consider the

Environment Agency's concerns and had placed too much weight on the interests of the company's creditors. The payment of any fine by the company would necessarily reduce the assets available for distribution to its creditors. After the Court of Appeal's decision, the local magistrates' court fined the company £20,000 with £11,365 costs for failing to comply with the condition of its licence that required it to cap waste.

12.5 INSOLVENCY PRACTITIONERS

A solicitor who acts as an administrative receiver, administrator, liquidator, supervisor of a voluntary arrangement, or an LPA receiver, that is, a receiver appointed under the Law of Property Act 1930, may face potential environmental liabilities. As discussed below, the potential liabilities differ depending on the position held by the insolvency practitioner.

12.5.1 Administrative receivers

General

A receiver appointed by a bank or other lender under the terms of a normal floating charge debenture taking over the whole or substantially the whole of a company's assets will be an 'administrative receiver' by virtue of IA 1986, s.29.

The main implications and effects of this are that:

- IA 1986 provides that such an individual will be the agent of the company (s.44); and
- the appointee is given very wide powers to deal with the assets of the company, together with wide powers of management.

The breadth of the powers of the administrative receiver are, to some extent, a cause for concern in that, very often, the receiver becomes very closely allied to the activities of the company over which he is appointed. This can link him with its environmental liabilities. However, he enjoys statutory exemption for liability for contaminated land so long as he acts normally in the execution of his functions.

Criminal liability

DIRECT LIABILITY

Notwithstanding the statutory protection in respect of contaminated land, receivers may still be criminally liable directly under the following legislation:

(a) under the Environmental Permitting Regulations if:

- they carry on a business in breach of an environmental permit or without a required permit; or
- they cause, knowingly cause or knowingly permit a water pollution, water discharge or a groundwater offence;

(b)   under EPA 1990 if:

- they deposit, knowingly cause or knowingly permit the deposit of waste;
- they breach the duty of care; or
- they are responsible for a statutory nuisance and fail to comply with an abatement notice; and

(c)   under WIA 1991 if:

- they occupy trade premises and discharge trade effluent in breach of a sewerage undertaker's consent or without a required consent.

Whether this is possible depends on the ability of the prosecuting authority to prove the receiver's causal involvement in the incident, and this in turn depends on the extent of the receiver's actual involvement in the management of the business.

A typical receiver will normally be wishing to sell the business as a going concern and will, therefore, be thinking in terms of keeping the operation going until a buyer is found. He will therefore be continuing the activities of the company under his powers of management. If offences are committed in this period, the receiver may be exposed to the risk of prosecution if his activities have 'caused' the offence.

At the very least, the receiver will be expected to understand the nature of the business over which he is appointed, and so must be said to be 'knowingly permitting' any offences which occur. A receiver must therefore investigate the potential environmental liabilities and risks fully before appointment.

Most of the offences are strict liability offences. A receiver is therefore likely to be personally liable unless he can take advantage of some statutory defence, e.g. under EPA 1990, s.33(7) or the Environmental Permitting Regulations, reg. 40.

A receiver's agency will not protect him from prosecution for a criminal offence.

INDIRECT LIABILITY

Receivers may be made indirectly liable by virtue of EPA 1990, s.157 (or sister provisions including the Environmental Permitting Regulations, reg.41 and WIA 1991, s.210), if it can be said that a receiver is 'a person who was purporting to act' in the capacity of a company officer.

A receiver is an 'office-holder' within the meaning of IA 1986 and successor legislation. Whether a receiver is an 'officer' of the company, however, is debatable, but he may be 'someone purporting to act in that capacity', in that the receiver has *de facto* power of control over company operations once appointed.

There may, in addition, be liability under EPA 1990, s.158 (or sister provisions including the Environmental Permitting Regulations and WIA 1991) if he commits some 'act or default' which results in an offence being committed. This may possibly include merely continuing existing business operations.

Civil liability

NUISANCE

A receiver may be liable in nuisance if he is appointed over the assets of a company, one of which is land giving rise to a nuisance, for example, due to contamination.

The receiver could arguably be said to be an occupier of the land or, depending on the circumstances, the creator of the nuisance and, as such, could be sued in tort.

After *Cambridge Water Company Ltd* v. *Eastern Counties Leather plc* [1994] 2 AC 264, HL, it seems clear that if it is beyond the power of the receiver to rectify a contaminating situation, he will not be liable in nuisance.

However, if it is within the receiver's power to rectify a situation, it matters not that the nuisance had begun before the receiver was appointed; failing to abate or prevent it from continuing after that date may be sufficient to attach liability for all the foreseeable consequences of the activity.

Of course, the receiver will be strictly liable in civil law for the foreseeable consequences of any operations carried on by him while in office.

It is perhaps unlikely that, given the short time of his occupation, a claimant would be able to show all the necessary elements of the claim against the receiver, so the risk of civil suits should not be overstated.

Clean-up costs

ENVIRONMENTAL PERMITTING REGULATIONS

Receivers may be liable under reg. 44 of the Environmental Permitting Regulations for the cost of remedying damage caused by an environmental permitting offence only if they are convicted of the appropriate offence.

EPA 1990, PART II – WASTE MATTERS

Receivers can be liable under EPA 1990, s.59 (cost of removal of waste) if they are the 'occupier' of the land in question. Is a receiver an 'occupier'? The term is not defined in the Act, but case law would have it that the person in possession of the property is its occupier. A receiver will be so regarded as he is generally provided with full power to possess and control the property.

Section 59 requires the deposit to constitute an offence under s.33 before the power to recover costs from an occupier exists, so a receiver could raise the statutory defences in s.33 as a defence to a claim for clean-up costs.

If there is no occupier of the land or the occupier cannot be found without the authority incurring unreasonable expense, the owner of the land may be liable for the cost of removing the waste under s.59ZA. It is unlikely, however, that a receiver would be regarded as the owner of the land.

EPA 1990, PART III – STATUTORY NUISANCES

A receiver can be liable for the cost of abating a statutory nuisance if his act or default caused the statutory nuisance.

It is debatable, therefore, whether the cost of abating a nuisance which arose before the receiver's appointment but continues after that date would be recoverable from him. It probably is not, though it is possible to argue that continued inactivity by a receiver with regard to known problems could amount to 'default'.

WATER RESOURCES ACT 1991

A receiver could be liable under WRA 1991, ss.161–161D for the costs of preventing or remedying a water pollution incident if he can be said to have caused or knowingly permitted it.

It is submitted that the test of causing or knowingly permitting will be the same as in criminal law, i.e. strict liability for matters which the receiver should or could have known about. Receivers can therefore expect to be made personally liable for these costs, though the receiver's agency, as long as it subsists, should protect him from clean-up costs.

12.5.2 Administrators

Administrators appointed by the court under IA 1986 and successor legislation have the function of taking control of the activities of a company, in the shoes of the directors, in order to achieve one or more of the purposes specified in the Act broadly, the financial regeneration of the company, or a better realisation of its assets.

An administrator enjoys very wide powers of management over the company, and therefore faces potentially the same sort of exposure to environmental liability as a receiver, and for the same reasons. Likewise, he may well be regarded as an occupier of land owned by the company, but probably not its owner.

There are, however, certain differences in the nature of the two appointments, and the legislation surrounding them, that put an administrator in a stronger position.

First, an administrator is an appointee of the court, not merely of some party in contract with the company. Second, he benefits from a statutory stay on all proceedings or actions while in office. Moreover, the insolvency legislation provides that the administrator's discharge, at the end of his period in office, releases him from 'all liabilities'.

It is suggested that this combination of provisions effectively means that an administrator cannot be prosecuted for his activities while in office, and is exonerated on his departure.

12.5.3 Liquidators

The function of a liquidator, by contrast, is to wind up the company. In the process, liquidators are given very wide powers to deal with the assets of the company and manage its business. Notably though, and unlike the situation in a bankruptcy, the assets do not actually vest in the liquidator. He is merely given powers to deal with them. He would probably be regarded as the occupier of any land, but not its owner.

Potentially, then, a liquidator faces similar potential exposure to environmental liabilities as receivers do. However, it is not the possession of powers which is fatal to the office-holder but the exercise of them.

Can the liquidator be said to have committed an offence by the actions which he took? This requires activity, and whereas a receiver is usually carrying on the business activities pending sale, a liquidator will usually be running them down. If, in that process, a liquidator takes steps or performs activities which have a polluting impact, then he would be exposed to liability on the same principles as set out above, but in the absence of such direct involvement, liquidators should be safe.

A related question is whether the liquidator can become personally liable if an insolvency estate contains an environmental permit and the estate has insufficient funds to comply with its terms and conditions. In *Re Mineral Resources Ltd; Environment Agency* v. *Stout* [1999] 1 All ER 746, Neuberger J stated that 'a conscientious honest liquidator' would not be personally liable for failing to spend his own money complying with the permit.

12.5.4 Supervisors of voluntary arrangements

The function of supervisors is, as the name suggests, implementation of an agreed scheme between the company and its creditors for the payment of its debts. There are no powers beyond this. As such, it is difficult to see how such office-holders could be made liable for any of the risks that are set out above.

To the extent that the regulatory agencies and potential civil claimants can be said to be creditors of the company, they may be affected by the rules relating to advertisement of creditors' meetings, and the voting rules at such meetings where arrangements for the payment of liabilities, including environmental liabilities, are discussed and approved. Once approved by the requisite majority attending the meeting, the scheme is binding on all creditors who could have attended the meeting – whether or not they did so.

12.5.5   LPA receivers

Rather like supervisors, an LPA receiver usually has no powers to run the company or deal with its assets. They are usually appointed merely to collect rent from property and, as such, it is difficult to see how they could be saddled with any of the liabilities mentioned above.

However, such powers of management can be given by contract between the company and the person appointing the receiver, and, if such powers are given and in fact used by the receiver, then liability may follow, depending on the circumstances and the extent of the receiver's involvement in the polluting event.

It is generally thought unlikely, however, that such receivers would be treated as occupiers or owners of any property owned by the company.

12.6   PROTECTION FOR INSOLVENCY PRACTITIONERS CONCERNING CONTAMINATED LAND

Part IIA of EPA 1990 (s.78X) provides that:

> a person acting [as a liquidator, provisional liquidator, administrator, administrative receiver or nominee or supervisor of a voluntary arrangement] shall not be personally liable, under this Part [i.e. for remediating contaminated land] unless that thing is to any extent referable to substances whose presence in, on or under the contaminated land in question is a result of any act done or omission made by him which it was unreasonable for a person acting in that capacity to do or make ...

It follows that an insolvency practitioner is in danger of liability for remediating contaminated land under Part IIA only if the contamination is caused by some negligent act or omission on his part. Provided the practitioner acts with reasonable care while in office, he should be safe.

Even where there is a negligent act or omission, the practitioner will only be liable to the extent that the contamination is caused by that act or omission.

If a situation arises in which an insolvency practitioner is potentially liable under Part IIA, the main difficulty would seem to be determining if and when the practitioner contributed a contaminant and if and when a contaminant was contributed by the insolvent company. This difficulty is likely to render actions against the practitioner a dead letter.

It should be noted, however, that the protection for insolvency practitioners is limited to Part IIA; there is no similar protection under other environmental liability legislation. Nor would the defence be available to any action at common law.

CHAPTER 13

Environmental insurance

13.1 INTRODUCTION

Environmental insurance policies have been generally available in the UK since the early 1990s. The main reasons for their introduction were the increase in the number and scope of environmental liabilities and the exclusion of cover for harm caused by gradual pollution incidents in public liability policies.

Policies are available for a wide range of environmental liabilities including third-party bodily injury and property damage claims arising from pollution, the remediation of historic and future contamination on third-party land and on land that is owned or controlled by an insured (including residences), unforeseen costs incurred in the remediation of contamination and liabilities arising from the acts and omissions of environmental consultants, remediation and general contractors and environmental laboratories.

New policies are continually being introduced to meet the needs of potential insureds and to keep pace with the introduction of new environmental liabilities, for example, the Environmental Damage Regulations (see Chapter 3). In addition, products such as finite risk programmes, which typically combine an insurance element with a funding element, continue to be developed.

13.2 PUBLIC LIABILITY POLICIES

Before deciding whether to purchase an environmental insurance policy, a potential insured should consider the scope of cover that is already included in its general liability insurance policies, in particular, its public liability policy.

Public liability policies provide limited cover for environmental liabilities. These policies, which are purchased by practically all commercial and industrial businesses, together with employers' liability, property, motor and other general policies, provide cover for claims against an insured by third parties for bodily injury and property damage and, in some cases, other risks.

Public liability policies are written on an 'occurrence' basis, i.e. the policies provide cover for bodily injury and property damage that occurs during the policy period. In many cases, the injury or damage occurs at the same time as the event that caused it. Examples include injury and damage caused by an explosion at a factory or the rupture of a large above-ground storage tank containing chemicals.

13.2.1 Cover for past pollution incidents

In some cases, however, it is not easy to determine when the injury or damage occurred. Examples include the development of mesothelioma or asbestosis from exposure to asbestos fibres, following a long latency period, or the death of cattle from drinking groundwater that has been polluted by chemicals that seeped to the groundwater.

The vast majority of courts in the United States that have considered the issue have determined that bodily injury or property damage may occur, in the context of general liability policies, before the manifestation of the injury or damage. The so-called 'triggers of coverage' that have been adopted, depending on the applicable state law, include the 'exposure' trigger, the 'injury in fact' trigger and the 'continuous' trigger as well as the 'manifestation' trigger.

Under the 'exposure' trigger, policies on the risk at the time of the exposure of an individual or property to pollutants are triggered. Under the 'injury in fact' trigger, policies on the risk at the time that the injury or damage occurs are triggered. Under the 'continuous' trigger, policies on the risk at the time of exposure, the occurrence of injury or damage and its manifestation (and even beyond) are triggered.

An English court has determined that the applicable trigger under a public liability policy for mesothelioma from exposure to asbestos is either the 'injury in fact' or the 'manifestation' trigger. In *Bolton Metropolitan Borough Council* v. *Municipal Mutual Insurance Ltd* [2006] 1 WLR 1492, the Court of Appeal concluded that the policies on the risk when the claimant developed the malignant tumour in about 1980 or when the mesothelioma was capable of being diagnosed in 1990 covered the claim and not those that were on the risk when the exposure to asbestos fibres occurred during the 1960s and 1970s.

If a court applies this trigger to pollution-related claims, policies that were purchased in the 1970s, or even before that time, could be triggered. The potential for claims to be brought against public liability policies long after the bodily injury or property damage has led to such policies being said to have a 'long tail' of liability.

Depending on the type of policy, the exposure trigger may apply. In *Durham* v. *BAI (Runoff) Ltd* [2010] EWCA Civ 1096, known as the employers' liability policy trigger litigation, the Court of Appeal concluded that the exposure trigger applies to employers' liability policies with insuring clauses containing terms such as 'disease contracted' during the policy period; reading the word 'contracted' as synonymous with 'caused'. The court nevertheless concluded that the 'injury in fact' trigger applies to policies with insuring clauses containing terms such as 'injury sustained' during the policy period. That is, the policy that responds is the policy on the risk when the mesothelioma tumour begins to develop. Leave to appeal to the UK Supreme Court has been granted.

13.2.2   Cover for gradual pollution

In 1990, the Association of British Insurers (ABI) recommended to its members that they should exclude cover for gradual pollution in public liability policies. Since that time, virtually every public liability policy for UK risks has excluded cover for such pollution.

The most commonly used exclusion in public liability policies is the ABI model pollution exclusion which bars cover for:

> ... all liability in respect of Pollution or Contamination other than caused by a sudden identifiable unintended and unexpected incident which takes place in its entirety at a specific time and place during the Period of Insurance.

The term 'Pollution or Contamination' is defined broadly (and circuitously) to mean:

> ... all pollution or contamination of buildings or other structures or of water or land or the atmosphere; and . . . all loss or damage or injury directly or indirectly caused by such pollution or contamination.

The ABI model exclusion is designed to concentrate all claims arising from a pollution incident into one public liability policy and, thus, one policy limit by further providing that 'All Pollution or Contamination which arises out of one incident shall be deemed to have occurred at the time such incident takes place'. If a pollution incident that occurred in, say, 1995 resulted in individuals becoming ill from its effects during the next five or 10 years, the only policy that would be triggered by the incident would be the policy that was in effect in 1995 and, thus, the only indemnity limit that would apply would be the limit of that policy.

Some insurers have adapted some or all of the clauses in the ABI model pollution exclusion to their policies. Other insurers have simply included some or all of the clauses without adapting them.

The second most widely used pollution exclusion in public liability policies was drafted by the Lloyd's Underwriters Non-Marine Association and is known as NMA 1685. NMA 1685 bars cover for bodily injury and property damage that is:

> ... directly or indirectly caused by seepage, pollution or contamination [except for] seepage, pollution or contamination [that] is caused by a sudden, unintended and unexpected happening during the period of this Insurance.

Like the ABI exclusion, NMA 1685 is a qualified pollution exclusion, i.e. the clause begins by excluding all cover for harm from pollution and then writes back cover for non-gradual pollution.

At the time of writing, no English court had interpreted the meaning of the ABI model pollution exclusion or NMA 1685. One court has interpreted the meaning of the word 'sudden' in another pollution exclusion to hold that it bars cover for pollution that occurred over a period of many weeks.

13.2.3 Cover for remediating contamination

A public liability policy does not necessarily provide cover for costs incurred in remediating contaminated land or polluted water. A typical coverage clause in a public liability policy provides that the insurer agrees to indemnify the insured in respect of 'all sums which the insured shall become legally liable to pay as damages [or compensation]' for accidental bodily injury or property damage.

If a pollutant from an insured's site causes damage to an adjoining site, the claim against the insured by the adjoining landowner for the costs of remediating its site may be covered, depending on other terms and conditions in the policy, in particular, any pollution exclusion.

If, however, an insured who has been notified that he is an appropriate person under EPA 1990, Part IIA or has caused or knowingly permitted water pollution, then conducts remedial works, or the local authority or Environment Agency conducts them and seeks reimbursement, the costs may not be covered.

In *Bartoline Ltd* v. *Royal & Sun Alliance plc and Heath Lambert Ltd* [2006] EWHC 3598, the High Court concluded that the cost of remediating watercourses that had been polluted during a massive fire at Bartoline's factory was not covered by a public liability policy that provided cover 'against legal liability for damages in respect of … accidental loss of or damage to property … nuisance, trespass to land or trespass to goods or interference with any easement right of air, light, water or way'. The cost of remediating the pollution from the escape of solvents and fire-fighting water and foam into the watercourses was nearly £775,000. HHJ Hegarty QC concluded that the cost was a statutory liability and not 'damages' under the policy language.

A subsequent non-pollution case has concluded that some statutory liabilities that are akin to torts are covered by a public liability policy but, as always, it is necessary to examine the specific policy language at issue.

Since *Bartoline*, insurers have issued so-called Bartoline endorsements that provide cover for some statutory environmental liabilities under public liability policies. The endorsements tend, however, to be narrow in scope.

Public liability policies do not provide cover for damage to an insured's own site.

13.3 PROFESSIONAL INDEMNITY INSURANCE POLICIES

PII policies provide cover for the acts or omissions of advisers such as solicitors, accountants, surveyors and environmental consultants. The policies are underwritten on a 'claims made' basis rather than the 'occurrence' basis used in public liability policies. This means that a PII policy provides cover, subject to its terms and conditions, for a claim that is made against an insured during the policy period. The policy does not, therefore, have a long tail of liability.

Some professional indemnity insurers included pollution exclusions in their policies in the mid-1990s. The vast majority of, if not all, professional indemnity insurers, however, no longer exclude cover for pollution. Indeed, some professional bodies prohibit the use of pollution exclusions in PII policies for their members.

Solicitors must purchase the required minimum cover of £2 million (£3 million for LLPs) from insurers which are approved by the Law Society. The approved insurers must provide the mandatory policies on terms that are at least as broad as the terms that are set out in the Law Society's minimum terms and conditions. The minimum terms and conditions do not permit an exclusion for injury or damage caused by pollution. The same restrictions do not apply to top-up cover, i.e. PII policies that provide cover in excess of the required minimum cover. Few, if any, top-up policies for solicitors include pollution exclusions.

Another profession whose minimum terms and conditions for PII policies do not permit the inclusion of pollution exclusions is accountants. Top-up policies for accountants are also highly unlikely to contain pollution exclusions.

Conversely, the RICS has included a pollution exclusion in the wording for RICS-compliant professional indemnity policies since 1 January 1994. The RICS offers cover for losses arising from pollution for its members who wish to 'buy back' cover for such losses. Few surveyors have purchased the cover, however. Top-up policies for surveyors do not automatically contain a pollution exclusion.

Although there is no professional body for environmental consultants which requires them to purchase PII, it is common practice for potential clients to require environmental consultants to provide evidence that they have cover for pollution-related claims of between £1 and £3 million before instructing them. The limit is virtually always provided on an aggregate basis, i.e. the indemnity limit is for all claims that are made against the environmental consultant during the policy period. The environmental consultant may purchase a higher limit of cover that is specific to a client's project but generally charges the client the premium for the additional cover. There has been one case involving cover for environmental consultants in which the High Court considered the scope of cover provided by the policy.

A common misconception exists that an environmental consultant's policy provides cover for a client. This is incorrect. First, the consultant is not liable unless the consultant has been negligent or has breached the terms and conditions of the contract with the client. Second, the policy is for the benefit of the consultant not the client. The policy may, therefore, provide cover to the consultant in challenging the client's claim.

13.4   PROPERTY POLICIES

Property policies provide cover for loss or damage to property that is owned or controlled by the insured. The loss or damage must occur during the policy period in order to be covered.

Most property policies contain either a qualified or an absolute pollution exclusion. In addition, they virtually never provide cover for remediating contamination because they cover only 'insured property' such as specified buildings and other structures, not land.

A clause that provides cover for the removal of debris from a fire or other insured risk or peril may well state that it does not cover debris from property that is not insured property. Such a debris removal clause would not, therefore, provide cover for the remediation of soil or water that is polluted by a leak of petrol from a storage tank or another pollution incident.

13.5 HOMEOWNERS POLICIES

A homeowners policy is a combination of a public liability policy that provides cover for third-party claims against the homeowner and a property policy that provides cover for the loss of, or damage to, the residence or other insured property. It is increasingly common for homeowners policies to contain a qualified and/or absolute pollution exclusion in one or both parts of the policy.

13.6 ENVIRONMENTAL INSURANCE POLICIES

The only way to ensure that environmental liabilities are insured is to purchase an environmental insurance policy. The policies are underwritten on a claims-made-and-reported basis with the exception of contractors pollution liability policies which are underwritten on an occurrence basis as well as a claims-made-and-reported basis, the former for a higher premium (see **13.6.4**).

A claims-made-and-reported policy provides cover for a claim that is made against the insured and reported by the insured to the insurer during the policy period. The policies generally provide cover for losses and related legal defence costs arising from a pollution incident or a pollution condition, as specified in the policy.

The limits of indemnity for environmental insurance policies have increased substantially since the late 1990s. Limits in the tens or even hundreds of thousands of pounds or more are generally available.

13.6.1 Differences between commercial environmental insurance policies and general liability policies

Environmental insurance policies have three main characteristics that distinguish them from general liability policies.

First, underwriters of environmental insurance policies have environmental skills as well as underwriting skills. The former enable an underwriter, among other things, to assess risks arising from the environmental condition and the management of polluting activities at sites, or for businesses, that the underwriter is considering insuring and to review environmental assessments and other reports prepared by environmental consultants and other environmental advisers to the potential insured.

Second, environmental insurance policies for owners and occupiers of land do not generally provide cover for unspecified sites. The sites that are covered by the policy are listed in its schedule or endorsements to it.

Third, with limited exceptions for policies for low-risk sites, the terms and conditions of environmental insurance policies are generally negotiated by an insurer and the insured's agents, i.e. brokers and also, in some cases, solicitors. The finalised policy tends to include a standardised (specimen) wording with standardised and/or manuscript endorsements. The endorsements tend to supersede coverage and exclusionary clauses in the body of the policy as well as other terms and conditions. If the policy provides cover for more than one site, endorsements may note the addition or deletion of sites from coverage during the policy period as the insured acquires or disposes of them.

If the limit of indemnity of a policy is particularly high and the risks covered by it are particularly complex, the entire policy may be a manuscript policy, i.e. a bespoke policy. Such a policy is, however, the exception rather than the rule.

Environmental insurance policies for low-risk sites and the homeowners contaminated land policy are underwritten on a site-specific basis but their terms and conditions are not generally negotiated. This is due primarily to their relatively low limits and the documentation on which they are based being standardised environmental reports (see **13.6.4**).

13.6.2 Placing environmental insurance policies

The procedure that should be followed when a solicitor is involved in placing an environmental insurance policy for a client (other than an environmental insurance policy for low-risk sites or a homeowners contaminated land policy) is to contact a broker on behalf of the client or to advise the client to contact its broker directly (the major environmental insurance brokers are listed in **13.10**). The broker will determine the client's needs, gather necessary information from the client and contact insurers who offer policies that provide the required cover (the major environmental insurers are also listed in **13.10**). In turn, insurers will provide quotes, generally with a range of indemnity limits, deductibles and policy periods, and specifications of the scope of the proposed policy.

It is unadvisable for a solicitor to place policies directly for a client. Most importantly, since 14 January 2005, a solicitor who recommends and places insurance products must comply with the legislation that transposed the Insurance Mediation Directive (2002/92/EC) into English law. In addition, a solicitor does not have the necessary skills to ensure that the client purchases the most beneficial policy for the best premium. As a general rule, a solicitor does not possess the expertise to advise a client, among other things, about the range of environmental insurance policies that are available or the adequacy of a potential insurer's security (to ensure that the insurer has the necessary financial capability to pay any claims if and when they arise).

It is beneficial for a client who is purchasing a site-specific policy to provide potential insurers with as much information as possible about the environmental conditions and potentially polluting operations at the sites to be insured. The submission of such information may lead an underwriter to offer a lower premium or to offer cover for risks that it would otherwise have carved out of the policy. The documentation needed typically includes existing environmental assessment reports and any reports describing the completion and verification of remedial works at the site(s) to be insured. Insurers do not require environmental assessments to be conducted at potential sites by an insurer-approved environmental consultant or, indeed, any environmental consultant. This practice ceased in the mid-1990s.

An underwriter may ask to visit one or more of the sites to be insured. In the case of a property transfer policy (see **13.6.4**), the main purpose of the visit is to review the environmental condition of the site(s). In the case of a policy for operational risks (see **13.6.4**), another purpose is to review the potential insured's management of its potentially polluting operations. In the latter instance, the underwriter may visit one of the sites to be insured and reach a conclusion about the environmental risks at all of the sites to be insured based on its assessment of the client's management of potentially polluting operations at that site.

The broker, together with an environmental solicitor in some cases, on behalf of the client, generally negotiates the terms and conditions of a policy with the underwriter. Negotiations include topics such as the addition of any endorsements to the policy to revise its terms and conditions as well as other matters such as the policy period, the limit of indemnity for the policy and the premium to be paid for it.

If negotiations continue, the underwriter will ask the potential insured to complete an application, also called a proposal form, for the policy. The form includes questions such as the number and nature of any pollution incidents that have occurred at the site(s) to be insured, any contamination at the site(s) that is known to the potential insured, the nature and amount of chemicals stored on the site(s), any underground storage tanks and their condition, waste disposal procedures at the site(s) and so on. Known underground storage tanks must be listed in an endorsement to the policy in order to be covered.

If the negotiations conclude successfully, the insurer will issue the policy agreed by the parties in exchange for payment of the agreed premium.

The terms and conditions of the environmental insurance policy for low-risk sites and the homeowners contaminated land policy are not generally negotiated and, therefore, do not necessarily require the assistance of a broker. Solicitors who recommend or place such a policy for clients must, however, ensure that their activities comply fully with the legislation transposing the Insurance Mediation Directive (2002/92/EC) into English law.

In purchasing an environmental insurance policy, the client must not misrepresent facts or fail to disclose material issues such as an environmental assessment that identifies contamination at one of the sites to be insured. If the client does so and the insurer issues the policy and subsequently discovers a misrepresentation or non-disclosure, the insurer is entitled to void the policy.

13.6.3   Structure of a policy

Environmental insurance policies, like other general liability policies, include a schedule and a wording.

The schedule sets out the name of the insured and any additional insureds, the dates on which the policy period begins and ends, the limit of liability and any sub-limits and/or aggregate limit, the amount of the deductible (also called an excess) and the amount of the premium. The schedule in a site-specific policy may also list the sites that are covered by it.

The wording generally contains the following sections, not necessarily in the following order. The sections, some of which are the same as, or similar to, those in general liability policies, are as follows.

Introductory provisions

The introductory section of the policy generally explains that the policy is under-written on a claims-made-and-reported basis. The section also generally states that the insured and the insurer agree to the provisions of the policy. It may also state that the insured warrants the truthfulness of its answers in the proposal form and that the insurer has relied on the statements in issuing the policy.

Insuring agreement(s)

One or more clauses specify the cover that the insurer agrees to provide in the policy. Nearly all environmental insurance policies set out a 'menu' of coverage clauses in order to allow a potential insured to choose the required cover. Otherwise, the policy sets out the specified cover only.

Definitions

This section sets out the definitions of various words and terms that are used in the policy. The defined words and terms appear in the policy in bold, capital letters or a similar manner to denote that they are defined.

Exclusions

Typical exclusions, depending on the type of policy, are: employers' liability (cover for employees is provided by employers' liability policies which are mandatory under English law); fines (it is against public policy for an insurer to provide cover for fines for criminal offences); nuclear risks; terrorism; asbestos in buildings (but not generally in the ground); disposal sites that are not owned by the insured;

contamination that is known to the insured but not disclosed to the insurer at the commencement of the policy; known underground storage tanks that are not listed on a schedule attached to the policy; contractual liability that has been assumed by an insured unless the liability exists in the absence of the contract; and the cost of remediating contamination for a changed use of an insured site.

Limits of indemnity and deductibles

As well as a limit of indemnity for each and every claim against the policy and an aggregate limit, the policy may include sub-limits. This section of the policy, and/or the schedule, includes clauses that state how the limits and deductibles are to be applied.

Notification and reporting provisions

The notification provisions in this section specify the requirements with which an insured must comply in notifying the insurer of circumstances which may lead to a claim and in notifying a claim itself. The section also sets out the details that an insured must provide to an insurer about a claim and the legal documents such as pleadings that an insured must forward to the insurer following a claim.

The notification and reporting provisions (and some other provisions of the policy) may be conditions precedent. The failure of an insured to comply with a condition precedent in respect of a claim means that the claim is not covered by the policy.

Claims cooperation provisions

Environmental insurance policies generally include provisions that set out the insured's duties and responsibilities if it makes a claim against the insurer. Typical clauses state that the insured shall cooperate with the insurer in the defence of a claim against the insured and shall not admit liability or settle a claim without prior notification to, and approval by, the insurer.

Extended reporting periods

Environmental insurance policies may include extended reporting periods that apply if a policy is cancelled by the insured or not renewed. The periods do not apply if the insured has purchased the same type of environmental insurance policy for the same period as the extended reporting period from another insurer.

An automatic extended reporting period, which is generally up to 60 days in length, entitles an insured to submit a claim that it has received during that period to the insurer provided the claim arises from a pollution incident (as specified in the

217

policy) that occurred at an insured site during the policy period and was not discovered by, or otherwise known to, the insured until after the policy period terminated.

An optional reporting period, which is generally between one and five years and for which the insured pays an additional premium, similarly entitles the insured to submit a claim that it has received during that period to the insurer provided that the claim arises from a pollution incident (as specified in the policy) that occurred at an insured site during the policy period but was not discovered by, or otherwise known to, the insured until after the policy period terminated.

General conditions

The general conditions section of the policy, which may be lengthy, contains clauses that cover topics such as the territory covered by the policy (unless this clause is in a separate section), choice of law, choice of jurisdiction, the insurer's subrogation rights, the insurer's cancellation rights (which are generally restricted to non-payment of the premium, misrepresentation, non-disclosure and fraud), assignment of the policy, and so on.

A particularly important clause is a declaration that the insurer has relied on the statements in the insured's proposal form in issuing the policy or that the insured warrants the accuracy of the answers provided in that form. This clause, which is known as a 'basis of the contract clause', means that representations in the form are warranties. Under English insurance law, the breach of a warranty by an insured entitles the insurer to void the policy regardless of the seriousness (or not) of the breach of warranty and/or its materiality to the risk.

13.6.4   Types of environmental insurance policies

There are three main types of environmental insurance policies for commercial risks:

- site-specific policies;
- policies for professionals; and
- policies for remediation, asbestos and general contractors.

Insurers who provide such policies are listed in **13.10**, which also lists the major environmental insurance brokers.

Site-specific policies and other protection also exist for homeowners in respect of remediation notices for contaminated land.

Site-specific policies

Site-specific environmental insurance policies provide cover for third-party claims for bodily injury, property damage and works to remediate contamination as well as first-party claims for works to remediate contamination.

Six types of site-specific policies are available for commercial risks. All of the policies provide cover to the owner and/or occupier of land, as listed in the schedule or an endorsement to a policy, and the directors and officers of insured companies. The insured's lender, a trustee, a developer and the seller may be listed in the policy as additional insureds.

The policies are:

- third-party environmental liability:
- first-party pollution and environmental damage;
- property transfer policies;
- remediation cost cap;
- lender liability; and
- environmental insurance policies for low-risk sites.

Some of the above policies, in particular the third-party environmental liability, first-party pollution and property transfer policy are offered as a combined policy. A remediation cost cap policy may also be included in such a policy, as appropriate. Such policies are issued in a 'menu' format, which allows the parties to select the applicable coverage parts.

Property transfer and post-remediation policies are generally available for periods up to 10 years. Policies for operational risks, i.e. third-party environmental liability and first-party pollution policies, are generally available for periods up to five years. Both types of policies tend to be triggered by: a 'request' by the Environment Agency to the insured to remediate water pollution, rather than only the service of a works notice; or a notification of contaminated land by a local authority under EPA 1990, Part IIA, rather than only the service of a remediation notice. Insurers do not make a distinction between a sudden and accidental incident or a gradual and accidental incident; both are covered.

A remediation cost cap policy is available for the length of the remediation project. A lender liability policy is available for the length of relevant loan periods. An environmental insurance policy for low-risk sites is available for a one-year period on a renewable basis.

THIRD-PARTY ENVIRONMENTAL LIABILITY

These policies, or coverage parts in a policy, provide cover for third-party bodily injury and property damage claims and the costs of remediating contamination that result from a pollution incident (as specified in the policy), that occurs on the insured's site(s) during the policy period, environmental damage (which includes, but is not limited to, pollution or contamination) that occurs on the insured's site(s) under the Environmental Damage Regulations, plus related defence costs. Additional cover that may be provided includes business interruption for the insured and third parties, economic loss such as the loss of rental income or the diminution in value of third-party property and relocation costs during remediation.

FIRST-PARTY POLLUTION AND ENVIRONMENTAL DAMAGE

These policies provide cover for bodily injury, property damage and the costs of remediating contamination that results from a pollution incident (as specified in the policy) that occurs on the insured's site(s) or environmental damage on the insured's site under the Environmental Damage Regulations during the policy period plus related legal costs. Additional cover that may be offered includes business interruption and economic loss such as the loss of rental income or the diminution in value of the insured's property.

PROPERTY TRANSFER

Property transfer policies are the most popular environmental insurance policies in the UK. They provide cover for the costs of remediating contamination that existed on an insured's site(s) before the policy commenced provided that the insured did not know that the contamination existed or the insured disclosed it to the insurer, both when the policy commenced. In the latter instance, the insurer may agree to cover the risk of remediating the contamination depending on its nature or may 'carve out' the known contamination from the policy. Property transfer policies also cover bodily injury and property damage caused by the contamination and related legal costs as well as environmental damage under the Environmental Damage Regulations.

Additional cover that may be provided includes on-site bodily injury, business interruption costs, costs incurred by delays in commencing construction due to remedial works, economic loss such as the loss of rental income or the diminution in value of third-party property and relocation costs during remediation.

A variant of a property transfer policy provides cover for an environmental indemnity and other environmental clauses in a sale and purchase agreement that is specified in the policy.

REMEDIATION COST CAP

Remediation cost cap policies, which are also called stop loss remediation policies, cover landowners and developers who are remediating contamination from unforeseen costs arising from the contamination. The cause of the unforeseen costs may be undiscovered contamination, cost over-runs or failure of the remedial works. The policy provides cover up to a limit of indemnity for costs above the estimated costs of the remedial works, as agreed by the insured and the insurer, and a self-insured retention or buffer. Remediation cost cap policies are generally only offered for remedial works exceeding £2 million.

LENDER LIABILITY

These policies, which have not proved popular for UK risks, provide cover to a lender who has accepted a site as collateral for a loan for either the borrower's principal loan balance or the costs of remediating required contamination if the borrower defaults. The policy may also provide cover for first-party remediation costs, third-party bodily injury and property damage and any related legal costs.

ENVIRONMENTAL INSURANCE POLICY FOR LOW-RISK SITES

This policy, which is issued on an annual basis, is designed for low-risk sites, including property portfolios, with no known environmental problems. Its purpose is to provide a low-cost policy for such properties without the need to negotiate wordings.

Policies for professionals

The two main types of environmental insurance policies for professionals are policies for environmental consultancies and environmental laboratories.

ENVIRONMENTAL CONSULTANCIES

An environmental insurance policy for an environmental consultancy provides cover for losses arising from its professional services. The policy, which may also provide cover for related legal costs and/or completed projects, is for a specified project or a specified period of time.

ENVIRONMENTAL LABORATORIES

An environmental insurance policy for a laboratory that conducts environmental work provides cover for losses arising from its professional services. The policy may also cover related legal costs and/or completed professional services.

Policies for remediation, asbestos and general contractors

A remediation contractor, i.e. a contractor which remediates contamination, may purchase an environmental insurance policy to cover losses arising from its services. Similarly, an asbestos contractor, i.e. a contractor which conducts works in respect of asbestos in buildings, may purchase a policy to cover losses arising from its services. In addition, a contractor which conducts industrial, maintenance, electrical, cleaning and other general work may purchase a policy to cover losses arising from its services. The policies may also provide cover for pollution-related errors and omissions, related defence costs and completed operations. Cover is available for a specified project or a specified period of time. An 'occurrence'-based policy is available for a higher premium than a claims-made-and-reported policy.

Homeowner contaminated land protection

There are two main types of protection for homeowners in respect of their homes being built on contaminated land. They are warranty protection for new or converted residences and a homeowner contaminated land policy.

WARRANTY PROTECTION

The National House-Building Council (NHBC) offers cover for the cost of remediating contamination at a residence under its product, Buildmark, as part of warranties provided by it for owners of new or converted residences. Premier Guarantee and BLP Secure offer similar cover. Zurich Building Guarantees Insurance Company offered a similar warranty until September 2009 when it withdrew from the market.

HOMEOWNER CONTAMINATED LAND POLICY

The Homecheck Professional Land Insurance policy, which is offered by Countrywide Legal Indemnities and is underwritten by Liberty Legal Indemnities at Lloyd's (Syndicate 190), covers the cost of remediating contamination that was not known to the insured homeowner or the homeowner's advisers when the policy period commenced. The policy also covers the diminution in the value of the home if it is sold during the policy period plus related legal costs. The trigger for the policy, which is not assignable, is a notification of contaminated land or a remediation notice that is served on the homeowner under EPA 1990, Part IIA. The policy has a limit of indemnity of £1 million and a policy period of up to 10 years. It may be purchased from Landmark in conjunction with the Homecheck Professional Environmental Report, or directly from Countrywide Legal Indemnities. Premiums are from £50 depending on the size of the residence.

13.7 FINITE RISK PROGRAMMES

A finite risk programme for environmental liabilities has a funding element and an insurance element. The funding element generally covers the estimated costs of remediating contamination whilst the insurance element generally covers the risk of the costs exceeding the estimate and/or the timing of the remedial works. Remedial costs may exceed the estimate as a result of a difference in the extent or nature of the contamination, inflation, or a change in the standard of remediation

13.8 SELF INSURANCE

A company may decide to retain the risk of liabilities and thus act as a self insurer instead of purchasing insurance. A decision by a company not to purchase an environmental insurance policy, however, is generally due to a lack of knowledge about environmental insurance policies and a perception that its public liability policy provides cover for remediating contamination (which is generally incorrect) rather than a decision to self insure the risk of incurring environmental liabilities.

13.9 CAPTIVES

A large company may decide to establish a captive insurance company instead of purchasing environmental (and/or other) insurance from commercial insurers. Captives tend to be, but are not always, wholly owned by a single company. A major purpose in establishing a captive is generally the favourable tax implications. A captive does not necessarily retain all the liabilities of its parent company but may reinsure them to commercial reinsurers.

13.10 MAJOR ENVIRONMENTAL INSURERS AND BROKERS

The environmental insurers, which offer a wide range of policies and which are all located in London, are:

- ACE Europe Group;
- Chartis;
- Chubb Insurance Company of Europe S.A.;
- Liberty International Underwriters Europe Ltd; and
- XL Environmental.

Other insurers, such as AXA, Allianz Global and Gerling have also entered the environmental insurance market.

The major environmental brokers are:

- Aon Ltd;
- Argyll Insurance Services Ltd;
- Bridge Insurance Brokers Ltd;
- Heath Lambert Ltd;
- Marsh Ltd;
- Tyser & Co Ltd; and
- Willis Ltd.

Argyll Insurance Services Ltd is located in Brighton; Bridge Insurance Brokers Ltd is located in Manchester. The other environmental brokers listed above are located in London.

In addition to broking environmental insurance policies, environmental brokers assist in structuring finite risk programmes and other products.

Clauses intended to pass liability for contaminated land to a purchaser

EXCLUSION TEST 2 – PAYMENTS FOR REMEDIATION

(i)   [Seller hereby pays to the buyer the sum of £ […] in respect of] [The purchase price of the property has been reduced by the sum of £[…]to take account of] the cost of the remediation of the property, of which details are set out in [Schedule […]] and which includes but is not limited to the removal and/or treatment of all and any matters which may have the result that the property be designated as contaminated land [the meaning of Part IIA of the Environmental Protection Act 1990 or any consolidations or re-enactments thereof].

(ii) The parties acknowledge that the said sum would be sufficient to achieve the result that the property is not designated as contaminated land if such remediation were to be carried out effectively and the parties further acknowledge that, accordingly, the Seller is therefore entitled to be excluded from the categories of person liable to contribute to the cost of any remediation works at on or under the property [the said Part IIA etc] and that the Buyer will bear any such liability for such cost as would otherwise have attached to the Seller.

(iii) The Buyer shall indemnify and keep indemnified the Seller against any liability which may be incurred by the Seller for the costs of remediation works at on or under the property occasioned by the failure of any body of competent authority to exclude the Seller from such liability [the terms of the said Part IIA etc.] in accordance with this clause.

EXCLUSION TEST 3 – SOLD WITH INFORMATION

(i)   [Full details have been disclosed to the Buyer of the nature and broad measure of all and any matters which may have the result that the property be designated as contaminated land within the meaning of Part IIA of the Environmental Protection Act 1990 or any consolidations or re-enactments thereof] [The buyer has had full opportunity to inspect and survey the property and carry out investigations thereon] and the Buyer accepts and acknowledges that the Seller is therefore entitled to be excluded from the categories of person liable to contribute to the cost of any remediation works at on or under the property [under the said Part IIA etc.] and that the Buyer will bear any such liability for such cost as would otherwise have attached to the Seller.

(ii) The Buyer shall indemnify and keep indemnified the Seller against any liability which may be incurred by the Seller for the costs of remediation works at on or under the property occasioned by the failure of any body of competent authority to exclude the Seller from such liability [under the terms of the said Part IIA etc.] in accordance with this clause.

Precedent agreement on liabilities under Part IIA

SCHEDULE
AGREEMENT ON LIABILITY FOR REMEDIATION UNDER
PART IIA EPA
PART I

1   Background

The Parties acknowledge that they are or may be held to be responsible for all or part of the costs of a Remediation Action in respect of the Property and have agreed the basis on which they wish to divide that responsibility

2   Definitions and interpretation

In this schedule:

'Body of Competent Authority' means the body specified as being the regulator of contaminated land in accordance with the Environmental Protection Act 1990 Part IIA the Contaminated Land (England) Regulations 2006 and all and any guidance notes circulars and other documentation issued thereunder or any statutory modification or re-enactment thereof.

'Exclusion' 'Apportionment' and 'Attribution' have the meanings attributed to them by the Environmental Protection Act 1990 Part IIA the Contaminated Land (England) Regulations 2006 and all and any guidance notes circulars and other documentation issued thereunder or any statutory modification or re-enactment thereof.

'Legislation Relating to Contaminated Land' means the Environmental Protection Act 1990 Part IIA the Contaminated Land (England) Regulations 2006 and all and any guidance notes circulars and other documentation issued thereunder or any statutory modification or re-enactment thereof.

'Limitation On The Recovery Of Remediation Costs' has the meaning attributed to it by the Environmental Protection Act 1990 Part IIA the Contaminated Land (England) Regulations 2006 and all and any guidance notes circulars and other documentation issued thereunder or any statutory modification or re-enactment thereof.

'the Parties' means [the Seller and the Buyer *or* [*as the case may be*]].

'the Property' means [all of the Properties *or* Property No(s) [*numbers*]].

'Remediation Action' means any action specified as being required to cause land to cease to be contaminated within the meaning of the Environment Protection Act 1990 Part IIA the

Contaminated Land (England) Regulations 2006 and all and any guidance notes circulars and other documentation issued thereunder or any statutory modification or re-enactment thereof.

'Remediation Notice' means the document served by the Body of Competent Authority which specifies any Remediation Action.

3 Apportionment of liabilities

3.1 If a Body of Competent Authority serves a Remediation Notice in respect of the Property on persons which include the Parties the provisions of this paragraph of this schedule shall come into effect.

3.2 The Parties shall pay the costs of any Remediation Action or part thereof in accordance with the provisions set out in Part II of this schedule.

3.3 The Parties confirm that they are content for the provisions of Part II of this schedule to be applied to the costs of the Remediation Action and that a copy of this agreement may be provided to the Body of Competent Authority concerned.

3.4 The Parties confirm and accept that the provisions of Part II of this schedule shall be applied and that the Body of Competent Authority shall as between the Parties make such determinations on the questions of Exclusion Apportionment and Attribution as shall give effect to the terms of Part II of this schedule and that the Body of Competent Authority shall not as between the Parties apply the tests set out in any Legislation Relating to Contaminated Land for the time being in force.

3.5 The Parties confirm that the transaction the subject of this agreement and the terms of Part II of this schedule are not intended nor are they part of any larger series of transactions which are intended to have the effect of increasing the share of costs theoretically to be borne by any person who would benefit from a Limitation On The Recovery Of Remediation Costs and that the Body of Competent Authority should not therefore seek to disregard this agreement.

3.6 If the Body of Competent Authority should notwithstanding paragraph 3.5 disregard this agreement and apply the normal tests set out in any Legislation Relating to Contaminated Land for the time being in force and this has the effect that the Parties share the costs of the Remediation Action in a way other than that set out in Part II of this schedule Part II of this schedule shall nevertheless apply as between the Parties and they shall be entitled to insist on reciprocal indemnities the one against the other such that the costs of the Remediation Action shall be adjusted as between them in order to restore the financial position to that which would have prevailed had the Body of Competent Authority applied Part II of this schedule and not disregarded this agreement.

PART II

[Insert substantive details of apportionment and payment of the costs of the Remediation Action agreed by the parties, e.g. 100%, 0%, 80%, 20%, etc.]

APPENDIX A3

Sample environmental search report[1]

 **Consultants**
RISK MANAGEMENT

in association with

home check professional
A Landmark service

Certificate

This Certificate is issued in respect of the Homecheck Professional Environmental Report 31099763_1 dated 04/05/2010 for the property described as:

Sample House
1 The High Street
Newtown
Your Reference: Sample_HCP_HCP

Contaminated Land Assessment
RPS certifies that the level of environmental risk identified in the Homecheck Professional Environmental Report is not likely to be sufficient for the property to be described as "contaminated land" as defined by section 78(A)2 of Part IIA of the Environmental Protection Act 1990.

Lending Assessment
As the subject property has received a Certificate, it is the opinion of RPS that "contaminated land" issues should not have a significant impact on the security of the property for normal lending purposes.

Completed by:
RPS Environmental Risk Team

Dated 4 May 2010

This Certificate is based only on the information relating to historical land uses as shown by data sources collected by Sitescope Ltd and stated within the Homecheck Professional Environmental Report. This Certificate should be read in conjunction with both that Report and the Guide to the RPS Environmental Risk Certificate provided with this Certificate. No physical inspection of the Property has been carried out. This Certificate is subject to our prevailing terms of business as set out in the document entitled Sitescope Terms and Conditions.

---

[1]   Reproduced by kind permission of Landmark Information Group Limited.

Guide to the RPS Environmental Risk Certificate

1 Purpose of the Certificate

The purpose of the RPS Environmental Certificate is to assist the conveyancer in assessing the implications of the environmental risks identified in the Homecheck Professional Environmental Report and their possible impact on the security of the property for normal lending purposes. Such risks are identified from eleven key recorded environmental datasets which on their own or in combination and subject to their proximity to the subject site could lead to the property being described as "contaminated land" as defined by section 78(A)2 of Part IIA of the Environmental Protection Act 1990.

Under this legislation Local Authorities have a duty placed on them to identify land within their Borough, which falls within the statutory definition of being "contaminated land". Where land is identified as being "contaminated land", the Local Authority (or the Environment Agency in certain circumstances) must ensure that the site is remediated to ensure that the land is safe for its current usage.

For a site to be identified as "contaminated land" there must be a source of contamination that can find a pathway to affect the underlying groundwater, watercourse, people, building materials, or the natural environment (the receptor) AND be causing significant harm or likely to cause significant harm to the receptor. That is: for land to officially be deemed "contaminated land" a linkage must exist between the source, the pathway and the receptor. If any one of these is absent, then it cannot be classed as contaminated land under the Part IIA guidance. Each Local Authority has a contaminated land inspection strategy which explains the process they will be following.

2 Lending Assessment

In addition to the Certificate and to add further clarification to the result of the report, RPS provide an Opinion on whether the potential risk associated with the likelihood of the property being defined as "contaminated land" will have a significant impact on the security of the property for normal lending purposes.

3 Review Procedure

Where a sufficient level of potential risk has been identified within the report such that the property does not immediately receive a Certificate, the report is automatically forwarded to RPS for manual review by a qualified environmental consultant. The outcome of the manual review will either be a Certificate (in the majority of cases) or a detailed report on the outstanding matters that require further information to be obtained and other actions that may be necessary. Where a Certificate is not issued after a review, this does not necessarily mean there is a likelihood of contamination but that further information/action is required before a Certificate can be issued. The review will normally be completed within 2 working days. There is then the choice of instructing RPS to assist and carry out this further investigation or sourcing the information independently and forwarding it to RPS for further review.

The Certificate is based solely on the 11 key recorded environmental datasets defined below and as detailed in the Homecheck Professional Environmental Report and is NOT based on any physical inspection of the site or condition of the land. Whilst Sitescope uses the best available public sources of information to identify possible risks and sources of land use, Sitescope does not warrant that all potentially contaminative land uses or features whether past or current will be identified in the Homecheck Professional Environmental Report using these sources. Where sufficient risk is identified in the Homecheck Professional Environmental Report it does not necessarily mean that a property will be designated as contaminated land or a special site. It is the duty of the Local Authority to inspect the land in its area to determine if it meets the definition of contaminated land (as mentioned in Section 1 above). Until such investigations have taken place it will not be possible to confirm whether the site is likely to be designated as contaminated.

Under Part IIA of the Environmental Protection Act 1990, Local Authorities have a duty to inspect their land from time to time. This means that they may gather information at a later date, which may lead them to alter their decision on whether the land can be classed as contaminated. We recommend that for additional protection insurance cover be obtained. Please contact the Homecheck Professional Environmental Helpline (0844 844 9966) for further details on Land Insurance.

4 Other Matters

Other matters identified in the Homecheck Professional Environmental Report, which the conveyancer may wish to bring to the attention of the client, are set out together with appropriate guidance in the "Other Matters" section of the Certificate. These risks are outside the definition of contaminated land because they are outside the scope of Part IIA of the Environmental Protection Act 1990.

These risks are:
Flooding, Radon Gas and Coal Mining. Where relevant, reference is also made to the report commissioned by DEFRA in relation to the impact on property values caused by their proximity to active landfill sites.

Where indicative flood plain is identified in close proximity to the property, enquiries should be made to confirm that insurance cover is available for this risk.

The Certificate ONLY applies to residential property with a valid planning consent, not to commercial/industrial property.

For any enquiries in relation to this report (including queries for RPS), please contact the Homecheck Professional Environmental Helpline on 0844 844 9966 or at helpdesk@homecheck.co.uk

5 Methodology and Scope

The RPS Certificate is based on a risk assessment model designed by RPS specifically for the purpose described above. The model uses details set out in this Homecheck Professional Report to assess the risk from 11 key recorded environmental datasets. Using a point allocation system based on the contaminative nature of each land use identified and distance from the search site, the model determines if sufficient risk is present. The data used to assess sufficient risk is limited to:

1. Historical Industrial land uses
2. Potentially Infilled land
3. Historical Tanks and Energy Facilities
4. BGS Recorded Landfill Sites
5. Registered Landfill Sites
6. Local Authority Recorded Landfill Sites

7. Licensed Waste Management Facilities
8. Waste Treatment Sites
9. Scrap Yards
10. Fuel Station Entries
11. Contaminated Land Register Entries and Notices

Areas of Military Land depicted on historical maps often comprise large expanses of land. Although parts of these areas can have the potential for a degree of contamination, a substantial proportion have often only been occupied by open land (e.g. fields) or subject to non-contaminative activities (e.g. as a training ground or barracks). In addition some areas of past Military Land were left blank for defence reasons. Consequently, given this inconsistency and to avoid over-caution, areas of Military Land have been excluded from assessment within this report.

6 Who is RPS?

RPS is part of the RPS Group plc, the largest Environmental Consultancy in Europe with over 4000 staff. As a leading advisor to the financial and property sector on potential environmental liabilities, RPS has developed statistical models to try to ensure that potential environmental liabilities are placed in a suitable risk context. RPS acts as a panel advisor to the majority of UK clearing banks.

7 Other Information

It is not possible to identify from records and historical mapping all contaminative land uses. For example, illegal tipping of chemical substances by an unknown business or person could result in a remediation notice being issued on the current occupier of the land.

8 Contact Details

For any enquiries in relation to this report (including queries for RPS), please contact the Homecheck Professional Environmental Helpline on 0844 844 9966 or at helpdesk@homecheck.co.uk

Environmental Report

Residential Property at
Sample House
1 The High Street
Newtown

Grid Reference: 491043E 106947N

Order Reference: 31099763_1

Your Reference: Sample_HCP_HCP

Tuesday, 4 May 2010

Requested by
Landmark Po Sample Account
6 - 7 Abbey Court
Eagle Way
Exeter
Devon
EX2 7HY

Homecheck Professional is provided by Sitescope Limited, part of Landmark Information Group. Sitescope is a leading UK provider of spatially-enabled property and environmental risk information to lawyers, banks, insurance companies, home inspectors and other property professionals.

 The campaign for increased awareness of flood risk
Join at: www.knowyourfloodrisk.co.uk

Sitescope is a value added reseller for

232

**Environmental
Report**

Introduction

Introduction

This report is for use by lawyers and other professionals involved in residential conveyancing. It presents information in the following four key areas that are not covered by Standard Enquiries of Local Authorities:

Section A - Statutory Registers

This section of the report sets out information from statutory registers kept by the Environment Agency, local authorities and the Health and Safety Executive. It identifies any nearby industrial processes or installations which might have an environmental impact on the property.

The key areas covered are the existence of landfill and waste management sites, industrial processes regulated by the Environment Agency, the storage of hazardous substances, discharges to air, and industrial installations regulated by the Health and Safety Executive under NIHHS and COMAH Regulations.

Section B - Site History

This section of the report seeks to identify both past and present industrial land use. Its purpose is to identify any land which may have been put to a potentially contaminative use.

Section C - Mining and Radon

This section concerns coal mining, underground cavities and radon, which are the principal cause of insurance claims. It is designed to highlight potential issues which may affect the value or enjoyment of the property.

Section D - Flooding

This section provides a high level overview of potential flood risks.

The Summary section of the report presents enquiries in a familiar and easy-to-understand question and answer format. Where a reply to an enquiry is Yes, further details are given for each question in the Additional Information section of the report.

Unless otherwise stated in the enquiry, the answers cover two search bands, 0-250 metres and 251-500 metres from the property. Contact details for the data providers are given in the Contacts section at the end of this report.

Footnotes
(1) The report should only be used in connection with one residential parcel of land (for the purpose of defining a single parcel of land Rule2(2) of the Local Land Charges Act 1997 is used). The report is based on the address and grid reference shown on the cover of this report and the replies are given in reliance on the accuracy and completeness of this information.
(2) The report is supplied subject to our current standard terms and conditions.
(3) The search is based on a UK National Grid Reference for the property. The grid reference used is shown on the cover of this report.
(4) The information in the report is supplied under licence to Sitescope Limited from various sources including: Environment Agency, British Geological Survey and Ordnance Survey.
(5) This report is a search of statutory and non-statutory sources of information which does not include any on-site survey or inspection of the property or its environs. Accordingly the report cannot in any way provide information as to the actual state of the property or land.
(6) The replies in this report are based on information currently supplied to Sitescope Limited by its data providers. Sitescope cannot guarantee the accuracy or the completeness of any information supplied to it by its data providers.
(7) Homecheck Professional is a Sitescope Product provided by Landmark Information Group Limited.

Environmental Report

Aerial Photo

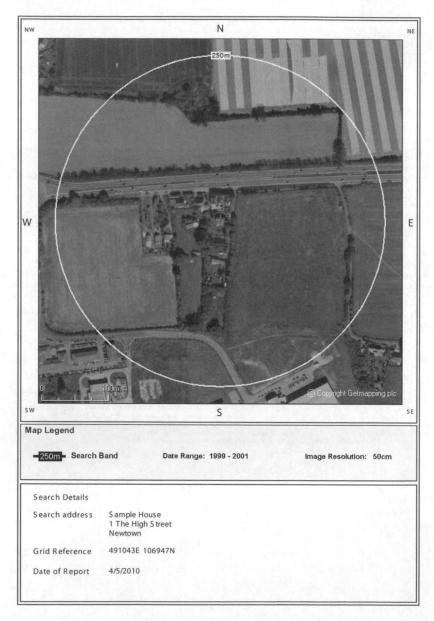

Map Legend

250m Search Band   Date Range: 1999 - 2001   Image Resolution: 50cm

Search Details

Search address   Sample House
                    1 The High Street
                    Newtown

Grid Reference   491043E 106947N

Date of Report   4/5/2010

Environmental Report

Site Location

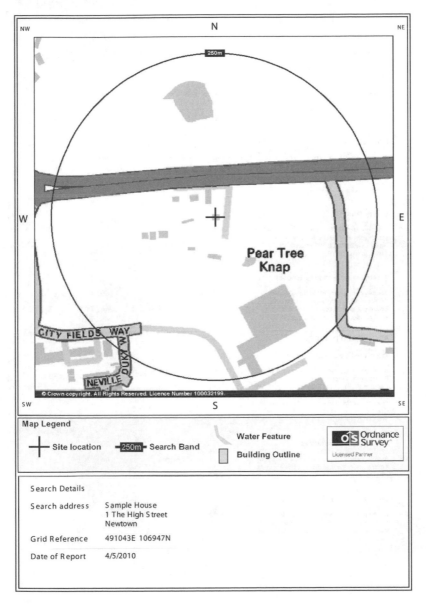

Map Legend

┼ Site location	▬250m▬ Search Band	Water Feature
		Building Outline

Ordnance Survey
Licensed Partner

Search Details

Search address	Sample House 1 The High Street Newtown
Grid Reference	491043E 106947N
Date of Report	4/5/2010

APPENDIX A3

| Environmental Report | Report Summary |

Section A - Statutory Registers

LANDFILL AND WASTE

Local Authority Landfill Sites

A.1.1 Are there any Local Authority recorded landfill sites?

within 0 - 250 metres? No

within 251 - 500 metres? No

Are there any Local Authority recorded landfill sites? The following list shows if local authorities covering the area of search have made landfill data available.

Chichester District Council - Has no landfill data to supply

West Sussex County Council - Has supplied landfill data

Please refer to the Contacts section for contact information.

Landfill Sites

A.1.2 Are there any landfill sites or waste management facilities licensed by the environment Agency under Part II of Environmental Protection Act 1990 or any BGS Recorded Landfill sites?

within 0 - 250 metres? No

within 251 - 500 metres? No

Waste Transfer

A.2 Are there any Waste Transfer Sites (including scrapyards) licensed by the environment Agency under Part II of Environmental Protection Act 1990?

within 0 - 250 metres? No

within 251 - 500 metres? No

Waste Treatment and Disposal

A.3 Are there any other sites licensed by the environment Agency under Part II of Environmental Protection Act 1990 to treat, keep or dispose of controlled waste?

within 0 - 250 metres? No

within 251 - 500 metres? No

REGULATED INDUSTRIES

Integrated Pollution Control (IPC) Regulations

A.4 Are there sites authorised under Part 1 of the Environmental Protection Act 1990 or the Pollution Prevention and Control (England and Wales) Regulations 2000 to carry out processes subject to Integrated Pollution Control (IPC) or Integrated Pollution Prevention and Control (IPPC)?

within 0 - 250 metres? No

within 251 - 500 metres? No

Radioactive Substances

A.5 Are there any sites registered by environment Agency under the Radioactive Substances Act 1993 to keep or use radioactive materials?

within 0 - 250 metres? No

within 251 - 500 metres? No

Storage of Hazardous Substances

A.6 Are there any sites subject to hazardous substances consents granted by the relevant local authority under the Planning (Hazardous Substances) Act 1990?

within 0 - 250 metres? No

within 251 - 500 metres? No

Environmental Report

Report Summary

Storage of Dangerous Substances

A.7 Are there any sites regulated by the Health and Safety Executive for storing specific dangerous substances under the Notification of Installations Handling Hazardous Substances (NIHHS) Regulations 1982?

| within 0 - 250 metres? | No |
| within 251 - 500 metres? | No |

Control of Major Accident Hazards

A.8 Are there any sites regulated by the Health and Safety Executive under the Control of Major Accident Hazards (COMAH) Regulations 1999?

| within 0 - 250 metres? | No |
| within 251 - 500 metres? | No |

AIR

Emissions to Air

A.9 Are there any sites subject to Local Authority Pollution Prevention and Control (LAPPC) under Part I of the Environmental Protection Act 1990 or the Pollution Prevention Control Act 1999?

| within 0 - 250 metres? | No |
| within 251 - 500 metres? | No |

DISCHARGE LICENCES

Discharges to Water

A.10 Are there any authorisations issued by the environment Agency (and its predecessor, the National Rivers Authority) to discharge to the watercourse from non-IPC processes in accordance with the Water Resources Act 1991?

| within 0 - 250 metres? | No |
| within 251 - 500 metres? | No |

CONTAMINATED LAND REGISTER

Contaminated Land Register Entries and Notices

A.11 Are there any Contaminated Land Register Entries and Notices from the Local Authority as defined by 78(A) 2 of Part IIA of the Environmental Protection Act 1990?

| within 0 - 250 metres? | No |
| within 251 - 500 metres? | No |

CONTRAVENTIONS

Contraventions

A.12 Are there any records of any enforcements, prohibitions, or prosecutions relating to questions in Section A or any Substantiated Pollution Incidents?

| within 0 - 250 metres? | No |
| within 251 - 500 metres? | No |

Environmental Report

Report Summary

Footnotes:

Question A.1 The Landfill Sites and Licensed Waste Management Facilities have been provided by the relevant environment agency or Local Authority (where available). At present no complete national data set exists for landfill site boundaries, therefore, a point grid reference, provided by the data supplier, is used for some landfill sites. In certain cases the point grid references supplied provide only an approximate position, and can vary from the site entrance to the centre of the site. For Registered Landfill Sites, where the positional accuracy of the site is unclear, a "buffer" is constructed around the point to warn of the possible presence of landfill.

Question A.2. The Waste Transfer Sites comprise both current and historic sites sourced from the relevant environment Agency. In certain cases it has been possible to source site boundaries.

Question A 3. The Waste Treatment and Disposal Sites comprise both current and historic sites sourced from the relevant environment Agency. In certain cases it has been possible to source site boundaries.

Question A.6 The response to this question is based on data supplied by Local Planning Authorities.

Question A.10 The response to this question is based on details of consents issued by the relevant environment Agency to discharge to the watercourse.

Question A.11 The contaminated land regulations, enacted in 2000, give effect to relevant sections of the Environmental Protection Act (1990) in regards to contaminated land. There are three sets of regulations that relate to England, Scotland and Wales. They are Contaminated Land (England) Regulations 2000 (SSI227), Contaminated Land (Scotland) Regulations 2000 (SI 178), and Contaminated Land (Wales) Regulations 2001 (WSI 2197) respectively. There is also statutory guidance that complements the regulations. The regulations give power to define special sites, contaminated land and to remediate any land defined as contaminated as well as exclude and apportion liability for remediation.

Environmental Report

Report Summary

Section B - Site History

LAND USE

Past Industrial Land Use

B.1 Are there any industrial sites (indicating potentially contaminative land use) shown on historical Ordnance Survey maps?

within 0 - 250 metres? Yes

Please refer to the Additional Information section for details of records found.

Current Industrial Land Use

B.2 Are there any industrial sites (indicating potentially contaminative land use) in Trade Listings?

within 0 - 250 metres? No

Footnotes:

Question B.1 Historical maps are a valuable and recognised source of information for investigating site history. They assist in identifying any previous potential contaminative uses or potential infilling of land which may have been carried out at a particular location.

The Historical Industrial Land Use data used in this reply is the result of a systematic analysis of 1:10,560 scale Ordnance Survey maps dating from the 1880s, as well as selected 1:10,000 scale Ordnance Survey National Grid Series.

Evidence of past potential contamination and potentially infilled land is drawn from a series of up to six historic map editions. The first of these editions will be the earliest County Series maps, which date from between 1860 and 1890 and are to a scale of 1:10,560. The second edition of County Series maps dates from circa 1900, and the third circa 1930.

In addition, evidence of Historical Tanks and Energy Facilities has been identified from the location of text on 1:2,500 and 1:1,250 historical Ordnance Survey maps covering a period from 1943-1996.

Question B.2 The reply to this question is based on contaminative industrial uses identified from current published trade directories.

 **Environmental Report**

Section C - Mining and Radon

MINING

Coal Mining Areas

C.1   Is the property in a coal mining area or in an area (without past or present, deep or open-cast, coal mining activity) in which coal bearing strata are known or expected to be present?   No

RADON AND RADON PROTECTION MEASURES

Radon Affected Area

C.2   Is the property in a radon-affected area as defined by the Health Protection Agency (HPA) and if so what percentage of homes are above the action level?   Between 1% and 3% of homes are above the Action Level

Whether or not a home actually has a basic or high radon concentration can only be established by having the building tested. The HPA provides a radon testing service, please refer to the Contacts section of this report.

Radon Protection Measures

C.3   Is the property in an area where radon protection measures are required for new properties or extensions to existing ones?   No radon protective measures are necessary

Footnotes:

Question C.1 The reply to this question indicates whether it is advisable to obtain a coal mining search from the Coal Authority.

Question C.2 The HPA recommends an 'Action Level' of 200 Becquerels per cubic metre. Areas are defined as radon-affected for existing dwellings where there is 1% chance or more of a house having a radon concentration at or above the Action Level.

Question C.3 In areas with 3% chance or more of a house having a radon concentration at or above the Action Level, protective measures need to be installed in new buildings and extensions to existing buildings. These areas are estimated through a combined analysis of geological data from the British Geological Survey (BGS) and measurement data from the Health Protection Agency (HPA). This forms the basis for the Building Research Establishment guidance on radon protective measures for new buildings (BR211, 2007)

Environmental Report

Section D - Flooding

FLOODING

Defended Flood

D.1.1 Is the property in or within 250m of an area potentially affected by flooding, taking flood defences into account?   No

Undefended Flood

D.1.2 Is the property in or within 250m of an area potentially affected by flooding, assuming the absence of flood defences?   No

Pluvial Flood

D.1.3 Is the property in or within 250m of an area at potential risk of surface water flooding?   Yes

Tidal Flood

D.1.4 The property is not within an area of potential tidal flooding.

Footnotes:

Question D.1 RMS flood data is based on analyses of historical data, using mathematical and statistical models and the encoded experience of scientists and engineers, and is inherently imprecise. It is provided "AS IS", without any warranty of any kind. The information provided is not intended to constitute professional advice or an endorsement by RMS of any kind regarding the use and suitability of the information. You rely on this information solely at your own risk. RMS shall not be liable for any damages (whether direct or consequential damages, including loss of profits) suffered by any recipient of this report or any third party relying upon or using this report. Please refer to the report user guide for further information

Question D.1.1 The potential risk has been modelled on the basis of a flood occurring on average every 75, 100 or 1000 years. Flood defences in this model are assumed to withstand the flood heights for which they were designed. For further information you should consider purchasing the Homecheck Professional Flood Report.

Question D.1.2 The potential risk has been modelled on the basis of a flood occurring on average every 75, 100 or 1000 years. This model assumes that no flood defences are present, representing the possible outcome if defences fail earlier than designed. For further information you should consider purchasing the Homecheck Professional Flood Report.

Question D.1.3 The potential risk has been modelled on the basis of a flood occurring on average every 75, 100 or 1000 years. Surface water flooding is due to flooding from minor rivers, water flowing across the ground or raised groundwater levels. For further information you should consider purchasing the Homecheck Professional Flood Report.

Question D.1.4 Where the property is in or within 250m of an area of potential tidal flooding we report the overall flood risk for that property as generated by Norwich Union. For further information you should consider purchasing the Homecheck Professional Flood Report.

Environmental Report

Additional Information

Section B - Site History

B.1 - Past Industrial Land Use - Records within 0 - 250m

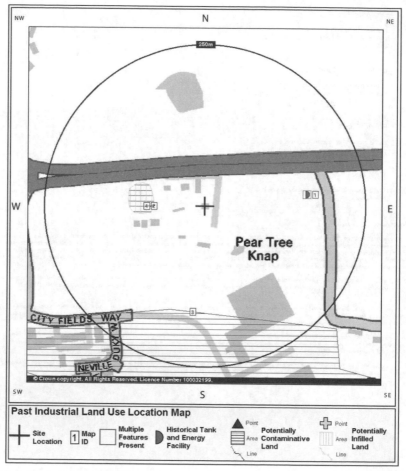

Past Industrial Land Use Location Map

Historical Tanks And Energy Facilities

Map ID	1
Direction	East
Distance	160m
Use:	Electrical Sub Station Facilities
Scale of Mapping:	1:2,500
Date of Mapping:	1975

Environmental
Report

Additional Information

Map ID   1
Direction   East
Distance   171m
Use: Electrical Sub Station Facilities
Scale of Mapping: 1:2,500
Date of Mapping: 1990

Potentially Contaminative Industrial Uses (Past Land Use)

Map ID   2
Direction   West
Distance   80m
Use: Quarrying of sand & clay, operation of sand & gravel pits
Date of Mapping: 1951

Map ID   3
Direction   South
Distance   166m
Use: Military Land
Date of Mapping: 1961

Potentially Infilled Land (Non-Water)

Map ID   4
Direction   West
Distance   80m
Use: Unknown Filled Ground (Pit, quarry etc)

 **Environmental Report**

Chichester District Council - Environmental Health Department
East Pallant House
1 East Pallant
Chichester
West Sussex
PO19 1TY

Telephone 01243 785166 Fax 01243 776766

Website www.chichester.gov.uk

Health Protection Agency - Radon Survey, Centre for Radiation, Chemical and Environmental Hazards
Chilton
Didcot
Oxfordshire
OX11 0RQ

Telephone 01235 822622 Fax 01235 833891

Email radon@ hpa.org.uk

Website www.hpa.org.uk

Anyone concerned about the radon levels in their home can obtain a free information pack about radon (including details of how to obtain a test kit) by leaving their name, address and postcode on the free telephone number 0800 614529. Further information is also available on the HPA website.

Landmark Information Group Limited
5 - 7 Abbey Court
Eagle Way
Sowton
Exeter
Devon
EX2 7HY

Telephone 01392 441761 Fax 01392 441709

Email cssupport@ landmarkinfo.co.uk

Website www.landmarkinfo.co.uk

Landmark Information Group Limited
Legal And Financial
The Smith Centre
Fairmile
Henley-On-Thames
Oxon
RG9 6AB

Telephone 0844 844 9966 Fax 0844 844 9980

Email info@ landmarkinfo.co.uk

Website www.landmarkinfo.co.uk

West Sussex County Council - Environment & Development
County Hall
Tower Hall
Chichester
West Sussex
PO19 1RH

Telephone 01243 777100

Website www.westsussex.gov.uk

**Environmental
Report**

Contacts

British Geological Survey - Enquiry Service
British Geological Survey
Kingsley Dunham Centre
Keyworth
Nottingham
Nottinghamshire
NG12 5GG

Telephone 0115 936 3143 Fax 0115 936 3276

Email enquiries@ bgs.ac.uk

Website www.bgs.ac.uk

The BGS can provide a detailed geological report on the area in which the property is located.

Sitescope Limited - Homecheck Professional Environmental Helpline
Legal And Financial
The Smith Centre
Fairmile
Henley-On-Thames
Oxon
RG9 6AB

Telephone 0844 844 9966 Fax 0844 844 9980

Email helpdesk@ homecheck.co.uk

Search Code

Important Consumer Protection Information

This search has been produced by Landmark Information Group of The Smith Centre, Fairmile, Henley on Thames, RG9 6AB (Tel: 0844 844 9966, Fax: 0844 844 9980, Email: helpdesk@landmarkinfo.co.uk), which is registered with the Property Codes Compliance Board as a subscriber to the Search Code.

The Search Code provides protection for homebuyers, sellers, conveyancers and mortgage lenders, who rely on property search reports carried out on residential property within the United Kingdom. It sets out minimum standards which organisations compiling and/or selling search reports have to meet. This information is designed to introduce the Search Code to you.

By giving you this information, Landmark Information Group is confirming that they keep to the principles of the Search Code. This provides important protection for you.

The Code's main commitments

The Search Code's key commitments say that search organisations will:

- Provide search reports which include the most up-to-date available information when compiled and an accurate report of the risks associated with the property.
- Deal promptly with queries raised on search reports.
- Handle complaints speedily and fairly.
- At all times maintain adequate and appropriate insurance cover to protect you.
- Act with integrity and ensure that all search services comply with relevant laws, regulations and industry standards.

Keeping to the Search Code

How search organisations maintain compliance with the Search Code is monitored independently by the Property Codes Compliance Board (PCCB). If you have a query or complaint about your search, you should raise it directly with the firm, and if appropriate ask for your complaint to be considered under their formal internal complaints procedure. If you remain dissatisfied with the firm's final resolution after your complaint has been formally considered or if the firm has exceeded the response timescales, you may refer your complaint to the Independent Property Codes Adjudication Scheme (IPCAS). IPCAS can award compensation of up to £5,000 to you if it finds that you have suffered loss as a result of your search provider failing to keep to the Code.

Please note that all queries or complaints regarding your search should be directed to your search provider in the first instance, not to IPCAS.

IPCAS Contact Details

Telephone: 020 7520 3800
Email: info@idrs.ltd.uk

You can also get more information about the PCCB and IPCAS from Property Codes Compliance Board website at: www.propertycodes.org.uk

Please contact our Customer Service Team on 0844 844 9966 if you would like a copy of the full search code.

Search Code

Complaints Procedure - Information for customers

If you wish to make a complaint, we will deal with it speedily and fairly. We will:

- Respond to your complaint within 2 working days of receipt.
- Try and resolve your complaint fully within 2 weeks of receipt. If there are valid reasons for consideration of the complaint taking longer, we will keep you fully informed in writing or via telephone or email as you prefer and you will receive a response at the very latest within 8 weeks.
- Liaise with counselling organisations acting on your behalf, if you ask us to.
- Send you a final decision on the complaint in writing.

If you are not satisfied with the final decision, you may refer the complaint to the Independent Property Codes Adjudication Scheme (IPCAS) and we will give you contact details. We will co-operate fully with the independent adjudicator during the consideration of a complaint by the IPCAS and comply with any decision.

Complaints should be sent to:

Customer Relationship Manager
Landmark Information Group Limited
Legal & Financial
The Smith Centre
Fairmile
Henley-on-Thames
RG9 6AB

Telephone: 0844 844 9966
E-mail: helpdesk@landmarkinfo.co.uk

IPCAS can be contacted at:

IDRS Ltd, 24 Angel Gate, City Road, London EC1V 2PT
Phone: 020 7520 3800
Fax: 020 7520 3829
E-mail: info@idrs.ltd.uk

APPENDIX A3

SITESCOPE TERMS AND CONDITIONS

Definitions

"Authorised Reseller" means an agent or reseller of Sitescope whom Sitescope has duly appointed to resell its Reports and Services.
"Content" means any data, computing and information services and software, and other content and documentation or support materials and updates included in and/or supplied by or through the Websites, in Reports or Services or in any other way by Sitescope and shall include Sitescope developed and Third Party Content.
"First Purchaser" means the first person, or legal entity to purchase the Property Site following provision of a Report;
"First Purchaser's Lender" means the funding provider for the First Purchaser
"Information Pack" means a pack compiled by or on behalf of the owner or prospective buyer of the Property Site, designed to aid the marketing or purchase of the Property Site and containing information provided by or on behalf of the owner or prospective buyer of the Property Site.
"Intellectual Property Rights" means copyright, patent, design right (registered or unregistered), service or trade mark (registered or unregistered), database right or other data right, moral right or know how or any other Intellectual property right;
"Order" means the request for Services from Sitescope by You.
"Property Site" means a land site on which Sitescope provides a Service.
References to "We", "Us" and "Our" are references to Sitescope Limited ("Sitescope"), whose registered office is 7 Abbey Court, Eagle Way, Exeter, EX2 7HY. Where You are not ordering the Services directly from Sitescope, but from an Authorised Reseller, references to "Sitescope" or "We", "Us" and "Our" shall be construed so as to mean either Sitescope and/or the Authorised Reseller as the context shall indicate.
References to "You/Your/Yourself" refer to the contracting party who accesses the Website or places an Order with Sitescope.
"Report" includes any information that Sitescope supplies to You including all reports, services, datasets, software or information contained in them.
"Services" means the provision of any service by Sitescope pursuant to these Terms, including without limitation, any Report.
"Sitescope Fees" means any charges levied by Sitescope for Services provided to You.
"Suppliers" means any organisation who provides data or information of any form to Sitescope.
"Terms" means these Terms and Conditions.
"Third Party Content" means the services, software, information and other content or functionality provided by third parties and linked to or contained in the Services.
"Websites" means websites hosted by Sitescope and includes the Content and any report, service, document, data-set, software or information contained therein, derived there from or thereby.

1. Terms and Conditions

a. These Terms govern the relationship between You and Sitescope whether You are an unregistered visitor to the Website or are purchasing Services. Where these Terms are not expressly accepted by You they will be deemed to have been accepted by You, and You agree to be bound by these Terms when You place any Order, or pay for any Services provided
b. If the person communicating with Sitescope is an Authorised Reseller, they must ensure that You agree to these Terms.
c. The headings in these Terms are for convenience only and shall not affect the meaning or interpretation of any part of these Terms.
d. Sitescope may modify these Terms, and may discontinue or revise any or all other aspects of the Services at our sole discretion, with immediate effect and without prior notice, including without limitation changing the Services available at any given time. Any amendment or variation to these Terms shall be posted on our Websites. Continued use of the Services by You shall be deemed an acceptance by You to be bound by any such amendments to the Terms.
e. These Terms, together with the prices and delivery details set out on our Websites, Sitescope's Privacy Policy and Your Order comprise the whole agreement relating to the supply of Services to You by Sitescope. No prior stipulation, agreement, promotional material or statement whether written or oral made by any sales or other person or representative on our behalf should be understood as a variation of these Terms. Save for fraud or misrepresentation, Sitescope shall have no liability for any such representation being untrue or misleading.
f. These Terms shall prevail at all times to the exclusion of all other terms and conditions including any terms and conditions which You may purport to apply even if such other provisions are submitted in a later document or purport to exclude or override these Terms and neither the course of conduct between parties nor trade practice shall act to modify these Terms.

2. Services

a. Sitescope will use reasonable care and skill in providing the Services to You, however, the Services are provided on the express basis that the information and data supplied in the Services are derived from third party sources and Sitescope does not warrant the accuracy or completeness of such information or data. Such information is derived solely from those sources specifically cited in the Services and Sitescope does not claim that these sources represent an exhaustive or comprehensive list of all sources that might be consulted.

3. Intellectual Property

a. You acknowledge that all Intellectual Property Rights in the Services are and shall remain owned by either Sitescope or our Suppliers and nothing in these Terms purports to transfer, assign or grant any rights to You in respect of the Intellectual Property Rights.
b. Subject always to these Terms You may, without further charge, make the Services available to;
   i. the owner of the Property at the date of the Report,
   ii. any person who purchases the whole of the Property Site,
   iii. any person who provides funding secured on the whole of the Property Site,
   iv. any person for whom You act in a professional or commercial capacity,
   v. any person who acts for You in a professional or commercial capacity; and
   vi. prospective buyers of the Property Site as part of an Information Pack but for the avoidance of doubt, Sitescope shall have no liability to such prospective buyer unless the prospective buyer subsequently purchases the Property Site, and the prospective (or actual) buyer shall not be entitled to make the Service available to any other third party.
   Accordingly Sitescope shall have the same duties and obligations to those persons in respect of the Services as it has to You.
c. Each of those persons referred to in clause 3.b. shall have the benefit and the burden of Your rights and obligations under these Terms. The limitations of Sitescope's liability as set out in clause 6 shall apply to all users of the Service in question in aggregate and Sitescope shall not be liable to any other person.
d. All parties given access to the Services agree that they will treat as strictly private and confidential the Services and all information which they obtain from the Services and shall restrict any disclosure to employees or professional advisors to enable the relevant party to conduct its internal business. The requirement in this clause to treat the Services as confidential shall include a requirement to maintain adequate security measures to safeguard the Services from unauthorised access, use or copying.
e. Each recipient of the Services agrees (and agrees it will cause its employees, agents or contractors who may from time to time have access to the Services to agree) it will not, except as permitted herein or by separate agreement with Sitescope:-
   i. effect or attempt to effect any modification, merger or change to the Service, nor permit any other person to do so; or
   ii. copy, use, market, re-sell, distribute, merge, alter, add to or carry on any redistribution, reproduction, translation, publication, reduction to any electronic medium or machine readable form or commercially exploit or in any other way deal with or utilise or (except as expressly permitted by applicable law) reverse engineer, decompile or disassemble the Services, Content or Website; or
   iii. remove, alter or in any way change any trademark or proprietary marking in any element of the Services and You shall acknowledge the ownership of the Content, where such Content is incorporated or used into Your own documents, reports, systems or services whether or not these are supplied to any third party.
   iv. create any product which is derived directly or indirectly from the data contained in the Services
f. The mapping contained in any Services is protected by Crown Copyright and must not be used for any purpose outside the context of the Services or as specifically provided by these Terms.
g. You are permitted to make five copies of any Report, but are not authorised to re-sell the Report, any part thereof or any copy thereof unless you are an Authorised Reseller. Further copies may not be made in whole or in part without the prior written permission of Sitescope who shall be entitled to make a charge for each additional copy.

4. Charges

a. VAT at the prevailing rate shall be payable in addition to the Sitescope Fees. You shall pay any other applicable indirect taxes related to Your use of the Services.
b. An individual or a monthly invoice showing all Orders created by You will be generated subject to these Terms. You will pay the Sitescope Fees at the rates set out in Sitescope's or its Authorised Reseller's invoice. The Sitescope Fees are payable in full within 30 days without deduction, counterclaim or set off. You acknowledge that time is of the essence with respect to the payment of such invoices. Sitescope reserve the right to amend the Sitescope Fees from time to time and the Services will be charged at the Sitescope Fee applicable at the date on which the Service is ordered.
c. We may charge interest on late payment at a rate equal to 3% per annum above the base lending rate of National Westminster Bank plc.
d. Sitescope or its Authorised Reseller shall not be obliged to invoice any party other than You for the provision of Services, but where Sitescope or its Authorised Reseller does so invoice any third party at Your request, and such invoice is not accepted or remains unpaid, Sitescope or its Authorised Reseller shall have the option at any time to cancel such invoice and invoice You direct for such Services. Where Your order comprises a number of Services or severable elements within any one or more Services, any failure by Sitescope or its Authorised Reseller to provide an element or elements of the Services shall not prejudice Sitescope's or its Authorised Reseller's ability to require payment in respect of the Services delivered to You.

5. Termination

a. Sitescope may suspend or terminate Your rights under these Terms without any liability to You with immediate effect if at any time:-
   i. You fail to make any payment due in accordance with clause 4;
   ii. You repeatedly breach or commit or cause to be committed any material breach of these Terms; or
   iii. You commit a breach and You fail to remedy the breach within 7 days of receipt of a written notice to do so; additionally, without prejudice to the foregoing, Sitescope may remedy the breach and recover the costs thereof from You.
b. If Your rights are terminated under this clause and You have made an advance payment We will refund You a reasonable proportion of the balance as determined by Us in relation to the value of Services previously purchased.
c. Sitescope reserves the right to refuse to supply any or all Services to You without notice or reason.

6. Liability

a. We provide warranties and accept liability only to the extent stated in this clause 6 and clause 7.
b. Nothing in these Terms excludes either party's liability for death or personal injury caused by that party's negligence or wilful default, and the remainder of this clause 6 is subject to this provision and Your statutory rights.
c. As most of the information contained in the Services is provided to Sitescope by others, Sitescope cannot control its accuracy or completeness, nor is it within the scope of Sitescope's Services to check the information on the ground. Accordingly, Sitescope will only be liable to You for any loss or damage caused by its negligence or willful default and subject to clause 6.o below neither Sitescope nor any person providing information contained in any Services shall in any circumstances be liable for any inaccuracies, faults or omissions in the Services, nor shall Sitescope have any liability if the Services are used otherwise than in accordance with these Terms.
d. Save as precluded by law, Sitescope shall not be liable for any indirect or consequential loss, damage or expenses (including loss of profits, loss of contracts, business or goodwill) howsoever arising out of any problem, event, action or default by Sitescope.
e. In any event, and notwithstanding anything contained in these Terms, Sitescope's liability in contract, tort (including negligence or breach of statutory duty) or otherwise howsoever arising by reason or in connection with this Contract (except in relation to death or personal injury) shall be limited to an aggregate amount not exceeding £1 million if the complaint is in relation to a Report on residential property and an aggregate amount not exceeding £10 million in respect of any other Report or Service purchased from Sitescope.
f. Sitescope will not be liable for any defect, failure or omission relating to Services that is not notified to Sitescope within six months of the date of the issue becoming apparent and in any event, within twelve years of the date of the Service.
g. You acknowledge that:-
   i. Subject to clause 6.o below You shall have no claim or recourse against any Third Party Content supplier nor any of our other Suppliers. You will not in any way hold us responsible for any selection or retention of, or the acts of omissions of Third Party Content suppliers or other Suppliers (including those with whom We have contracted to operate various aspects or parts of the Service) in connection with the Services (for the avoidance of doubt Sitescope is not a Third Party Content supplier). Sitescope does not promise that the supply of the Services will be uninterrupted or error free or provide any particular facilities or functions, or that the Content will always be complete, accurate, precise, free from defects of any other kind, computer viruses, software locks or other similar code although Sitescope will use reasonable efforts to correct any inaccuracies within a reasonable period of them becoming known to us;
   ii. Sitescope's only obligation is to exercise reasonable skill and care in providing environmental property risk information to persons acting in a professional or commercial capacity who are skilled in the use of property and environmental information and You hereby acknowledge that You are such a person;
   iii. no physical inspection of the Property Site reported on is carried out as part of any Services offered by Sitescope and Sitescope do not warrant that all land uses or features whether past or current will be identified in the Services. The Services do not include any information relating to the actual state or condition of any Property Site nor should they be used or taken to indicate or exclude actual fitness or unfitness of a Property Site

for any particular purpose nor should it be relied upon for determining saleability or value or used as a substitute for any physical investigation or inspection. Sitescope recommends that You inspect and take other advice in relation to the Property Site and not rely exclusively on the Services.

iv. Subject to clause 6.o below, Sitescope shall not be responsible for error or corruption in the Services resulting from inaccuracy or omission in primary or secondary information and data, inaccurate processing of information and data by third parties, computer malfunction or corruption of data whilst in the course of conversion, geo-coding, processing by computer or electronic means, or in the course of transmission by telephone or other communication link, or printing.

v. Sitescope will not be held liable in any way if a Report on residential property is used for commercial property or more than the one residential property for which it was ordered.

vi. the Services have not been prepared to meet Your or anyone else's individual requirements; that You assume the entire risk as to the suitability of the Services and waive any claim of detrimental reliance upon the same; and You confirm You are solely responsible for the selection or omission of any specific part of the Content;

vii. Sitescope offer no warranty for the performance of any linked internet service not operated by Sitescope;

viii. You will on using the Services make a reasonable inspection of any results to satisfy Yourself that there are no defects or failures. In the event that there is a material defect You will notify us in writing of such defect within seven days of its discovery;

ix. Any support or assistance provided to You in connection with these Terms is at Your risk;

All liability for any insurance products purchased by You rests solely with the insurer. Sitescope does not endorse any particular product or insurer and no information contained within the Services should be deemed to imply otherwise. You acknowledge that if You Order any such insurance Sitescope will deem such as Your consent to forward a copy of the Report to the insurers. Where such policy is purchased, all liability remains with the insurers and You are entirely responsible for ensuring that the insurance policy offered is suitable for Your needs and should seek independent advice. Sitescope does not guarantee that an insurance policy will be available on a Property Site. All decisions with regard to the offer of insurance policies for any premises will be made solely at the discretion of the insurers and Sitescope accepts no liability in this regard. The provision of a Report does not constitute any indication by Sitescope that insurance will be available on the property.

Professional opinions contained in Reports are provided to Sitescope by third parties, and such third parties are solely liable for the opinion provided. For the avoidance of doubt, those parties providing assessments or professional opinions on Sitescope products include RPS Plc & Wilbourn Associates Limited, and any issues with regard to the provision of such opinion should be taken up with the relevant third party.

If Sitescope provides You with any additional service obtained from a third party, including but not limited to any interpretation or conclusion, risk assessment or environmental report or search carried out in relation to a Report on Your Property Site, subject to clause 6.o below, Sitescope will not be liable in any way for any information contained therein or any issues arising out of the provision of those additional services to You. Sitescope will be deemed to have acted as an agent in these circumstances and the supply of these additional services will be governed by the terms and conditions of those Third Parties.

In any event no person may rely on a Service more than 12 months after its original date.

If You wish to vary any limitation of liability as set out in these Terms, You must request such variation prior to ordering the Service. Sitescope shall use its reasonable endeavours to agree such variation but shall not be obliged to do so.

Time shall not be of the essence with respect to the provision of the Services.

Ordnance Survey have undertaken a positional accuracy improvement programme which may result in discrepancies between the positioning of features used in datasets in the Services and the updated Ordnance Survey mapping.

Subject to clause 6.o below Sitescope and its Suppliers exclude all and any liability incurred as a result of the implementation of such positional accuracy improvement programme.

Where Sitescope provides its own risk assessment in connection with any Report, Sitescope shall carry out such assessment with all reasonable skill and care but shall have no liability for any such risk assessment conclusion which is provided for information only, save where Sitescope conducted the same negligently, in which case the provisions of clause 6 shall apply. Notwithstanding the provision of any such risk assessment conclusion you should carefully examine the remainder of the Report and should not take or refrain from taking any action based solely on the basis of the risk assessment. For the avoidance of doubt, the provisions of this clause 6n apply solely to risk assessments conducted by Sitescope, and the provision of any other risk assessment by a third party shall be governed by such third party's terms in accordance with the provisions of clause 6i above.

Sitescope obtains much of the information contained in its Report from third parties. Sitescope will not accept any liability to You for any negligent or incorrect entry, or error or corruption in the Third Party Content supplied to Sitescope, but Sitescope's Suppliers may be liable for such negligent or incorrect entries, or errors or corruptions, subject to the terms and conditions on which they supply the Third Party Content to Sitescope.

Contribution

Save where expressly provided, this clause 7 shall apply solely to those Homecheck Professional Environmental Reports where RPS certify that the level of environmental risk identified in the report is not likely to be sufficient for the property to be described as "contaminated land" as defined by section 78(A)2 of Part IIA of the Environmental Protection Act 1990 and where RPS should have identified such risk. Nothing in this clause 7 shall operate to override or vary the provisions of clause 6.

Sitescope are prepared to offer, at their sole discretion, and without any admission or inference of liability a contribution towards the costs of any remediation works required under a Notice (as defined below) on the terms of this clause 7 ("the Contribution")

In the event that a Remediation Notice is served on the First Purchaser or First Purchaser's Lender of a Property Site under Part II(A) of the Environmental Protection Act 1990 ("the Notice") Sitescope will contribute to the cost of such works as either the First Purchaser or First Purchaser's Lender (but not both) are required to carry out under the Notice subject to the provisions of this clause 7 and on the following terms:

i. the Contribution shall only apply to contamination or a pollution incident present or having occurred prior to the date of the Report;

ii. The Contribution shall only apply where the Property Site is a single residential dwelling house or a single residential flat within a block of flats. For the avoidance of doubt, this obligation does not apply to any commercial property, nor to any Property Site being developed or redeveloped whether for residential purposes or otherwise;

iii. The Contribution is strictly limited to the cost of works at the Property Site and at no other site.

iv. The Contribution will not be paid in respect of any of the following:
Radioactive contamination of whatsoever nature, directly or indirectly caused by or contributed to or arising from ionising radiations or contamination by radioactivity from any nuclear fuel or from any nuclear waste from the combustion of nuclear fuel or the radioactive toxic explosive or other hazardous properties of any explosive nuclear assembly or nuclear component thereof.
Asbestos arising out of or related in any way to asbestos or asbestos-containing materials on or in structures or services serving the structures.
Naturally occurring materials arising from the presence or required removal of naturally occurring materials except in circumstances where such materials are present in concentrations which are in excess of their natural concentration.
Intentional non-compliance arising from the intentional disregard of or knowing, wilful or deliberate non-compliance by any owner or occupier of the Property Site with any statute, regulation, administrative complaint, notice of violation, or notice letter of any Regulatory Authority.
Any condition which is known or ought reasonably to have been known to the First Purchaser or the First Purchaser's Lender prior to the purchase of the Report.
Any condition which is caused by acts of War or an Act of Terrorism
Any property belonging to or in the custody or control of the First Purchaser which does not form a fixed part of the Property Site or the structure.
Any fines liquidated damages punitive or exemplary damages.
Any bodily injury including without limitation, death, illness or disease, mental injury, anguish or nervous shock.
Any financial loss in respect of any loss of any rental, profit, revenue, savings or business or any consequential indirect or economic loss damage or expense including the cost of rent of temporary premises or business interruption.
Any losses incurred following a material change in use of, alteration or development of the Property Site.

d. The maximum sum that shall be contributed by Sitescope in respect of any Contribution shall be limited to £60,000. In the event that more than one Report is purchased on the Property Site the Contribution will only be payable under the first Report purchased by or on behalf of any First Purchaser or First Purchaser's Lender and no Contribution will be made in respect of subsequent Reports purchased by or on behalf of such First Purchaser, First Purchaser's Lender or any person connected to them

e. Sitescope shall only pay a Contribution where the Notice is served within 36 months of the date of the Report.

f. Any rights to a Contribution under this Clause 7 are not assignable in the event of a sale of the Property Site and Sitescope will not make any Contribution after the date of completion of such sale.

g. In the event the First Purchaser or First Purchaser's Lender wishes to claim any Contribution, it shall notify Sitescope in writing within 3 months of the date of the Notice. The First Purchaser or First Purchaser's Lender (as applicable) shall comply with all reasonable requirements of Sitescope with regard to the commission and conduct of the remediation works to be carried out under the Notice, and in the event the First Purchaser or First Purchaser's Lender (as applicable) does not do so, including without limitation, obtaining Sitescope's prior written consent to any estimates for such works or complying with any other reasonable request by Sitescope, Sitescope shall not be required to pay any Contribution. Notwithstanding the payment of the Contribution by Sitescope the First Purchaser or First Purchaser's Lender as applicable shall take all reasonable steps to mitigate any costs incurred in connection with the conduct of works required under the terms of any Notice.

h. In the event that the First Purchaser or First Purchaser's Lender receives any communication from a statutory authority to the effect that there is an intent to serve a notice received under PartII(A) of the Environmental Protection Act 1990 they will advise Sitescope within a maximum period of two months from receipt of such communication. This clause 7h and the service of any notice under it shall not affect the provisions of clauses 7 e and g, and any such communications, even if advised to Sitescope will not operate as notice under clause 7e.

i. Sitescope reserve the right at any time prior to a claim for Contribution being made in accordance with clause 7g above, to withdraw the offer of payment of Contributions without further notice.

8. Events Beyond Our Control

a. You acknowledge that Sitescope shall not be liable for any delay, interruption or failure in the provision of the Services which are caused or contributed to by any circumstance which is outside our reasonable control including but not limited to, lack of power, telecommunications failure or overload, computer malfunction, inaccurate processing of data, or delays in receiving, loading or checking data, corruption of data whilst in the course of conversion, geo-coding, processing by computer in the course of electronic communication, or printing.

9. Severability

a. If any provision of these Terms are found by either a court or other competent authority to be void, invalid, illegal or unenforceable, that provision shall be deemed to be deleted from these Terms and never to have formed part of these Terms and the remaining provisions shall continue in full force and effect.

10. Governing Law

a. These Terms shall be governed by and construed in accordance with English law and each party agrees irrevocably submit to the exclusive jurisdiction of the English courts If any dispute arises out of or in connection with this agreement (a "Dispute") the parties undertake that, prior to the commencement of Court proceedings, they will seek to have the Dispute resolved amicably by use of an alternative dispute resolution procedure acceptable to both parties with the assistance of the Centre for Dispute Resolution (CEDR) if required, by written notice initiating that procedure. If the Dispute has not been resolved to the satisfaction of either party within 60 days of initiation of the procedure or if either party fails or refuses to participate in or withdraws from participating in the procedure then either party may refer the Dispute to the Court.

11. General; Complaints

a. Sitescope may assign its rights and obligations under these Terms without prior notice or any limitation.

b. Sitescope may authorise or allow our contractors and other third parties to provide to Sitescope and/or to You services necessary or related to the Services and to perform Sitescope's obligations and exercise Sitescope's rights under these Terms, which may include collecting payment on Sitescope's behalf.

c. No waiver on Sitescope's part to exercise, and no delay in exercising, any right, power or provision hereunder shall operate as a waiver thereof, nor shall any single or partial exercise of any right, power or provision hereunder preclude the exercise of that or any other right, power or provision.

d. Unless otherwise stated in these Terms, all notices from You to Sitescope must be in writing and sent to the Sitescope registered office (or in the case of an Authorised Reseller, to its registered office address) and subject to paragraph e below all notices from Sitescope to You will be displayed on our Websites from time to time.

e. Any complaints in relation to the Services should, in the first instance, be in writing addressed to the Customer Service Support Manager at the Sitescope registered office. Sitescope or its agents will respond to any such complaints in writing as soon as practicably possible.

f. A person who is not a party to any contract made pursuant to these Terms shall have no right under the Contract (Right of Third Parties) Act 1999 to enforce any terms of such contract and Sitescope shall not be liable to any such third party in respect of any Services supplied.

g. Sitescope's Privacy Policy as displayed on the Website governs the use made of any information You supply to Sitescope.

Sitescope Limited, 7 Abbey Court, Eagle Way, Exeter, EX2 7HY Email: info@landmarkinfo.co.uk

Version 3.05 28 Jul 2007

Standard questions to ask following an environmental search report

IN RELATION TO POLLUTING DISCHARGES

1. When and to whom was the discharge consent or permit identified at [*location*] granted? Who is the current holder of the consent? [*Note: The answer to this question may already be included in the search report.*]

2. What substances are the proprietors of the consent or permit authorised to discharge, and into what environmental medium?

3. Have there ever been any breaches of the terms of the discharge consent or permit resulting in a criminal prosecution against anyone? [*Note: The answer to this question may already be included in the search report.*]

4. Is there any history of non-compliance with consent or permit conditions by anyone, whether resulting in prosecution or not?

5. Does any permitted discharge, past or current, of which you are aware, pose any risk or threat to health or property, or constitute a nuisance, at [*address*]?

6. Are you aware of any past or current unauthorised discharges into any environmental medium from any location which pose, or might pose, any risk or threat to health or property, or constitute a nuisance, at [*address*]?

7. Are you aware of any past or current unauthorised discharges into any environmental medium from [*address*] which might result in prosecution or pose a risk or threat to health or property, or constitute a nuisance, at other locations?

IN RELATION TO POTENTIALLY CONTAMINATED OR POLLUTED LAND

8. Does the authority have any information in its possession regarding the presence or possible presence of pollutants or contaminants at [*address/grid reference/nature of feature (e.g. brickworks)*] whether or not such location has been designated as 'contaminated land' under EPA Part IIA? If so, please provide it. Does the Authority have any intention of visiting or investigating the property at [*address*] in discharge of its duties under Part IIA of EPA 1990?

9. Does the authority have any information in its possession regarding the presence or possible presence of pollutants or contaminants at any location adjacent or reasonably close to [*address/grid reference/nature of feature (e.g. brickworks)*] whether or not such location has been designated as 'contaminated land' under EPA Part IIA? If so, please provide it.

10. Does the authority have any concerns regarding the presence or possible presence of

pollutants or contaminants at [*address/grid reference/nature of feature (e.g. brickworks)*] or any location adjacent or reasonably close to it that, in the authority's view, may pose a risk or threat to health or property at [*address/grid reference/nature of feature (e.g. brickworks)*]? If so, please provide it.

11. Does the authority have any information or concerns regarding the presence or possible presence of pollutants or contaminants at [*feature*] in [*grid referenced location*] or any location adjacent or reasonably close to it that, in the authority's view, may pose a risk or threat to health or property at [*address*]? If so, please provide it.

12. In the authority's view, is the [*feature*] at [*grid referenced location*] likely to give rise to any risk or threat to health or property, or constitute a nuisance, at [*address*]?

13. In the authority's view, is the land, or any pollutants, contaminants or possible pollutants or contaminants, at [*address/grid reference/nature of feature (e.g. brickworks)*] likely to give rise to any risk or threat to health or property, or constitute a nuisance, at [*address*] or any other location?

14. At the time of the development of the [*address*] were any planning conditions imposed on the developer relating to the treatment, removal or other works regarding any pollution or contamination concerns? If so, what works have been carried out in compliance or purported compliance with such conditions? Were all required works carried out to the satisfaction of the relevant planning authority?

15. At the time of the development of the [*address*] were any treatment, removal or other works carried out regarding any pollution or contamination concerns? If so, what works? Please provide details [*copies of any documents*] relating to such works, including any environmental reports and investigations carried out prior to, during or after the development of [*address*].

16. In the developer's view, is the land, or any pollutants, contaminants or possible pollutants or contaminants, at [*address*] or any adjacent location likely to give rise to any risk or threat to health or property, or constitute a nuisance, at [*address*] or any other location?

Clauses to include in client care letter regarding environmental risks

[[In this case, your lender requires us to undertake] [The expenses we will incur on your behalf include the sum of £[....] in respect of] an environmental data search report. We obtain this report in case there are any environmental matters which may be of concern to you, or your mortgage lender. Whilst it is unlikely that there will be any substantial problem, it is always best to check as such problems are not always evident from a visit and a survey may not reveal them either. If any factors are revealed which we feel ought to be investigated further, we will of course let you know. If you have any queries about this – or any other specific concerns – please do not hesitate to contact us.]

[Our professional body suggests that we draw to your attention the possibility that the property you intend to buy may be affected by contamination. In fact, there are many matters which may affect the use and enjoyment of your new home such as the risk of flooding, the presence of naturally-occurring but harmful substances such as radon gas, an odour problem from an industrial process nearby or some potentially costly expenses to clean up historic contamination which may already be on your land. We intend to undertake an initial search on the property to ascertain whether any of these problems may exist. The cost of this will be £[....] plus VAT. If any factors are revealed which we feel ought to be investigated further, we will of course let you know. If you have any queries about the matters mentioned – or any other concerns – please do not hesitate to contact us.]

[Like many clients and their lenders, you may wish us to undertake an environmental data search report, to determine whether or not your property might be affected by contamination. In fact, there are many matters which may affect the use and enjoyment of your new home such as the risk of flooding, the presence of naturally-occurring but harmful substances such as radon gas, an odour problem from an industrial process nearby or some potentially costly expenses to clean up historic contamination which may already be on your land. An initial data search on the property can help us to ascertain whether any of these problems may exist. The cost of this will be £[....] plus VAT. If any factors are revealed which we feel ought to be investigated further, we will of course let you know.

If you do not wish us to undertake such a search, please tell us by return that you do not wish us to proceed with this important step. Please appreciate, however, that in declining such a report, you may fail to appreciate risks associated with the property that you may have wished to avoid, and we will not be in a position to advise you about them.]

[*NB: Similar clauses could mention the availability and desirability of planning searches.*]

Enquiries of the seller

[NB: These enquiries focus on land contamination. Other enquiries may be added concerning energy performance certificates, environmental permits, etc. for commercial transactions.]

1. Uses of the property

1.1 Please give details of the current use of and the activities carried on at the property.

1.2 Has there been a change in the nature of the use of or activities carried on at the property during the seller's ownership or occupation? If so, please give details.

1.3 Please give details of the use of, and activities carried on at, the property prior to the seller's period of ownership or occupation, and, in particular, whether the property has ever been used for any one or more of the following:

1.3.1 Agriculture: burial of diseased livestock.

1.3.2 Extractive industry: coal mines, coal preparation plants, oil refineries and petrochemicals; mineral workings, mineral processing works. (NB: includes loading, transport, sorting, forming and packaging and similar operations.)

1.3.3 Energy industry: gas works; coal carbonisation plants; oil refineries; power stations.

1.3.4 Production of metals: metal processing; heavy engineering; electroplating and metal finishing. (NB: includes scrap metal treatments.)

1.3.5 Production of non-metals and their products: mineral processing; asbestos works; cement, lime and gypsum manufacture, brickworks and associated processes.

1.3.6 Glass-making and ceramics: including glazes and vitreous enamel.

1.3.7 Production and use of chemicals.

1.3.8 Engineering and manufacturing processes: manufacture of metal goods (including mechanical engineering industrial plant or steel work, motor vehicles, ships, railway or tramway vehicles, etc.); storage, manufacture or testing of explosives, propellants, small arms, etc.; electrical and electronic equipment manufacture and repair.

1.3.9 Food processing industry: pet foods or animal feedstuffs; processing of animal by-products (including rendering or maggot farming but excluding slaughterhouses and butchering).

1.3.10 Paper, pulp and printing industry.

1.3.11 Timber and timber products industry: chemical treatment and coating of timber and timber products.

1.3.12 Textile industry: tanning, dressing, fellmongering or other process for preparing, treating or working leather; fulling, bleaching, dyeing or finishing fabrics or fibres; manufacture of carpets or other textile floor-coverings (including linoleum works).

1.3.13   Rubber industry: processing natural or synthetic rubber (including tyre manufacture or retreading).

1.3.14   Infrastructure: marshalling, dismantling, repairing or maintenance of railway rolling-stock; dismantling, repairing or maintenance of marine vessels (including hovercraft); dismantling, repairing or maintenance of road transport or road haulage vehicles; dismantling, repairing or maintenance of air and space transport systems.

1.3.15   Waste disposal: treating sewage or other effluent or storage, treatment or disposal of sludge (including sludge from water treatment works); treating, keeping, depositing or disposing of waste including scrap (to include infilled canal basins, docks or river courses); storage or disposal of radioactive materials.

1.3.16   Miscellaneous: dry-cleaning operations; laboratories for educational or research purposes; demolition of buildings, plant or equipment for any of the activities mentioned above.

1.4   Is any neighbouring property used for:

1.4.1   any industrial purposes which, in the event of a major accident, may require immediate evacuation of the property?

1.4.2   any purposes involving handling hazardous, explosive or radioactive substances?

1.5   Are there any storage tanks over or underground on the property or on any adjoining or neighbouring property? If so please provide details of:

1.5.1   their location;
1.5.2   their age and condition;
1.5.3   any substances stored in them, including details of nature and volume;
1.5.4   any spillages or leakages from them;
1.5.5   facilities for inspection;
1.5.6   results of any inspections carried out.

1.6   Are there, or has there ever been, any electricity sub-station transformers, capacitors or other oil-filled electrical switchgear containing PCBs located on the property or any neighbouring property? If so, please give details of their location and condition and any steps proposed or taken to remove them from the property.

1.7   Are any neighbouring properties used, or have they ever been used, for any of the uses mentioned above or for any other purpose which does or may lead to interference of an environmental nature on the property?

1.8   Is the seller aware of any proposal to use the property or any neighbouring property for any of the uses mentioned above or for any other purpose which does or may lead to interference of an environmental nature on the property?

2.   Condition of the property

2.1   Is there any contamination or pollution on the property, or in or on any adjoining or neighbouring property? If so, please give details.

2.2   Is there any stained soil or significant evidence of damage to vegetation on the property?

2.3   Are there currently, or have there been previously, any flooring, drains, or walls located within the property that are stained by substances other than water or are emanating noxious odours?

2.4   Please confirm that no hazardous substances have been used in the structure or fabric of any building on the property. If such confirmation cannot be given please give full details of the materials used and of any action taken to identify and remove any such materials from the property.

2.5   Has the seller any reason for believing or suspecting that some potential liability or detriment arising from pollution or related environmental matters, whether of the property or neighbouring property, may attach to the owners or occupiers of the property at any foreseeable future date?

2.6　Please confirm that no polluting incident has taken place, or is taking place on the property. If such an incident is taking, or has taken, place please provide the following particulars:

2.6.1　full details of the accident or incident;

2.6.2　copies of any reports, correspondence, court orders, notices or recommendations relating to the accident or incident;

2.6.3　details of any remedial work carried out, including certificates of satisfactory completion.

3.　Waste

3.1　Is there any waste on the property? If so, please indicate the quantity, and whether it is industrial, commercial, domestic or hazardous waste.

3.2　Is the property being or has it ever been used as, or does it or has it ever comprised in whole or in part a waste landfill site, including any infilling of the ground? If so, please provide copies of any Environmental Permits or Waste Management Licences or other permits or authorisations granted in respect of the property and any reports or material correspondence relating thereto. In particular, please specify what measures have been taken to close the landfill, and what steps are being or have been taken to limit, control, contain and/or monitor any emissions of any substance likely to emanate from the property.

3.3　Has any adjoining or neighbouring land been used in any way (including, but not limited to, use for the deposit, disposal or treatment of waste) which might impact on the state and condition of the property by pollution or contamination, either directly or indirectly (e.g. by watercourses or otherwise)? If so, please provide details.

3.4　Is the seller aware of any proposal to deposit waste on the property or any adjoining land?

4.　Inspections, complaints, notices and proceedings

4.1　Have there been any complaints from or disputes with the Environment Agency, the local authority, any other statutory authority or any other person regarding the state and condition of the property or the use of the property, or any neighbouring property? If so, please supply full details.

4.2　Has the Environment Agency or the local authority inspected the property or given notice of its intended inspection of the property or any neighbouring property? Please supply copies of any survey or test results carried out in relation to the property pursuant to such inspection.

4.3　Has any notice been served in respect of the property or any neighbouring property by the Environment Agency, the local authority or any other statutory authority which is of current effect? If so, please give details of such notices and any appeals.

4.4.　Is there any reason why any statutory body might enter the property or any neighbouring property and/or take any steps to avoid pollution to the environment or harm to health, or any indication that the authority might do any of those things? If so, please supply full details.

4.5　Are there any proceedings in progress or in prospect, or any circumstances which may result in such proceedings, which have led or may lead to the owner of the property being liable to fines, penalties and/or costs of remedial measures? If so, please supply full details.

4.6　Are there any proceedings in progress or in prospect, or any circumstances which may result in such proceedings, which have led or may lead to the owner of the property being liable to pay damages in respect of any environmental incident, accident, escape or emission? If so, please supply full details.

4.7 Has the seller ever had cause to make a complaint about any neighbouring property or institute, or bring any claim, action or proceedings against the owners of any neighbouring property in respect of any environmental matter?

Sample lease clauses

SUGGESTED LEASE DEFINITIONS

'Environmental Closure' means any closure of the Premises: caused by any requirements for Remedial and Clean-Up Action at the Premises or in its locality: or, otherwise caused by the presence of Environmental Contamination at the Premises or in its locality;

'Environmental Contamination' means any release, leakage, discharge, deposit, emission, spillage or other escape of Hazardous Substances into the atmosphere, water or on to land occurring or having occurred (in any case) on or from the Premises and/or any other property;

'Environmental Laws' means all Laws, in so far as they relate to: the control and prevention of pollution of the land, water or the atmosphere due to the release, discharge, spillage, entry, deposit, emission or other escape of Hazardous Substances; the conservation maintenance and management of environmental resources on land, in water or in the atmosphere; the production, transportation, storage, treatment, recycling or disposal of waste; the protection of human health and life;

'Environmental Liabilities' means:

all costs of Remedial and Clean-Up Action incurred or suffered by [the Landlord/Tenant] in order to meet the requirements of any court of competent jurisdiction or any competent authority in respect of such action;

all costs of Remedial and Clean-Up Action to the extent that [the Landlord/Tenant] is liable for such costs and such action is carried out by any person other than [the Landlord/Tenant] pursuant to the orders or directions of any court of competent jurisdiction or any competent authority;

all costs of Remedial and Clean-Up Action which would meet the requirements of any court of competent jurisdiction or any competent authority; all liabilities of [the Landlord/Tenant] to third parties who have suffered injury, loss or damage as a result of any Environmental Contamination;

all fines and awards made in proceedings before a court or tribunal of competent jurisdiction (and all costs and expenses reasonably incurred in connection with such proceedings);

'Environmental Notice' means any document served by any body of competent authority which specifies any Remedial and Clean-Up Action;

'Hazardous Substances' means any organism, products, wastes, pollutants, contaminants or other substances (whether in solid or liquid form or in the form of a gas or vapour and whether alone or in combination with any other substance) which may, either alone or in combination, be harmful to man or to the life or health of any other living organisms or constitute a nuisance;

'Remedial and Clean-Up Action' means:

investigation of the effects of the relevant incident of Environmental Contamination giving rise to any Environmental Liability;

physical exposure of, and all actions reasonably necessary to ascertain the nature and extent of the relevant Environmental Contamination;

relevant treatment, removal and/or destruction of contaminated soil, water, materials, substances, or living organisms being the cause or likely cause of or resulting from the relevant Environmental Contamination, abatement or prevention of the releases, discharges. spillages, deposits, emission or other escapes of Hazardous Substances into the atmosphere or water or onto the land being the cause or likely cause of or resulting from the relevant Environmental Contamination; and

reinstating any property, goods or equipment affected by Remedial and Clean-Up Action.

'Waste' means any packaged or stored substance which constitutes scrap material, effluent or other unwanted surplus substance arising from the application of any process or operation (whether toxic, dangerous or otherwise).

SAMPLE CLAUSES FAVOURING LANDLORD

Covenant to observe all laws and notices

To heed observe and at all times comply with all Environmental Laws and Environmental Notices pertaining to the demised premises.

Without prejudice to the generality of the foregoing the Tenant agrees not to discharge or permit or suffer to be discharged any solid matter or any fluid of a poisonous or noxious nature (with the exception of human sewage) from the demised premises into any drains or sewers as aforesaid that does in fact destroy, sicken or injure the fish in or contaminate or pollute the water of any stream or river and further not to do or omit or permit or suffer to be done any act or thing whereby the waters of any stream or river may be polluted or the composition thereof so changed as to render the landlord liable to any action or proceedings by any person whatsoever. [*adapt for other risks*]

Covenant to pay all outgoings

The Tenant shall pay all and any outgoings, liabilities, costs, expenses and other burdens arising from any Environmental Liability or from compliance with any applicable Environmental Law or Environmental Notice served in relation to the demised premises.

Covenant to indemnify Landlord

The Tenant hereby agrees to indemnify the Landlord against all and any outgoings, liabilities, costs, expenses and other burdens arising from any Environmental Liability or from compliance with any applicable Environmental Law or Environmental Notice served in relation to the demised premises.

Notwithstanding any provision of this Lease the Landlord shall not be liable to the Tenant for any Environmental Contamination in relation to the Premises and the Tenant [and the Tenant's Guarantor] hereby jointly and severally irrevocably and unconditionally indemnify the Landlord against all Environmental Liabilities.

SAMPLE CLAUSES FAVOURING TENANT

Cessor of rent

In case the Premises or any part thereof shall be subject to Environmental Closure then and in any such case the rents and the further rents hereby reserved or a fair and just proportion thereof according to the nature and extent of the Environmental Closure shall from and after such Environmental Closure and until the cessation of such Environmental Closure be suspended and cease to be payable and any dispute as to the amount of such proportion shall be referred to arbitration.

Tenant's right to determine in the event of Environmental Closure

1. This Clause applies if the period of any Environmental Closure has commenced more than six months previously and continues at the date of service of the Tenant's notice under the provisions of Clause 2.
2. If this Clause applies the Tenant may by notice served on the Landlord terminate this Lease.
3. Upon service of that notice the Term will absolutely cease but without prejudice to any rights or remedies that may have accrued to either party against the other.

Tenant's right to determine in the event of an Environmental Notice

In the event that any competent authority or court of competent jurisdiction shall serve a notice or make an order (whether under any Environmental Law or otherwise) which exposes the Tenant to any Environmental Liability in relation to the Premises then the Tenant may terminate this Lease by giving the Landlord within 28 days of receipt of such notice or order written notice to that effect but such termination shall not prejudice the rights of either party in respect of any antecedent breach of obligations of the other.

Environmental Indemnity

Notwithstanding any provision of this Lease the Tenant shall not be liable to the Landlord for any Environmental Contamination in relation to the Premises and the Landlord and the Landlords Guarantor hereby jointly and severally irrevocably unconditionally indemnify the Tenant against all Environmental Liabilities.

Service Charge

The Tenant will not be obliged to contribute whether through the Service Charge or otherwise any sums in relation to any Environmental Liabilities whether in respect of the Premises or in respect of any other property.

Illustrative environmental clauses for inclusion in a share purchase agreement

[NB: These illustrative clauses are intended to cover the major environmental issues that may arise in a share purchase agreement. They do not purport to cover all such issues. The clauses should, of course, be adapted to ensure that they are compatible with the rest of the share purchase agreement.]

DEFINITIONS

1.1   In this Agreement:

'Environmental Contamination' means any release, leakage, discharge, deposit, emission, spillage or other escape of Hazardous Substances into the atmosphere, water or on to land occurring or having occurred (in any case) on or from the Property and any buildings, Plant and Equipment situated therein or thereon;

'Environmental Indemnity' means the indemnity given by the Vendor to the Purchaser in Clause [ ];

'Environmental Law' means all laws (whether statutory or common law and whether civil or criminal), in so far as they relate to the control and prevention of pollution of land, water or the atmosphere due to the release, discharge, spillage. entry, deposit. emission or other escape of Hazardous Substances or to noise, odour or other nuisances and the production, transportation, storage, treatment, recycling or disposal of waste and the protection of human health and life;

'Environmental Liabilities' means:

(a)   any fines or penalties (whenever imposed) in respect of any breaches prior to Completion by the Vendor or the Company or its predecessors in title or their officers, agents or employees of any Environmental Law and all costs and expenses reasonably incurred in connection with such proceedings;

(b)   any liability to third parties (whenever arising) resulting wholly or partly from:

(i)   the state or condition of the Property prior to or at Completion;

(ii)   activities or operations of the Vendor or the Company or its predecessors in title or those deriving title therefrom at the Property;

(c)   all costs of remedial or clean-up action incurred or suffered by the Purchaser in order to meet the requirements of any competent authority or a Court of competent jurisdiction and arising in consequence of (i) or (ii) above and whether carried out by the Purchaser, the competent authority or another;

(d)   all costs of remedial or clean-up action arising in consequence of (i) or (ii) above which the Independent Environmental Consultant, appointed pursuant to Clause [ ] hereof, has reported as being, in his opinion, necessary to meet the reasonable requirements of any competent authority or Court of competent jurisdiction had such authority or Court been made fully aware of the condition of the Property;

(e) the cost of reasonable measures taken in respect of the Property to prevent or mitigate any risks presented by the Property to human health or safety, property, air quality, surface or underground water or soil by reasons of Environmental Contamination arising prior to Completion;

(f) for the purposes of clause (d) above and Clause 6 and the Warranties it is agreed that the expression 'remedial and clean-up action' shall include proper investigation of the Environmental Contamination giving rise to any Environmental Liability, removal of defective plant or structures contributing to Environmental Contamination and appropriate treatment of contaminated material, whether by destruction, removal, containment or otherwise;

'Environmental Licences' means the permits, licences, authorisations, consents or other approvals required by any Environmental Law;

'Hazardous Substances' means any organism, products, wastes, pollutants, contaminants or other substances (whether in solid or liquid form or in the form of a gas or vapour and whether alone or in combination with any other substance) which may, either alone or in combination, be harmful to man or to the life or health of any other living organisms or deleterious to the environment;

'Independent Environmental Consultant' means the independent environmental consultant appointed pursuant to Clause [ ];

'Licences' means all licences, authorisations and approvals (including but not limited to the Environmental Licences and the other permits) that are required for the exploitation of the Business;

'Prudent Operating Practice' means the standard of practice attained by exercising that degree of skill, diligence, prudence and foresight which could reasonably be expected from a skilled and experienced operator engaged in the same or a similar type of undertaking as or to that of the Vendor in operating the Business under the same or similar circumstances;

'Waste' means any packaged or stored substance which constitutes material or effluent or other unwanted surplus substance arising from the application of any process (whether toxic, dangerous or otherwise) which requires to be disposed of.

CONDUCT OF BUSINESS PRIOR TO COMPLETION

2.1 The Vendor covenants and agrees that, prior to the Completion Date, it shall in respect of the Business comply with each of the following:

2.1.1 it shall comply with the provisions of any Laws applicable to operation of the Business, and in particular any Environmental Laws, and shall make sure that none of the warranties granted hereunder are breached or otherwise materially affected;

2.1.2 it shall comply with the provisions of all Licences, the terms and conditions of all contracts to which the Vendor is a party and any requirements, obligations, covenants or like matters associated with title in the Property;

2.1.3 it shall maintain in full force and effect insurance coverage of a type and amount customary in its business.

ENVIRONMENTAL INDEMNITY

3.1 The Vendor hereby agrees to indemnify the Purchaser and the Company against all Environmental Liabilities whether current or future arising under Environmental Laws and without limitation under Part IIA of the Environmental Protection Act 1990 or any statutory replacement, amendment or re-enactment thereof and also agrees that it will join in notifying any competent authority of the existence and terms of this agreement and in requesting the competent authority to give effect to the said agreement for the purposes of the said Part IIA.

3.2 Each of the Warranties, Indemnities and Environmental Indemnity shall be construed as a separate warranty or indemnity, as the case may be, and shall not be limited or restricted by reference to, or inference from, the terms of any other warranty or indemnity or any other term of this Agreement.

3.3 The Environmental Indemnity shall be limited to 75 per cent of all Environmental Liabilities arising in connection with the Business provided that any such Environmental Liability occurred on or before the Completion Date. Where any incident of Environmental Contamination is or shall be discovered at the Property at any time after the Completion Date, the Purchaser shall, where there is any dispute as to the existence or scope of the Vendor's liability as a result of such incident under any Environmental Liability:

3.3.1 instruct the Independent Environmental Consultant to make such enquiries and investigations as he shall consider appropriate and to determine as soon as practicable to what extent the instance of Environmental Contamination was reasonably likely to have occurred in whole or in part on or prior to the Completion Date; and

3.3.2 instruct the Independent Environmental Consultant to determine whether the remedial and clean-up action proposed to be undertaken by the Purchaser is the minimum reasonably required in order to bring the [premises] into compliance with Environmental Law.

3.4 The Independent Environmental Consultant shall be appointed by mutual agreement of the Vendor and the Purchaser upon notification by the Purchaser to the Vendor that it wishes an Independent Environmental Consultant to be appointed to resolve any dispute as described in Clause [ ]. If the Vendor and the Purchaser shall fail to agree upon an appointee within 14 days of the Purchaser notifying the Vendor of its wish to make an appointment, either the Vendor or the Purchaser may apply to the President for the time being of the British Chambers of Commerce to appoint an Independent Expert.

3.5 The Vendor and the Purchaser shall jointly instruct the Independent Environmental Consultant to report in accordance with Clause [ ] above. The professional fees of the Independent Environmental Consultant shall be borne by the Vendor and the Purchaser proportionally in 75:25 shares respectively. The Vendor and the Purchaser shall provide such information and all necessary access to their respective properties, plant, equipment, records and personnel as the Independent Environmental Consultant shall reasonably require. The opinion of the Independent Environmental Consultant pursuant to this clause shall be conclusive and binding on the parties, but without prejudice to the right of the Purchaser to commence and serve legal proceedings to the extent that any damage to the Purchaser or liability to third parties would not be eliminated by the remedial and clean-up action as determined under Clause [ ].

3.6 The Vendor hereby unconditionally and irrevocably undertakes to the Purchaser that it shall. prior to Completion or as soon as reasonably practicable thereafter (and in any event within one month of the day of Completion), remove or have removed, and dispose or have disposed from the Property in accordance with all Environmental Laws any Waste. The Vendor shall indemnify and keep indemnified the Purchaser against any and all costs, damages, fines, judgments and expenses (including legal fees) and liabilities whatsoever incurred in connection with the removal of such Waste.

3.7   Any sum due from the Vendor to the Purchaser under the Environmental Indemnity shall be paid within [ ] days of:

3.7.1   completion of any remedial and clean-up action undertaken by the Purchaser;

3.7.2   the Purchaser incurring the cost of the remedial and clean-up action carried out by any person other than the Purchaser; or

3.7.3   the date of payment of any liabilities to third parties, fines or awards (and all expenses incurred in connection therewith);

provided that the Purchaser shall at the same time pay 25 per cent of any such sum due under the Environmental Indemnity.

LIMITATIONS ON WARRANTIES, INDEMNITY AND ENVIRONMENTAL INDEMNITY

4.1   The Purchaser acknowledges that in entering into this Agreement it has not relied on any warranties or representations whatsoever other than the Warranties, Indemnities or the Environmental Indemnity contained in this Agreement and that it has relied on the Disclosure Letter and no other warranties or representations whatsoever have been made by or on behalf of the Vendor.

4.2   The Purchaser shall not be entitled to make any claim under this Agreement (whether in contract or tort) if or to the extent that:

4.2.1   the facts, matters or circumstances in respect of which the claim arises are fairly and reasonably disclosed (and nothing has been knowingly withheld by the Vendor which would render them untrue, inaccurate or misleading) in the Disclosure Letter (or in any documents annexed to the Disclosure Letter); or

4.2.2   in respect of any claim made under the Environmental Indemnity, the claim arises or is increased as a result of the passing, or any change in, any Environmental Law made after the Completion Date; or

4.2.3   the facts, matters or circumstances in respect of which the claim arises occurred with the prior written consent of the Purchaser after the date hereof but on or before Completion.

4.3   The Purchaser shall not be entitled to make any claim under this Agreement (whether in contract or tort) unless the Purchaser gives to the Vendor written notice of the claim (giving details of the breach or nature of the claim and the Purchaser's best estimate of the amount of the claim) as soon as reasonably practicable after the Purchaser has become aware of the facts giving rise to the claim and in any event within, in the case of any claim under the Environmental Indemnity, [ ] years of the Completion Date and, in any other case, within [ ] years of the Completion Date, and commences and serves legal proceedings in respect of any such claim within [ ] months of the date any such notice is given.

4.4   If the Purchaser becomes aware of any claim or threatened claim against the Purchaser which may constitute or give rise to a claim under the Warranties or becomes aware of any Environmental Liability, the Purchaser shall as soon as practicable thereafter notify the Vendor giving full details thereof. The Purchaser shall not compromise, settle or discharge any such claim or make any admission of liability without first consulting with the Vendor and the Purchaser shall consider any reasonable request of the Vendor in connection with any negotiations or proceedings concerning any claim or potential claim under the Warranties or any Environmental Liability.

4.5   The following limitations shall apply:

4.5.1   the Vendor shall have no liability in respect of any single claim under this Agreement (whether in contract or tort) if the amount for which the Vendor would (in the absence of this Clause [ ]) be liable to the Purchaser in respect of that claim is equal to or less than £[*amount*];

4.5.2   the Vendor shall have no liability in respect of any claims under this Agreement (whether in contract or tort) if the aggregate amount for which the Vendor would (in the absence of this Clause [ ]) be liable to the Purchaser in respect of that claim is equal to or less than £[*amount*].

4.6   The Purchaser shall take all reasonable steps to avoid or mitigate any loss, damage or liability which might give rise to a claim against the Vendor under this Agreement (whether in contract or tort).

4.7   Any amount payable or paid by the Vendor to the Purchaser under the Warranties shall be treated as a reimbursement of the Purchase Price payable hereunder.

4.8   In the event of any circumstances arising which do or may give rise to an Environmental Liability and which fall within the terms of the Environmental Indemnity, the Purchaser shall not (where practicable) make any public statement regarding such circumstances without prior consultation with the Vendor on the text of any such public statement before it is made.

4.9   Subject to Clause [ ], no breach of the Warranties or of any other provisions of this Agreement nor any misrepresentation or statement of fact whatsoever shall give rise to any right of the Purchaser to rescind or terminate this Agreement following its signing by the parties hereto.

4.10   The aggregate liability of the Vendor in respect of (a) all claims including, where relevant, the fees of the Independent Environmental Consultant, made under the Environmental Indemnity shall be 75 per cent of £[*amount*] and (b) all other claims under this Agreement (whether in contract or tort) shall not in any event exceed the further amount of £[*amount*].

4.11   The Purchaser shall not be entitled to recover under the Warranties if and to the extent that the Purchaser has recovered any indemnity under any applicable insurance.

TERMINATION BY THE PURCHASER

5.1   This Agreement may be terminated by the Purchaser from the date hereof prior to the Completion Date if:

5.1.1   physical damage has occurred or hazard has arisen at the Property after the date hereof or any proceedings have been issued by a third party against the Vendor which (whether (in any case) alone or where the effect of which when combined with the effect of other such events) would render the Vendor unable to carry on the Business (or a material part thereof) from the Properties on or after the Date of Completion; or

5.1.2   any incident of material Contamination shall have occurred after the date hereof which would give rise to Environmental Liability.

SCHEDULE 1: WARRANTIES

1.   Environmental Matters

1.1   The Company has obtained all Environmental Licences necessary to own and operate the Assets and to carry on the Business at the Property and has at all times complied with all applicable Environmental Law and the terms and conditions of the Environmental Licences (whether express or implied) and, without undue expenditure and effort on the part of the Company, can continue to so comply.

1.2 The Company has not received any notice or other communication (including without limitation any abatement, enforcement, prohibition, revocation, remediation, works, charging, or other notice of a relevant nature, judgment, demand letter or communication relating to clean-up action in relation to pollution or protection of the environment or nuisance or any communication) from which it appears that it may be or is alleged to be in violation of any Environmental Law or Environmental Licence or that any Environmental Licence may be subject to modification, suspension or revocation and there are no circumstances likely to give rise to such violation or modification, suspension or revocation.

1.3 The Company is not engaged in and the Vendors are not aware of any facts which make it likely or desirable that it should be engaged in any appeal in respect of any Environmental Licence or any conditions contained therein or any review thereof or any refusal of any Environmental Licence and the Vendors have no reason to believe that those Environmental Licences which have been applied for but which have not yet been granted or are pending will not be granted within a reasonable period of time and on acceptable terms.

1.4 Full details of any remedial work carried out at the Property and affecting Environmental Contamination and of any environmental assessment, audit, review or investigation conducted by or on behalf of the Company are contained in or annexed to the Disclosure Letter.

1.5 There are no facts or circumstances which interfere with or prevent compliance with any Environmental Law or which may give rise to any common law or legal liability or otherwise form any claim or action related to the pollution or protection of the environment.

1.6 The Company has not refused to comply with or prevented or sought to prevent any other person from complying with the requirements of any inspector or other officer appointed under the Environmental Laws.

1.7 During the [ ] years prior to the date hereof, the Company has not used, disposed of, generated, stored, transported, dumped, released, deposited, buried or emitted any Hazardous Substance at, on, from or under any of the Property or at, on, from or under any other premises.

1.8 No other person has used, disposed of, generated, stored, transported, dumped, released, deposited, buried or emitted any Hazardous Substance at, on, from or under any of the Property or at, on, from or under any other premises.

1.9 During the [ ] years prior to the date hereof, the Company has not disposed of any Hazardous Substance in the past in connection with the business in such a way that its disposal would now constitute a breach of any Environmental Law.

1.10 To the best of the Vendors' knowledge and belief warranties [ ] to [ ] (inclusive) would be true if given in respect of any other person who owns or occupies or carries on business on property which adjoins either the Property or any property occupied by the Company in so far as relates to his adjoining property or to activities carried on there or in respect of whose activities or business wherever carried on the Company or its activities is or is likely to be affected.

1.11 Full details have been disclosed to the Purchaser of all expenditure which has been incurred or which the Vendor is aware will be required to be incurred by the Purchaser to comply with any applicable Environmental Law or any condition attaching to any Environmental Licence.

Illustrative terms for inclusion in a facility agreement

DEFINITIONS

'Environmental Claim' means, with respect to any person, any notice, claim, demand or similar communication (written or not) by any other person alleging potential liability for investigatory costs, clean-up costs, governmental response costs, natural resources damages, property damages, personal injuries, fines or penalties arising out of, based on or resulting from:

(a) the presence, or release into the environment, of any Material of Environmental Concern at any location, whether in surface or ground water or on or under land and whether or not owned by such person; or

(b) circumstances forming the basis of any violation, or alleged violation, of any Environmental Laws or Environmental Consent;

'Environmental Consent' means any consent, permit, licence, approval, ruling, exemption or other authorisation required under applicable Environmental Laws:

'Environmental Laws' means any law (which includes an order or decree, any form of delegated legislation, a treaty and a directive or regulation made by virtue of powers conferred by a treaty) of a Governmental Authority regulating, relating to or imposing liability or standards of conduct concerning, environmental protection matters, including without limitation, in relation to the manufacture, processing, distribution, use, treatment, storage, disposal, transfer or handling of Materials of Environmental Concern, as now or may at any time hereafter be in effect;

'Environmental Report' means the environmental report dated [ ] [201[ ] prepared by the Borrower with respect to the Borrower [and its Subsidiaries];

'Governmental Authority' means any nation or government, any state or political subdivision thereof and any entity exercising executive, legislative, judicial, regulatory or administrative functions of any of the foregoing;

'Material of Environmental Concern' means any poisonous, noxious or polluting matter, including but not limited to chemicals, pollutants, contaminants, wastes, toxic substances, petroleum and petroleum products and distillates, and all hazardous substances defined or regulated as such in or under any Environmental Laws.

CONDITIONS PRECEDENT

(a) The Lender receiving a copy of an Environmental Report from an environmental consultant acceptable to the Lender accompanied by a certificate from an officer of the

Borrower confirming that, after having made all appropriate inspections and investigations, the Borrower [and its Subsidiaries] [is/are] in compliance in all material respects
with the Environmental Laws in the jurisdictions in which [it/they] carr[ies/y] on
business and that the property occupied by the Borrower is not, nor is likely to be,
designated as contaminated land within the meaning of Part IIA of the Environmental
Protection Act 1990.

(b) The Lender receiving a collateral warranty from the environmental consultant in
relation to the Environmental Report in a form acceptable to the Lender.

(c) Evidence being provided to the Lender in a form acceptable to the Lender that effective
insurance cover is in place for risks in relation to Environmental Claims to such extent
as is in accordance with industry practice.

REPRESENTATIONS AND WARRANTIES

[(a) The Environmental Report is true. complete and accurate in all material respects, does
not omit any material fact in relation to the compliance by the Borrower [and its
Subsidiaries] with Environmental Laws and the Borrower is not aware of any material
fact or circumstance which has not been disclosed to [the Managers,] the Agent or the
Banks which, if disclosed, would be likely at the date of this Agreement to be relevant in
relation to any material liability of the Borrower [or any of its Subsidiaries], or any
liability of the [Managers,] the Agent or the Banks in their respective capacities as such
under this Agreement, under or in respect of Environmental Laws;]

(b) [each of] the Borrower [and its Subsidiaries] is in full compliance with all Environmental Laws which are currently applicable to its business and all Environmental Consents
required in respect thereof have been obtained from the appropriate authorities and are
in full force and effect [except where the failure to comply with any such Environmental
Laws or to obtain any such Environmental Consents would not reasonably be expected
(i) materially and adversely to affect the ability of the Borrower to fulfil its obligations
under this Agreement or (ii) to result in any liability to [the Managers,] the Agent or the
Banks in their respective capacities as such during the normal course of this Agree-
ment];

(c) no litigation, arbitration or administrative proceeding is current, pending or, to the
knowledge of the Borrower, threatened under any Environmental Laws to which the
Borrower [or any of its Subsidiaries] is or will be named as a party;

(d) there are no material compliance or enforcement orders currently outstanding against
the Borrower [or any of its Subsidiaries] arising under any Environmental Laws; and

(e) there is no Environmental Claim pending or, to the knowledge of the Borrower,
threatened against the Borrower [or any of its Subsidiaries] and, so far as the Borrower
is aware after due enquiry. there are no past or present actions, activities, circumstances,
conditions, events or incidents including without limitation the release, emission,
discharge or disposal of any Material of Environmental Concern, which could reasonably be expected to form the basis of any Environmental Claim against the Borrower [or
any of its Subsidiaries].

COVENANTS

(a) Comply with [, and ensure compliance by its Subsidiaries with,] all Environmental
Laws applicable to the operations of the Borrower [and its Subsidiaries] and obtain
from the appropriate authorities all Environmental Consents required in respect thereto
[, except where the failure to comply with any such Environmental Laws or to obtain
such Environmental Consents would not reasonably be expected:

      (i)   materially and adversely to affect the ability of the Borrower to fulfil its obligations under this Agreement; or

      (ii)   to result in any liability to [the Managers,] the Agent and the Banks in respect thereof in their respective capacities as such during the normal course of this Agreement];

(b)   maintain [, and ensure that each of its Subsidiaries maintains,] insurance on and in relation to [its/their respective] business[es] and assets with reputable underwriters or insurance companies against such risks, including, without limitation, risks in relation to Environmental Claims, and to such extent as in accordance with good industry practice; [as soon as practicable, and in any event within [ ] days, after the end of each of its financial years, deliver to the Agent in sufficient copies for the Banks a certificate of an officer of the Borrower stating that there has been no change to any of the matters set out in the Environmental Report or, if there has been any change, setting out of the details thereof its effect on the Borrower's obligations regarding Environmental Laws as set out in this Agreement and the steps the Borrower is taking in respect thereof;]

[(c)   if the Borrower fails to provide a certificate in respect of the Environmental Report as required by Clause [ ] and without prejudice to the rights of the Banks under Clause [ ] ([Events of Default]), permit [, and cause its Subsidiaries to permit,] any representative of the Agent and/or the Banks at any reasonable time (i) to visit and inspect any of the places at which the Borrower [or any of its Subsidiaries] carries on its business and (ii) to examine any of the books and records of the Borrower [and any of its Subsidiaries], for the purpose of conducting an environmental audit of the business of the Borrower; the cost of such audit to be reimbursed by the Borrower on demand if such audit establishes that the Borrower is in breach of this Agreement in relation to Environmental Laws;]

(d)   if:

      (i)   the Borrower [or any of its Subsidiaries] receives any notice alleging that it is not in compliance with any applicable Environmental Law; or

      (ii)   the Borrower [or any of its Subsidiaries] becomes aware that there is any Environmental Claim pending or threatened against it; or

      (iii)   there occurs any (or any threatened) release, emission, discharge or disposal of any substance which could reasonably be expected to form the basis of any Environmental Claim against the Borrower [or any of its Subsidiaries]; and, in the case of any of the foregoing, there is a reasonable likelihood that the same could materially and adversely affect the ability of the Borrower to perform its obligations under this Agreement or result in liability to [the Managers,] the Agent and/or the Banks in their respective capacities as such during the normal course of this Agreement then:

(e)   the Borrower shall promptly upon the occurrence of any of the foregoing provide to the Agent a certificate of an officer of the Borrower specifying in detail the nature of such event and the actions which the Borrower [or, as the case may be, such Subsidiary] intends to take in response thereto; and

(f)   upon the written request of the Agent, submit to the Agent at reasonable intervals a report providing any update of the situation resulting from such event;

(g)   neither the Borrower [nor any of its Subsidiaries] will make or permit any material change in the nature of its business or commence any new type of business materially different from its business at the date of this Agreement [or commence any business which is a potential source of any Material of Environmental Concern or which may have the result of causing any land of the Borrower to be designated as contaminated or a special site within the meaning of Part IIA of the Environmental Protection Act 1990.]

INDEMNITY

The Borrower shall indemnify [the Managers,] the Agent and the Banks [and any receiver appointed under any of the Security Documents] and their respective employees, agents, directors and officers (the 'Indemnified Parties') against all claims, costs, expenses or liabilities (a 'Liability') of whatever kind or nature suffered or incurred by any Indemnified Party arising out of or in connection with any order, requirement or demand made against any Indemnified Party by any Governmental Authority in respect of a breach or alleged breach by the Borrower [or any of its Subsidiaries] of any Environmental Law or arising out of or in connection with any action taken by the Indemnified Parties to clean up, improve, remove any substance (hazardous or otherwise) or take any other action of whatever kind taken with a view to disposing of the assets subject to the Security Documents.

AGREEMENT IN RESPECT OF CONTAMINATED LAND LIABILITY

(a) If any Governmental Authority designates any land belonging to the Borrower or any of its Subsidiaries as contaminated land within the meaning of Part IIA of the Environmental Protection Act 1990 or serves or indicates an intention to serve on [the Managers,] the Agent or the Bank [or any receiver appointed under any of the Security Documents] any remediation notice or other Environmental Claim under Part IIA of the Environmental Protection Act 1990, the Borrower hereby agrees that it will bear 100 per cent of the cost of complying with the said notice or intended notice.

(b) The Parties hereto confirm that they are content for the provisions of this paragraph to be applied to the costs of the Environmental Claim and that they will join together in notifying, confirming the contents of and if necessary providing a copy of this agreement to, the Governmental Authority concerned.

(c) The Parties confirm and accept that the provisions of this paragraph shall be applied and that the Governmental Authority shall as between the Parties make such determinations on the questions of exclusion, apportionment and attribution as shall give effect to the terms of this paragraph and that the Governmental Authority shall not as between the Parties apply the tests set out in any Environmental Laws relating to contaminated land for the time being in force.

(d) The Parties confirm that the transaction the subject of this agreement and the terms of this paragraph are not intended nor are they part of any larger series of transactions which are intended to have the effect of increasing the share of costs theoretically to be borne by any person who would benefit from any limitation on the recovery of remediation costs and that the Governmental Authority should not therefore seek to disregard this agreement.

(e) If the Governmental Authority should notwithstanding paragraph [ ] disregard this agreement and apply the normal tests set out in any Environmental Laws relating to contaminated land for the time being in force and this has the effect that the Parties share the costs of the Environmental Claim in a way other than that set out in this paragraph, this paragraph shall nevertheless apply as between the Parties and they shall be entitled to insist on reciprocal indemnities the one against the other such that the costs of the Environmental Claim shall be adjusted as between them in order to restore the financial position to that which would have prevailed had the Governmental Authority applied this paragraph and not disregarded this agreement.

CLAUSES TO BE INSERTED IN THE CERTIFICATE OF TITLE OR IN THE FACILITY AGREEMENT AS REPRESENTATIONS AND WARRANTIES

(a) [So far as the Borrower is aware [during the Borrower's occupation]] there has been no storage disposal generation or treatment of any hazardous substances or Material of Environmental Concern at the Property in contravention of any statute or regulation relating thereto.

(b) [During the Borrower's period of ownership] there has been no spill, discharge, leak, emission, injection, escape, dumping or release of any kind onto the Property with respect to any business carried on at the Property or into the environment surrounding the Property other than releases as permissible or allowable under applicable Environmental Consents or licences.

Terms and conditions of engagement

[The clauses contained in this suggested agreement have been drafted on the basis of other well-established precedents for similar consultancy agreements, adapted for use in the environmental field.

Most firms of consultants have standard terms and conditions which are substantially briefer and usually much more restrictive of the client's rights than this model, and those standard terms may well be adequate, once the main restrictions have been dealt with (for commentary please see text).

As a clean-sheet approach, the aim of which is to protect the client first and foremost, the following model is suggested as the basis for initial bargaining. Many consultants will relent and accept conditions other than their own if the client is assertive enough on the important points.]

[From a drafting perspective, practitioners may prefer to have a short section of operative provisions, referring to details as set out in Schedules.]

Date:

Parties:

1. 'The Client': [ ] [Limited][PLC] (registered no. [ ]) whose registered office is at [ ]
2. 'The Consultant':[ ] [Limited][PLC] (registered no. [ ]) whose registered office is at [ ]

Recitals:

(A) The Consultant is engaged in business offering consultancy services in relation to environmental matters and has considerable skill, knowledge and experience in that field.

(B) In reliance upon that skill, knowledge and experience, the Client wishes to engage the Consultant to provide services in relation to environmental matters and the Consultant agrees to accept the engagement on the following terms.

1. Interpretation

1.1 In this Agreement:

'Affiliate' means any company, partnership or other entity which directly or indirectly controls, is controlled by or is under common control of either the Client or the Consultant;

'Control' means the legal power to direct or cause the direction of the general management and policies of the party in question;

271

'Agreement' means this instrument and any and all Schedules to this Agreement as the same may be amended, modified or supplemented from time to time in accordance with these provisions;

'The Board' means the Board of Directors from time to time of the Client; [*Clearly, if the client is not a company but, say, a firm of solicitors, this will need redefining.*]

'The Commencement Date' means [insert date];

'Confidential Information' means all unpatented designs, drawings, data, specifications, manufacturing processes, testing procedures and all other technical business and similar information relating to the Project or relating to the business of the Consultant or its operation including all readable or computer or other machine readable data, logic, logic diagrams, flow charts, orthographic representations coding sheets, coding, source or object codes, listings, test data, test routines, diagnostic programs or other material relating to or comprising software which is part of the Project;

'Documents' means all records, reports, documents, papers and other materials whatsoever originated by or on behalf of the Consultant pursuant to this Agreement;

'The Project' means the job specification set out in Schedule 1; 'Services' means the services more particularly set out in Schedule 2; and 'The Site(s)' means the property and places more particularly set out in Schedule 3. [*Relevant definitions have been relegated to Schedules in view of the potentially complex definition of the type of works required which may be necessary.*]

1.2 The headings in this Agreement are inserted only for convenience and shall not affect its construction.

1.3 Where appropriate, words denoting a singular number only shall include the plural and vice versa.

1.4 Reference to any statute or statutory provision includes a reference to the statute or statutory provisions as from time to time amended, extended or re-enacted.

2. Duration

2.1 The Consultant shall commence the provision of the Services on the Commencement Date and shall continue to provide the Services until termination of this Agreement as provided in Clause 6.

3. Positive obligations of the Consultant

3.1 The Consultant shall provide the Services at the Site provided that it may provide the Services at such other place or places as may be necessary for the due performance of them.

3.2 The Consultant shall keep detailed records of all acts and things done by it in relation to the provision of the Services and at the Client's request shall make them available for inspection and/or provide copies to the Client.

3.3 The Consultant shall at all times during the period of this Agreement:

3.3.1 faithfully and diligently perform using such skill and care as may reasonably be expected of a properly qualified and competent environmental consultant those duties and exercise such powers consistent with them which are from time to time necessary in connection with the provision of the Services;

3.3.2 obey all lawful and reasonable directions of the Board; [*Clearly, if the client is not a company but, say, a firm of solicitors, use of the term 'Board' is inappropriate.*]

3.3.3 use its best endeavours to promote the interests of the Client and its Affiliates and to ensure that the Services are carried out in such a manner as to cause as little inconvenience, disturbance or damage as is reasonably possible;

3.3.4   ensure that it and its personnel comply with all applicable laws, legislation, statutes, codes of practice, authorisation conditions, requirements of regulatory authorities and all lawful requirements of the Client or the Board;

3.3.5   ensure that it obtains and complies in full with the requirements of any authorisation or consent as may be necessary in connection with the performance of the Services.

3.4   *Confidentiality*

3.4.1   The Consultant agrees to treat as secret and confidential and make no disclosure of and to ensure that its personnel shall treat as secret and confidential and make no disclosure of the Confidential Information, the Documents and all other matters arising or coming to its or their attention in connection with the provision of the Services and not at any time for any reason whatsoever to disclose them or permit them to be disclosed to any third party except as permitted hereunder to enable the Consultant to carry out its duties and obligations. The Consultant shall procure that its personnel and all others of its employees having access to any of the Confidential Information, the Documents or such matters shall be subject to the same obligations as the Consultant and shall enter into a suitable secrecy agreement in a form approved by the Client or, in so far as this is not reasonably practicable, the Consultant shall take all reasonable steps to ensure that its employees are made aware of and perform such obligations.

3.4.2   The Consultant agrees to treat as secret and confidential and not at any time for any reason to disclose or permit to be disclosed to any person or persons or otherwise make use of or permit to be made use of any information relating to the Client's technology, technical processes, business affairs or finances or any such information relating to any Affiliate, suppliers, or customers of the Client where knowledge or details of the information was received during the period of this Agreement.

3.4.3   The obligations of the parties under this Clause 3.4 shall survive the expiry or the termination of this Agreement for whatever reason.

3.5   *Liability*

3.5.1   The Client will be relying upon the Consultant's skill, expertise and experience and also upon the accuracy of all representations or statements made and the advice given by the Consultant in connection with the provision of the Services and the accuracy of any Confidential Information or Documents conceived, originated, made or developed by the Consultant in connection with the provision of the Services and the Consultant hereby agrees to indemnify the Client against all loss, damage, costs, legal costs and professional and other expenses of any nature whatsoever incurred or suffered by the Client or by a third party whether direct or consequential including but without limitation any economic loss or other loss of turnover, profits, business or goodwill as a result of such reliance.

3.5.2   The Consultant accepts:

3.5.2.1   liability for death or personal injury howsoever resulting from the Consultant's negligence or that of its employees or subcontractors; and

3.5.2.2   liability for damage to property howsoever resulting from the Consultant's negligence or that of its employees or subcontractors where such negligence has arisen or arises in connection with the provision of the Services or in connection with any other activities undertaken by the Consultant pursuant to or for any purpose related to this Agreement.

3.5.3   The Consultant's liability under Clauses 3.5.1 and 3.5.2 above shall be limited to the sum of £[ ]. [*One could seek to omit any clause voluntarily limiting the liability of the consultant, but this is unlikely to escape scrutiny. One will inevitably have to concede some limitation – the question is how much. Suitable limits would be a sum equivalent to the consultant's insurance cover, typically £1m–£5m. This has to be balanced against the value of the work to the consultant. It should nevertheless be borne in mind that insurance can be difficult to obtain, and in any event, if a claim has already been brought against a consultant, the limit of £5m may already have been exhausted.]*

3.5.4   The Consultant expressly acknowledges that the provisions of this Clause 3.5 satisfy the requirements of reasonableness specified in the Unfair Contract Terms Act 1977 and that it shall be estopped from claiming the contrary at any future date in the event of any dispute with the Client concerning the Consultant's liability hereunder.

3.5.5   The Consultant undertakes and agrees to take out and maintain for the whole period of the Project adequate insurance cover with an insurance office of repute to cover the liability accepted by it in this Clause 3.5 and agrees to produce at the Client's request a copy of the insurance policy or policies and relevant renewal receipts for inspection by the Client. [*Insurance is available for consultants on the specialist market, so one should resist inclusions which seek to limit this requirement in some way, e.g. by adding words such as 'in so far as such cover is commercially available at suitable premiums'.*]

3.5.6   The provisions of this Clause 3.5 shall survive the termination of this Agreement for any reason.

3.6   If the Consultant shall consider it necessary to use the services of a third party whether for information or for the supply of goods or services including without limitation manufacture of models, prototypes, mock-ups, artwork, drawings, printing, photography, testing and the like, the Consultant shall, except in matters of a minor and obvious nature, obtain the prior consent of the Client before using such services.

3.7   The Consultant shall indemnify the Client against all and any liability, loss, damage, cost and expense of whatsoever nature incurred or suffered by the Client or any third party as a result of the activities of the Consultant in undertaking the Project.

4.   Payment

4.1   In consideration of the provision of the Services, the Client shall pay to the Consultant the fees as set out in Schedule 4.

4.2   All payments to the Consultant shall be made against the Consultant's invoices which shall be presented at the end of each calendar month during the term of this Agreement in respect of the provision of the Services provided in each such month. All payments shall be made by the Client within [30] days following receipt by the Client of the Consultant's invoice. All payments shall be made by the Client by a cheque or bank transfer to the account of the Consultant at a bank to be nominated in writing by the Consultant.

4.3   Payment by the Client shall be without prejudice to any claims rights which the Client may have made against the Consultant and shall not constitute any admission by the Client as to the performance by the Consultant of its obligations hereunder. Prior to making any such payment, the Client shall be entitled to make deductions or deferments in respect of any disputes or claims whatsoever with or against the Consultant.

5.   Obligations of the Client

5.1   Throughout the period of this Agreement, the Client shall [if applicable] in so far as possible afford the Consultant such access to the Site and the Client's information records and other material relevant to the Project as the Consultant may require to provide the Services provided always that the Client shall [if applicable] be obliged to afford such access only during its normal business hours. Further, the Client shall [if applicable]:

5.1.1   advise the Consultant of the rules and regulations which are then in force for the conduct of personnel at the Site. The Consultant shall ensure that its personnel comply with any such rules and regulations;

5.1.2   make available such working space and facilities at the Site as the Consultant may reasonably require. Such working space and facilities shall be comparable to but not better than those given by the Client to its own personnel of similar status;

5.1.3   make available appropriate personnel to liaise with the Consultant;

5.1.4   secure and otherwise keep safe all and any property of the Consultant.

[Clearly, this clause has no function if the client is not the owner of the site, but the investigation is being carried out in anticipation of an acquisition.]

6.   Termination

6.1   This Agreement shall terminate automatically on completion of the Project by the Consultant to the satisfaction of the Client by the service of a written notice to that effect from the Client, but such termination shall be without prejudice to any provision intended to operate thereafter.

6.2   Upon any breach by the Consultant of any of its duties and obligations under this Agreement in relation to the provision of the Services, the Client shall have the rights specified in Clauses 6.2.1 and 6.2.2.

6.2.1   The Client shall have the right to seek an order for specific performance together with a mandatory injunction against the Consultant in addition to bringing a claim in damages. The Consultant expressly acknowledges that the Client is relying upon the Consultant to perform all the Consultant's duties and obligations in connection with the provision of the Services and that, upon any breach by the Consultant of any such duties and obligations, the Client may not wish to exercise its right to terminate this Agreement pursuant to Clause 6.2.2 and thereafter to engage the services of another consultant to complete the provision of the Services seeking to recover the cost thereof as damages from the Consultant since any such other consultant will not have the familiarity with the Client's business affairs necessary to enable such other consultant to provide the Services pursuant to the terms of this Agreement. By reason of the foregoing the Consultant hereby agrees that, in circumstances where it is in breach of its duties and obligations in connection with the provision of the Services and the Client elects to affirm this Agreement and claim for damages, the claim for damages will be an inadequate remedy for the Client and, subject always to the discretion of the Court, the Client shall be entitled to an interlocutory order for specific performance together with a mandatory injunction (if the circumstances are appropriate to the grant of such an injunction) either or both in terms compelling the Consultant and its personnel thereafter to provide the Services pursuant to this Agreement. The Consultant further hereby agrees that such relief shall not affect the Client's right to seek to recover any loss and damage suffered by it in respect of the Consultant's prior breach of its duties and obligations in connection with the provision of the Services.

6.2.2   The Client shall have the right to terminate this Agreement forthwith by notice in writing to the Consultant and to engage another consultant to complete the provision of the Services. Following any such termination of this Agreement the Consultant shall indemnify the Client against all loss, damage, cost including management and similar costs, expenses including professional fees and expenses and all other expenditure or loss of opportunity or revenue whatsoever incurred or suffered by the Client as a result of the Consultant's breach. This indemnity shall survive the termination of this Agreement.

275

6.3 In addition to and notwithstanding the Client's rights of termination pursuant to Clause 6.2 either party may terminate this Agreement forthwith by notice in writing to the other if the other:

6.3.1 commits a breach of this Agreement which in the case of a breach capable of remedy shall not have been remedied within 30 days of the receipt by the other of a notice from the innocent party identifying the breach and requiring its remedy;

6.3.2 is unable to pay its debts or enters into compulsory or voluntary liquidation (other than for the purpose of effecting a reconstruction or amalgamation in such manner that the company resulting from such reconstruction or amalgamation if a different legal entity shall agree to be bound by and assume the obligations of the relevant party under this Agreement) or compounds with or convenes a meeting of its creditors or proposes a voluntary arrangement with its creditors or has a receiver or manager or administrative receiver, or administrator appointed or ceases for any reason to carry on business or takes or suffers any similar action which in the opinion of the party giving notice means that the other may be unable to pay its debts.

6.4 The Client shall have the right to terminate this Agreement forthwith by written notice to the Consultant if the Consultant shall have been prevented by any cause from providing the services for an aggregate period of [20] working days in any period of [12] calendar months.

6.5 Upon termination of this Agreement:

6.5.1 for whatever reason, the Consultant shall deliver up to the Client all of the Confidential Information, Documents and copies thereof in the possession, power. custody or control of either of them at the time and shall execute all such deeds and documents as the Client's legal advisers may require to transfer and assign to the Client the property and intellectual property in such Confidential Information and Documents and the Consultant shall not thereafter utilise or exploit the Confidential Information or Documents in any way whatsoever;

6.5.2 for whatever reason, the Client shall have the right to utilise and exploit the Confidential Information and the Documents in any way whatsoever without restriction;

6.5.3 by the Consultant pursuant to Clause 6.3 the Client shall remain liable to pay to the Consultant all sums which have accrued due and owing to the Consultant hereunder.

6.6 Termination of this Agreement for whatever reason shall not affect the accrued rights of the parties arising in any way out of this Agreement as at the date of termination and, in particular but without limitation, the right to recover damages against the other and all provisions which are expressed to survive this Agreement shall remain in force and effect.

7. Assignment

7.1 Subject to the provisions of Clause 7.2 below neither party shall assign, transfer, subcontract or in any other manner make over to any third party the benefit and/or burden of this Agreement without the prior written consent of the other.

[The question of the assignability of rights under the agreement is a vexed one. It is common practice for persons other than the client (e.g. a purchaser of assets from the client) to want the right to sue the consultant if they have in some way relied on the report in their assessment of risk. They will usually demand the assignment of rights under the contract, and the client could be advised to include a term allowing the unilateral assignment of rights by the client alone.

Most environmental consultants recognise this and, subject to limiting the number of assignments or reliance letters (also known as duty of care letters), will permit this, as long as they are advised when initially entering into the agreement, and not, say, two years after the work has been completed.

In addition, consultants will resist any attempt to force them to act as the client's 'insurer' against environmental risk – the right to sue being traded off against a contract price in a transaction. Their view is that the client should be more concerned to get the right information for their own purposes, and to look no further.

Including this clause will, however, give the client freedom to negotiate assignment on an ad hoc basis when and if required, although the consultant is likely to want to charge a further fee for any assignment not agreed prior to entering the agreement.

One freedom which the client may need to reserve is the freedom to provide a duty of care letter to a funder.]

7.2 The Client shall be entitled without the prior written consent of the Consultant to assign, transfer or in any manner make over the benefit and/or burden of this Agreement to an Affiliate or to any 50/50 joint venture company where it is the beneficial owner of 50 per cent of the issued share capital thereof or to any company or partnership with which it may merge or to any company or partnership to which it may transfer its assets and undertaking provided that such Affiliate or other company or partnership undertakes and agrees in writing to assume, observe and perform the rights and powers and/or duties and obligations of the Client under the provisions of this Agreement being assigned, transferred or otherwise made over.

7.3 This Agreement shall be binding upon the successors and assigns of the parties hereto and the name of a party appearing herein shall be deemed to include the names of its successors and assigns provided always that nothing shall permit any assignment by either party except as expressly provided.

8. Governing law jurisdiction

8.1 The validity, construction and performance of this Agreement shall be governed by English law.

8.2 All disputes, claims or proceedings between the parties relating to the validity, construction or performance of this Agreement shall be subject to the non-exclusive jurisdiction of the High Court of Justice in England to which the parties hereto irrevocably submit. Each of the parties irrevocably consents to the award or grant of any relief in any such proceedings before the High Court of Justice in England. Either party shall have the right to take proceedings in any other jurisdiction for the purposes of enforcing a judgment or order obtained from the High Court of Justice in England.

9. *Force majeure*

9.1 Neither party shall be in breach of this Agreement if there is any total or partial failure of performance by it of its duties and obligations under this Agreement occasioned by any act of God, fire, act of government or state, war, civil commotion, insurrection, embargo, prevention from or hindrance in obtaining any raw materials, energy or other supplies and any other reason beyond the control of either party. If either party is unable to perform its duties and obligations under this Agreement as a direct result of the effect of one of those reasons, that party shall give written notice to the other of the inability which sets out full details of the reason in question.

The operation of this Agreement shall be suspended during the period (and only during the period) in which the reason continues. Forthwith upon the reason ceasing to exist the party relying upon it shall give written notice to the other of this fact. If the reason continues for a period of more than [90] days and substantially affects the commercial intention of this Agreement, the party not claiming relief under this Clause

9 shall have the right to terminate this Agreement upon giving 30 days' written notice of such termination to the other party.

10. Illegality

10.1 If any provision or term of this Agreement or any part thereof shall become or be declared illegal, invalid or unenforceable for any reason whatsoever including but without limitation by reason of the provisions of any legislation or other provisions having the force of law or by reason of any decision of any Court or other body or authority having jurisdiction over the parties or this Agreement including the EU Commission and the European Court of Justice, such terms or provisions shall be divisible from this Agreement and shall be deemed to be deleted from this Agreement in the jurisdiction in question provided always that, if any such deletion substantially affects or alters the commercial basis of this Agreement, the parties shall negotiate in good faith to amend and modify the provisions and terms of this Agreement as may be necessary or desirable in the circumstances.

11. Amendment, etc.

11.1 This Agreement shall not be amended, modified, varied or supplemented except in writing signed by a duly authorised representative of each of the parties.

11.2 No failure or delay on the part of either party hereto to exercise any right or remedy under this Agreement shall be construed or operated as a waiver thereof nor shall any single or partial exercise of any right or remedy as the case may be. The rights and remedies provided in this Agreement are cumulative and are not exclusive of any rights or remedies provided by law.

11.3 The text of any press release or other communication to be published by or in the media concerning the subject matter of this Agreement shall require the approval of each party.

11.4 Each of the parties hereto shall be responsible for its respective legal and other costs incurred in relation to the preparation of this Agreement.

12. Notice

12.1 Any notice or other document to be given under this Agreement shall be in writing and shall be deemed to have been duly given if left or sent by:

12.1.1   first class post or express or air mail or other fast postal service; or

12.1.2   registered post; or

12.1.3   telex, facsimile, email or other electronic media to a party at the address or relevant telecommunications number for such party or such other address as the party may from time to time designate by written notice to the other[s].

12.2 All such notices and documents shall be in the English language. Any notice or other document shall be deemed to have been received by the addressee two working days following the date of dispatch of the notice or other document by post or, where the notice or other document is sent by hand or is given by telex, facsimile, email or other electronic media, simultaneously with the delivery or transmission. To prove the giving of a notice or other document it shall be sufficient to show that it was dispatched.

SIGNATURE AND EXECUTION CLAUSE
SCHEDULES

APPENDIX B

Contaminated Land Warning Card[1]

WARNING – TO ALL SOLICITORS – CONTAMINATED LAND LIABILITIES

The advice contained on this Card is not intended to be a professional requirement for solicitors. Solicitors should be aware of the requirements of Part IIA of the Environmental Protection Act 1990 but they themselves cannot provide their clients with conclusive answers. They must exercise their professional judgement to determine the applicability of this advice to each matter in which they are involved and, where necessary, they should suggest to the client obtaining specialist advice. In the view of the Law Society the advice contained in this Card conforms to current best practice.

Solicitors should be aware that environmental liabilities may arise and consider what further enquiries and specialist assistance the client should be advised to obtain.

Contaminated land

1. The contaminated land regime was brought into effect in England on 1 April 2000. It applies to all land, whether residential, commercial, industrial or agricultural. It can affect owners, occupiers, developers, and lenders. The legislation, which is contained in Part IIA, Environmental Protection Act 1990 and in regulations and statutory guidance issued under it (see Contaminated Land (England) Regulations 2000 SI 2000/227 and DETR Guidance on Contaminated Land April 2000) is retrospective. It covers existing and future contamination.

The National Assembly is expected shortly to introduce similar regulations regarding contaminated land in Wales.

2. Local authorities must inspect and identify seriously contaminated sites. They can issue remediation notices requiring action to remediate contamination, in the absence of a voluntary agreement to do so. In certain cases ('Special Sites') responsibility for enforcement lies with the Environment Agency.

A negative reply to the standard local authority enquiries from the local authority may merely mean the site has not been inspected. It does not necessarily mean there is no problem.

Compliance can be costly, and may result in expenditure which could exceed the value of the property.

Liability falls primarily on those who 'cause or knowingly permit' contamination (a Class A person). If the authority cannot identify a Class A person, liability falls on a Class B person, the current owner, or occupier of the land. Class B persons include lenders in possession. There are complex exclusion provisions for transferring liability from one party to another. Some exclusions apply only on the transfer of land, or the grant of a lease. The applicability of any relevant exclusion needs to be considered before entering such transactions.

In every transaction you must consider whether contamination is an issue.

Conveyancing transactions

In purchases, mortgages and leases, solicitors should:

1.   Advise the client of potential liabilities associated with contaminated land.

Generally clients should be advised of the possibility and consequences of acquiring interests in contaminated land and the steps that can be taken to assess the risks.

2.   Make specific enquiries of the seller.

In all commercial cases, and if contamination is considered likely to be a risk in residential cases (e.g. redevelopment of brown field land):

3.   Make enquiries of statutory and regulatory bodies.

4.   Undertake independent site history investigation, e.g. obtaining site report from a commercial company.

In commercial cases, if there is a likelihood that the site is contaminated:

5.   Advise independent full site investigation.

6.   Consider use of contractual protections and the use of exclusion tests.

This may involve specific disclosure of known defects, possibly coupled with price reduction, requirements on seller to remedy before completion, and in complex cases the use of warranties and indemnities.

Unresolved problems, consider

7.   Advising withdrawal, and noting advice;

8.   Advising insurance (increasingly obtainable for costs of remediation of undetected contamination and any shortfall in value because of undisclosed problems).

Specific transactions

1. Leases

Consider if usual repair and statutory compliance clauses transfer remediation liability to tenant, and advise.

2. Mortgages

Advise lender, if enquiries reveal potential for or existence of contamination, and seek instructions.

In enforcement cases, consider appointment of receivers, rather than steps resulting in lender becoming mortgagee in possession, and so treated as a Class B person.

3. Share sales and asset purchases

Consider recommending the obtaining of specialist technical advice on potential liabilities, use of detailed enquiries, warranties and indemnities.

Other relevant legislation

Other legislation and common law liabilities (e.g. nuisance) may also be relevant when advising on environmental matters including:

Water Resources Act 1991
Groundwater Regulations 1998
Pollution Prevention and Control (England and Wales) Regulations 2000

Further information

Law Society's *Environmental Law Handbook.*
DETR's Website **www.detr.gov.uk**

CON 29R Enquiries of Local Authority (2007)[1]

PLANNING AND BUILDING REGULATIONS

1.1. Planning and building decisions and pending applications

Which of the following relating to the property have been granted, issued or refused or (where applicable) are the subject of pending applications?

- (a) a planning permission
- (b) a listed building consent
- (c) a conservation area consent
- (d) a certificate of lawfulness of existing use or development
- (e) a certificate of lawfulness of proposed use or development
- (f) building regulations approval
- (g) a building regulation completion certificate and
- (h) any building regulations certificate or notice issued in respect of work carried out under a competent person self-certification scheme

1.2. Planning designations and proposals

What designations of land use for the property or the area, and what specific proposals for the property, are contained in any existing or proposed development plan?

ROADS

2. Roadways, footways and footpaths

Which of the roads, footways and footpaths named in the application for this search (via boxes B and C) are:

- (a) highways maintainable at public expense
- (b) subject to adoption and, supported by a bond or bond waiver
- (c) to be made up by a local authority who will reclaim the cost from the frontagers
- (d) to be adopted by a local authority without reclaiming the cost from the frontagers

---

[1] © The Law Society 2007. Reproduced with the kind permission of Oyez Straker.

CON 29R Enquiries of local authority (2007)

The Law Society

A duplicate plan is required for all searches submitted directly to a local authority.
If submitted manually, this form must be submitted in duplicate. Please type or use BLOCK LETTERS

A.

Local authority name and address	Search No:...
	Signed:...
	On behalf of: .... Local authority/private search company/ member of the public (indicate as applicable)
	Dated: ....

B.

Address of the land/property

UPRN(s):

Secondary name/number:

Primary name/number:

Street:

Locality/village:

Town:

Postcode:

C.

Other roadways, footways and footpaths in respect of which a reply to enquiry 2 is required

D.

Fees

£_____ is enclosed/is paid by NLIS transfer (delete as applicable)

Signed:

Dated:

Reference:

Telephone No:

Fax No:

E-mail:

E. (For HIPs regulations compliance only)

Names of those involved in the sale (this box is only completed when the replies to these enquiries are to be included in a Home Information Pack)

Name of vendor:

Name of estate agents:

Name of HIP provider:

Name of solicitor/conveyancer:

Your personal data – name and address – will be handled strictly in accordance with the requirements of the Data Protection Act. It is required to pass on to the relevant authority(ies) in order to carry out the necessary searches.

Notes

A. Enter name and address of appropriate Council. If the property is near a local authority boundary, consider raising certain enquiries (e.g. road schemes) with the adjoining Council.
B. Enter address and description of the property. Please give the UPRN(s) (Unique Property Reference Number) where known. **A duplicate plan is required for all searches submitted directly to a local authority.** The search may be returned if land/property cannot easily be identified.
C. Enter name and/or mark on plan any other roadways, footways and footpaths abutting the property (in addition to those entered in Box B) to which a reply to enquiry 2 is required.
D. Details of fees can be obtained from the Council, your chosen NLIS channel or search provider.
E. Box E is only to be completed when the replies to these enquiries are to be included in a Home Information Pack. Enter the name of the individual(s) and firms involved in the sale of the property.
F. Enter the name and address/DX address of the person or company lodging or conducting this enquiry.

F.

Reply to

DX address:

© Law Society 2007   4.2007 F7618

5033382

Conveyancing 29R (Enquiries)

OTHER MATTERS

3.1. Land required for public purposes

Is the property included in land required for public purposes?

3.2. Land to be acquired for road works

Is the property included in land to be acquired for road works?

3.3. Drainage agreements and consents

Do either of the following exist in relation to the property?

(a) an agreement to drain buildings in combination into an existing sewer by means of a private sewer

(b) an agreement or consent for (i) a building, or (ii) extension to a building on the property, to be built over, or in the vicinity of a drain, sewer or disposal main

3.4. Nearby road schemes

Is the property (or will it be) within 200 metres of any of the following?

(a) the centre line of a new trunk road or special road specified in any order, draft order or scheme

(b) the centre line of a proposed alteration or improvement to an existing road involving construction of a subway, underpass, flyover, footbridge, elevated road or dual carriageway

(c) the outer limits of construction works for a proposed alteration or improvement to an existing road involving

    (i) construction of a roundabout (other than a mini roundabout), or

    (ii) widening by construction of one or more additional traffic lanes;

(d) the outer limits of

    (i) construction of a new road to be built by a local authority,

    (ii) an approved alteration or improvement to an existing road involving construction of a subway, underpass, flyover, footbridge, elevated road or dual carriageway,

    (iii) construction of a roundabout (other than a mini roundabout) or widening by construction of one or more additional traffic lanes

(e) the centre line of the proposed route of a new road under proposals published for public consultation

(f) the outer limits of

    (i) construction of a proposed alteration or improvement to an existing road involving construction of a subway, underpass, flyover, footbridge, elevated road or dual carriageway,

    (ii) construction of a roundabout (other than a mini roundabout),

    (iii) widening by construction of one or more additional traffic lanes, under proposals published for public consultation

3.5. Nearby railway schemes

Is the property (or will it be) within 200 metres of the centre line of a proposed railway, tramway, light railway or monorail?

3.6. Traffic schemes

Has a local authority approved but not yet implemented any of the following for the roads, footways and footpaths (named in Box B) which abut the boundaries of the property?

    (a)   permanent stopping up or diversion
    (b)   waiting or loading restrictions
    (c)   one way driving
    (d)   prohibition of driving
    (e)   pedestrianisation
    (f)   vehicle width or weight restriction
    (g)   traffic calming works including road humps
    (h)   residents parking controls
    (i)   minor road widening or improvement
    (j)   pedestrian crossings
    (k)   cycle tracks
    (l)   bridge building

3.7. Outstanding notices

Do any statutory notices which relate to the following matters subsist in relation to the property other than those revealed in a response to any other enquiry in this form?

    (a)   building works
    (b)   environment
    (c)   health and safety
    (d)   housing
    (e)   highways
    (f)   public health

3.8. Contravention of building regulations

Has a local authority authorised in relation to the property any proceedings for the contravention of any provision contained in Building Regulations?

3.9. Notices, orders, directions and proceedings under Planning Acts

Do any of the following subsist in relation to the property, or has a local authority decided to issue, serve, make or commence any of the following?

    (a)   an enforcement notice
    (b)   a stop notice
    (c)   a listed building enforcement notice
    (d)   a breach of condition notice
    (e)   a planning contravention notice
    (f)   another notice relating to breach of planning control
    (g)   a listed building repairs notice
    (h)   in the case of a listed building deliberately allowed to fall into disrepair, a compulsory purchase order with a direction for minimum compensation
    (i)   a building preservation notice

(j)   a direction restricting permitted development

(k)   an order revoking or modifying planning permission

(l)   an order requiring discontinuance of use or alteration or removal of building or works

(m)   a tree preservation order

(n)   proceedings to enforce a planning agreement or planning contribution

3.10.   Conservation area

Do the following apply in relation to the property?

(a)   the making of the area a conservation area before 31st August 1974

(b)   an unimplemented resolution to designate the area a conservation area

3.11.   Compulsory purchase

Has any enforceable order or decision been made to compulsorily purchase or acquire the property?

3.12.   Contaminated land

Do any of the following apply (including any relating to the land adjacent to or adjoining the property which has been identified as contaminated land because it is in such a condition that harm or pollution of controlled waters might be caused on the property)?

(a)   a contaminated land notice

(b)   in relation to a register maintained under section 78R of the Environmental Protection Act 1990

      (i)   a decision to make an entry

      (ii)   an entry

(c)   consultation with the owner or occupier of the property conducted under section 78G(3) of the Environmental Protection Act 1990 before the service of a remediation notice

3.13.   Radon gas

Do records indicate that the property is in a 'Radon Affected Area' as identified by the Health Protection Agency?

NOTES:

(1)   References to the provisions of particular Acts of Parliament or Regulations include any provisions which they have replaced and also include existing or future amendments or re-enactments.

(2)   The replies will be given in the belief that they are in accordance with information presently available to the officers of the replying Council, but none of the Councils or their officers accept legal responsibility for an incorrect reply, except for negligence. Any liability for negligence will extend to the person who raised the enquiries and the person on whose behalf they were raised. It will also extend to any other person who has knowledge (personally or through an agent) of the replies before the time when he purchases, takes a

tenancy of, or lends money on the security of the property or (if earlier) the time when he becomes contractually bound to do so.

(3)   This Form should be read in conjunction with the guidance notes available separately.

(4)   Area means any area in which the property is located.

(5)   References to the Council include any predecessor Council and also any council committee, sub-committee or other body or person exercising powers delegated by the Council and their approval includes their decision to proceed. The replies given to certain enquiries cover knowledge and actions of both the District Council and County Council.

(6)   Where relevant, the source department for copy documents should be provided.

CON 290 Optional Enquiries of Local Authority (2007)[1]

ROAD PROPOSALS BY PRIVATE BODIES

4. What proposals by others, still capable of being implemented, have the Council approved for any of the following, the limits of construction of which are within 200 metres of the property?

    (a)   the construction of a new road

    (b)   the alteration or improvement of an existing road, involving the construction, whether or not within existing highway limits, of a subway, underpass, flyover, footbridge, elevated road, dual carriageway, the construction of a roundabout (other than a mini roundabout) or the widening of an existing road by the construction of one or more additional traffic lanes

This enquiry refers to proposals by bodies or companies (such as private developers) other than the Council (and where appropriate the County Council) or the Secretary of State. A mini roundabout is a roundabout having a one-way circulatory carriageway around a flush or slightly raised circular marking less than 4 metres in diameter and with or without flared approaches.

PUBLIC PATHS OR BYWAYS

5.1. Is any footpath, bridleway, restricted byway or byway open to all traffic which abuts on, or crosses the property, shown in a definitive map or revised definitive map prepared under Part IV of the National Parks and Access to the Countryside Act 1949 or Part III of the Wildlife and Countryside Act 1981?

5.2. If so, please mark its approximate route on the attached plan.

ADVERTISEMENTS

Entries in the register

6.1. Please list any entries in the register of applications, directions and decisions relating to consent for the display of advertisements.

---

[1]   © The Law Society 2007. Reproduced with the kind permission of Oyez Straker.

CON 290 Optional enquiries of local authority (2007)

The Law Society

A duplicate plan is required for all searches submitted directly to a local authority.
If submitted manually, this form must be submitted in duplicate. Please type or use BLOCK LETTERS

A.

Local authority name and address	Search No:...
	Signed:...
	On behalf of: Local authority/private search company/ member of the public (indicate as applicable)
	Dated:...

B.

Address of the land/property

UPRN(s):

Secondary name/number:

Primary name/number:

Street:

Locality/village:

Town:

Postcode:

C.

Optional enquiries (please tick as required)

☐ 4. Road proposals by private bodies

☐ 5. Public paths or byways

☐ 6. Advertisements

☐ 7. Completion notices

☐ 8. Parks and countryside

☐ 9. Pipelines

☐ 10. Houses in multiple occupation

☐ 11. Noise abatement

☐ 12. Urban development areas

☐ 13. Enterprise zones

☐ 14. Inner urban improvement areas

☐ 15. Simplified planning zones

☐ 16. Land maintenance notices

☐ 17. Mineral consultation areas

☐ 18. Hazardous substance consents

☐ 19. Environmental and pollution notices

☐ 20. Food safety notices

☐ 21. Hedgerow notices

☐ 22. Common land, town and village greens

D.

Fees

£_____ is enclosed/is paid by NLIS transfer (delete as applicable)

Signed:

Dated:

Reference:

Telephone No:

Fax No:

E-mail:

Notes

A. Enter name and address of appropriate Council. If the property is near a local authority boundary, consider raising certain enquiries (e.g. road schemes) with the adjoining Council.

B. Enter address and description of the property. Please give the UPRN(s) (Unique Property Reference Number) where known. **A duplicate plan is required for all searches submitted directly to a local authority.** The search may be returned if land/property cannot easily be identified.

C. Questions 1-3 appear on CON 290 Enquiries of local authority (2007).

D. Details of fees can be obtained from the Council, your chosen NLIS channel or search provider.

E. Enter the name and address/DX address of the person or company lodging or conducting this enquiry.

E.

Reply to

DX address:

Oyez 7 Spa Road, London SE16 3QQ

© Law Society 2007   4.2007 F7619

5033384

Conveyancing 290 (Optional Enquiries)

6.2.   If there are any entries, where can that register be inspected?

Notices, proceedings and orders

6.3.   Except as shown in the official certificate of search:
   (a)   has any notice been given by the Secretary of State or served in respect of a direction or proposed direction restricting deemed consent for any class of advertisement
   (b)   have the Council resolved to serve a notice requiring the display of any advertisement to be discontinued
   (c)   if a discontinuance notice has been served, has it been complied with to the satisfaction of the Council
   (d)   have the Council resolved to serve any other notice or proceedings relating to a contravention of the control of advertisements
   (e)   have the Council resolved to make an order for the special control of advertisements for the area

COMPLETION NOTICES

7.   Which of the planning permissions in force have the Council resolved to terminate by means of a completion notice under s.94 of the Town and Country Planning Act 1990?

PARKS AND COUNTRYSIDE

Areas of outstanding natural beauty

8.1.   Has any order under s.82 of the Countryside and Rights of Way Act 2000 been made?

National Parks

8.2.   Is the property within a National Park designated under s.7 of the National Parks and Access to the Countryside Act 1949?

PIPELINES

9.   Has a map been deposited under s.35 of the Pipelines Act 1962, or Schedule 7 of the Gas Act 1986, showing a pipeline laid through, or within 100 feet (30.48 metres) of the property?

HOUSES IN MULTIPLE OCCUPATION

10.   Is the property a house in multiple occupation, or is it designated or proposed to be designated for selective licensing of residential accommodation in accordance with the Housing Act 2004?

NOISE ABATEMENT

Noise abatement zone

11.1.   Have the Council made, or resolved to make, any noise abatement zone order under s.63 of the Control of Pollution Act 1974 for the area?

Entries in register

11.2.   Has any entry been recorded in the noise level register kept pursuant to s.64 of the Control of Pollution Act 1974?

11.3.   If there is any entry, how can copies be obtained and where can that register be inspected?

URBAN DEVELOPMENT AREAS

12.1.   Is the area an urban development area designated under Part XVI of the Local Government, Planning and Land Act 1980?

12.2.   If so, please state the name of the urban development corporation and the address of its principal office.

ENTERPRISE ZONES

13.   Is the area an enterprise zone designated under Part XVIII of the Local Government, Planning and Land Act 1980?

INNER URBAN IMPROVEMENT AREAS

14.   Have the Council resolved to define the area as an improvement area under s.4 of the Inner Urban Areas Act 1978?

SIMPLIFIED PLANNING ZONES

15.1.   Is the area a simplified planning zone adopted or approved pursuant to s.83 of the Town and Country Planning Act 1990?

15.2.   Have the Council approved any proposal for designating the area as a simplified planning zone?

LAND MAINTENANCE NOTICES

16.   Have the Council authorised the service of a maintenance notice under s.215 of the Town and Country Planning Act 1990?

MINERAL CONSULTATION AREAS

17.   Is the area a mineral consultation area notified by the county planning authority under Schedule 1 para 7 of the Town and Country Planning Act 1990?

HAZARDOUS SUBSTANCE CONSENTS

18.1.   Please list any entries in the register kept pursuant to s.28 of the Planning (Hazardous Substances) Act 1990.

18.2.   If there are any entries:
    (a)   how can copies of the entries be obtained
    (b)   where can the register be inspected

ENVIRONMENTAL AND POLLUTION NOTICES

19.   What outstanding statutory or informal notices have been issued by the Council under the Environmental Protection Act 1990 or the Control of Pollution Act 1974? (This enquiry does not cover notices under Part IIA or Part III of the EPA, to which enquiries 3.12 or 3.7 apply.)

FOOD SAFETY NOTICES

20.   What outstanding statutory notices or informal notices have been issued by the Council under the Food Safety Act 1990 or the Food Hygiene Regulations 2006?

HEDGEROW NOTICES

21.1.   Please list any entries in the record maintained under regulation 10 of the Hedgerows Regulations 1997.

21.2.   If there are any entries:
    (a)   how can copies of the matters entered be obtained
    (b)   where can the record be inspected

COMMON LAND, TOWN AND VILLAGE GREENS

22.1.   Is the property, or any land which abuts the property, registered common land or town or village green under the Commons Registration Act 1965 or the Commons Act 2006?

22.2.   If there are any entries, how can copies of the matters registered be obtained and where can the register be inspected?

NOTES:

(1)   References to the provisions of particular Acts of Parliament or Regulations include any provisions which they have replaced and also include existing or future amendments or re-enactments.

(2)   The replies will be given in the belief that they are in accordance with information presently available to the officers of the replying Council, but none of the Councils or their officers accept legal responsibility for an incorrect reply, except for negligence. Any liability for negligence will extend to the person who raised the enquiries and the person on whose behalf they were raised. It will also extend to any other person who has knowledge (personally or through an agent) of the replies before the time when he purchases, takes a tenancy of, or lends money on the security of the property or (if earlier) the time when he becomes contractually bound to do so.

(3)   This form should be read in conjunction with the guidance notes available separately.

(4)   Area means any area in which the property is located.

(5)   References to the Council include any predecessor Council and also any council committee, sub-committee or other body or person exercising powers delegated by the Council and their approval includes their decision to proceed. The replies given to certain enquiries cover knowledge and actions of both the District Council and County Council.

(6)   Where relevant, the source department for copy documents should be provided.

CON 29DW Standard Drainage and Water Enquiries (2007)[1]

Public sewer map

1   Where relevant, please include a copy of an extract from the public sewer map.

Foul water

2   Does foul water from the property drain to a public sewer?

Surface water

3   Does surface water from the property drain to a public sewer?

Public adoption of sewers and lateral drains

4   Are any sewers or lateral drains serving or which are proposed to serve the property the subject of an existing adoption agreement or an application for such an agreement?

Public sewers within the boundaries of the property

5   Does the public sewer map indicate any public sewer, disposal main or lateral drain within the boundaries of the property?

Public sewers near to the property

6   Does the public sewer map indicate any public sewer within 30.48 metres (100 feet) of any buildings within the property?

Building over a public sewer, disposal main or drain

7   Has a sewerage undertaker approved or been consulted about any plans to erect a building or extension on the property over or in the vicinity of a public sewer, disposal main or drain?

---

[1]   © The Law Society 2007.

CON 29DW Standard drainage and water enquiries (2007)

This search form must be submitted with the appropriate fee and a copy of the location plan.

A. Name and address of water company

(For use by water company only)

B. Address of the land/property

UPRN(s)

House name/number

Street

Locality

Town

County

Postcode

If the enquiries are made of a plot of land or of a property less than 5 years old:

Name of developer

Plot no.

Site name and phase

C. Your details

Signed ....

Name/contact name

Company name

Date

Your reference

Telephone

Fax

Email

Account no.

D. Fees

Search	Fee
CON 29DW Standard drainage and water enquiries 2007	
Total	

E. Reply to

DX

Notes

The standard drainage and water enquiries are listed on page 2 of this form. These enquiries comply with the Home Information Pack (No.2) Regulations 2007.

Completing and submitting this form to a water company indicates an acceptance of that water company's terms and conditions. Terms and conditions may vary between water companies. Request a copy of the terms and conditions from the water company or see its website for details.

A. Ensure that search forms are sent to the correct water company, see www.drainageandwater.co.uk for details.

B. Enter the address of the property. Please give the Unique Property Reference Number if known. If the enquiries are made of a plot of land or the property is less than 5 years old, please give the developer's details.

C. Sign, date and enter your details. Account customers of water companies may enter their account number.

D. Enter the fee for the enquiries. Fees may differ between water companies. Consult the water company or see www.drainageandwater.co.uk for the current fees.

E. Enter the name and address/DX address of the person or company conducting this enquiry.

Map of waterworks

8   Where relevant, please include a copy of an extract from the map of waterworks.

Adoption of water mains and service pipes

9   Is any water main or service pipe serving or which is proposed to serve the property the subject of an existing adoption agreement or an application for such an agreement?

Sewerage and water undertakers

10   Who are the sewerage and water undertakers for the area?

Connection to mains water supply

11   Is the property connected to mains water supply?

Water mains, resource mains or discharge pipes

12   Are there any water mains, resource mains or discharge pipes within the boundaries of the property?

Current basis for sewerage and water charges

13   What is the current basis for charging for sewerage and water services at the property?

Charges following change of occupation

14   Will the basis for charging for sewerage and water services at the property change as a consequence of a change of occupation?

Surface water drainage charges

15   Is a surface water drainage charge payable?

Water meters

16   Please include details of the location of any water meter serving the property.

Sewerage bills

17   Who bills the property for sewerage services?

Water bills

18   Who bills the property for water services?

Risk of flooding due to overloaded public sewers

19   Is the dwelling-house which is or forms part of the property at risk of internal flooding due to overloaded public sewers?

Risk of low water pressure or flow

20   Is the property at risk of receiving low water pressure or flow?

Water quality analysis

21   Please include details of a water quality analysis made by the water undertaker for the water supply zone in respect of the most recent calendar year.

Authorised departures from water quality standards

22   Please include details of any departures –

    (a)   authorised by the Secretary of State under Part 6 of the 2000 Regulations from the provisions of Part 3 of those Regulations; or

    (b)   authorised by the National Assembly for Wales under Part 6 of the 2001 Regulations from the provisions of Part 3 of those Regulations.

Sewage treatment works

23   Please state the distance from the property to the nearest boundary of the nearest sewage treatment works.

NOTES

(i)   The terms used in these enquiries have the meaning given to them by the Home Information Pack (No.2) Regulations 2007, Sched.8, Part 1.

(ii)   The report prepared by a water company in response to these enquiries will include those enquiries and replies which are relevant to the property. The numbering and order of enquiries may differ between this form and a report.

Model planning conditions for development on land affected by contamination

www.communities.gov.uk
community, opportunity, prosperity

30 May 2008

The Chief Planning Officer:
    County Councils in England
    District Councils in England
    Unitary Authorities in England
    London Borough Councils
    Council of the Isles of Scilly;

The Town Clerk, City of London;

The National Park Officer,
    National Park Authorities in England;

The Chief Planning Officer,
    The Broads Authority

Dear Chief Planning Officer

MODEL PLANNING CONDITIONS FOR DEVELOPMENT ON LAND AFFECTED BY CONTAMINATION

This letter is to circulate a new set of model conditions (attached at Appendix 1) intended for use by local planning authorities during development on land affected by contamination. This has been developed in conjunction with the Chartered Institute of Environmental Health's Standing Conference on Land Contamination Planning Subgroup and I am very grateful for their work on this.

Background:

The Government attaches great importance to making better use of land, and the re-use of land affected by contamination is at the heart of a range of Government policies. As you will be aware, PPS23: Planning and Pollution Control and its supporting Annex 2: Development on Land Affected by Contamination set out how the planning system can assist in the remediation of contaminated land through the process of development.

The principal planning objective when considering development on land affected by contamination is to ensure that any unacceptable risks to human health, buildings and other property, and the natural and historical environment from the contaminated condition of land are identified, so that appropriate action can be considered and then taken to address those risks. Annex 2 of PPS23 advises on the circumstances when it may be appropriate for local planning authorities to grant planning permission subject to conditions relating to the condition of the land and provides advice in respect to their use at 2.61 – 2.65.

Department for Communities and Local Government   Tel 020 7944 3865
Communities and Local Government
Eland House
Bressenden Place
London SW1E 5DU

The publication of PPS23 in 2004 had the effect that there are now two sets of planning conditions published in national planning policy relating to the issue of contamination. In addition to examples of conditions used by local planning authorities provided at Appendix 2B of Annex 2 of PPS23, there are suggested models of acceptable conditions in Appendix A of Circular 11/95 (conditions 56 – 59). These latter model conditions have been overtaken by the policy in PPS23. The intention of circulating these new conditions is to establish a single set of model conditions that is consistent with PPS23 policy. As such I would encourage their use to you. They replace Appendix 2B of Annex 2 of PPS23 and conditions 56 – 59 in Appendix A of Circular 11/95 which are hereby cancelled.

The new set of model conditions:

The new model conditions attached at Appendix 1 are intended to support effective implementation of PPS23 policy. At 2.62, PPS23 Annex 2 advises that local planning authorities should consider the use of three-stage conditions. Model conditions 1 – 3 follow this approach. At 2.63 the Annex advises that local planning authorities should consider imposing a condition in respect of the possibility of unsuspected contamination being discovered during the course of the development. Model condition 4 is intended for this purpose. At 2.65 Annex 2 advises that the use of a condition may be appropriate in respect of subsequent monitoring. Model condition 5 is intended for this purpose.

You will note that model condition 3 refers to the requirement for the local planning authority to receive a *verification* report that demonstrates the effectiveness of the remediation scheme, rather than the *validation* report referred to at 2.62 of PPS23 Annex 2. This is to conform to terminology in Defra and the Environment Agency's 'Model Procedures for the Management of Land Contamination, CLR 11'.

I would reiterate advice in Circular 11/95 that no condition should be imposed unless, having regard to the circumstances of each case, it meets the tests set out in the Circular. The attached conditions are only models, and may need adaptation to the circumstances of particular cases. Text in square brackets in the model conditions, [*thus*] are words that will commonly need variation.

I would also remind local planning authorities of advice in Circular 11/95 with regard to the compiling their own lists of model conditions (at paragraph 8).

If you have any queries please contact James Henderson at james.henderson@communities.gsi.gov.uk, or telephone 020 7944 3865.

Yours faithfully,

f. Hurst

Steph Hurst
Deputy Director
Planning – Resources and Environment Policy

Appendix 1:

Model planning conditions for development on land affected by contamination:

Unless otherwise agreed by the Local Planning Authority, development other than that required to be carried out as part of an approved scheme of remediation must not commence until conditions 1 to 4 have been complied with. If unexpected contamination is found after development has begun, development must be halted on that part of the site affected by the unexpected contamination to the extent specified by the Local Planning Authority in writing until condition 4 has been complied with in relation to that contamination.

1. Site Characterisation

An investigation and risk assessment, in addition to any assessment provided with the planning application, must be completed in accordance with a scheme to assess the nature and extent of any contamination on the site, whether or not it originates on the site. The contents of the scheme are subject to the approval in writing of the Local Planning Authority. The investigation and risk assessment must be undertaken by competent persons and a written report of the findings must be produced. The written report is subject to the approval in writing of the Local Planning Authority. The report of the findings must include:

(i)   a survey of the extent, scale and nature of contamination;

(ii)   an assessment of the potential risks to:
  - human health,
  - property (existing or proposed) including buildings, crops, livestock, pets, woodland and service lines and pipes,
  - adjoining land,
  - groundwaters and surface waters,
  - ecological systems,
  - archeological sites and ancient monuments;

(iii)   an appraisal of remedial options, and proposal of the preferred option(s).

This must be conducted in accordance with DEFRA and the Environment Agency's *'Model Procedures for the Management of Land Contamination, CLR 11'.*

2. Submission of Remediation Scheme

A detailed remediation scheme to bring the site to a condition suitable for the intended use by removing unacceptable risks to human health, buildings and other property and the natural and historical environment must be prepared, and is subject to the approval in writing of the Local Planning Authority. The scheme must include all works to be undertaken, proposed remediation objectives and remediation criteria, timetable of works and site management procedures. The scheme must ensure that the site will not qualify as contaminated land under Part 2A of the Environmental Protection Act 1990 in relation to the intended use of the land after remediation.

3. Implementation of Approved Remediation Scheme

The approved remediation scheme must be carried out in accordance with its terms prior to the commencement of development other than that required to carry out remediation, unless otherwise agreed in writing by the Local Planning Authority. The Local Planning Authority must be given two weeks written notification of commencement of the remediation scheme works.

Following completion of measures identified in the approved remediation scheme, a verification report (referred to in PPS23 as a validation report) that demonstrates the effectiveness of the remediation carried out must be produced, and is subject to the approval in writing of the Local Planning Authority.

4. Reporting of Unexpected Contamination

In the event that contamination is found at any time when carrying out the approved development that was not previously identified it must be reported in writing immediately to the Local Planning Authority. An investigation and risk assessment must be undertaken in accordance with the requirements of condition 1, and where remediation is necessary a remediation scheme must be prepared in accordance with the requirements of condition 2, which is subject to the approval in writing of the Local Planning Authority.

Following completion of measures identified in the approved remediation scheme a verification report must be prepared, which is subject to the approval in writing of the Local Planning Authority in accordance with condition 3.

5. Long Term Monitoring and Maintenance

A monitoring and maintenance scheme to include monitoring the long-term effectiveness of the proposed remediation over a period of [x] years, and the provision of reports on the same must be prepared, both of which are subject to the approval in writing of the Local Planning Authority.

Following completion of the measures identified in that scheme and when the remediation objectives have been achieved, reports that demonstrate the effectiveness of the monitoring and maintenance carried out must be produced, and submitted to the Local Planning Authority.

This must be conducted in accordance with DEFRA and the Environment Agency's *'Model Procedures for the Management of Land Contamination, CLR 11'.*

Reason (common to all): To ensure that risks from land contamination to the future users of the land and neighbouring land are minimised, together with those to controlled waters, property and ecological systems, and to ensure that the development can be carried out safely without unacceptable risks to workers, neighbours and other offsite receptors [in accordance with policy _____ of the adopted Local Plan (date)].

APPENDIX G

Contacts

British Gas
PO Box 4805
Worthing
BN11 9QW
Tel: 0800 048 0202
Web: www.britishgas.co.uk

British Geological Survey
Kingsley Dunham Centre
Keyworth
Nottingham NG12 5GG
Tel: 0115 936 3100
Fax: 0115 936 3200
Web: www.bgs.ac.uk

British Water
1 Queen Anne's Gate
London
SW1H 9BT
Tel: 020 7957 4554
Fax: 020 7957 4565
Email: info@britishwater.co.uk
Web: www.britishwater.co.uk

British Waterways

Head Office
64 Clarendon Road
Watford
Herts WD17 1DA
Tel: 01923 201 120
Fax: 01923 201 304
Web: www.britishwaterways.co.uk

Regional Offices

Central Shires
Peel's Wharf

Lichfield Street
Fazeley
Tamworth
Staffordshire B78 3QZ
Tel: 01827 252 000
Fax: 01827 288 071

East Midlands
The Kiln
Mather Road
Newark NG24 1FB
Tel: 01636 704 481
Fax: 01636 705 584

Kennet & Avon
The Locks
Bath Road
Devizes
SN10 1QR
Tel: 01380 722 859

London
British Waterways London
1 Sheldon Square
Paddington Central
London W2 6TT
Tel: 020 7985 7200
Fax: 020 7985 7201

Manchester & Pennine
Red Bull Yard
Congleton Road South
Church Lawton
Stoke on Trent
ST7 3AP
Tel: 01782 785 703

305

North East
Fearns Wharf
Neptune Street
Leeds LS9 8PB
Tel: 0113 281 6860
Fax: 0113 281 6886

North Wales and Borders
Navigation Road
Northwich
Cheshire CW8 1BH
Tel: 01606 723800

North West
Waterside House
Waterside Drive
Wigan WN3 5AZ
Tel: 01942 405700

South East
510–524 Elder House
Elder Gate
Milton Keynes MK9 1BW
Tel: 01908 302500
Fax: 01908 302510

Campaign to Protect Rural England
CPRE National Office
128 Southwark Street
London SE1 0SW
Tel: 020 7981 2800
Fax: 020 7981 2899
Email: info@cpre.org.uk
Web: www.cpre.org.uk

Church Commissioners for England
Church House
Great Smith Street
London SW1P 3AZ
Tel: 020 7898 1000
Web: www.cofe.anglican.org/about/
churchcommissioners

Coal Authority
200 Litchfield Lane
Berry Hill
Mansfield
Nottingham NG18 4RG
Tel: 01623 637 000 (switchboard)
Tel: 0845 762 6848 (mining reports)
Email: thecoalauthority@coal.gov.uk
Web: www.coal.gov.uk

Commission of the European Communities
The European Commission
Representation in the United Kingdom
8 Storey's Gate
London SW1P 3AT
Tel: 020 7973 1992
Fax: 020 7973 1900
Web: http://ec.europa.eu/unitedkingdom/
index_en.htm

Companies House
Crown Way
Maindy
Cardiff CF14 3UZ
Tel: 0303 1234 500
DX: 33050 Cardiff
Web: www.companieshouse.gov.uk

Council for Licensed Conveyancers
16 Glebe Road
Chelmsford
Essex CM1 1QG
Tel: 01245 349 599
Fax: 01245 341 300
DX: 121925 Chelmsford-6
Web: www.conveyancer.org.uk

Council of Mortgage Lenders
Bush House
North West Wing
Aldwych
London WC2B 4PJ
Tel: 0845 373 6771 (switchboard)
Fax: 0845 373 6778
Web: www.cml.org.uk

Country Land and Business Association
16 Belgrave Square
London SW1X 8PQ
Tel: 020 7235 0511
Fax: 020 7235 4696
Email: mail@cla.org.uk
Web: www.cla.org.uk

Countryside Council for Wales
Maes-y-Ffynnon
Penrhosgarnedd
Bangor
Gwynedd LL57 2DW
Tel: 0845 130 6299
Fax: 01248 355782
Web: www.ccw.gov.uk

Department for Environment, Food and Rural Affairs (Defra)
Customer Contact Unit
Eastbury House
30–34 Albert Embankment
London SE1 7TL
Tel: 08459 33 55 77
Fax: 020 7238 2188
Email: helpline@defra.gsi.gov.uk
Web: ww2.defra.gov.uk

Department for Transport
Great Minster House
76 Marsham Street
London SW1P 4DR
Tel: 0300 330 3000
Fax: 020 7944 9643
Email: FAX9643@dft.gsi.gov.uk
Web: www.dft.gov.uk

DG Environment (The Directorate-General for the Environment)
Avenue de Beaulieu 5
1160 Brussels
Postal address:
Environment Directorate-General
European Commission, B-1049 Brussels
Web: http://ec.europa.eu/dgs/environment/index_en.htm

DG Climate Action (The Directorate-General for Climate Action)
Avenue de Beaulieu 5
1160 Brussels
Postal address:
Environment Directorate-General
European Commission, B-1049 Brussels

Drinking Water Inspectorate
Room M03
55 Whitehall
London SW1A 2EY
Tel: 030 0068 6400
Fax: 030 0068 6401
Email: dwi.enquiries@defra.gsi.gov.uk
Web: dwi.gov.uk

English Heritage
Customer Services Department
PO Box 569
Swindon SN2 2YP
Tel:0870 333 1181
Fax: 01793 414 926

Email: customers@english-heritage.org.uk
Web: www.english-heritage.org.uk

Environment Agency

National Customer Contact Centre
PO Box 544
Rotherham S60 1BY
Enquiry line: 08708 506 506
Incident hotline: 0800 807 060
Floodline: 0845 988 1188 (24 hour service)
Hazardous waste registration:
08708 502 858
Agricultural waste registration:
0845 603 3113
Email: enquiries@environment-agency.gov.uk
Web: www.environment-agency.gov.uk

Regional legal departments

Anglian Region
Legal Services
Kingfisher House
Goldhay Way
Peterborough
PE2 5ZR
Tel: 01733 464 487
Fax: 01733 371 811
DX: 701640-Orton

Environment Agency Wales
Legal Services
Ty Cambria House
29 Newport Road
Cardiff
CF24 0TP
Tel: 029 2046 6417
Fax: 029 2077 0088
DX: 121376 CARDIFF

Head Office
Legal Services
Block 1, Government
Burghill Road,
Bristol
BS10 6BF
Tel: 0117 915 6220
Fax: 0117 915 6203
DX: 130055

Midlands Region
Legal Services
550 Streetsbrook
Solihull
B91 1QT
Tel: 0121 711 5895
Fax: 0121 711 2324
DX: 702280-Solihull 3

North East Region
Legal Services
Rivers House
21 Park Square South
Leeds
LS1 2QG
Tel: 0113 231 2483
Fax: 0113 244 0191
DX: 706953 LEEDS

North West Region
Legal Services
Richard Fairclough House
Knutsford Road
Warrington
WA4 1HT
Tel: 01925 574 736
Fax: 01925 653 999
DX: 709290-Warrington

South West Region
Legal Services
Manley House
Kestrel Way
Exeter
EX2 7LQ
Tel: 01392 442 112
Fax: 01392 444 000
DX: 121350-Exeter 12

Southern Region
Legal Services
Guildbourne House
Chatsworth Road
Worthing
BN11 1LD
Tel: 01903 832 058
Fax: 01903 832 000
DX 3713

Thames Region
Legal Services
Kings Meadow House
Kings Meadow Road

Reading
RG1 8DQ
Tel: 0118 950 9440
DX 121325-Reading
Fax: 0118 953 5000

Environmental Data Systems Ltd (ENDS)
11–17 Wolverton Gardens
London
W6 7DY
Tel: 020 8267 8100
Fax: 020 8267 8150
Email: post@ends.co.uk
Web: www.ends.co.uk

Environmental Law Foundation
2–10 Princeton Street
London
WC1R 4BH
Tel: 020 7404 1030
Fax: 020 7404 1032
Email: info@elflaw.org
Web: www.elflaw.org

European Environment Agency
Kongens Nytoru 6
DK-1050 Copenhagen K
Denmark
Tel: 00 45 3336 7100
Fax: 00 45 3336 7199
Web: www.eea.europa.eu

Forestry Commission England
England National Office
620 Bristol Business Park
Coldharbour Lane
Bristol
BS16 1EJ
Tel: 0117 906 6000
Email: fcengland@forestry.gsi.gov.uk
Web: www.forestry.gov.uk

Forestry Commission Scotland
Silvan House
231 Corstorphine Road
Edinburgh EH12 7AT
Tel: 0131 334 0303
Fax: 0131 314 6152
Email: fcscotland@forestry.gsi.uk

Forestry Commission Wales
Welsh Assembly Government
Rhodfa Padarn
Llanbadarn Fawr
Aberystwyth SY23 3UR
Tel : 0300 068 0300
Fax : 0300 068 0301
Email: fcwenquiries@forestry.gsi.gov.uk

Health Protection Agency (Radiation Division)
Centre for Radiation, Chemical and Environmental Hazards
Chilton
Didcot
OX11 0RQ
Tel: 01235 831 600
Web: www.hpa.org.uk

Health and Safety Executive
Infoline: 0845 345 0055
Web: www.hse.gov.uk

Institute of Environmental Management and Assessment
St Nicholas House
70 Newport
Lincoln
LN1 3DP
Tel: 01522 540 069
Fax: 01522 540 090
Email: info@iema.net
Web: www.iema.net

Institute of Historic Building Conservation (IHBC)
Jubilee House
High Street
Tisbury
SP3 6HA
Tel: 01747 873133
Fax: 01747 871718
Email: admin@ihbc.org.uk
Web: www.ihbc.org.uk

International Network for Environmental Management
Osterstrasse 58
20259 Hamburg
Germany
Tel: 00 49 89 18935 200
Fax: 00 49 89 18935 199
Web: www.inem.org

Joint Committee of National Amenity Societies
c/o Secretary Matthew Slocombe
The Society for the Protection of Ancient Buildings (SPAB)
37 Spital Square
London E1 6DY
Email: secretary@jcnas.org.uk
Web: www.jcnas.org.uk

Landmark Information Group Ltd
5–7 Abbey Court
Eagle Way
Sowton Industrial Estate
Exeter EX2 7HY
Tel: 01392 441 700
Fax: 01392 441 709
Web: www.landmark.co.uk

Lands Tribunal
43–45 Bedford Square
London
WC1B 3AS
Tel: 020 7612 9710
Fax: 020 7612 9723
DX: 149065 Bloomsbury 9
Email: lands@tribunals.gsi.gov.uk
Web: www.landstribunal.gov.uk

Landscape Institute
Charles Darwin House
12 Roger Street
London WC1N 2JU
Tel: 020 7685 2640
Web: www.landscapeinstitute.org

Law Society of England and Wales
The Law Society's Hall
113 Chancery Lane
London WC2A 1PL
Tel: 020 7242 1222
Fax: 020 7831 0344
DX: 56 London/Chancery Lane
Web: www.lawsociety.org.uk

Local Government Association
(FAO LGconnect)
Local Government Group
Local Government House
Smith Square
London SW1P 3HZ
Tel: 020 7664 3000
Fax: 020 7664 3030

Email: info@local.gov.uk
Web: www.lga.gov.uk

Natural England
1 East Parade
Sheffield S1 2ET
Tel: 0300 060 3078
Fax: 0300 060 1622
Email: enquiries@naturalengland.org.uk
Web: www.naturalengland.org.uk

National Monuments Record
(part of English Heritage)
Kemble Drive
Swindon SN2 2GZ
Tel: 01793 414 700
Fax: 01793 414 770
Email: nmrinfo@english-heritage.org.uk
Web: www.english-heritage.org.uk

National Radiological Protection Board
Now part of the **Health Protection Agency**

OECD Paris Centre
2 rue André Pascal
75775 Paris Cedex 16
France
Tel.: 0033 1 45 24 82 00
Fax: 0033 1 45 24 85 00
Web: www.oecd.org

Network Rail
Kings Place
90 York Way
London
N1 9AG
National Helpline: 08457 11 41 41
Tel: 020 7557 8000
Web: www.networkrail.co.uk

Office of Water Services (OFWAT)
Centre City Tower
7 Hill Street
Birmingham B5 4UA
Tel: 0121 644 7500
Fax: 0121 644 7699
Email: enquiries@ofwat.gsi.gov.uk
Web: www.ofwat.gov.uk

Planning Inspectorate
Registry/Scanning
Room 3/05 Kite Wing
Temple Quay House

2 The Square
Temple Quay
Bristol BS1 6PN
Customer support: 0117 372 6372
Email: enquiries@planning-inspectorate.
gsi.gov.uk
Web: www.planning-inspectorate.gov.uk

Planning Inspectorate for Wales
Crown Buildings
Cathays Park
Cardiff CF1 3NQ
Tel: 029 2082 3866
Fax: 029 2082 5150
Email: wales@planning-inspectorate.gsi.
gov.uk
Web: www.planning-inspectorate.gov.uk/
cymru/wal/index_e.htm

Ramblers Association
2nd Floor
Camelford House
87–90 Albert Embankment
London SE1 7TW
Tel: 020 7339 8500
Fax: 020 7339 8501
Email: ramblers@london.ramblers.org.uk
Web: www.ramblers.org.uk

Royal Commission on the Ancient and Historical Monuments of Wales
Crown Buildings
Plas Crug
Aberystwyth
SY23 1NJ
Tel: 01970 621 200
Fax: 01970 627 701
Email: nmr.wales@rcahmw.gov.uk
Web: www.rcahmw.org.uk

Royal Courts of Justice
Strand
London WC2A 2LL
Tel: 020 7936 6000
DX: 44450 Strand
Web: www.hmcourts-service.gov.uk

Royal Institute of British Architects
66 Portland Place
London W1B 1AD
Tel: 020 7580 5533
Fax: 020 7255 1541

Email: info@inst.riba.org
Web: www.architecture.com

Royal Institution of Chartered Surveyors
12 Great George Street
Parliament Square
London SW1P 3AD
Tel: 0870 333 1600
Fax: 020 7334 3811
DX: 2348 Victoria SW1
Email: london@rics.org.uk
Web: www.rics.org.uk

Royal Town Planning Institute
41 Botolph Lane
London EC3R 8DL
Tel: 020 7929 9494
Fax: 020 7929 9490
Web: www.rtpi.org.uk

Town and Country Planning Association
17 Carlton House Terrace
London SW1Y 5AS
Tel: 020 7930 8903
Web: www.tcpa.org.uk

United Kingdom Environmental Law Association Ltd
PO Box 487
Dorking RH4 9BH
Tel: 01306 500 090
Web: www.ukela.org

Water and sewerage companies

Anglian Water Services Ltd
Head Office Address:
Anglian House
Ambury Road
Huntingdon PE29 3NZ
Tel: 01480 323 000
Fax: 01480 323 115
Web: www.anglianwater.co.uk

Dwr Cymru Cyfyngedig (Welsh Water)
Head Office Address:
Pentwyn Road
Nelson
Treharris
CF46 6LY
Tel: 01443 452 300
Fax: 01443 452 323
Web: www.dwrcymru.co.uk

Northumbrian Water Ltd
Head Office Address:
Abbey Road
Pity Me
Durham DH1 5FJ
Tel: 08706 084820
Fax: 0191 384 1920
Web: www.nwl.co.uk

Severn Trent Water Ltd
Head Office Address:
2297 Coventry Road
Sheldon
Birmingham B26 3PU
Tel: 0121 722 4000
Fax: 0121 722 4800
Web: www.stwater.co.uk

South West Water Ltd
Head Office Address:
Peninsula House
Rydon Lane
Exeter EX2 7HR
Tel: 01392 446 688
Fax: 01392 434 966
Web: www.southwestwater.co.uk

Southern Water Services Ltd
Head Office Address:
Southern House
Yeoman Road
Worthing
BN13 3NX
Tel: 01903 264 444
Fax: 01903 262 185
Web: www.southernwater.co.uk

Thames Water Utilities Ltd
Head Office Address:
Clearwater Court
Vastern Road
Reading RG1 8DB
Tel: 0845 9200 888
Fax: 01793 424 291
Web: www.thameswater.co.uk

United Utilities Water plc
Head Office Address:
Haweswater House
Lingley Mere Business Park
Lingley Green Avenue
Great Sankey
Warrington WA5 3LP

Tel: 01925 237 000
Fax: 01925 237 073
Web: www.unitedutilities.com

Wessex Water Services Ltd
Head Office Address:
Claverton Down Road
Claverton Down
Bath BA2 7WW
Tel: 01225 526 000
Fax: 01225 528 000
Web: www.wessexwater.co.uk

Yorkshire Water Services Ltd
Head Office Address:
Western House
Western Way
Bradford BD6 2LZ
Tel: 01274 691 111
Fax: 01274 604 764
Web: www.yorkshirewater.com

Water only companies

Bournemouth & West Hampshire Water plc
Head Office Address:
George Jessel House
Francis Avenue
Bournemouth BH11 4NX
Tel: 01202 591 111
Fax: 01202 597 022
Web: www.bwhwater.co.uk

Bristol Water plc
Head Office Address:
PO Box 218
Bridgwater Road
Bristol BS99 7AU
Tel: 0117 966 5881
Fax: 0117 963 4576
Web: www.bristolwater.co.uk

Cambridge Water Company plc
Head Office Address:
90 Fulbourn Road
Cambridge
CB1 9JN
Tel: 01223 706 050
Fax: 01223 214 052
Web: www.cambridge-water.co.uk

Cholderton & District Water Company Ltd
Head Office Address:
Estate Office
Cholderton
Salisbury
SP4 0DR
Tel: 01980 629 203
Fax: 01980 629 307
Web: www.choldertonwater.co.uk

Dee Valley Water plc
Head Office Address:
Packsaddle
Wrexham Road
Rhostyllen
Wrexham
LL14 4EH
Tel: 01978 846 946
Fax: 01978 846 888
Web: www.deevalleygroup.com

Essex & Suffolk Water plc
(now part of Northumbrian Water Ltd)
Head Office Address:
Sandon Valley House
Canon Barns Road
East Hanningfield
Chelmsford
CM3 8BD
Tel: 01245 491 234
Fax: 01245 212 345
Web: www.eswater.co.uk

Hartlepool Water plc
(now part of Anglian Water Services Ltd)
Head Office Address:
3 Lancaster Road
Hartlepool TS24 8LW
Tel: 01429 858 050
Fax: 01429 858 000
Web: www.hartlepoolwater.co.uk

Portsmouth Water plc
Head Office Address:
PO Box 8
West Street
Havant
PO9 1LG
Tel: 0239 249 9888
Fax: 0239 245 3632
Web: www.portsmouthwater.co.uk

South East Water Ltd
Head Office Address:
Rockfort Road
Snodland
Kent
ME6 5AH
Tel: 0845 223 5111
Fax: 01634 242 764
Web: www.southeastwater.co.uk

South Staffordshire Water plc
Head Office Address:
Green Lane
Walsall
WS2 7PD
Tel: 01922 638 282
Fax: 01922 723 631
Web: www.south-staffs-water.co.uk

Sutton & East Surrey Water plc
Head Office Address:
London Road
Redhill
RH1 1LJ
Tel: 01737 772 000
Fax: 01737 766 807
Web: www.waterplc.com

Veolia Water Central Ltd
(formerly Three Valleys Water plc)
Head Office Address:
Tamblin Way
Hatfield
AL10 9EZ
Tel: 01707 268 111
Fax: 01707 277 333
Web: https://central.veoliawater.co.uk/
index.aspx

Veolia Water East Ltd
(formerly Tendring Hundred Water Services
Ltd)

Head Office Address:
Mill Hill
Manningtree
CO11 2AZ
General and Billing Enquiries
0845 1489288
Fax: 01206 399 210
Web: https://east.veoliawater.co.uk/index.
aspx

Veolia Water Southeast Ltd
(formerly Folkestone and Dover Water
Services Ltd)
Head Office Address:
Cherry Garden Lane
Folkestone
CT19 4QB
Tel: 01303 298 800
Fax: 01303 276 712
Web: https://southeast.veoliawater.co.uk/
index.aspx

The Wales Office
Office of the Secretary of State for Wales
Gwydyr House
Whitehall
London SW1A 2NP
Tel: 020 7270 0534
Email: wales.office@walesoffice.gsi.
gov.uk
Web: www.walesoffice.gov.uk

Welsh Assembly Government
Cathays Park
Cardiff CF10 3NQ
Tel (English): 0300 060 3300 or
0845 010 3300
Tel (Welsh): 0300 060 4400 or
0845 010 4400
Email: wag-en@mailuk.custhelp.com
Web: http://wales.gov.uk

Index

Abatement notice
    commercial property transactions
      7.2.1
    content 2.11.1
    failure to comply 1.6.1, 7.2.1
    person served 1.6.1
Administration
    prosecutions during 12.4
    see also **Insolvency**
Administrative receivers
  12.5.1
    administrators compared 12.5.2
    as agent 12.5.1
    civil liability 12.5.1
    clean-up costs 12.5.1
    contaminated land 2.9.1, 2.19.2,
      12.5.1, 12.6
    criminal liability 12.5.1
    environmental permitting offences
      12.5.1
    nuisance 12.5.1
    as occupier of land 12.5.1
    as office holder 12.5.1
    powers 12.5.1
    statutory nuisances 12.5.1
    waste offences 12.5.1
    water pollution 12.5.1
    see also **Insolvency; Insolvency**
      practitioners
Administrators 12.5.2
    see also **Insolvency; Insolvency**
      practitioners
Agriculture
    environmental damage 3.5.2
Air conditioning systems
    inspection 4.3.3
Air pollution
    environmental damage 3.6
Airborne pollutants 3.6
Alarms
    statutory nuisance 1.6.1

Annoyance
    covenant not to create 7.6.1
Areas of Outstanding Natural
  Beauty (AONBs) 1.7.1
Artificial light
    statutory nuisance 1.6.1
Asbestos
    exposure to 1.8.5
Asbestos contractors
    environmental insurance 13.6.4

Banks
    contaminated land and 2.9.1
Best available techniques
  (BAT) 1.3.1
Biodiversity liabilities 1.7
    protecting client against 1.10
Birds
    conservation 1.7.1
Borrowing transactions *see*
  Lenders
Buildings
    zero carbon buildings 4.2
    see also **CRC Energy Efficiency**
      Scheme; Energy certificates
Buncefield Oil Terminal
  explosion 1.4.3

Certificate of title 11.2.1
Chartered environmental
  surveyor (CES) 10.3.4
Civil liability
    administrative receivers 12.5.1
    commercial property transactions
      7.2.2, 7.5
    contaminated land 1.6.1
    corporate transactions 8.2
    CRC Energy Efficiency Scheme
      4.4.7
    insuring against *see* **Environmental**
      insurance

Civil liability – *continued*
negligence *see* **Negligence**
nuisance *see* **Nuisance**
property transactions 6.2.2, 7.2.2
residential property transactions
6.2.2, 6.5
sanctions *see* **Civil sanctions**
subterranean migration of
contaminants 2.3.3
see also **Tort liability**
Civil sanctions 1.5
appeals 1.5.2
combining 1.5.1
compliance notice 1.5.1
enforcement cost recovery notice
1.5.2
enforcement undertaking 1.5.1
Environment Agency 1.5
failure to comply 1.5.2
fixed monetary penalty (FMP) 1.5.1,
1.6.1
Natural England 1.5
procedure 1.5.2
publication of results of enforcement
actions 1.5.2
representations and objections 1.5.2
restoration notice 1.5.1
restoration order 1.7.1, 1.7.2
standard of proof 1.5.2
stop notice 1.5.1
types 1.5.1
variable monetary penalty (VMP)
1.5.1
Clean-up costs 1.4.3, 1.6
administrative receivers 12.5.1
agreements on liabilities 2.9.4, 2.18.2,
8.5.3
commercial property transactions
7.2.3
contaminated land 1.6.1, 2.9, 2.18,
6.2.3, 7.2.3
controlled waste 1.6.1
current and future pollution 1.6
environmental permitting 7.2.3,
12.5.1
exemption from liability 2.9
historic events 1.6
insolvency and 2.9.1, 12.5.1
insurance 1.10
lenders 11.1, 11.2.2
property transactions 6.2.3, 7.2.3
protecting client against 1.10
recovery by lender 11.2.2

residential property transactions
6.2.3
scope 1.6
statutory nuisances 1.6.1, 7.2.3, 12.5.1
'suitability for use' standard 1.6
waste 1.6.1, 7.2.3, 12.5.1
water pollution 1.6.2, 6.2.3, 7.2.3,
12.5.1
Climate change 4.1
zero carbon buildings 4.2
see also **CRC Energy Efficiency**
Scheme; **Energy certificates**
Commercial freehold
transactions 7.4
advice to client on potential for
problems 7.4.2
agreements on liabilities 7.4.8
contractual protections against
seller 7.4.8
enquiries of statutory and regulatory
bodies 7.4.4
environmental search report 7.4.6
full enquiries of seller 7.4.3
full information, requiring 7.4.8
full site investigation 7.4.7
indemnities 7.4.8
insurance policy 7.4.8
lenders' position 7.4.5
local authority searches 7.4.4
Con 29R 7.4.4, App C
price reductions/specific payments
7.4.8
retention by buyer 7.4.8
searches 7.4.1
site history investigations 7.4.5
withdrawal from purchase 7.4.9
Commercial property
transactions 7.1
abatement notice 7.2.1
advice to sellers 7.5
civil liability 7.2.2, 7.5
clean-up costs 7.2.3
contaminated land 7.2.1, 7.5
Contaminated Land Warning Card
7.1, 7.3, App B
controlled waste 7.2.1
criminal liability 7.2.1
environmental permitting offences
7.2.1
freehold *see* **Commercial freehold**
transactions
hazardous substances and 7.2.4
legal issues 7.2.1–7.2.5

nature conservation regime 7.2.1
non-legal issues 7.2.6
nuisance 7.2.2
radioactive substances and 7.2.4
sewers 7.2.1, 7.5
statutory nuisances 7.2.1, 7.5
water pollution 7.2.1, 7.5
Common law defences 1.9.1
Company officers
administrative receivers 12.5.1
liability 1.4.1, 8.2
Compliance notice *see* **Civil sanctions**
Consultants *see*
Environmental consultants
Contacts App G
Contaminated land 2.1.1
administrative receivers 2.9.1, 2.19.2,
12.5.1, 12.6
agreements on liabilities 2.9.4, 2.18.2,
8.5.3
apportioning liability and costs 2.9
banks and 2.9.1
basis for designation 2.2.2, 2.2.3
charging notice 2.15.1
civil liability 1.6.1
Class A liability group 2.9.2, 2.9.3,
2.9.5, 2.18.1
Class B liability group 2.9.2, 2.18.1
clean-up costs 1.6.1, 2.9, 2.18, 6.2.3,
7.2.3
commercial property transactions
7.2.1, 7.5
concentrations of pollutants 2.2.2
'contaminated state', definition 1.6.1
cost recovery 2.10
criminal liability 1.6.1, 6.2.1, 7.2.1
cumulative impact of two or more
sites 2.2.1
definition 2.3.1
designation 2.2.2, 2.2.3
determination 2.3
development works and 9.4
environmental damage 3.5.1, 3.5.2,
3.6.1
environmental permitting and 2.17.5
environmental search report 7.2.1
escapes of substances to other land
2.9.6
exclusionary tests 2.9.2, 2.9.3, 2.18.1,
6.2.1, 7.2.1, 9.4
exemption from liability 2.9
administrative receivers 12.5.1

financial institutions and 2.9.1
fines 1.4.2, 2.14.1
formulation of scheme 2.6
harm, definition 2.3.1, 2.3.3
health, impact on 2.3.1, 2.3.2, 2.3.3
health and safety issues 2.17.2, 3.6.1
homeowner insurance 13.6.4
identifying contaminated sites 2.2.1
identifying interested persons 2.5,
2.8.2
informal clean-ups 2.1.1, 2.21
insolvency practitioners 2.9.1, 2.19.2,
12.5.1, 12.6
inspection and investigation 2.2
insurance 6.4.8
land remediation tax relief 9.5.1
landfill tax 2.17.4
legal transactions 2.18
lenders for 2.9.1, 2.19.1
liability groups 2.9.2, 2.9.3, 2.9.5,
2.18.1
local authority contaminated land
officers 1.2.1
major accident hazards 2.17.3
model planning conditions for
development App F
mortgagee not in possession 2.9.1
notice 2.3.3
notification and consultation 2.7.1,
2.8.2, 2.11.2
occupiers 2.9.1, 2.9.2, 2.9.5, 2.18.1,
6.2.1, 7.2.1
offences 6.2.1, 7.2.1
original polluter 2.9.1, 2.9.2, 2.9.3,
2.9.5, 2.18, 2.18.1, 6.2.1, 7.2.1
overall summary of procedure 2.1.2
owner 2.9.1, 2.9.2, 2.9.5, 2.18.1, 6.2.1,
7.2.1
passing liability 2.18.1, App A1
penalties 1.4.2, 2.14.1
planning law and 2.17.1
pollutant linkage 2.2.2, 2.3.2, 2.9.3,
2.11.2, 3.6.1
precedent agreement on liabilities
App A2
property transactions 6.2.1, 6.2.3, 6.5,
7.2.1, 7.5, 9.4
protecting the client 2.20
purchaser, passing liability to 2.18.1,
App A1
radioactive substances 2.3.2
reasons for designation 2.2.2, 2.2.3
receptors 2.3.2, 2.3.3

Contaminated land – *continued*
  registers *see* **Registers of**
    contaminated land
  remediation notice *see* **Remediation**
    notice
  residential property transactions
    6.2.1, 6.2.3, 6.5
  risk assessment 2.3.2
  risk management 2.2.2
  risk-based criteria 2.2.2
  sales with information 2.9.3, 2.13.3,
    8.4
  shared collective action 2.9.2
  shared common action 2.9.2
  significant harm 2.2.1, 2.2.2, 2.3.1
  significant pollution linkage 2.6,
    2.9.3
  special sites 1.6.1, 2.2.1
  statutory nuisance and 1.6.1, 2.17.6
  strategies 2.2.2, 2.2.3
  subterranean migration of
    contaminants 2.3.3
  tax relief 9.5.1
  urgency of works 2.4
  warning card 6.1, 6.3, 7.1, 7.3, App B
  water pollution and 2.2.2, 2.3.2,
    2.17.7
Contaminated Land Warning
  Card 6.1, 6.3, 7.1, 7.3, App B
Contractors
  asbestos contractors 13.6.4
  criminal proceedings 1.4.1
  pollution liability insurance 13.6,
    13.6.4
Corporate transactions 8.1
  agreement on liabilities 8.5.3
  assets purchase 8.4, 8.5.3
  authorised processes 8.4
  civil liability 8.2
  company officers' liability 1.4.1, 8.2
  criminal liability 8.2
  directors' liability 1.4.1, 8.2
  documenting 8.5
  environmental audit 8.1
  environmental indemnities 8.4, 8.5.2
  environmental investigation 8.1
  environmental warranties 8.4, 8.5.1,
    App A8
  historical use of site 8.3
  insurance 8.1, 8.4
  licences 8.3
  licensed processes 8.4
  local inspection 8.3

  occupation of former sites 8.3
  'pie-crust' leases 8.4
  the process 8.3
  the product 8.3
  raw materials 8.3
  remedial work 8.4
  risk allocation 8.1
  sales with information 8.4
  share purchase agreement 8.5
    illustrative environmental clauses
      App A8
  site inspection 8.3
  waste disposal 8.3
Countryside Council for
Wales
  civil sanctions 1.5
CRC Energy Efficiency
Scheme (CRC Scheme) 4.4
  appeals 4.4.7
  application 4.4.4
  audits 4.4.7
  buying and selling allowances 4.4.3
  civil liability 4.4.7
  criminal offences 4.4.7
  electricity supply 4.4.2
  enforcement 4.4.7
  Environment Agency 1.2.2
  evidence packs 4.4.3
  exclusions 4.4.2
  franchises 4.4.4
  full participation 4.4.2
  groups of undertakings 4.4.4
  information disclosure 4.4.2, 4.4.6
  joint ventures (JVs) 4.4.4
  landlords and tenants 4.4.4
  league tables 4.4.3
  levels of involvement 4.4.2
  operation of scheme 4.4.3
  overseas undertakings 4.4.4
  private finance initiatives (PFIs)
    4.4.4
  public sector organisations 4.4.5
    bodies corporate 4.4.5
    the Crown 4.4.5
    grouping of public bodies 4.4.5
    local authorities 4.4.5
    mandated participants 4.4.5
    schools 4.4.5
  qualification 4.4.2
  recycling payments 4.4.3
  significant group undertaking
    (SGU) 4.4.4
  timelines 4.4.3

undertakings 4.4.4
Criminal liability
 administrative receivers 12.5.1
 avoidance 1.9.1
 commercial property transactions
  7.2.1
 common law defences 1.9.1
 company officers 1.4.1, 8.2
 contaminated land 1.6.1, 6.2.1, 7.2.1
 corporate transactions 8.2
 CRC Energy Efficiency Scheme
  4.4.7
 defences 1.9.1
 duplicity of informations 1.9.1
 environmental damage 3.3, 3.15, 3.25
 environmental permitting 7.2.1,
  12.5.1
 evidential gaps 1.9.1, 1.9.2
 guilty plea 1.9.2
 the hearing 1.9.2
 identity of defendant 1.9.1
 impact of conviction 1.9.4
 indirect 12.5.1
 initial source of contamination,
  proving 1.9.1
 insurance and 1.9
 mitigation *see* **Mitigation**
 nature conservation regime 1.7, 6.2.1,
  7.2.1
 not guilty plea 1.9.2
 procedural problems 1.9.2
 property transactions 6.2.1, 7.2.1
 protecting client against 1.9
 public nuisance 1.8.2
 relationship with regulatory bodies
  1.9.1
 remediation notice, non-compliance
  1.4.2, 2.14, 7.2.1
 reporting of incidents 1.9.3
 reputation of company 1.9.4
 residential property transactions
  6.2.1
 statutory defences 1.9.1
 statutory nuisances 1.6.1, 7.2.1
 trade effluent discharges to sewers
  7.2.1, 12.5.1
 waste 1.4.1, 7.2.1, 12.5.1
 water pollution 6.2.1, 7.2.1, 12.5.1
Criminal proceedings 1.4
 contractors 1.4.1
 directors and officers 1.4.1, 8.2
 employees 1.4.1
 lenders 1.4.1

 parent companies 1.4.1
 penalties 1.4.2
 proceeds of crime 1.4.3
 prosecutions 1.4.1
 strict liability 1.4
Crown
 CRC Energy Efficiency Scheme
  4.4.5

Damages
 personal injury 1.8.2
Development works 9.4
Diffuse pollution 3.9, 3.9.2
Directors
 liability 1.4.1, 8.2
Discharge consents 6.2.1, 6.2.5,
 6.2.1
**Display Energy Certificates
 (DECs)** 4.3.2
Domestic purchasers *see*
 **Residential property
 transactions**

Eco-systems protection 6.2.1,
 7.2.1
**Electrical and electronic
 equipment**
 waste 1.3.2
Employees
 criminal proceedings 1.4.1
End-of-life vehicles 1.3.2
Energy certificates 4.3
 Display Energy Certificates (DECs)
  4.3.2
 Energy Performance Certificates
  (EPCs) 4.3.1
 inspection of air conditioning
  systems 4.3.3
**Energy Performance
 Certificates (EPCs)** 4.3.1
**Enforcement cost recovery
 notice** 1.5.2
Enforcement notice
 failure to comply 1.3.5
 water-related offences 1.3.1
Enforcement undertaking *see*
 Civil sanctions
Enforcing authorities 1.2
 formal cautions 1.4
 warning letters 1.4
Environment Agency 1.2.2
 civil sanctions 1.5

Environment Agency – *continued*
CRC Energy Efficiency Scheme
1.2.2
duties and responsibilities 1.2.2, 2.2.1
Enforcement and Prosecution
Policy 1.2.2, 1.4
as enforcing authority 1.2.2, 2.2.1
environmental damage 1.2.2, 3.10.2
environmental information 5.2.1, 5.3
environmental permitting 1.2.2, 1.3.1
formal cautions 1.4
packaging waste 1.3.2
prosecutions 1.3.2, 1.4.1, 1.4.3
registers 5.2.1
searches 5.3, 6.4.4
special sites 1.2.2, 2.2.1
warning letters 1.4
water quality 1.2.2
water resources 1.2.2
Environmental audit 5.6, 10.1
corporate transactions 8.1
environmental investigation
distinguished 5.6
risk evaluation 11.2.1
Environmental consultants
accreditation 10.3.4
appointment 10.3.4, 10.3.5
assignability of rights 10.3.5
chartered environmental surveyor
(CES) 10.3.4
confidentiality 10.3.5
copyright 10.3.5
costs information 10.3.5
directories 10.3.4
environmental audit 10.1
Environmental Consultants Group
(ECG) 10.3.4
environmental investigations 10.1
full site investigation 6.4.7, 7.4.7
insurance
environmental insurance 13.6.4
professional indemnity insurance
10.3.5, 13.3
intellectual property rights 10.3.5
legal professional privilege 10.2.2,
10.3.5
membership of professional bodies
10.3.5
multi-disciplinary practices 10.3.5
need for 10.3.3
previous experience 10.3.5
professional institutions 10.3.4, 10.3.5
references 10.3.4, 10.3.5

reports 10.2.1
privilege 10.2.2, 10.3.5
readability/accessibility 10.3.5
selection criteria 10.3.4
specification of works 10.3.5
standard contracts 10.3.5
terms and conditions of
engagement App A10
types of consultancy 10.3.2, 10.3.5
use 10.3.2
see also **Environmental
investigations**
**Environmental Consultants
Group (ECG)** 10.3.4
Environmental damage
agricultural activities 3.5.2
airborne pollutants 3.6
appeals to notifications 3.19
charges on premises 3.23
compensation, duty to grant and
pay 3.24
costs, recovery 3.22
criminal liability 3.3, 3.25
determination 3.3, 3.16
diffuse pollution 3.9, 3.9.2
duty to notify 3.15
emergency actions 3.3
enforcing authorities 3.10
Environment Agency 1.2.2, 3.10.2
exemptions 3.9
damage after 1 March 2009 3.9.1
diffuse pollution 3.9.2, 3.9
fines 3.25
genetically modified organisms
(GMOs) 3.5.1
imminent threat 3.14
information notices 3.13
interested parties 3.11
investigations 3.12
land 3.5.1, 3.5.2, 3.6.1, 3.18.1
liability 1.6.3, 1.7.3, 3.5
criminal liability 3.3, 3.15
exemptions 3.9
joint and several liability 3.7
non-Schedule 2 operators 3.5.2
operators 3.5
Schedule 2 operators 3.5.1
limitation periods 3.8
local authority enforcement 3.10.1
Marine Management Organisation
3.10.4
meaning 3.5
Natural England 1.2.3, 3.10.3

natural habitats 3.5.1, 3.5.2, 3.6.3,
   3.18.2
natural resources 3.5
notification to authorities 3.3, 3.15
notification of liability 3.17
   appeals 3.19
   offences 3.25
   penalties 3.25
   prevention duty 3.14
   prevention notice 3.14
   procedures 3.3
   protected species 3.5.1, 3.5.2, 3.6.3,
      3.18.2
   regime 3.1
   remedial measures 3.18
      compensatory remediation 3.3,
         3.18.2
      complementary remediation 3.3,
         3.18.2
      primary remediation 3.18.2
   remediation notices 3.3, 3.20
   remediation proposals 3.3
   sanctions 3.25
   SSSIs 1.2.3, 1.7.3, 3.5.1, 3.5.2, 3.6.4,
      3.18.2
   structure of regime 3.2
   thresholds 3.6
   water 1.7.3, 3.5.1, 3.5.2, 3.6.2, 3.18.2
**Environmental data search
report** *see* **Environmental
search report**
**Environmental impact
assessment** 9.2.5
Environmental indemnities
8.4, 8.5.2
Environmental information
5.1
   access 5.2
      Environmental Information
         Regulations 2004 5.2.1
   discharge consents 6.2.1
   Environment Agency searches 5.3
   environmental data providers 5.5.1
   hazardous substances 1.3.4, 6.2.4,
      7.2.4
   local authority searches 5.4, 6.4.4,
      7.4.4
      Con 29R 2.3.3, 2.16.2, 5.4, 6.4.4,
         7.4.4, App C
   occurrence-based policies 13.6,
      13.6.4
   previous pollution incidents 6.2.1
   search reports *see* **Environmental
      search report**

sources 5.1
withholding 5.2.1
Environmental insurance 1.1,
   1.10, 13.1, 13.6
   asbestos contractors 13.6.4
   captives 13.9
   claims cooperation provisions 13.6.3
   claims-made-and-reported policies
      13.6.4, 13.6
   commercial freehold transactions
      7.4.8
   contaminated land 6.4.8
   contractors pollution liability
      policies 13.6, 13.6.4
   deductibles 13.6.3
   endorsements 13.6.1
   environmental consultancies 13.6.4
   environmental laboratories 13.6.4
   exclusions 13.6.3
   extended reporting periods 13.6.3
   finite risk programmes 13.7
   first-party pollution and
      environmental damage policy
      13.6.4
   general conditions 13.6.3
   general liability policies
      distinguished 13.6.1
   homeowner contaminated land
      protection 13.6.4
   lender liability policy 13.6.4
   limits of indemnity 13.6, 13.6.1,
      13.6.3
   low-risk sites policy 13.6.4
   major insurers and brokers 13.10
   manuscript policies 13.6.1
   negotiation of terms and conditions
      13.6.2
   notification and reporting
      provisions 13.6.3
   placing policies 13.6.2
   professionals, policies for 13.6.4
   property transfer policy 7.4.8, 13.6.4
   remediation contractors 13.6.4
   remediation cost cap policy 13.6.4
   residential freehold transactions
      6.4.8
   self insurance 13.8
   site-specific policies 13.6.4
   structure of policy 13.6.3
   third-party environmental liability
      policy 13.6.4
   types 13.6.4
   warranty protection 13.6.4

Environmental insurance – *continued*
  see also **Insurance**
Environmental investigations
  5.6, 10.1
    carrying out investigations 10.3
    compliance investigations 5.6.1,
      10.3.1
    confidentiality 10.2.1
    consultants, using *see*
      Environmental consultants
    corporate transactions 8.1
    desk study 5.6.1, 7.4.1
    environmental audits distinguished
      5.6
    follow-up 5.6.1
    historical review 5.6.1
    internal matters 10.3.1
    legal professional privilege 10.2.2,
      10.3.5
    meaning 5.6
    monitoring 5.6.1
    objectives 5.6.1
    Phase 1 survey 10.1
    Phase 2 site investigation 10.1
    recommendations 5.6.1
    remediation programme 5.6.1
    risk evaluation 11.2.1
    risks 10.2
      consultants' reports 10.2.1, 10.2.2
      damaging information 10.2.1
    site inspections 5.6.1, 6.4.7, 7.4.7
    transactional investigation 5.6.1
    types 5.6.1
    walk through production process
      5.6.1
Environmental liabilities 1.1
    administrative receivers 12.5.1
    administrators 12.5.2
    directors and others 1.4.1, 8.2
    enforcing authorities 1.2
    Environmental Damage Regulations
      1.6.3, 1.7.3
    indirect costs 1.11
    liquidators 12.5.3
    LPA receivers 12.5.5
    nature conservation and biodiversity
      liabilities 1.7
    regulatory liabilities 1.3
    see also **Environmental**
      Permitting Regulations
    strict liability 1.4, 1.8.3, 1.9.1, 12.5.1
    supervisors of voluntary
      arrangements 12.5.4

    see also **Civil sanctions**; **Clean-up**
      costs; **Criminal liability**;
      Criminal proceedings; **Tort**
      liability
Environmental management
  systems 11.2.1
Environmental permitting
(EP)
    A1/A2 installations 1.3.1
    administrative receivers 12.5.1
    best available techniques (BAT)
      1.3.1
    clean-up costs 7.2.3, 12.5.1
    clean-up powers 2.17.5
    commercial property transactions
      7.2.1
    conditions 1.3.1
    contaminated land and 2.17.5
    criminal liability 7.2.1, 12.5.1
    defences 1.3.5
    emission limit values 1.3.1
    groundwater contamination 1.3.1
    land returned to 'satisfactory state'
      1.3.1
    non-compliance with condition 1.3.5
    nuisance and 1.6.1
    offences 7.2.1, 12.5.1
    pollution prevention and control
      1.3.1
    raw materials monitoring 8.3
    site reports 1.3.1
    soil contamination 1.3.1
    statutory nuisances 1.6.1
    waste management 1.3.1
Environmental Permitting
  Regulations 1.3, 1.3.1
    application 1.3.1
    defences 1.3.5
    Environment Agency 1.2.2, 1.3.1
    general offences 1.3.1
    guidance 1.3.1
    pollution prevention and control
      1.3.1
    waste management 1.3.1
    water-related offences 1.3.1
Environmental search report
  5.5
    clear search/no perceived problem
      5.5.3, 6.4.6, 7.4.6
    contaminated land 7.2.1
    environmental data providers 5.5.1
    environmental permitting 7.2.1
    flooding data 5.5.2

hazardous substances 6.2.4, 7.2.4
interpreting 5.5.3, 6.4.6, 7.4.6
mining enquiries 5.5.2
natural perils enquiries 5.5.2
nature conservation regime 6.2.1, 7.2.1
radon enquiries 5.5.2
reading 5.5.2
risk certificate 5.5.2
sample App A3
searches revealing entries 5.5.3, 6.4.6, 7.4.6
site history enquiries 5.5.2
site plan with polygon features indicated 5.5.2
standard questions following App A4
statutory register enquiries 5.5.2
terms of issue 5.5.2
water pollution 6.2.1, 7.2.1
Environmental warranties 8.4, 8.5.1, App A8
Escapes of substances to other land 2.9.6
European Union 1.3
Explosives 1.3.4, 6.2.4, 7.2.4

Facility agreement
illustrative terms for inclusion App A9
Financial institutions
contaminated land and 2.9.1
Fines
aggravating factors 1.4.4
contaminated land 1.4.2, 2.14.1
daily default fines 1.4.2, 2.14.1
environmental damage 3.25
environmental offences 1.4.2–1.4.4
failure to comply with remediation notice 1.4.2, 2.14.1
illustrative fines 1.4.3
level of fines 1.4.3
manifestly excessive/unjust 1.4.4, 1.9.3
mitigating factors 1.4.4
reduction of fines 1.4.4
remediation notice 1.4.2, 2.14.1
Fire-fighting water
run-off into controlled waters 1.3.1
Fish Legal 1.4.1
Flooding
environmental search report 5.5.2

Freehold transactions *see* **Commercial freehold transactions; Residential freehold transactions**
Funding transactions *see* **Lenders**

General Permitted Development Order (GPDO) 9.2.5
Genetically modified organisms (GMOs)
deliberate release 3.5.1
environmental damage 3.5.1
Groundwater *see* **Water**

Hazardous substance consents 1.3.4, 7.2.4
Hazardous substances 1.3.4
commercial property transactions and 7.2.4
explosives 1.3.4, 6.2.4, 7.2.4
information to public 1.3.4, 6.2.4, 7.2.4
legislation 1.3.4
major accident hazards 1.2.4, 2.17.3
radioactive substances 1.3.4, 2.3.2, 6.2.4, 7.2.4
residential property transactions and 6.2.4
storage 1.3.4, 3.5.2, 6.2.4, 7.2.4
Hazardous waste 1.3.1, 1.3.2
Health and safety
airborne pollutants 3.6
contaminated land and 2.17.2
Health and Safety Executive (HSE) 1.2.4
Historic contamination
liability for 1.8.1
nuisance 1.8.1
Historic events
clean-up costs 1.6
Historical review 5.6.1
Historical use of site 8.3
Homeowner insurance 13.5
homeowner contaminated land protection 13.6.4
Housing
energy certificates *see* **Energy certificates**
zero carbon buildings 4.2
Human rights issues 1.8.7

Indemnities
  commercial freehold transactions
    7.4.8
  corporate transactions 8.4, 8.5.2
  environmental indemnities 8.4, 8.5.2
  leasehold transactions 7.6.1
  lenders App A9
Industrial Emissions Directive
  (IED) 1.3.1
Information notices
  environmental damage 3.13
Insects
  statutory nuisance 1.6.1
Insolvency
  clean-up costs and 2.9.1, 12.5.1
  disposal of land 12.2
  land containing waste 12.3
  prosecutions during administration
    12.4
Insolvency practitioners 12.5
  administrative receivers *see*
    Administrative receivers
  administrators 12.5.2
  contaminated land 2.9.1, 2.19.2,
    12.5.1, 12.6
  liquidators 12.5.3
  LPA receivers 12.5.5
  supervisors of voluntary
    arrangements 12.5.4
Insurance
  clean-up costs 1.10
  commercial freehold transactions
    7.4.8
  corporate transactions 8.1, 8.4
  criminal liability and 1.9
  environmental consultants 10.3.5,
    13.3
  homeowners policies 13.5, 13.6.4
  professional indemnity insurance
    (PII) 6.3, 10.3.5, 13.3
  property policies 13.4
  residential freehold transactions
    6.4.8
  self insurance 13.8
  see also **Environmental insurance**;
    Public liability insurance
Integrated Pollution Control
  (IPC)
  replacement by EP regime 2.17.5
Investigations *see*
  Environmental
  investigations

Joint ventures (JVs)
  CRC Energy Efficiency Scheme
    4.4.4

Land
  disposal 12.2
  environmental damage 3.5.1, 3.5.2,
    3.6.1
    remedial measures 3.18.1
    threshold 3.6.1
Land remediation tax relief
  9.5.1
Landfill
  closure notice 1.3.5
  grading and landscaping of sites
    9.2.4
  insolvency of operators 12.3
  prohibitions/restrictions on specified
    waste 1.3.1
  remediation works 9.2.4
  waste acceptance criteria (WAC)
    1.3.1
Landfill tax 2.17.4, 9.5.2
  contaminated land and 2.17.4
  exemption 2.21, 9.5.2
  rates 9.5.2
Leasehold transactions
  clauses restricting user 7.6.1
  covenants
    to comply with statutory
      obligations 7.6.1
    not to commit waste 7.6.1
    not to create nuisance, etc. 7.6.1
    repairing covenants 7.6.1
  existing leases 7.6.1
  indemnities 7.6.1
  new leases 7.6.1
  'pie-crust' leases 7.6.2, 8.4
  prohibition on assignment, etc. 7.6.1
  sample lease clauses App A7
  standard lease 7.6.1
Legal professional privilege
  environmental consultants and
    10.2.2, 10.3.5
Lenders 11.1
  certificate of title 11.2.1, App A9
  clean-up costs 11.1, 11.2.2
  commercial freehold transactions
    7.4.5
  for contaminated land 2.9.1, 2.19.1
  criminal proceedings 1.4.1
  existing facilities 11.2.3

illustrative terms for inclusion in
facility agreement App A9
indemnity App A9
liability App A9
mortgagee in possession 2.9.1
new proposals and ongoing
protection 11.2.2
conditions precedent 11.2.2, App A9
covenants and undertakings 11.2.2,
App A9
events of default 11.2.2
recovery of clean-up costs 11.2.2
representations and warranties
11.2.2, App A9
protection for 11.2
recovery of clean-up costs 11.2.2
representations and warranties
11.2.2, 11.2.1, App A9
reputational risks 11.1
residential freehold transactions
6.4.5
risk evaluation 11.2.1
certificate of title 11.2.1
consents and licences 11.2.1
environmental investigations or
audits 11.2.1
environmental management systems
11.2.1
representations and warranties
11.2.1
security 11.1
**Licensed insolvency
practitioner (LIP)**
contaminated land 2.9.1
Liquidators 12.5.3
see also **Insolvency**; **Insolvency
practitioners**
Local authorities
contaminated land officers 1.2.1
CRC Energy Efficiency Scheme
4.4.5
duties and responsibilities 1.2.1
as enforcing authorities 1.2.1, 3.10.1
environmental health office 1.2.1
Local authority searches 5.4,
6.4.4, 7.4.4
Con 29DW standard drainage and
water enquiries App E
Con 29O optional enquiries App D
Con 29R enquiries 2.3.3, 2.16.2, 5.4,
6.4.4, 7.4.4, App C
Local nature reserves 1.7.1
LPA receivers 12.5.5

see also **Insolvency**; **Insolvency
practitioners**
Major accident hazards 1.2.4
contaminated land 2.17.3
see also **Hazardous substances**
**Marine Management
Organisation**
environmental damage 3.10.4
Media releases 1.9.4
Mining sites
grading and landscaping 9.2.4
Mitigation 1.9.3
age and history of defendant 1.9.3
aggravating factors 1.9.3
behaviour since offence 1.9.3
circumstances surrounding offence
1.9.3
indirect effect of conviction or
sentence 1.9.3

National nature reserves 1.7.1
Natural England 1.2.3
civil sanctions 1.5
Enforcement Policy 1.2.3
Enforcement Strategy 1.2.3
as enforcing body 1.2.3
environmental damage 1.2.3, 3.10.3
Natural habitats
commercial property transactions
and 7.2.1
conservation 1.7.1–1.7.3
criminal liability 6.2.1
environmental damage 3.5.1, 3.5.2,
3.6.3
enforcing authorities 3.10.1, 3.10.3,
3.10.4
remedial measures 3.18.2
threshold 3.6.3
marine waters 3.10.4
residential property transactions
and 6.2.1
Nature conservation regime
commercial property transactions
7.2.1
criminal liability 1.7, 6.2.1, 7.2.1
offences 6.2.1
residential property transactions
6.2.1
Nature reserves 1.7.1
Negligence 1.8.5
duty of care 1.8.5
exposure to asbestos 1.8.5

Negligence – *continued*
 foreseeable harm 1.8.5
 latent damage 1.8.5
 liability 1.8.5
 limitation period 1.8.5
Noise
 human rights issue 1.8.7
 statutory nuisance 1.6.1, 1.8.7
Nuisance
 commercial property transactions
  7.2.2
 continuing nuisance 1.8.1, 6.2.2, 7.2.2
 covenants not to create 7.6.1
 damages 1.8.2
 historic contamination 1.8.1
 human rights issues 1.8.7
 private nuisance 1.8.1
  continuing nuisance 1.8.1
  historic contamination 1.8.1
  limitation 1.8.1
  reasonable foreseeability 1.8.1,
   1.8.3
  successors in title 1.8.1
 property transactions 6.2.2, 7.2.2
 public nuisance 1.8.2
  damages for personal injury 1.8.2
 residential property transactions
  and 6.2.2
 Rylands v. *Fletcher* rule 1.8.3
 strict liability 1.8.3, 12.5.1
 see also **Statutory nuisances**

**Packaging and packaging
 waste** 1.3.2
Passing liability clause 2.18.1,
 App A1
Personal injury
 damages 1.8.2
'Pie-crust' leases 7.6.2, 8.4
**Planning implications of
 property transactions** 9.2
 aftercare conditions 9.2.4
 categories of occupier 9.2.2
 contamination as 'material
  consideration' 9.2.1
 enforcement powers 9.2.6
 environmental impact assessment
  9.2.5
 General Permitted Development
  Order (GPDO) 9.2.5
 modification powers 9.2.7
 notification requirement 9.2.3
 passing risk to purchaser 9.4

 planning obligations 9.2.4, 9.2.8
 Planning Policy Statement 23 (PPS
  23) 9.2.9
 restoration conditions 9.2.4
 revocation powers 9.2.7
 special planning zone (SPZ)
  scheme 9.2.5
 undertaking the works 9.3
Planning law
 contaminated land and 2.17.1
Pollution insurance *see*
 Environmental insurance
**Pollution prevention and
 control (PPC)**
 replacement by EP regime 1.3.1,
  2.17.5
Press releases 1.9.4
Prevention notice
 environmental damage 3.14
**Private finance initiatives
 (PFIs)**
 CRC Energy Efficiency Scheme
  4.4.4
Private nuisance *see* **Nuisance**
Privilege
 environmental consultants and
  10.2.2, 10.3.5
**Professional indemnity
 insurance (PII)** 6.3, 13.3
 environmental consultants 10.3.5,
  13.3
 see also **Insurance**
Prohibition notice
 failure to comply 1.3.5
Property insurance 13.4
 homeowner policies 13.5, 13.6.4
Property transactions *see*
 **Commercial property
 transactions; Leasehold
 transactions; Residential
 property transactions**
Protected species 1.7.1, 1.7.2
 commercial property transactions
  and 7.2.1
 criminal liability 6.2.1
 environmental damage 3.5.1, 3.5.2,
  3.6.3
  enforcing authorities 3.10.1, 3.10.3,
   3.10.4
  remedial measures 3.18.2
  threshold 3.6.3
 marine water 3.10.4

residential property transactions
and 6.2.1
Public liability insurance
10.3.5, 13.2
    ABI model pollution exclusion
        13.2.2
    gradual pollution 13.2.2
    homeowners policies 13.5
    past pollution incidents 13.2.1
    remediating contamination 13.2.3
Public nuisance *see* **Nuisance**

Radioactive substances 1.3.4,
2.3.2, 6.2.4, 7.2.4
Radon levels
    environmental search report 5.5.2
Ramsar wetland sites 1.7.1
Raw materials
    monitoring 8.3
Receivers *see* **Administrative
receivers**
**Registers of contaminated
land** 2.16
    access 2.16.1
    appeals 2.16.1
    clean-up details 2.16.2
    contents 2.16.1
    conveyancing transactions 2.16.2
    exclusions 2.16.1
Remediation notice 1.6.1, 2.1.1
    agreements on liabilities 2.9.4, 2.18.2,
        8.5.3
    appeals
        contaminated land 2.13
        environmental damage 3.21
    application for planning permission,
        effect 2.8.2
    apportioning liability and costs 2.9
    appropriate person 2.2.2, 2.9.1
        exemptions 2.9
    banks 2.9.1
    carrying out remediation works 2.12
    compensation for access 2.12.1
    confirmation 2.13.1
    content 2.11.1
    cost recovery 2.10, 2.11.2, 2.15
    criminal liability 1.6.1
    defences 1.3.5, 2.8.2
    definition of 'remediation' 2.11.1
    delaying service 2.8.2
    environmental damage 3.3, 3.20
        appeals 3.21

escapes of substances to other land
    2.9.6
exclusionary tests 2.9.2, 2.9.3, 6.2.1
exempt persons 2.9
failure to comply 1.3.5, 1.4.2, 2.1.1,
    2.14, 7.2.1
financial institutions 2.9.1
fines 1.4.2, 2.14.1
hardship 2.10, 2.15.1
liability group 2.9.2
local authority complete works and
    recover costs 2.15
material defect 2.13.1
modification 2.13.1
mortgagee not in possession 2.9.1
multiple appropriate persons 2.9.1,
    2.9.2
'must not' be served, where 2.8.1,
    2.11.1
non-compliance 1.3.5, 1.4.2, 2.1.1,
    2.14, 7.2.1
notice of intention to serve 2.7.1
notification and consultation 2.7.1,
    2.8.2, 2.11.2
numbers served 2.1.1
occupiers 2.9.1, 2.9.2, 2.9.5, 6.2.1
offences 1.6.1
original polluter 2.9.1, 2.9.2, 2.9.3,
    2.9.5, 6.2.1
owners 2.9.1, 2.9.2, 2.9.5, 6.2.1
penalties 1.4.2, 2.14.1
person served 1.6.1
persons having short-term interest
    only 2.9.3
planning permission, effect of
    application 2.8.2
quashing 2.13.1
remediation statement 2.8.1
restrictions on service 2.8.1, 2.11.1,
    2.11.2
sales with information 2.9.3, 2.13.3,
    8.4
service 2.2.2, 2.9, 2.11, 7.2.1
shared collective action 2.9.2
shared common action 2.9.2
specification of steps to be taken
    2.11.1
third-party intervener 2.9.3
time limits 2.13
Remediation statement 2.8.1
Repairing covenants 7.6.1
Reporting of incidents 1.9.3
**Residential freehold
transactions** 6.4

Residential freehold
transactions – *continued*
advice to client on potential for
problems 6.4.2
client care letter App A5
amendment of Standard Conditions
of Sale 6.4.8
contractual protections against
seller 6.4.8
enquiries of seller 6.4.3, App A6
enquiries of statutory and regulatory
bodies 6.4.4
Environment Agency searches 6.4.4
environmental search report 6.4.6
full site investigation 6.4.7
lenders' position 6.4.5
local authority searches 6.4.4
Con 29R 6.4.4, App C
new insurance 6.4.8
site history investigations 6.4.5
withdrawal from purchase 6.4.9
Residential property
transactions 6.1
advice to sellers 6.5
civil liability 6.2.2, 6.5
clean-up liabilities 6.2.3
contaminated land 6.2.1, 6.5
Contaminated Land Warning Card
6.1, 6.3, App B
criminal liability 6.2.1
environmental risks 6.1
advice to client 6.4.2
client care letter App A5
explosives and 6.2.4
freehold *see* **Residential freehold**
transactions
hazardous substances and 6.2.4
legal issues 6.2.1–6.2.5
nature conservation regime offences
6.2.1
non-legal issues 6.2.6
nuisance 6.2.2
radioactive substances and 6.2.4
statutory nuisances 6.5
water pollution 6.2.1, 6.5
Restoration notice 1.5.1
Restoration order 1.7.1, 1.7.2
Risk assessment
contaminated land 2.3.2
water pollution 2.3.2

Sales with information 2.9.3,
2.13.3, 8.4

Schools
CRC Energy Efficiency Scheme
4.4.5
Scrapyards 1.3.1
Sewers
offences 6.5, 7.2.1, 7.5, 9.4
trade effluent discharges 7.2.1, 12.5.1
Share purchase agreement 8.5
illustrative environmental clauses
App A8
Site inspections 5.6.1, 6.4.7,
7.4.7, 8.3
Sites of special scientific
interest (SSSIs) 1.7.1
criminal offence 1.7.1
environmental damage 1.2.3, 1.7.3,
3.5.1, 3.5.2, 3.6.4
enforcing authorities 3.10.1, 3.10.2,
3.10.3
remedial measures 3.18.2
threshold 3.6.4
Natural England 1.2.3
restoration of damaged site 1.7.1
Soil
contamination 1.3.1
environmental permitting 1.3.1
Industrial Emissions Directive
(IED) 1.3.1
unexcavated 1.3.1
Special areas of conservation
1.7.1
Special nature conservation
order 1.7.2
Special planning zone (SPZ)
scheme 9.2.5
Special protection areas 1.7.1
Stamp duty land tax (SDLT)
relief for zero carbon buildings 4.2
Statutory nuisances
abatement notice 1.6.1, 2.11.1, 7.2.1
administrative receivers 12.5.1
alarms 1.6.1
artificial light 1.6.1
best practicable means 1.3.5
clean-up costs 1.6.1, 7.2.3, 12.5.1
commercial property transactions
7.2.1, 7.5
contaminated land and 1.6.1, 2.17.6
'contaminated state', definition 1.6.1
criminal liability 1.6.1, 7.2.1
defences 1.3.5
development works and 9.4
environmental permitting and 1.6.1

insects 1.6.1
noise 1.6.1, 1.8.7
offences 7.2.1
property transactions 6.5, 7.5, 9.4
residential property transactions 6.5
see also **Nuisance**
Stop notice *see* **Civil sanctions**
Storage
hazardous substances 1.3.4, 3.5.2,
6.2.4, 7.2.4
waste 1.3.2
**Supervisors of voluntary
arrangements** 12.5.4
see also **Insolvency**; **Insolvency
practitioners**
Suspension notice
failure to comply 1.3.5
water-related offences 1.3.1
Sustainable homes
zero carbon buildings 4.2

Tax *see* **Land remediation tax
relief, Landfill tax**
Tort liability 1.8
human rights issues 1.8.7
negligence *see* **Negligence**
non-natural/non-reasonable use of
land 1.8.3
nuisance *see* **Nuisance**
reasonable foreseeability 1.8.1, 1.8.3
Rylands v. *Fletcher* rule 1.8.3
statutory torts 1.8.4
trespass 1.8.6
**Trade effluent discharges to
sewers** 7.2.1, 12.5.1
Trespass 1.8.6

Warning letters 1.4
Warranties
environmental warranties 8.4, 8.5.1,
App A8
lenders and 11.2.2, 11.2.1
Waste
acceptance criteria (WAC) 1.3.1
clean-up costs 1.6.1, 7.2.3, 12.5.1
commercial property transactions
and 7.2.1
controlled waste 1.3.2, 7.2.1
corporate transactions and 8.3
covenants not to commit waste 7.6.1
criminal liability 1.4.1, 7.2.1, 12.5.1
defences 1.3.5
definition 1.3.1

depositing or causing or permitting
deposit 1.3.2, 1.8.4
discarded material 1.3.1
disposal 8.3
electrical and electronic equipment
1.3.2
emergency activities 1.3.5
end-of-life vehicles 1.3.2
environmental permitting 1.3.1
extractive waste 1.3.2
hazardous 1.3.1, 1.3.2
identifying 1.3.2
'intention to discard' 1.3.1
keeping 1.3.2
labelling 1.3.2
landfill tax 2.17.4
leakages 1.3.1, 1.3.2, 6.2.1
offences 1.3.2, 1.4.1, 7.2.1, 12.5.1
packaging waste 1.3.2
permitting 1.3.2
prevention 1.3.1
proceeds of crime prosecutions 1.4.3
property transactions and 7.2.1
prosecutions 1.4.1
recycling 1.3.1
reduction 1.3.1
site waste management plans 1.3.2
spillages 1.3.1
statutory duty of care 1.3.1, 1.3.2
storage 1.3.2
transfer notes 1.3.2
unexcavated soil 1.3.1
**Waste acceptance criteria
(WAC)** 1.3.1
Waste facility closure notice
1.3.5
Waste management licensing
replacement by EP regime 1.3.1,
2.17.5
Water
discharge activities 1.3.1
discharge consents 6.2.1, 6.2.5
environmental damage *see* Water
pollution
environmental permitting 1.3.1
groundwater
discharge activities 1.3.1
remediation costs 1.4.3
Industrial Emissions Directive
(IED) 1.3.1
legislation 1.3.1, 1.3.3
Marine Management Organisation
3.10.4

Water – *continued*
offences 1.3.3
privatised water companies 1.3.3
water-related offences 1.3.1
Water pollution
administrative receivers 12.5.1
agricultural activities 1.3.3
airborne pollutants 3.6
'causing' water pollution 1.3.1
clean-up costs 1.6.2, 6.2.3, 7.2.3,
12.5.1
clean-up powers 2.17.7
commercial property transactions
7.2.1, 7.5
contaminated land and 2.2.2, 2.3.2,
2.17.7
controlled waters 6.2.1
criminal liability 6.2.1, 7.2.1, 12.5.1
defences 1.3.5
development works and 9.4
discharge activities 1.3.1
discharge consents 6.2.1, 6.2.5
environmental damage 1.7.3, 3.5.1,
3.5.2, 3.6.2
enforcing authorities 3.10.1, 3.10.2,
3.10.4
remedial measures 3.18.2
threshold 3.6.2
environmental search report 6.2.1,
7.2.1

fire-fighting water run-off 1.3.1
knowingly permitting 1.3.1
offences 1.3.1, 1.3.3, 1.4.1, 6.2.1, 7.2.1,
12.5.1
permitting pollution 1.3.1
private prosecutions 1.4.1
property transactions 6.2.1, 6.2.3, 6.5,
7.2.1, 7.5, 9.4
remediation works 2.9.5
residential property transactions
6.2.1, 6.2.3, 6.5
risk assessment 2.3.2
sampling procedures 1.9.1
silage 1.3.3
slurry 1.3.3
testing of discharge 1.9.1
trade effluent discharges to sewers
7.2.1, 12.5.1
vandalism 1.3.1
works notice 1.10, 2.17.7
Wetlands
conservation 1.7.1
Ramsar sites 1.7.1
Wild birds conservation 1.7.1
Wildlife conservation 1.7.1
Works notice 1.10, 2.17.7

Zero carbon buildings 4.2
see also **Energy certificates**